The Soul of Success

Volume 2

12/3/15

Dear Lizzy & Josh,

It has been an honor to be a part of your life milestones. Thank you for your support and friendship. Wishing you continued success and much happiness.

I CARE

that all your

DREAMS

Come true!

Warmest regards,
Becky Cafen

Published by CelebrityPress®, Orlando, FL

CelebrityPress® is a registered trademark.

Printed in the United States of America.

ISBN: 978-0-9961978-4-7
LCCN: 2015942404

This publication is designed to provide accurate and authoritative information with regard to the subject matter covered. It is sold with the understanding that the publisher is not engaged in rendering legal, accounting, or other professional advice. If legal advice or other expert assistance is required, the services of a competent professional should be sought. The opinions expressed by the authors in this book are not endorsed by CelebrityPress® and are the sole responsibility of the author rendering the opinion.

Most CelebrityPress® titles are available at special quantity discounts for bulk purchases for sales promotions, premiums, fundraising, and educational use. Special versions or book excerpts can also be created to fit specific needs.

For more information, please write:
CelebrityPress®
520 N. Orlando Ave, #2
Winter Park, FL 32789
or call 1.877.261.4930

Visit us online at: www.CelebrityPressPublishing.com

The Soul of Success
Volume 2

CELEBRITYPRESS®
Winter Park, Florida

CONTENTS

CHAPTER 1

DARE TO ASK!

BY JACK CANFIELD

If there is something to gain and nothing to lose by asking,
by all means ask!

~ W. Clement Stone,
Author of *The Success System That Never Fails*

My first mentor was a multi-millionaire insurance mogul, publisher, and author by the name of W. Clement Stone. When I was in my early 20s, he took me under his wing and taught me a series of success principles that still form the core of my work today. He taught me to take 100 percent responsibility for everything in your life, to totally give up blaming others, complaining about things, and making excuses for myself. He taught me to only think positive thoughts and to always focus on what I wanted, not what I didn't want. He taught me how to set specific and measurable goals and why it was so important. He taught me to visualize and affirm all of my goals as already complete, and to act as if they were all a done deal. He also taught me to take action as soon as I had an inspiration, what he referred to as "always do it now!"

Mr. Stone also taught me to limit the amount of time I spent watching television, which he referred to as "the income reduction box." He constantly reminded me that eliminating one hour of television a day would add up to 365 extra hours a year (that's a little over nine 40-hour workweeks, or two months) of extra time to devote to being productive.

He also chided me to become what he called an "inverse paranoid"—someone who believes the world is plotting to do him good instead of harm.

But most important, Mr. Stone taught me the importance of asking. He would repeatedly remind me, "If there is something to gain by asking and nothing to lose by asking, by all means ask." This one principle has reaped great rewards in my life, and it can do the same for you.

Unfortunately, many of us are not great at asking. For any number of reasons stemming from childhood conditioning to traumatic rejections later in life, we have become afraid of the word "no." To be successful, you have to be willing to ask! ask! ask! and keep asking until you get a yes. No's are just part of the journey to finally getting to a yes. And it only takes one yes to radically change your life forever.

YOU HAVE TO REJECT REJECTION

When Mark Victor Hansen and I finished the first *Chicken Soup for the Soul* book, we flew to New York with our literary agent Jeff Herman. We met with about 20 publishers over the course of three days, and none of them were interested in publishing our book. "Collections of short stories don't sell," we were told. "The title doesn't work." "The stories are to Pollyanna—too nicey-nice." Later we submitted the manuscript by mail to 20 more publishers. They also said no! At that point, our agent gave us the book back and said he couldn't sell it.

Of course we were disappointed, but we never got discouraged. When the world said "no," we said "next!" We continued to reach out to publishers on our own. We also asked every member of our speaking and training audiences to fill out a "Commitment to Buy" form we created, indicating how many copies they would commit to buy when the book was finally published. We eventually had promises to buy more than 20,000 books!

Armed with copies of these forms and a backpack full of spiral-bound copies of our best 30 stories, we headed off to the American Booksellers Convention in Anaheim, California, where we walked the floor of the exhibit hall for two days talking to one publisher after another about publishing our book. But again we heard no, no, no! And hour after hour, booth after endless booth, we said next! next! next!

At the end of the second very long day, Peter Vegso and Gary Seidler, the co-presidents of Health Communications Inc., a small publisher from Deerfield Beach, Florida, agreed to read the manuscript when they got back home. Later that week Gary Seidler took the manuscript to the beach and read it. He loved it, and he and Peter decided to publish it. After more than 140 rejections, the book was finally published and went on to sell more than 210 million copies in 47 languages, launched a series of more than 250 books that has gone on to sell more than 500 million books worldwide, and created a brand now worth more than $100 million! Those hundreds of nexts have really paid off!

This manuscript of yours that has just come back from another editor is a precious package. Don't consider it rejected. Consider that you've just addressed it "to the editor who can appreciate my work" and it has just come back stamped "not at this address." Just keep looking for the right address.

~ Barbara Kingsolver, Author of *The Poisonwood Bible*

In order to be successful, you have to reject rejection. Rejection doesn't mean no! It simply means not yet. It took us almost two years to get our book published and another 14 months before it got on the *New York Times* bestseller list. But once it did, it stayed in the number-one position for more than three years!

Don't get discouraged when you get a no. Just keep asking! You have to accept that you may get a lot of no's on the way to a yes.

JUST SAY "NEXT!"

Have you ever gone to a KFC restaurant? When Colonel Harlan Sanders left his home armed only with a pressure cooker and his special recipe for cooking Southern fried chicken he received more than 300 rejections, but he eventually found someone who believed in his dream. Today, because of his unwillingness to let the no's discourage him, there are now 5,200 KFC restaurants in the United States and more than 15,000 worldwide!

Remember, if one person tells you no, ask someone else. Remember this phrase:

SWSWSWSW

It stands for: **Some will. Some won't. So what! Someone's waiting!** Some people are out there waiting to be asked—waiting to say yes. Along the way you'll definitely get some no's. So what—just keep taking action and making requests.

WHAT IF THEY SAY NO?

I once was hired to speak at an annual sales meeting for a company that produces about half the world's eyeglass lenses. They are that big. Interestingly, I was the first outside speaker they had ever hired. I arrived there early and met with some of the salespeople earlier in the day. During the conversation, I asked them if they knew who the top producers in the company were. They all said the same three names. Everyone knew who the top salespeople were: Mary, Robert and Martin. These three were selling 200 percent or 400 percent more than anyone else in the company. That night I asked the audience of 300 salespeople to raise their hands if they thought they knew who were the top three producers in the company. Almost everybody raised their hands.

I then asked them to keep their hand up if they had ever gone up to any of those three people and asked them what their secrets of success were. What were they doing that made them so much more successful? Not one hand remained in the air. Whoa! What a revelation! I have spent my whole life seeking out the peak performers that had the answers, that knew more than I did, that were getting faster and better results than I was. "Teach me," I would say. "I want to learn." And yet not one person in this organization had reached out for the information that was readily available to them.

I then asked them why they hadn't asked these top producers for their success secrets, and the answers came fast and were almost unanimous. "Fear of rejection." "Why would they want to tell me? I have nothing to offer them." "I didn't want to risk them rejecting me." "I didn't want to look foolish or look like I didn't already know." In essence—I didn't want to risk rejection. I'd rather look good than do good.

Nobody makes it to the top without support from people who are ahead of them on the path—athletes need coaches and managers; businesspeople need coaches, mentors and consultants; artists need teachers, agents and gallery owners; entertainers need managers and agents; politicians need mentors and campaign managers. We all need to look to those who have gone before us, who know more than us, and use their experience, wisdom and knowledge.

ASK FOR GUIDANCE

A few years ago I was in the dressing room of a television station in Dallas, getting ready to appear on a morning news show to promote my book, *The Success Principles: How to Get From Where You Are to Where You Want to Be*. As I often do, I asked the woman who was putting on my makeup if she had a dream—some ultimate goal. She answered that she wanted to own her own salon someday. I said, "That's great. What are you doing to make that happen?" "Nothing," she replied. "That's a bad strategy," I said. Why aren't you doing anything to make your dream come true?" "I don't know what you have to do to own your own salon," she answered. "Well, I have a radical idea," I said. "Why don't you go find someone who owns a salon and ask them how they did it?" I was stunned when she said, "Wow, that's a great idea." I am always a bit taken aback when people don't see what is so obvious to me. But then most of us are not taught to ask others to help us. In fact, many of us get programmed by our parents to not ask, to not be a bother, to not impose ourselves on others.

MOST PEOPLE ARE WILLING TO HELP
IF THEY ARE ASKED

The truth that I have discovered is that most successful people are willing to share what they have learned with others who are sincere in their intention to succeed. It is a human trait to want to pass on what wisdom one has learned. Not everyone will take the time to mentor you, but most will—if they are asked! So you simply need to make a list of the people you would like ask for advice or to mentor you and ask them to devote a few minutes a month to you.

BE CREATIVE IN YOUR ASKING

Early in my career I had a very strong dream and desire to be an international peak performance trainer, impacting the lives of millions of people around the world. One of the people who was already doing that was Lou Tice, the co-founder and chairman of the Pacific Institute, whose work had positively affected tens of millions of people in more than 50 countries. Thinking that I could learn a lot from him, I called his office to ask if he would briefly mentor me. I was told that he was way too busy to do any individual mentoring. Undaunted, I sent him a personal letter suggesting that the next time he visited Los Angeles on business, instead of hiring a limousine service to transport him to his hotel and to his meetings, he permit me to pick him up and drive him to and from his various destinations in exchange for allowing me to ask him some questions.

Several weeks later I received a reply agreeing to my proposal. Not too long after that I picked him up at the Los Angeles airport, drove him to his hotel, and later to and from his speech. The whole time we were together I asked him question after question, which he graciously answered. In those few short hours, I learned a ton of valuable business lessons. Ironically, about a year later, both my company and his submitted proposals for a $750,000 training contract with the Los Angeles County Office of Education. Out of all the contenders, it finally came down to two proposals—The Pacific Institutes' and mine—and after two more days of interviews with the County Office, we won the contract. After Lou found out, he graciously called me, commented on what a fast learner I was, and congratulated me. My out-of-the-box creative ask had ultimately added $750,000 to our year's income!

ANOTHER CREATIVE ASK

Tim Ferriss, who later penned the bestseller *The 4-Hour Workweek*, also used a creative approach to get me to mentor him. At the time, Tim was about 26 years old and had not yet written his book. He knew he wanted to write a book and he knew he wanted me as one of his publishing mentors. He also knew I was very busy and most likely would say no. What he did was brilliant.

Tim joined a group called the Silicon Valley Association of Startup Entrepreneurs and volunteered to be their next program chair. He then called me and said he wanted me to speak there, and while they couldn't pay me anything, he would introduce me to some of the most powerful people in Silicon Valley who might be able to hire me as a consultant. Since the flight from Santa Barbara to Santa Jose is less than an hour, I agreed to come speak. Tim's real agenda, it turned out, was to get to know me, which was accomplished when we went out for food and drinks after the meeting. Tim is one of the most interesting and engaging people I have ever met, and we quickly became friends. Months later, when he asked me to be his mentor, it was a slam-dunk yes!

ASK AND YOU JUST MIGHT GET IT

Several years ago, Sylvia Collins flew all the way from Australia to Santa Barbara, California, to take one of my weeklong "Breakthrough to Success" seminars, where she learned about the power of asking. A year later, I received this letter from her:

I have taken a detour in my career path, and I'm now selling new developments on the Gold Coast with a company called Gold Coast Property. I work with a team of guys mostly in their 20s. The skills I have acquired through your seminars have helped me to perform and be an active part of a winning team! I must tell you how having self-esteem and not being afraid to ask has impacted this office!

At a recent staff meeting, we were asked what we would like to do for our once-a-month team-building day. I asked Michael, the managing director, "What target would we have to reach for you to take us to an island for a week?"

Everyone around the table just went silent and looked at me; obviously it was out of everyone's comfort zone to ask such a thing. Michael looked around and then looked at me and said, "Well, if you reach...(and then he set a financial target), I'll take the whole team (10 of us) to the Great Barrier Reef!"

Well, the next month we reached the target and off we went to Lady Elliott Island for four days—airfares, accommodations, food and activities all paid for by the company. We had the most amazing four days—we snorkeled together, had bonfires on the beach, played tricks on each other, and had so much fun!

Afterwards, Michael gave us another target and said he would take us to Fiji if we reached it, and we reached that target in December! Even though the company is paying for these trips, Michael is miles ahead from the enormous level of increased sales!

As Sylvia's letter so clearly illustrates, sometimes all you have to do is break out of your comfort zone and ask.

About Jack

Known as America's #1 Success Coach, Jack Canfield is the CEO of the Canfield Training Group in Santa Barbara, CA, which trains and coaches entrepreneurs, corporate leaders, managers, sales professionals and the general public in how to accelerate the achievement of their personal, professional and financial goals.

He is best known as the coauthor of the #1 New York Times bestselling *Chicken Soup for the Soul®* book series, which has sold more than 500 million books in 47 languages, including 11 New York Times #1 bestsellers. As the CEO of Chicken Soup for the Soul Enterprises he helped grow the Chicken Soup for the Soul® brand into a virtual empire of books, children's books, audios, videos, CDs, classroom materials, a syndicated column and a television show, as well as a vigorous program of licensed products that includes everything from clothing and board games to neutriceuticals and a successful line of Chicken Soup for the Pet Lover's Soul® cat and dog foods.

His other books include *The Success Principles™: How to Get from Where You Are to Where You Want to Be* (recently revised as the 10th Anniversary Edition,) *The Success Principles for Teens, The Aladdin Factor, Dare to Win, Heart at Work, The Power of Focus: How to Hit Your Personal, Financial and Business Goals with Absolute Certainty, You've Got to Read This Book, Tapping into Ultimate Success, Jack Canfield's Key to Living the Law Attraction,* and his recent novel—*The Golden Motorcycle Gang: A Story of Transformation.*

Jack is a dynamic speaker and was recently inducted into the National Speakers Association's Speakers Hall of Fame. He has appeared on more than 1000 radio and television shows including Oprah, Montel, Larry King Live, the Today Show, Fox and Friends, and 2 hour-long PBS Specials devoted exclusively to his work. Jack is also a featured teacher in 12 movies including *The Secret, The Meta-Secret, The Truth, The Keeper of the Keys, Tapping into the Source,* and *The Tapping Solution.*

Jack has personally helped hundreds of thousands of people on six different continents become multi-millionaires, business leaders, best-selling authors, leading sales professionals, successful entrepreneurs, and world-class athletes while at the same time creating balanced, fulfilling and healthy lives.

His corporate clients have included Virgin Records, SONY Pictures, Daimler-Chrysler, Federal Express, GE, Johnson & Johnson, Merrill Lynch, Campbell's Soup, Re/Max, The Million Dollar Forum, The Million Dollar Roundtable, The Entrepreneur Organization, The Young Presidents Organization, the Executive Committee, and the World Business Council.

He is the founder of the Transformational Leadership Council and a member of Evolutionary Leaders, two groups devoted to helping create a world that works for everyone.

Jack is a graduate of Harvard, earned his M.Ed. from the University of Massachusetts and has received three honorary doctorates in psychology and public service. He is married, has three children, two step-children and a grandson.

For more information visit: www.JackCanfield.com

CHAPTER 2

FIVE PRINCIPLES OF SUCCESS

BY MITSIE VARGAS, DVM

Several years ago, on a hot summer afternoon, I was speaking to a wonderful group of girls attending the after-school program at Girls Inc. of Polk County. There weren't any television cameras or media coverage, but this event became a pivotal point in my life; I had looked in the eyes of all these girls and told them my "success" story. It was then that the seeds of this chapter were sown. I wanted to inspire those girls who were growing up in poverty, hopelessness and dysfunctional environments to believe they can change the course of their lives. Here I was, telling them how I transcended the rampant examples of school dropouts, illiteracy, teen pregnancies, alcoholism, drug abuse and poverty that permeated my early childhood experiences. If I could achieve my life purpose and find happiness coming from a less than desirable situation, then they too could follow their dreams and be successful individuals.

The hope my heart felt in writing this chapter is that, in revealing the life-learned wisdom that serves as my north star, the readers gain insight that could be applied to guide them in their own personal situation. I believe we all are in constant search of inspiration and in my experience the most effective way to find it is by shifting our paradigms. When we are shown how others have conquered personal challenges and limitations to achieve their goals, then we all take a closer look at our situation and get to see all the possibilities we were not aware of.

So, I would like to share my story and the five simple principles that have led me along my journey and contributed to my success in my career and personal life:

1. Living your passion

I consider myself blessed to have always known what I wanted to be when I grew up. My earliest memory goes back to the tender age of seven. The epiphany came in the midst of a tragedy; losing my beloved tabby named Michigan.

Michigan was no ordinary cat because in fact, she was not officially my pet! She was a stray somebody dumped near my house and that I befriended. My parents were divorced and my mother had her hands full raising three kids and working two jobs to make ends meet. Mom had a 'no pets' rule, but I couldn't resist pretending Michigan was mine. In those times the school bus would drop off us by 3 pm, and mom would be back from her first job by 5 pm. Those two hours our sacred bonding time. I would bring her into my room to feed, brush and play with her. I really was a lonely child with many pent-up emotions stemming from seeing my parents separate. This kitty was a God-sent distraction that warmed my heart. She was alone too. She was my mentor in cat behavior and a trusted confidant. Her purring and her affectionate head bumps filled a big hole in my little girl's heart.

Therefore, the day I lost her was a traumatic one, filled with a sense of guilt for my part in the tragic accident. I was calling her and she was hunting across the street. One second I saw her running towards me, tail up in the air, the next she was being hit by a speeding car. Blood was everywhere, but she sprang up, still coming. I opened the front door and she ran under my bed where I quickly followed. Attempting to comfort her, I laid a hand on her head and prayed to God to save her. I was wailing and sobbing so loud when she finally passed, that my worried mother had to pick the bed apart to get us out. It was there, as I felt her life energy leave her little broken body that my moment of truth came. I remember feeling so powerless and defeated. I decided that if I knew how to fix what hurts, then I could save animals from suffering so much. I experienced an epiphany; my purpose in life was to heal animals.

From my experience, success is living your life knowing you are using your divine gifts to your own satisfaction. Living by this principle means that to achieve success, we need to engage in an activity we are innately good at, and love to do. Many people work hard at a job they hate because they believe they need to make some money, retire and then do what they really love to do. I pity those lost souls! I am here to tell you that the only sure way to success is to live your passion. You may earn lots of money at a job you hate, but you will have a deep sense of discontent that will bleed into other areas of your life. Only when you start doing what you love will you know true, bone-deep satisfaction.

How do you know you are living your passion? Simple; you love what you do so much that you lose sense of time. When you draw from your gifts, you could immerse yourself in your task and enjoy it so much that the world around you disappears. Many call this phenomenon being 'in the zone.' That is the time when you are at your peak creativity and cognitive functions. If you live your passion, you spend your days full of enthusiasm and joy. It is imperative you find what activities make use of your talents, then find a way to monetize them.

2. Goal setting

Goal setting starts by writing down exactly that which we want to accomplish. This simple process seems to ignite a change in the universe, and what was formerly just a longing, morphs into a tangible reality. I recommend to be as specific as you can and to set a deadline to achieve these goals. Whether it is being the top sales person for this year or opening/expanding your current business in the next five years, write it down! I find that subconsciously, we start working on our goals based on a perceived time constraint. Dare to dream big here; a goal too easily reached is not stretching your talents.

Who knew I could become a veterinarian when my family income was below the poverty level and my mother was a fourth grade drop out? Did I mention I lived in Puerto Rico and the few veterinary schools were only in the US? Knowing that I wanted to enter a highly competitive field, I learned early on to write down my goals and to set time lines in which to accomplish them. My goal was high; no one in my family had gone on to postgraduate studies. I knew the GPA I needed to keep, and dedicated myself to achieving those grades. I did all the research to compete for scholarships and student loans and realized I needed a financial miracle.

Even my high school counselor told me I couldn't do it; she encouraged me to apply for a "real" profession in Medicine instead of following my dream. So, I sat down and wrote a plan to get in vet school as soon as possible. I took AP courses in high school to shorten my undergraduate time, and completed 18 credit semesters plus summers to beat my own expectations by being accepted at 20 years old. If you really want to achieve something, you have got to give birth to it on paper before you get to experience it in your life.

3. Believe in yourself

Loving who you are, accepting that although flawed you are a unique creation, is essential for success. The by-product of self-love is confidence. Confidence is the fuel that keeps you going for your goals. The most common trait of all the successful people I know is confidence. People buy from you and trust your recommendations based on your ability to show confidence. I remember surviving my first years as a practitioner by faking confidence. I embraced the fact that I was a non-native English speaker and had an accent. I understood that I did not have connections nor the financial means to own a practice.

The one thing I had was an unwavering belief in myself and my abilities. I had certainty of purpose. I just knew success was the only option because I had dedication and single-minded focus. I trusted that if I continued putting forth my best efforts that surely success would be guaranteed. Even when I opened my practice, I drew from my inner confidence. Here I was, an unproven practitioner, daring to ask the bank for an unsecured loan. I was able to convince them that investing in me and my business was a safe bet. Two decades later I've more than substantiated my claims.

4. Expect success

All the successful people I know are optimistic in nature. A positive attitude brings the best out of everyone around you and it is contagious. Creativity feeds on positivity – resulting in better ideas, improved performance and efficiency. Remember to spend time daily visualizing the outcome you seek. I have always been a "glass half-full" person. I remember years ago, I went to a conference where they were discussing the high mortality of a certain disease process. I was baffled about the fact that, although I had seen many of those cases, I had not lost any of my patients to it. I attribute a lot of those recoveries to my optimistic attitude toward treating my patients. I believe that the owner's emotions, the hospital setting and the practitioner's outlook truly affect the outcome of medical cases. Therefore, I surround myself with positive employees and strive to maintain a positive workplace environment.

My clients know I am always expecting the best-case scenario, and would work tirelessly until I achieve it. A negative work environment is detrimental to your psyche. Expecting your business to just survive or your relationships to just get by is a sure way to keep you from getting good results. You don't have to be a new age guru to understand that what we think about most we end up attracting into our lives; so think and expect success!

5. Be a blessing to others

You do not need to be rich to be a giver or to make a difference in the lives of others. In fact, there is a lot of power in a kind word. Heart-felt advice means so much to people in need. Your smile is a gift to your family, customers and coworkers. The best reward for giving is the satisfaction in making a difference in other people's lives. After 21 years practicing (19 of them owning a successful business), I still enjoy networking, speaking at schools, mentoring future veterinary students, sponsoring local charities and helping stray animals.

I learned to be generous from my mother. Although she was barely getting by working two jobs and raising us, she was always a generous person. Sadly, I only learned how much she had helped her siblings and countless other people at her funeral. Tons of people came to her viewing, it was surprising how a simple factory worker in a forgotten rural neighborhood had influenced the lives of so many. She never bragged about what she did, she gave from her heart and without expectations. I learned that day that kindness' return on investment (ROI) is peace of mind. My mother had the guts to give even when her financial situation was dire, how could I ever do less? I learned from her that giving, despite not having excess resources, affirms to the universe that you are NOT in a place of Lack despite your current situation.

The most successful business people I know are philanthropists and considered pillars of their communities. The best reason for you to be financially successful is to be able to use money to help others. Money is a by-product of success and the engine that drives a generous heart to be a blessing to their family, community and the world. It is up to ourselves to take control of our lives and do it by believing in our own power and cultivating an attitude of positive expectation. Its important to keep our thoughts rooted in the belief that we can achieve a successful life.

This quote by Marcus Aurelius sums it up nicely: *Because your own strength is unequal to the task, do not assume that it is beyond the powers of man; but if anything is within the powers and province of man, believe that it is within your own compass also.*

About Dr. Mitsie

Dr. Mitsie Vargas received her DVM from Tuskeegee University in 1994. In 1996, she established her AAHA accredited Orchid Springs Animal Hospital inWinter Haven, FL.

In 2009 she started her studies at Chi Institute, eventually garnering certifications in Acupuncture, Food therapy and Tui Na. She is an assistant teacher at Chi Institute and a TCVM consultant for Disney Animal Kingdom. She is also a certified veterinary journalist and has published hundreds of articles including her Sunday newspaper pet care column. She serves as an AVMA Spokesperson for Hispanic market and has recorded many PSA's and radio interviews promoting responsible pet ownership.

Her passion for helping animals and her voluntarism has awarded her state and national recognition. Among her awards are the Purina National Pet Care Award, Bay News 9Medical Hero Award, Bright House Regional Business Award, Girls Inc. "She knows where she is going award" and the FVMA Gold award. Dr. Vargas has been selected as a top finalist in America's Favorite Veterinarian 2015.

CHAPTER 3

CAPTAIN OF MY RELATIONSHIPS: FAMILY, WORK & LIFE

BY MICHELLE BECHER, D.O., FACOOG

How do I define success?

If someone asked me to summarize what made my family life, my work life, my life, in general, a success, I could answer in just one word: Relationships.

Childbirth is one of the peak "relationship" experiences of life. It's an amazing, transforming moment, bringing a person into this world, hearing those first cries, and seeing new mothers exhausted, exhilarated and silenced by the awesomeness of it all. As an obstetrical-gynecological doctor and a mother myself, I've had the opportunity to participate in delivering life hundreds of times, and every time is magical for me.

It's not always easy. It's not always the happy ending we anticipate. But there can be meaning and connection even in the most agonizing situations.

Ten years ago, I was delivering a wonderful woman's baby. Her eighth child, it was an early birth at just 20 weeks. Full-term pregnancies typically last 40 weeks. Twenty weeks is an especially tragic time to deliver because babies born at this level of development are beautiful and look "perfect," and yet they do not have the organ structure to survive.

Within those first moments, it's easy for a mother to develop a strong attachment, to feel that bond. To see a beautiful baby delivered, and to know from a clinical standpoint that it just simply won't be able to survive breaks a doctor's heart. It broke my heart.

Although this infant did not survive childbirth, something magical happened in the delivery room that day. I picked it up in my arms. I held it. The grief-stricken mother, who knew what had happened but wasn't ready to accept it and couldn't bring herself to hold her baby, listened to me as I described what the infant looked like – its fingers, its toes, its eyelashes. And then, without thinking, and with no logical explanation, I began to instinctively rock the baby to and fro. It made no sense, but it consoled the mother. In her eyes, I was providing comfort and care to her baby when she couldn't.

Over the years, I have encountered this mother in the community several times. She has told me that my reaction to her stillborn infant made such an impact on her, such a meaningful difference in her life, that she will never forget it. She has told me that she could sense that I was "pouring love into that baby," and that I did something she wasn't able to do in her grief at that moment. "You doing that was so special for me," she said.

To have that connection, that memory, that relationship built, means so much to me – as a doctor, as a mother, as a human being. It's a powerful relationship even though it is based on this one experience. Not every interaction with a patient is this memorable, but I nurture the relationship I have with every one of my patients. To me, it's the most important part of my job.

I want to know my patients – to know about their passions, their interests, their concerns. I want to offer advice on the things that create stress in their lives. This is true with my work team, as well. For example, a surgical nurse was telling me recently about her child's misbehavior and how it was stressing her out. We discussed her situation and then I shared some tips that worked with my children. I explained to her that much of parenting has to do with our own attitudes; that as mothers, we should be grateful that our only challenge is having to parent through behavior issues, rather than experiencing something like having a child diagnosed with cancer. To offer her that perspective, that other mothers are sitting in hospitals with children who are ill or who are dying, helped her. She thanked me for helping her realize she was a lucky mom, and we then said a prayer together for a family friend with an ill child.

I'M THE CAPTAIN NOW

There's a thrilling action scene in the 2013 film "Captain Phillips," in which a Somali pirate says to Tom Hanks' captain character: "Look at me. I'm the captain now." Of course, I'm not hijacking a ship; I'm directing the many ships in my life, but those words – "I am the captain" – resonate with me. One of the ways I'm able to nurture and build the relationships in my life is through being a good captain.

Captains of fame and fortune – the captains' names you know from history and fiction – are predominantly men. Captain Ahab of Moby Dick fame, Christopher Columbus, Captain Phillips, Sir Francis Drake, and Captain Jack Sparrow for you Johnny Depp fans. And so it might seem strange that I am a female doctor who focuses on the care and nurturing of women, a doctor with three daughters for whom I want to serve as a strong role model, and I yet, here I am, navigating toward the analogy of serving as a captain. But I think it makes perfect sense.

Thinking of myself as a "captain" of success fits for at least three reasons:

1) A ship captain serves his or her crew, and is there to maintain order, direction and mission success, which I feel is something I do every day;

2) In medical school, this concept of being a captain was always used during our surgery and clinical training to emphasize the need for a surgeon to be in control, skillful, confident and clinically knowledgeable;

3) There are successful female captains! Sarah Breton of the United Kingdom was the first UK female cruise ship captain in 2010, when she took the helm of the 550-crew Artemis cruise ship. She is quoted as saying she has the best job in the world. And in 2011, Captain Jennifer Brokaw took command of the ship U.S.N.S. Victorious; she is only one of very few female special missions ship captains and gives the inspiring advice of, "Don't think twice, do it!"

MANY SHIPS IN MY SEA

As I've said, I captain many ships, not just one. These ships range from my household, which I co-captain with my husband, to the operating room, where I must assert myself as the captain in order to save lives and ensure the best outcomes for my patients. I also captain the ship of my many businesses – my multi-location OB-GYN practices called The Center for Women's HealthCare, my medical spa practice iWi MedSpa, and, yes, even an alpaca farm, all located in central Michigan.

There are smaller ships I command throughout the day, such as when I captain the technology of the da Vinci® Surgical System, in which I am certified. It sounds very "Star Trek," doesn't it? Because it is! This cutting-edge robot technology requires me to summon the focus and serenity of Captain James T. Kirk as I perform complex hysterectomies and other gynecologic procedures through tiny, one- to two-centimeter incisions.

What does a ship captain do? According to the career company, **Sokanu:** "A ship captain is the leader of an entire vessel, which can range in size from a small yacht to an entire cruise liner. He or she has vast experience with ships and their operation, and has likely worked their way through the ranks of other ship-related positions. Duties on the ship fall far beyond the scope of a management position, as the ship captain must be proficient in every aspect of running a ship, from ship operation to maintenance, and in the instance of touring ships, playing host to the passengers. The entire success of a ship's voyage lies on the captain's shoulders and how well he or she manages the crew."

I love that definition. And while commanding one's ship is essential to reaching your destination of success, it's not all about me. The captain is just one role of many. It takes a team, a crew, to make the ship sail and reach its destination.

In the O.R., when I'm performing surgery, our captain's log is the surgical-safety checklist that we follow. My crew can include an assistant surgeon, a scrub tech, a surgical nurse and an anesthesiologist, depending on the procedure. Although we work as a team, one person needs to assume command so there is one person responsible for ensuring everything proceeds as planned. For me, it's not about ego, but about the need for leadership in a situation that can be a life or death one.

There is also a crew at my office, and a different crew at the hospital obstetric department. Each crew I work with helps me to be the person I am, to succeed in my work. Within those crews are individual women (mostly women!) and such an array of personalities; I love each and every one of them, and each of them keeps me accountable in ways that keep everything running smoothly. I think about Gen who is so efficient with ordering supplies, Ronda who remembers everyone's name, Lori's kindness, and Shelly with her aptitude for technology. When we each bring forward our gift and contribute this knowledge to the crew, our ship sails happily off into the sunset.

WHAT IS THE SOUL TO MY SUCCESS?

There's a quote I just love from motivational speaker Sam Glenn's book, *A Kick In The Attitude*: "My perfect day boils down to that one word, relationships. Without meaningful relationships, your life suffers emptiness. A positive relationship is one that gives us life and a heart of gratefulness. Positive relationships are the key to great success."

My pastor's sermon on a recent Sunday had to do with the fact that the moment we accept Jesus into our hearts, we are given a gift, although many of us do not realize what our gift is here on Earth. He said he recognized that his gift was to preach. As he was speaking, I suddenly got goose bumps over my entire body when it struck me that I had been given two gifts and there were two "souls" to my success: the gift and soul of being both a mom and a surgeon.

I am constantly striving to be the best mother and guide for my daughters, directing them on the path toward the women they are meant to be, with a lot of praying and consulting with my husband! I know I have a finite amount time with them and yet so much to teach them. The love I feel for them is something I can't even put into words, it's so strong. I feel setting a good example for my daughters is so very important because I know they watch my every move. They make me accountable for the things I say I want to achieve, such as running 5K races on the weekends. These three girls watch what I do, listen to every discussion and – I hope – file this all away to be used in their futures.

CAPTAINS WHO HELP ME

The reason I'm acutely aware of my impact on my children is because there were adults in my life who shaped who I am today. One of the captains of my youth was an incredible second-grade teacher who told me for the first time that I could do whatever I wanted with my life. Not knowing at the time I'd truly achieve this goal, I had actually thought to myself at that young age, "I want to be a doctor."

My dad died when I was in the tenth grade, and that fueled a drive to want to find a cure for cancer. Of course, I realize I likely won't be curing cancer, but I am very passionate about helping my patients with cancer, improving their outcomes and improving their quality of life to the best of my ability. It's very personal for me.

My husband's father, Dr. Lawrence Brown – who passed away in 2009 – had a huge impact on me. As a doctor, he was a captain in his own right, holding many medical and leadership roles at the hospital where I now perform surgeries and deliver babies. This relationship was unique in that he was a mentor to me as a successful physician and he was also my father-in-law. He was also a much-loved character known for his witty expressions known as "Brown-isms," such as saying matter-of-factly when nothing else applied: "It is what it is!"

I've heard someone say, "You are one relationship away from success." I love that, and I believe in surrounding yourself with people who make you laugh, people who have good ethics and live lives built on character. I realize that I need to be this person for others. I need to be a captain, just as others have been a captain to me.

My relationships with my family and the support my husband and children give me allow the work I do to be successful. My mother supports me and helps me. My siblings do so much to help me be successful.

My relationship with God is one that is always changing. But one thing that never changes is that he is my rock and breathes life into me each day, giving me the strength to be my own captain.

About Dr. Michelle

Dr. Michelle Becher, D.O., FACOOG focuses on patient-care excellence with the same level of passion and love she gives to her three amazing daughters and husband of 20 years. A national speaker on health care and leadership topics, she is an inspiration to everyone who knows her. Dr. Becher is a Fellow in the American College of Osteopathic Obstetricians and Gynecologists, a member of the American Osteopathic Association, and Chief of Minimally Invasive Surgery at Sparrow Carson Hospital in Michigan. A board-certified obstetrical-gynecologist (OB), she provides a full range of services at her multiple practice locations. She completed her residency in OB at Metropolitan Hospital in Grand Rapids, Michigan, and her medical degree from Michigan State University-College of Osteopathic Medicine.

Her ties to Sparrow Carson Hospital run deep; known as Carson City Hospital for 75 years, Dr. Becher has had an affiliation here for decades. Her father-in-law and mentor – Dr. Lawrence Brown – also served in various leadership roles at this same hospital from 1987 until his death in 2009.

Active, engaged and present in everything she does, Dr. Becher does not feel the modern-day pressure to "find balance" in her life, because she has achieved it intuitively and organically by always following her heart, doing what she loves, caring deeply about her patients and being the "captain" of her patients' care. She lives this natural balance every day by focusing on relationships and spending time with the people that matter to her.

When she's not managing her many businesses, she enjoys downhill skiing, traveling the world, running 5K races, and reading books and blogs celebrating leadership and relationship-building.

The life she has built as an obstetrical gynecologist, a surgeon, and as a successful business owner with OB-GYN and medical spa services throughout Michigan, has made her a well-known, respected leader with a reputation for excellence in her community. Her focus on creating a unique space within which to care for her patients – gorgeous fixtures and décor in her offices, themed exam rooms featuring beachscapes and diamonds – has made her a natural at attracting local media attention and "wowing" her patients.

But it's the personal attention, clinical attention to detail and a desire to always advocate for and do what is best for her patients that has made her a loved and sought-after medical professional for decades.

Her staff members also get to come along for the ride with their inspirational captain. Four times a year, Dr. Becher coordinates and manages fun, team-building events for her staff and the Sparrow Carson Hospital obstetrical staff. She's known for her creative approaches to supporting community fundraising events, and for bringing her team on exciting field trips that enrich their perspectives.

If you'd like to invite Dr. Becher to speak on health care topics important to women, or to speak about how to be an inspiring leader, please contact her at:
Michelle Becher, D.O., FACOOG
Center for Women's HealthCare
639 E. Main St., Carson City, MI 48811
989.584.3107
97GynDoc@gmail.com

Please visit her online at one of her practice websites:
www.cfwhc.com or www.iwimedspa.com

CHAPTER 4

SUCCESS IS A COMEDY OF ERRORS...
THE FOUR MENTAL MUSCLES OF SUCCESS AND HOW YOU CAN LEARN THEM... BY DOING STAND-UP COMEDY

BY RAY BREHM

The lights were bright. The theatre was packed. I had been onstage earlier and had estimated close to 200 seats. Now they all were full. I could see my wife in the front row with her friends. Most of my routine was about marriage, specifically ours, which just added to the intensity of the moment. One week earlier, I had just given a presentation to around 100 people on "building culture," but this was different. I was backstage, and on deck for my first ever stand-up comedy routine. I was so far out of my comfort zone that I had both sweaty palms and an eerie calm at the same time. Then the comic ahead of me finished and said, "Please Welcome to the stage, a very funny guy, Ray Brehm!" It was go time . . .

That was a true "OMG" moment for me (if you don't know what OMG is, ask your teenager).

First of all, I am not a comedian (at least professionally). My skills are centered on Real Estate and Business Coaching. I love humor and entertainment, but by most accounts I had no business being up there. Most people I told about the show probably didn't believe me. The journey began two months earlier, when a colleague of mine from Entrepreneur's Organization had pushed me to take a stand-up comedy class. The class is two months long and culminates with the "graduates" participating in a real comedy show with other established comedians.

That night and the following personal post mortem were really insightful. When I reflected on that experience, it really tied in all of the keys to success that had been loosely floating around in my head for years.

FOUR MENTAL MUSCLES OF SUCCESS

I believe there are four mental muscles you must develop in order to be successful. They are beliefs, mindsets and universal understandings that you will find in most successful people. They cannot be developed overnight. They must be worked on continuously, just like exercise. My comedy routine was one non-business experiment that exercised all four of the mental muscles you need for business. These four muscles are:

1. Get out of your Comfort Zone
2. Belief without Proof
3. Adversity only makes you Stronger
4. Failure is a GOOD option

1. Get out of your Comfort Zone

I distinctly remember driving to that first comedy class. I called the guy who convinced me to do it and told him it had been a long time since I had been this far out of my comfort zone. I was sure I could start any business in any industry that day, and still not feel quite as uncomfortable as I was heading to that class. I had the same feeling two months later for the performance. But just like anything, after I did it, I wondered why I would ever question the outcome. I felt like so many more things were suddenly in my realm of possibility.

Your comfort zone may be the most critical muscle you can exercise on your way to success, and forever after. If running a mile scares you, it will always scare you until you just try to do it. Maybe you run

200 meters, and then you say that wasn't bad. In a week or two you are running 400, or maybe even that mile. Wait a second, now two miles doesn't seem that tough. Pretty soon you will start believing you can run a marathon, but it all starts with pushing past your mental limits. Any business, any skill, any project can be thought of in this way. You can strengthen this muscle in one area (like stand-up comedy), but it strengthens it for everything. Do you know anyone who thinks they can do anything? What do you think they spend their time doing? It almost becomes a game to strengthen it, pushing the limits of a comfort zone.

My most powerful way of stepping out of my comfort zone is constantly asking myself, "What is the worst that can happen here?" or "What if I fail?" When you actually analyze it, things aren't nearly as bad as you create in your head. What happens is this: you create this foggy image in your head of some kind of apocalypse occurring if you fail. Think about an extreme one, what if you were to go bankrupt tomorrow? What is the worst that can happen? Will your world end? No. So is it really that bad? What if your business fails? What if you can't pay all your bills one month? What if you start that company? What if you go freelance? What if you go travel the world?

The truth is you can do things to get out of your comfort zone - things that don't add any risk to your business, like take a comedy class, or join Toastmasters. They add no risk, but they push your comfort zone and that can have a lasting impact on your business later. You can constantly build this muscle in other areas (other than your business), and later flex that muscle in your business. Once you start building that muscle, you turn it into a game. You will also start building a reputation for trying more and more things. People start expecting you to leave your comfort zone all the time. And guess what, you will start expecting yourself to as well.

What can you do tomorrow, to get out of your comfort zone?

2. Belief without Proof

During one of my first stand-up comedy classes, our instructor gave us a kind of "if you build it, they will come" moment. He said not worry about the performance, people come to the show to laugh and they will. I believed him.

We had our final class only three days before that stand-up comedy performance. I had come up with what I thought was a funny topic, and made most of my jokes center around that. I had procrastinated a bit, not to mention I was running a business, so I had not tried my new jokes out on my classmates yet. The instructor hadn't heard these new jokes either, and by the end of class, I needed a rewrite. This was only three days out, I was new and I had nothing. This probably should have scared the crap out of me, but it didn't. I had no reason at that point to believe I could get it done, but I did believe it. I had other ideas, I just had to craft the jokes.

I heard a podcast one time, about entrepreneurs. On it they described one of the most profound definitions of entrepreneurs I have ever heard. They said what makes someone an entrepreneur is the ability to believe everything will work out, without any idea of how it will. I had never been able to put my finger on it prior, but that was my belief. So many times in my business I had partners, employees, or close friends wonder how I was going to do something or how I was going to get out of a jam. In most cases, I did not know either. I simply assumed I would work it out. What you need to develop is an unrelenting belief that things will work out.

I call it Belief without Proof. This success muscle requires a lot of work. It requires confidence of course. But it also requires effort. The more effort you make, the more confidence you will build. Confidence is not only built on success, however. In fact, success will only take this muscle so far. Failure becomes more important when you really strengthen that muscle (more on that in a minute).

The more you exercise this muscle of *belief without proof*, the stronger you will become at it and the stronger your success muscle becomes. Just don't start believing you can fly.

3. Adversity makes you Stronger

In my stand-up routine, there was lady who tried (and succeeded) in yelling out two punch lines to my jokes before I delivered them. She may have even thought she was helping me (in some strange way). I ignored it and kept going. The crowd would respond to me, not her. The next time a heckler says something, I probably won't even hear it. In fact, more advanced comics practice ignoring and if necessary responding to hecklers. Once they have had a few, they become very good at handling them.

When LeBron James decided to go to the Miami Heat, I remember they interviewed the legendary Kevin McHale of the Boston Celtics. The interviewer asked if LeBron would struggle because now every team was going to give them their best game every night. Kevin simply responded, that he didn't think that would be an issue at all, it would just make Miami stronger. They went to four straight NBA Finals, winning two.

If adversity makes you stronger, you must seek it out. Where do you find it? Anytime you try. The more you try to succeed, the more adversity you will encounter. The real key is to know every time you run into it, it is just making you that much stronger. This is an easy muscle to describe. But it can be very difficult to build or maintain. What entrepreneur does not ask (himself) daily why the heck he is doing what he is doing?

When I first started in Real Estate Property Management, if somebody complained, I was up all night stressed. Now someone could threaten to sue me, and I think, I will believe it when I see it.

Seek out adversity.

See it by doing.

Go do it.

4. Failure is a Good option

Comedians are constantly testing and measuring the success of their jokes? Know how they discover the very funniest ones? They push past those jokes that fail. They have to fail in order to actually create the best jokes. Many jokes start as flops, but because they tried and failed, they went back, fine-tuned them, changed the wording, and the delivery. Then all of the sudden, they look like a comedic genius. I watched and marveled at this first hand, as new comedians had a horrible joke one week, took feedback, and adjusted it and they became some of the best jokes in the show. They would never have discovered the really great joke if they had not tried the poor one.

Have you ever heard of exercising to the point of failure? You need to exercise your ideas and efforts past the point of failure. If you try to keep your track record perfect, you will never truly know what you are capable of. Failures are literally the most important part of success.

DO IT

By the way, if you are wondering how I performed that night, I killed it (at the very least in my mind and that of my wife). The audience laughed at every joke. I walked off the stage pumped, feeling like I could do anything. How did I do it? I decided first to get out of my comfort zone. I believed I could, before I even knew how to structure a joke. I pushed through the adversity of my changing routine and a heckler. I told jokes that were no good in class to find the ones that were.

You know who are good at the four mental muscles, our heroes. Whether movie heroes or real life heroes, they always excel at creating a limitless comfort zone, believing anything is possible, dealing with adversity and dismissing failures simply as steps closer to succeeding.

You can do it too. You be the hero. But you have to start. Start now. Push your comfort zone. Believe. Seek adversity. Fail often. Do it.

Be the hero of your story. Be the hero of your life. Be the hero to your wife. Be the hero to your kids. Be the hero to your Soul.

About Ray

Ray Brehm helps his clients manage passive income streams and grow their businesses. As a real estate investor for over 20 years, he found the quality of good property management companies truly lacking. In 2008, he co-founded a real estate property management company and quickly turned it into a multi-million dollar business. Ray is also a Certified Business Coach. When you put the two together, that is where it gets very interesting. Ray has a knack for applying principles of good business to real estate, in order to help investors manage their investments like true businesses. He also has a passion for helping business owners quickly convert their businesses into passive income streams. Ray believes "Passive Income is the Ninth Wonder of the World."

Ray graduated with a Bachelor of Science in Mathematics from Baldwin Wallace College in Berea, Ohio (now Baldwin Wallace University), where he was also a two-sport letterman. Ray started his career in corporate America, learning as much as he could, but always looking for his place. He found it as an entrepreneur.

As a business owner, Ray began learning and documenting what he calls the Mental Muscles of Success. By working these muscles, he found himself trying things most people wouldn't. "I went from obscurity one day to presenting alongside Dolf De Roos to real estate investors and being coached personally by Alex Charfen, the founder of one of the top business coaching firms in the country," he explains.

Ray's current projects include a book on how to run your real estate investments like a true business (with all of the hidden insights of both a business coach and real estate investor). Ray is also building a content marketing business to fill the much-needed niche of content for business owners' web presence.

Ray's dream is to build an Entrepreneur School for Youths, and teach as many of our future business owners as possible the power of owning your own business.

You can connect with Ray at:
info@raybrehm.com
RayBrehm.com
RPMPrivateWealth.com

CHAPTER 5

THE KEY TO SUCCESSFULLY GROWING A SMALL BUSINESS

BY CLATE MASK

It was December 2003 and we had no money. I remember it well, because my wife, Charisse, and I were trying to figure out how we would purchase Christmas presents for our children that year. I had partnered with Charisse's brothers, Scott and Eric Martineau, a year and a half earlier, and our startup was struggling – to put it mildly.

At the time we were taking home $2,500 a month, which barely covered the mortgage and living expenses for our family of six, not to mention the mounting credit card balances and $100,000 in student debt I had racked up in the process of getting a JD/MBA. Money was so tight back then that it caused some interesting exchanges with my wife and children.

I felt particularly embarrassed one night when my 8-year-old son asked, "Dad, why are you so mad?"

"Because a freakin' creditor called me on a Sunday!" I snapped.

The next question was, "What did he want?"

"He wanted to know why I haven't paid my bills."

"Well, Dad, did you tell him it's because you haven't made enough sales?"

At least my son knew the reason we didn't have enough money to pay the bills. You have to sell more to earn more.

On another occasion during those difficult times, an exasperated Charisse put it to me bluntly, "You have an MBA and a law degree, but we have no food in the cupboards. You need to quit working with my brothers and get a real job!" Thankfully, she had a change of heart, and we persisted until we made it through.

Back to December 2003. Since we had no money for presents, we decided Charisse would host a homemade jewelry party in order to make enough money to buy a few presents for the kids. On the night of the party, I worked on something that became the enabler for Infusionsoft's future success. What we learned in our business is an absolute game changer for any business that isn't already doing it.

Rather than beat around the bush, I want to get straight to the point and reveal **one of the most powerful secrets for growing your business**. In fact, of all the marketing and sales techniques you've heard, one will have a bigger impact on your business than any other.

If you want to be successful in your business, you must follow up consistently and effectively with ALL of your prospects and customers.

While Charisse was in the other room wowing people with her homemade wares, I sat down at a computer and created our first-ever automated follow-up campaign. The campaign featured six important pieces of content that readers would receive over the next six weeks. I wrote the first email and launched the campaign, knowing I would need to write the next email in the series by the time it was scheduled to go out the following week.

The next week I wrote the second email and it went out as scheduled. Then something magic happened. Someone called me, asked some questions about our software and was ready to buy. I need to underscore the point here… someone called me to buy our product. You have to understand that this had never happened before.

Prior to this sale, I had spent over a year doing everything we could imagine to drum up prospects and turn them into customers. It was hard work and the sales cycle was lengthy. We spent $5000 a month on marketing to generate leads (twice what we were taking home to support our families), but we had to work really, really hard to close every... single... sale!

I excitedly shared what happened with my co-founders, Scott and Eric, who were busy writing software, and they were happy that we got a sale but didn't fully realize the significance. And then, it happened again. And again! With much less effort, we were starting to get as many customers in a week as we used to scrape and claw to get in a month.

And the rest, as they say, is history. This year we plan to reach over $100M in sales and have more than 700 employees. I had no idea the impact that night in December 2003 would have on me and my family. Thankfully, Charisse was able to sell enough jewelry to buy some Christmas presents for our kids. And, even more important for the future well-being of my family, the power of personalized, automatic follow up became a reality in our business.

Now that you know the key to successfully growing a small business, let me tell you why it is the key.

You must be standing there the moment someone needs your product or service. You need to respond quickly when a customer makes a referral. And you better be on your A-game the moment a prospect finally turns to you for help. But why is follow up so important? Why is it the one thing that causes you to stand out from your competitors and drives more revenue to your bank account?

It all goes back to one basic marketing principle:

PEOPLE BUY WHEN THEY ARE READY TO BUY!

You don't think this applies to your business? Think again. Let's take the example of an attorney's law practice. Unlike many consumer goods and services, no one hires an attorney "just because." Hiring legal counsel is not an impulse decision. No one is going to seek those services...until they need them. Just because a prospect doesn't need legal services at this precise moment, it doesn't mean they won't need them in the future.

If you've been following up with ALL your prospects and customers, guess who's getting a phone call when the need arises for the products or services you sell. You! And here's why:

1. You're Building Relationships of Trust

Let's face it - the first time you speak with a prospective customer, they're assessing your personality, and, in most cases, they are putting up their best "you can't sell me" protective barrier. They're sizing you up; figuring out what they are going to say to you if you ask for the sale before they are ready to buy.

However, if you've done some relationship building with your prospects before you've even met, you've done what your competition only wishes they could do. You've already created some trust with your contacts. In place of distrust and skepticism, you've built loyalty and security. And guess what? When your prospects need your product or service (and they eventually will or they wouldn't be a prospect in the first place) they'll reach out to you, no matter what your competitors might be offering.

2. You're Keeping Your Name Fresh in Your Contacts' Mind

As great as your products and services might be, your prospects and past customers aren't likely sitting around thinking about you all of the time. They're busy, and they've got other things on their minds. They're thinking about work, things going on at home, running that pesky little errand that never gets done, etc.

When the need for your services arise, chances are that your prospects aren't thinking about your company. Back to our law firm example… suppose you are a lawyer. If someone is at a family reunion and mentions lawyers or legal services, others wouldn't typically think of mentioning your name. Unless…you have consistently reminded your contacts who you are, what you do, and what makes your services different from the competition.

With consistent, effective follow up, you never give your contacts a chance to forget about you. If **anything** related to what you do comes up in the course of their daily living, you're the first person your contacts think about.

3. You're Building the Loyalty of Your Prospects and Customers

The last benefit of keeping in touch with your contacts is that no one else is doing it. It's too hard. For the new business with only a handful of contacts, following up with people is easy. But the longer you're in business, the more difficult it becomes.

However, if you're taking the time to reach out to your contacts, they're going to feel it. And they'll appreciate it. You see, the primary reason customers don't refer friends, or give you repeat business, is because they don't feel appreciated. They feel as though they are simply one of many customers.

But you have the power to change that. With simple follow up, you can make your customers feel they are getting very personalized attention from you. And who wouldn't recommend service like that?

SO WHAT HAPPENS WHEN THERE'S NOT ENOUGH OF YOU TO GO AROUND?

If you've been in business very long, you've come to many of these conclusions yourself. You undoubtedly understand the value of consistent follow up. But like most business owners, you've stretched yourself too far as it is. How are you supposed to constantly follow up with all of your prospects and customers on top of everything else you've got to do?

It's not tough to figure out that the number one reason small business owners fail to follow up with prospects and customers is the lack of time. It's not an easy thing to run your business AND keep in touch with all of your contacts.

Unless…you automate your follow up.

With technology, it's easy to instantly send multi-step, multi-media, follow-up campaigns to exactly the right person at exactly the right time; and to create powerful, effective messages by personalizing those campaigns.

Let me give you an example of how this would work. Imagine you're an estate lawyer and a random prospect winds up on your website. They want to create a will and need an attorney. Right now, they're in the process of "researching" their options.

In an attempt to capture online leads, you've included a free report on your website entitled, "How to Draft Your Own Will (and Cut Down on Your Attorney Fees)." In exchange for someone's name, phone number, and email address, you're willing to part with an exclusive, valuable report.

The visitor is interested, so they sign up for the report. And since you understand the benefits of automation, rather than tracking their request, finding and sending the report, and following up with a phone call in a few days, you decide to let your automated follow-up marketing system take over. After all, you don't have the time to be constantly sending off free reports.

Once this visitor fills out the web form with their personal information, your automated system kicks in. Instantly, the new prospect is directed to a webpage that says, "Congratulations, your free report is being sent to the email address you gave us." (So far you don't have to do anything.)

The prospect goes to their email and finds the report. They like it. They appreciate the information you freely shared, and they are a little bit more interested in your firm. But not interested enough to take action yet. They're still looking at other options.

That's okay. You've got a plan. With an automated system at your disposal, the new prospect gets a "personal" email from you the next day. It says: *Hey, I hope you enjoyed the free report. Did you know a will is invalid if it's not properly created and witnessed?* And you send them more educational materials to go along with it. (As well as your contact information.)

Okay, you just moved this prospect to SERIOUS interest stage. Now whether the person requests your services at this moment or not is immaterial. With an automated process you can continue to send **predetermined, prewritten, personalized** letters, emails, postcards, texts and voice broadcasts at the right time. Can you see how this type of personalized automatic follow up makes you a strong contender when prospects need what you sell?

Anyone who knows me, knows that I love entrepreneurs. I love your courage. I love your creativity. I love the value you create. I want you to be successful.

Remember the impact of a simple email campaign in December of 2003. Business started to come to us without a ton of effort, and it changed everything. You can do the same thing in your business, and you'll be glad you did.

About Clate

Clate Mask is the Infusionsoft CEO and Co-Founder. He has been educating and inspiring entrepreneurs for over a decade, and is recognized by the small business community as a visionary leader. His passion for small business success stems from his personal experience, taking Infusionsoft from a struggling startup to an eight-time Inc. 500/5000 winner. As CEO, Clate is leading Infusionsoft on its mission to create and dominate the market of sales and marketing software for small businesses.

Under Clate's leadership, Infusionsoft has landed four rounds of venture capital including a $55 million Series D led by Bain Capital Ventures with contributions from prior investors, Signal Peak Ventures and Goldman Sachs. He was named an Ernst & Young Entrepreneur of the Year finalist, a Top 100 Small Business Influencer by Small Business Trends, one of the 100 Most Intriguing Entrepreneurs of 2013 by Goldman Sachs, and Business Leader of the Year by the Arizona Technology Council.

Clate is a national speaker on entrepreneurship and small business success, and co-author of *The New York Times* best-seller *Conquer the Chaos: How to Grow a Successful Small Business Without Going Crazy.* Clate has a BA in Economics from Arizona State University, as well as an MBA and a JD from Brigham Young University.

CHAPTER 6

TOP FIVE TIPS FOR SUCCESS

BY WARREN CLEVELAND

Becoming a pilot was the pursuit of my life. My dad was into aviation and flew remote control airplanes. I would go with him and watch those little planes soar with my father at the controls; it was our special time together. Cancer took him when I was only eight years old. After my dad died, the desire to become a pilot burned in me and I pursued it relentlessly.

I obtained a pilot's license at 17, when I was still in high school. In college, I got into a program where I could get my ratings. I was always focused and knew what I wanted to do. Everything I did was related to aviation. My first job in the field was to fly commuters, which I fulfilled for five years. I flew many different airplanes and was the youngest regional jack captain in the country at the age of twenty five.

Then I was hired with Continental Airlines. Walking onto the ground school of Continental, I felt this would be the last job I ever had. I was on the 737 as soon as I was able, and was upgraded to copilot on the 757 and 767, about ten months after that. I was flying out of Newark, but living in Florida, which is typical, but I wanted to move my family to PA so I could drive to work. This was in November, 2000. When September 11 happened, I lost my job October 1, 2001. I can remember crying on my wife's shoulder, saying, "What are we going to do? I worked my whole life to get here. Now it's being taken away from me." It was a real epiphany to figure out what to do next.

I had seen what the guy who helped sell my house in Florida made; and I thought it was a pretty nice payday for what he did. On October 2nd, I signed up for real estate school in PA, where I didn't know anyone. I'd only lived there a few months and had no idea what the hell I was doing, but I had the will to succeed… and few other options as failure was not one of them.

I went to work with a broker who taught the school. It turned out to be a complete disaster that accomplished nothing. I needed a mentor and coach, so I found a friend in real estate who said, "Hey, you should come with me and go to this Craig Proctor Training conference." This was in November of 2001, and my response was that I couldn't. I didn't have the money.

By May of that year, I was desperate and agreed to attend this training. I had to borrow the money, but I went. I attended the conference and then signed up for coaching. I didn't have the funds for that either, but I went ahead and registered, figuring I could make it happen. By August we were making money and my wife was able to quit her job because this new direction was outpacing her income. By following a system and having a coach, our new airplane took off, so to speak.

A year later, we were number one in the office of an established brokerage. We had done well and grown to where we had a couple of agents. Back in the '90s, I had sworn I'd never own my own business. I thought it was crazy; and said people who work that hard are truly "nuts". I was going to be an airline pilot the rest of my life, retiring number 11 on the seniority list at Continental.

But we succeeded in this new business. My wife set up the office as well as the back office, following Craig's system. Then in 2004, my seniority number was recalled. What that means in aviation terms is that I essentially had my job back if I wanted it. But we were in the middle of a big market up-turn; even in PA the markets were doing well. We had bought a couple properties and gone from almost bankrupt by the end of 2001, beginning of '02, to owning two houses in 2004. We had money to travel and life was good.

So I stayed out, by deferring my recall, but I went back in 2005 on the 777 as a copilot. I would bring all my real estate stuff with me because we flew long distance: NY to Tokyo, NY to Hong Kong, and occasionally we'd go to London. During this long haul flying, I started reading and working on my business. It was time away where I could work on the business with no phone calls. At one point, in Tokyo, I was making calls to sellers to book appointments and realized, "This is crazy!" I flew back and immediately had a listing appointment. I drove home, took a shower, and went straight to the appointment. The commission on that appointment would have equaled my entire salary as a pilot for the month.

I looked closely at my pilot status and said, "This is a waste of time. I don't need to do this anymore and it's a pain in the ass." I had discovered the entrepreneur spirit that I didn't know I had; and looking back on it, I was actually quite bored as an airline pilot, sitting up there. But I had worked my whole life to reach that goal, so it wasn't an easy realization to accept. However, I finally recognized what was right for me and resigned from Continental.

Many people thought I was out of my mind, to give up a world class career. But I wanted to be in charge of my own destiny. I wanted to have control over what happened to me; and if I was going to fail, it would be because I didn't try hard enough. It wouldn't be because of two idiots who flew airplanes into a few buildings, or because some CEO decided they needed to save money by laying off some of the workforce. I needed to be in complete control of where I was going and how my family fared.

So I resigned from Continental in December of 2006 and soon began to question why we were living in PA. We had moved there to get my flying career going, but I couldn't see any reason to stay. It took a little bit of time and effort, but in January of '08, I moved back to kickoff my south Florida business. I was licensed in Florida and began running TV commercials right away. It wasn't long before we realized that the market was in free-fall. I hadn't done the due diligence I should have; wasn't paying attention to the market. We were solely focused on getting out of the cold.

But in the first two weeks of January, I realized that the market was falling hard, like something had blown it up out of the sky, and it was just coming down. So I switched. I turned the TV off and decided to go into foreclosures. In one month I went from, "Hey, I'm the big man on campus with all my TV commercials" to "Alright, let's get down and dirty with bank-owned homes." Through a friend, I hooked up with a couple of guys out of NC who coached me to ramp up REOs quickly. Foreclosures and REOs are the same thing. REO stands for Real Estate Owned. It's the line item on a balance sheet for a lender that has loans that went bad and now they own the property.

Once again, I found a mentor and rather than reinvent the wheel, taking longer periods of time, I discovered a couple of brothers who knew what they were doing, who had a great reputation. I paid them a few bucks to coach and train me on how to sell bank-owned houses. Within a couple of months, I had cranked up that business, selling REOs where I had never done that before.

By June of '09, I was the number five Keller Williams agent in the country. This was in the middle of an absolutely devastating market crash. Everyone was struggling, but we were flourishing. We continued to hire and build our business; and were able to identify when it was time to transition out of REO and back into retail. At this time, I did TV commercials again and turned it all back on.

In the midst of this next transition, I hired another coach. I am a big believer in hiring people to help you, because success leaves clues; and if you want to be successful, you need to do the things that successful people do, and you will in turn be successful. It's almost guaranteed. Nothing's really new, it's just changed.

I realized we had to get more retail business, and to do that, I needed relevant presentations. I had to get back into sales. Our clients were bankers; they didn't need a sales pitch, just to be convinced of your skill and then they would send you property after property, where the average agent had to go out to 'hunt and kill' their business every day.

I am now a member of the National Association of Expert Advisors. I'm a mastermind member of that group. I'm fully expecting to increase my profitability this year by 20%. I anticipate selling fewer homes, but at a higher profit level. I will raise my sales price from the mid-100s to well over 200. I'm excited about where we are going.

In the course of my life, transitioning from what I thought was my dream to the discovery of what truly motivated me, I have identified five top tips which made all the difference in my success:

1. Reject Failure

I hate losing. Winning is OK, but losing tears me up inside. I hate losing more than I like winning. When you adopt the philosophy that failure is not an option, you propel yourself to do whatever it takes not to lose. It can be the motivation to move forward with the grit and determination that sets you apart from the rest. That mindset of being completely abhorrent of losing is the difference between someone who wants to be successful and someone who IS successful. Without that determination, most will give up when things get tough. If avoiding difficulty is more important to you that not losing, then you're set up for failure; but when failure is the worst thing imaginable, you can get through the challenges, because whatever they are, they are not worse than failure.

2. Don't be Afraid to be Different

It was by going against the proverbial grain that I found success. I quit a glamorous job, leaving the security of a pilot's retirement, to pursue what many saw as a risky business, without a safety net. If I had listened to the naysayers, and remained a pilot, I would not be where I am today. I could have made excuses, saying that a pilot is what I always wanted to be, but I knew in my heart I wanted more. Sometimes achieving greatness means not listening to those who question your decisions, and doing what no one else will attempt. It is when you go against traditional thought that untapped opportunities arise.

3. You need Accountability and a Coach

The most successful people on the plant have coaches. Sitting Presidents of the United States have called Tony Robbins when they needed advice. I was able to bypass the crowds and fast track to success by finding the right mentors. In many cases, there was an expense; and in the beginning, I took on the cost without knowing for sure how I would pay for it, but I knew that if I wanted to be successful, training from the right people was imperative. In every situation that I hired a coach, it set me on the path to tremendous success. I have proven this advice over and over again in my own life; and it is evident in the lives of most people you would label successful.

4. Work Hard

It's a simple concept, but hard work seems to be something people to go great lengths to avoid. Once you have the training from a mentor, while it will get you where you are heading faster, it does not replace hard work, only shows you where the effort should be spent. I literally worked 16 hour days for eight months to set up my business, but a year later, I could play golf any time I wanted; and I didn't need anyone's permission. I think it is Dave Ramsay who says, "Live like no one else, so you can live like no one else." The reference is: *Sacrifice a little now so that later on you'll reap the benefits*. You will reap the rewards of all the things you've done when you work hard.

5. Be Confident

Even when things aren't going the way you thought they would, believe in yourself. It isn't possible to succeed if you don't have faith in yourself first. Know that you are fully capable of success and that challenges, or downturns, are all part of the path to your goals. The minute you stop believing in yourself, you have lost, which circles back around to my first tip… rejecting failure happens when you have enough self confidence to know that you will never fail!

About Warren

Warren Cleveland began his career by achieving his dream to become a pilot of commercial aircraft. He flew many of the largest planes in the Continental fleet including the Boeing 737, 757/767, and 777 with destinations in the US, Europe, the Middle East, Asia, and Africa. After the events of 9/11 caused a reduction in capacity, he was furloughed; and he soon discovered a hidden entrepreneurial spirit.

Warren Cleveland began his new career as a real estate broker in 2001 and quickly rose up to be honored by the Keller Williams International franchise as being one of the TOP 10 Agents in the US for number of listings and closed transactions (out of 78,000 agents). Warren's personal business accounted for more than 50% of the overall office in which he worked, which was made up of over 200 agents. He did this in his first 12 months, despite being brand new to the market area.

In 2009, he founded the Every Florida Home brokerage. As the CEO, Warren oversees all operations and executive management decisions as well as provides leadership to the operation. In this new venture, he expanded the client list and facilitated significant growth by establishing relationships with over 20 corporate REO departments. This strategy established his team as one of the top 10 in the state of Florida for transactions during one of the worst real estate downturns ever witnessed.

Warren Cleveland has continually maintained high sales volume despite a reduction in overall supply during downturns in the market. He has also forged relationships with capital groups to initiate a rent-hold strategy through purchase of distressed assets throughout Florida. Last year alone, Warren sold over 340 homes. His unique programs offer sellers and buyers new and innovative customer experiences. Cleveland recently introduced a "Guaranteed Sale" program which offers sellers a guarantee should Warren not sell the home within 72 days.

Warren Cleveland currently resides in Palm Beach County, Florida where he manages his two businesses and enjoys time with his family while he pursues his hobbies of golf, fishing, and scuba diving.

If you are looking to buy or sell real estate in South Florida, you can contact Warren at:
Warren@WarrenCleveland.com
https://www.facebook.com/warren.cleveland.9
www.WarrenCleveland.com
Tel: 561-935-9772

CHAPTER 7

SUCCESS FOR YOUR CHILD STARTS TODAY: TIPS FOR FORMING PROPER HABITS

BY MARK KEMSLEY

Years ago my mother-in-law gave me a 24-karat gold ring. I didn't wear it often as it soon lost its shape. Gold is known for its great malleability, and is easily bent out of shape – and back in. Modern neuroscience is proving that, like pure gold, our minds and our habits are much more malleable than we once thought. Unlike early psychologists such as Freud, who believed that the habits and experiences of early childhood are doomed to be ingrained in us forever, modern neuroscientists and psychologists believe that the mind is basically open, flexible, and infinite in its potential to learn and create new habits—so long as we realize what those habits are and know how to change them.

Many of our children are not learning how to cultivate or use this basic mental flexibility. Instead, with the influence of dull routines, pop culture, and seductive media, they become mentally rigid and scattered by distractions. They accumulate a random collection of good and bad habits rather than an intentionally-chosen set of positive ones. Look at your parents or grandparents and it may be obvious that, as we age, we lose a great deal of our natural flexibility, and struggle to learn, retain, and comprehend new information. How can we help our children to fully realize their minds' potential while they are young?

I work with many incredible schools that are preparing their students for excellence. But it's not the schools alone that determine the success of a child – parents are the foundation for everything we educators accomplish in a classroom. As a parent of four, I know the amount of sacrifice and struggle that accompanies raising a child; even the most motivated, kindhearted and intelligent children need phenomenal amounts of support, guidance, and discipline from their parents.

Most of us, however, have felt inadequate or confused. Our children struggle, and we wish we could do more to help them, but we don't know how. In these few pages I hope to give you some practical concepts that can help you guide your child to success.

PARENTING THE BEST WE CAN

How our negative habits hinder our children:
Aggressive Parenting, Passive Parenting, Splitting,
and the Drama Triangle

Generally speaking, there are two harmful extremes we fall into as parents. First, aggressive parenting, or guiding too tightly; and second, passive parenting, or guiding too loosely.

Our parents may have hit us or yelled at us when they were unhappy with our behavior, but aggressive parenting isn't always abusive or physical – we stray into aggressive parenting when we attempt to control the uncontrollable: our children's actions.

No matter how tightly we attempt to govern their daily activities, access to media, and friend groups, children will always make their own choices. When we attempt to control them through harsh lectures, disproportionate punishments, or shaming them as stupid or lazy, we are being aggressive. The wisdom buried in aggressive parenting is the desire to provide structure and rules that are necessary for children, not only for their protection, but so they learn to have high standards and to respect the knowledge and guidance of their elders. However, when we aggressively shame, control, or punish our children, we are breeding resentment and anger in them, increasing the likelihood that they will rebel or sabotage themselves just to get back at us, and we are damaging their self-image.

The opposite extreme is just as harmful or perhaps worse. Passive parenting is when we back down from conflict and blindly believe nothing will go wrong. Passive parenting is letting children do whatever they please, often because we are afraid of making them unhappy with us. The wisdom buried in passive parenting is that we believe in our children and know they are intelligent and good. However, when we are too passive we can often set up little tyrants who manipulate the entire family, lack respect for others, and gain a sense of entitlement toward the world.

Often parents have both extremes going on. One parent is usually more aggressive, the other more passive. This leads to a dynamic called the drama triangle, a concept invented by Stephen Karpman to describe the most common form of dysfunction in most families. The triangle is made up of three roles: persecutor, rescuer, and victim. In spite of how they may sound, all of these roles are equally negative.

Persecutors feel insecure about lack of control. Perhaps their child's grades are slipping, and it makes them feel anxious. This anxiety quickly turns into anger or aggression, which they then unleash at the victim in an attempt to change the victim's behavior, exact punishment, or prevent the circumstance from happening again.

Rescuers feels uncomfortable with seeing the victim suffer. They may have empathy or compassion for the victim, or sometimes they rescue because of their own discomfort with the victim's emotions. In their constant attempts to help the victim avoid difficulty and stress, they teach the victim that he or she is weak and unable to deal with life independently.

Through acting helpless, persecuted, powerless, depressed, or overwhelmed, victims can avoid accountability for their mistakes. Children who grow up in households where splitting like this occurs, often learn to, as the Romans put it, *"Divide et impera"* – divide and conquer. They quickly learn to manipulate the conflict between their parents in order to gain whatever they want.

These children will tell one story at home and another at school, and succeed in pitting parents against teachers. This can be disastrous. Though we respect our children's perspectives, when we take their word over that of their teachers and react with anger or entitlement over a grade or a teaching style, we turn our children into victims. They no longer have to learn, change, grow, problem-solve, or accept responsibility for choices – they simply manipulate us into changing the world for them.

Splitting is especially dangerous for adolescents; they must learn that their parents and their mentors are all united in one purpose and that only their own hard work can help them. Instead of focusing on changing the personalities and choices of their teachers and parents, children must learn to focus on growing themselves. When we succeed in presenting a united front and a balanced parenting style, our children will develop healthier habits.

THE ANATOMY OF A HABIT

Cues, Behaviors, and Rewards

We've arrived at the heart of the chapter: an exploration of where habits come from, how they work, and how to use that knowledge to help our children succeed. I once heard somebody say that people are nothing more than a bundle of habits. That's a bit of an oversimplification, but it's true that the vast majority of our behaviors are habitual.

In his book *The Power of Habit*, Charles Duhigg outlines the basic anatomy of our habits, helping us gain power to change them. There are three parts to every habit: the cue, the behavior, and the reward. As I review the three parts, I'm going to use the powerful habit of smoking as an example.

Cues are the triggers or little signals that make us want to begin the behavior of a habit. They are usually associated with the structure of our lives: the routines and everyday events. If you've ever been a smoker, you know that certain situations will immediately make you want to smoke. Perhaps the end of a shift triggers you to smoke solely because your routine is to smoke every time you walk outside. Cues are the circumstances and situations that drive us to perform the behavior. Cues can be difficult to change because they are outside of us, and yet changing them can be the most important first step in gaining new habits or abandoning old ones.

For example, many of us have a much easier time breaking old habits when we are away from home on a vacation. Doctors have advised people for decades that it is easier to quit smoking while on vacation, where many of the old cues are missing. Instead of being surrounded by coworkers who trigger stress that makes you want to smoke, for example, you find yourself in a completely different environment where new cues are being made, like a new time for waking up every day.

The next part of a habit is the behavior, which is normally all that we think of when we consider of our habits. For example, smoking a cigarette is a behavior. We also tend to focus on the behavior when we want to change those habits. So many people decide, "I'm going to stop smoking!" but don't realize all the cues, rewards, and hidden difficulties until they really try to quit. We generally have little understanding of the reasons that make us continue smoking, or the reasons we don't exercise more or keep ourselves from overeating. This brings us to the third part, the reward.

The rewards are the obvious or hidden reasons we continue to perform the habit cycle. Generally, there are many rewards associated with any given habit. In the cigarette habit, you receive the obvious reward of satisfying a chemical craving, but you also receive less obvious rewards. Perhaps smoking is the way you bond with friends by sharing cigarettes after a meal, and this contributes to your feeling of emotional well-being.

Essentially, all of our habits help us fulfill a need. People have many needs, not only for very obvious things like food, water, and shelter, but for things like comfort, pleasure, companionship, affection, and even very abstract needs like a sense of meaning in life or connecting with something higher than ourselves. All of us have needs, and rewards are the parts of habits that feed into them.

As you can see, there are many reasons why we continue our habits, but we remain powerless to them until we become familiar with the cues that drive us to initiate the habits, and until we become aware of the subtle rewards we gain from the behavior. When we stop and think about the cues and rewards, this gives us tremendous power and insight by which we can replace the negative habits with positive ones that deliver equivalent rewards.

OUT WITH THE OLD, IN WITH THE NEW

Turning unwanted habits into good habits

Habits can be deliberately changed, and often we hear that the time it takes to develop or eliminate a habit is 21 days. This concept originates with research conducted in the 1950s, and much has been said in support, or refute, of it. Regardless, you can change a habit by understanding what causes you to do what you do, and by making a conscious decision to replace that habit with something that gives you a similar reward for a sustained period of time.

We often work with students to instill good study habits. We have them keep journals of homework and study they need to complete, and we guide them in creating and implementing plans for completion. In the process, we sometimes help them with other habits they are dealing with. A somewhat random habit that we helped a student to overcome was her inability to make a decision.

When Leah came to Kemsley Academy she could not make the simplest of decisions. We quickly learned not to even ask her what she preferred to eat as facing such a choice made her feel anxious.

After a couple of weeks I realized that she did not have a serious case of what Walter Kaufmann of Princeton University called "Decidophobia." She simply had lived a life in which her parents decided everything for her. The fact that Leah was now planning her study schedule, rather than just doing what she was told, seemed to give her a feeling of ownership that she learned to appreciate. She replaced the reward of freedom from making decisions with that of feeling empowered. Long story short – within a month Leah had no problem at all making the simple daily decisions of life.

This may not sound like an important change, but to Leah it was huge. She went from following everyone else all the time to being a leader in her own right. A year later she is demonstrating strong leadership qualities, becoming a self-appointed guidance counselor for new international students who attend her school.

But just as we can consciously replace bad habits with good, we must be careful not to unintentionally do the opposite. Consider the case of Julie.

Julie studied at a boarding school in New Hampshire. She made good grades and enjoyed associating with her friends. Over Spring Break of her Junior year, Julie returned to China for three weeks of good food, good fun, late nights, and no study. After the break she just couldn't seem to get herself back into the habit of studying. She attended classes, but didn't do her assignments.

It took two weeks for these new, lazy habits to catch up with her. She had an exam to take and had no idea how to do the material. Unfortunately,

Julie didn't react well to this problem. She made a bad decision, cheated on the test, and got expelled from school. This is how I met Julie. The school called me and asked if I could help her to find another school – a difficult task under the circumstances. The following year Julie graduated from a good high school, but it just wasn't the same caliber as the one she left behind. Obviously her bad decision was the pivotal factor here, but I can't help but think that this all wouldn't have happened if she hadn't let her good habits go during the three weeks that she was home in China.

Our campus in Massachusetts is a school break destination for international students who don't go home for holidays. Though the kids need to rest from their rigorous school schedules, we also make sure that they don't lose their good habits. They get up in the morning and attend classes for a couple of hours. They can enjoy the rest of the day as they like, but in the evening, we check in with them to ensure that they are ready for class the next day, reminding them of the need to retire at a reasonable hour to avoid "jet lag" when they start back at school. Your home is likely the primary school break destination for your kids. Giving them some structure during the holidays can go a long way to helping them pick up where they left off back at school.

I hope that in this very limited space I have triggered some thoughts that will contribute to the success of your child. You'll find many more ideas in my soon-to-be-published book *21 Days Can Change a Child's Life*.

About Mark

Mark Kemsley has helped change the lives of many adolescents – and their parents! After earning a degree in both Finance and International Business from Brigham Young University, he spent 20 years in Greater China. Based in Hong Kong, managing the Asian operations of an American corporation, he logged over 1300 flights and dealt with people from all levels of industry and government throughout the region.

Later as a business consultant, Mark was highly sought after as a speaker and trainer in Asia, and accumulated hundreds of hours on stage, presenting in English, Mandarin and Cantonese. Mark has appeared on a dozen television programs, and trained thousands of people. In 2008, he was nominated by American Business Awards as "Best Trainer of the Year."

A consulting assignment that Mark undertook in 2000 gave his career a new direction and new meaning. He spent two years helping to set up what is now the most successful English-language training company in China. He discovered then the joy of seeing people's lives change for the better as they acquired new skills. Having raised four tri-lingual children with his wife, Jenny, he was highly motivated to help kids in China to succeed through language acquisition as well. He began by renting school campuses and bringing teachers from the US to run summer camps in China. That evolved to purchasing a 15-acre campus in Massachusetts, where Kemsley Academy fills its dormitories with Chinese students each summer. The organization also helps international students to enter boarding schools in New England and manages them throughout their academic careers.

As he worked with the students, Mark became aware that most of them were not nearly as diligent as he had expected them to be. He soon came to realize that the stereotypical "hard working Chinese student" is often one who is being micro-managed in his study by his parents. Once in the US, freed from parental supervision, many of them are incapable of managing their own time and study. This prompted Mark to research the psychology of developing good study habits.

So what are all those kids doing at Kemsley Academy each summer? They're participating in a program called "21 Days Can Make A Difference," in which they receive English-language instruction in various school subjects, as well as learning and practicing study skills, forming new habits in the process. The results have been tremendous, and Mark is swarmed by grateful parents every time he travels to China. Perhaps not all habits can be changed in 21 days, but Mark is a strong advocate of setting clear objectives and developing patterns of behavior that will make the achievement of those objectives come naturally.

To learn more about Mark and Kemsley Academy, visit: www.kemsley.org
Or contact him via email at: mark@kemsley.org.

CHAPTER 8

SEVEN QUICK CASH FIXES FOR ANY BUSINESS

BY BETSI BIXBY

Cash in your business doesn't create happiness, but it sure makes life easier. All business owners I know want to increase their company's cash. Is that you?

Whether you are reading this chapter just to "tweak" your cash up a little for growth, or you know first-hand the gut-wrenching feeling of a true cash crunch – no money for payroll, having to fire long-term employees, selling off assets, or even closing down partial operations, this can help you.

When a business is short on cash repeatedly, owners lose sleep and lose confidence. When the problem persists, it strains marriages, tempers and in worst cases causes divorce or even suicide. Cash shortages affect entire families.

In the skinny margin world I live in, cash isn't a want, it's a need. While strong cash flow is vital to any business; it's the lifeblood of paper-thin margin businesses where gross profits are literally measured in pennies. These skinny-margin family businesses are my clients. Their profits are measured in tenths of a cent, not dollars. So they have no room for sloppiness or errors. If they lose money on one deal, it can take them dozens, even scores, of others to recoup their loss.

And I have a confession. Prior to the recession, the techniques in this chapter while proven, effective and highly practical, weren't personal to me. They were just for my clients. But shortly into the recession, after a vital division in my own company simply dried up from market forces, I suddenly found myself in the cash flow vice having to use these techniques to get my own company back on solid cash ground. They really work!

But let me digress. For over two decades, I've been privileged to help thousands of family-owned distribution companies avoid losses and increase their vital cash flow. I've introduced them to practices that have brought them consistent success. During that time, I've discovered that the techniques used in this specialized industry work just as well for companies in other businesses.

This chapter is to get you started on more cash and fast! With market forces hitting so many companies during and after the recession like a ton of bricks, and experiencing my own cash crunch, I felt compelled to get these quick fixes to business owners. Since these approaches have been so profitable for companies that operate on margins in fractions of pennies, imagine what they will do for a business like yours with margins measured in dollars.

ABOUT ME

Some folks think cash flow training should come from college courses. My cash flow knowledge didn't come from my MBA in Finance, but was first learned in the nation's premier commercial loan officer training program. Starting fresh out of college in the loan officer's chair, and later rising to the rank of Vice President, the Quick Fix cash flow concepts presented in this book were honed as I analyzed hundreds of businesses.

As my banking career progressed, I became frustrated. Often, I could clearly see why a company was not achieving peak cash flow, but banking practices tied my hands and prohibited me from offering help. When enough frustration built up, the entrepreneur in me grew restless, and thus the seeds for my present company, Meridian Associates, Inc., took root.

At about that same time, one of my banking clients was President of an industry trade association, and decided to hold a seminar for his fellow marketers on cash flow. At that time (early1991), bankers were disenchanted with the petroleum industry and reasonably priced bank debt was tough to get and keep. I presented my "Banker's Method of Cash Flow" talk to a group of about 125 petroleum marketers, who had annual sales between $2 million and $500 million, and cash flow that ranged from tight to severely tight. In my closing remarks, I invited them to call me if they needed help with cash flow or financing. That was a Saturday.

Monday morning, my phone at the bank began ringing, and the seeds for Meridian Associates, Inc. started bursting out of the ground. Since that first seminar, I've lost count of the actual number of family-owned petroleum distribution companies I've been blessed to help, but it's well over 3,500 companies.

PRACTICAL AND TESTED

The techniques here are not academic or theoretical—they're time-tested, proven methods that will boost your cash as well as your profits. And they will work for virtually all types of businesses, *if you act.* Make no mistake though; you cannot achieve the success you crave without taking action. While all really work, and fast, they take effort and some persistence. (I'm reminded of James 1:22, "Be doers of the word." God likes action too!) If you apply these quick-fix lessons of the tough petroleum distribution industry to your business, you can indeed begin making serious improvements in your cash.

Start building your bank account now with these seven quick fixes!

1. Collect one old receivable you previously wrote off.

Do you know that not being able to pay a bill can eat at an honest man's conscience for years? One of my clients had written off a farmer's account when a bad year made the farmer go belly up. When the farmer got back on his feet and started up business again, he went to a different supplier. My client figured it was because of the farmer's embarrassment.

He decided to call the farmer as he'd heard he was now doing well. Much to his surprise, the farmer took his call and proceeded to say how badly he had felt for years about that debt, how he now had the cash, and could he write him a check? What a blessing for both parties and now the farmer is buying from him again.

2. Ask for return of a cash deposit.

In the early years, before a company has established a good credit record, landlords, utility companies, vendors, insurance companies, and others often require it to post deposits. As time goes by, it's easy to forget about those deposits. Review your records. Do you have any deposits out there? If so, call and find out if you're entitled to have your deposit, or a portion of it, returned. Again, only one phone call could be standing between you and your money.

3. Get rid of just one non-turning or slow inventory item.

Return just one unsellable or unprofitable product to the original vendor for cash rebates or credits to your account. If the vendor won't accept returns, sell the item on the open market. Somebody, somewhere will want it.

Get the word out about the sale; post it on the internet. Try marking the item's price down, or group it with another product. For instance, if buyers purchase two high margin items of your choice, give them a bonus item at no additional cost — something you want to get rid of.

4. Pay one key supplier more slowly.

Vendor terms are like interest-free loans — the longer you have to pay, the better. Many vendors will negotiate terms, *but only if you ask*. If you've been a stellar account for a major supplier, ask for extended terms. If your supplier won't budge, seek out alternative suppliers who offer goods of similar quality and will give you longer or better terms. Check the Internet for alternate sources; it can make researching suppliers quick and easy.

If you have no other supply options, consider paying for items with a non-interest bearing credit card. Paying by credit card can provide you with the added bonus of airline miles or rebates.

5. Call your banker for a lower interest rate.

If you're not used to dealing with bankers, asking for interest rate reductions can be intimidating. But trust me, it works. Most businesses have a number of small loans for their vehicles, equipment and other expenses; it's a standard part of doing business.

So, call your banker. Ask if he or she hates having to process all those little, individual payments as much as you do, and question whether he or she finds it cost effective. See about getting all those little loans consolidated into one big note, and when you do, request an interest rate reduction.

6. Sell one unused asset.

We all have items we no longer use. They can range from anything as small as an extra computer to as big as a real estate parcel that isn't appreciating as much as we hoped it would. The sad fact is that most businesses have all sorts of stuff lying around that is not being used. Check with your team, take inventory, and figure out what you don't need. Then get rid of it in the most cost-effective manner to produce cash.

Some of the techniques you can use to convert assets into cash include telling your business associates, colleagues, employees, subcontractors, vendors and suppliers. Place classified ads in local publications, newsletters and blogs; put up *For Sale* signs at your business and other places; list property with agents; and use Internet sites.

7. Create an irresistible offer for existing customers.

When you need cash fast, no one is more likely to buy from you than your satisfied customers. The cheapest way to contact them is by email. (If you don't have email addresses for your customer base, you'll have to resort to alternative methods.) If your offer to your customers is special, something they would be nuts to refuse, it will work every time. Offer only items that they will pay for on the spot because you don't want to end up with receivables, especially from your present customers.

To make your proposition more attractive, offer your existing customers bonuses. Give them items from your inventory, services, or freebies from your suppliers or other businesses that would like to join you in a promotion that your customers would value. For instance, you could offer buyers of your items a free lunch at your friend's restaurant or a gift certificate for a free car wash. Just think about goods or services your customers would want and then call business owners who could supply them.

NEXT STEPS

As you experience cash success, please share it with me at: www.7QuickFixesBook.com

You'll find your success story could be worth even more cash as we'll be rewarding outstanding successes! And while there, be sure to check out all the business building help.

Enjoy this chapter and refer to it often.

About Betsi

Betsi Bixby and her company Meridian Associates, Inc. currently assist over 3,500 of this country's privately held, family-led petroleum companies increase cash flow and profits through education, strategic planning facilitation, merger mediation, business valuation and brokerage services. Her message is one of executable steps and core competencies that every business owner or manager needs to know.

Betsi has been the most widely-read cash flow expert in the petroleum industry, where pennies not dollars, have dictated success for over two decades. Through her *Money Matters* column published by the Petroleum Marketers Association of America (PMAA) and many state and regional petroleum, convenience store, and propane associations, years of publishing her newsletter *The Meridian Financial Advantage,* and now her PetroAnswers membership website, Betsi clarifies and simplifies complicated subjects into concrete step-by-step processes that dramatically impact company performance and profits.

A financial sharp shooter, Betsi is well known for the value she brings to businesses and the families that own them. By customer demand, Betsi began Meridian's highly-acclaimed Valuation and Brokerage Division in late 1999. Betsi and Meridian quickly earned a reputation for accurate market valuations and have continued to achieve great success facilitating highly confidential sales of family-owned companies.

Betsi Bixby is also well-known by major refiners, conducting training each year for the major gasoline brands. Betsi's background includes an MBA in Finance and serving as Vice President of Commercial Lending for a regional bank before founding Meridian. She captivates convention audiences throughout the U.S. with her hard-hitting, practical key note addresses and workshops.

In 2011, Betsi became a founding member of the John Maxwell Team, intensely studying John C, Maxwell and his leadership principles based on his premise that "Everything rises and falls on leadership." Betsi and her team coach family business CEOs and their executive teams to new levels of personal and professional success.

With Christ-centered personal ethics, Betsi strives to be a blessing to her customers, her employees and the family businesses she loves. Betsi resides in Weatherford, Texas where she enjoys a ranching lifestyle, complete with cattle and horses. Betsi's equestrian pursuits include a Top-Three national ranking by The American Competitive Trail Horse Association. In 2011, Betsi co-founded Freedom Horses, a non-profit

501(c)(3) organization that links survivors of domestic violence with volunteer horse owners to build courage, compassion and confidence. Betsi is former Chairman of the Tucson YMCA, former President of Greater Tucson Leadership, and former President of Soroptimist International of Tucson. Betsi considers her greatest accomplishment to be her daughter Sheila, who achieved a Masters in Behavioral Health Counseling and now resides in California.

If you have questions or comments, please email them to her at: betsi@7QuickFixesBook.com.

CHAPTER 9

STAIRWAY TO SUCCESS: A STORY OF TWO DENTISTS!

BY DR. BRUCE SEIDNER

When I look back at the last 29 years, there is a life lesson to be shared with all. We are going to look at two successful dental practices and see why one achieved overabundant success.

WHERE ARE THE PEOPLE?

It was a fall day in 1986 in northwest New Jersey. Here I am, this young 26-year-old about to embark on his destiny. Starting my career, in a town I never heard of until three months ago. What does this guy think he is doing? I was practicing as an associate dentist in Florida, and just got the urge to open my own practice. Originally from Brooklyn, NY, I decided the northeast is where I wanted to settle and raise a family. The suburbs are the American dream, with three kids, a dog and a yard to play in, unlike the concrete jungle I grew up in. By chance I stumbled upon a rural location in an area I could only hope would evolve into a growing community. I took a leap of faith and decided this would be my home. Commuting every other weekend from Florida to oversee the construction of the new office was a challenge to say the least, but with perseverance it was finally complete, and I was ready to open.

The day finally came to show my mother and father the office. It was a cloudy fall day when we made the one-hour journey from Brooklyn, NY. I was excited to show my parents how proud I was of what I had just accomplished (even though I had not earned a penny yet). The ride was quiet, not much conversation, as I was just hoping they would give me their approval, as every child would want from their parents.

For you people that are fans of the show Seinfeld, just imagine that Mr. and Mrs. Seinfeld are in the car with me. We arrive at the new office building and the first word out of my mother's mouth is, "WHERE ARE THE PEOPLE?" I don't see any people here."

Now to put this into context, being from Brooklyn and growing up in a 2-bedroom apartment where my brother and I slept feet-to-feet for 16 years, you could not avoid being surrounded by people. My parents both worked in Manhattan and commuted on the subway, in which there are people everywhere. To bring them, at the time, to a rural/suburban community was a little bit of a culture shock to say the least.

We do not even make it to the reception desk before my mom gasps, "What is he, crazy? Opening up in the middle of nowhere? How is he going to get patients? I don't know what he is going to do? Did he make a mistake? Dave, we have to go, I am starting to get sick."

But the sound of my mother's voice was in my head. Was I crazy? Am I doing the right thing? How am I going to get patients? Come to think of it, where **are** the people?

Let me tell you the ride back to Brooklyn was not an express route door-to-door. My mother did get ill, and we literally had to stop every ten or so minutes to find a bathroom for her.

We made it home and now the pressure was on. I had to make this work. I made my last trip to Florida, said my goodbyes, and packed up the U-Haul and made the trek to my new home in Randolph, NJ. I was a stranger in a town that I knew little about. It didn't take long to find the necessities, grocery store and of course the pizza shop.

The grand opening was in November of 1986, and the excitement was in the air. I did my demographic research and although there were other dentists in town, I knew there was room for one more. Then another bombshell hit. As I was reading the local newspaper in which I had placed an ad announcing my grand opening, on the next page there was another grand opening announcement. Holy Crap! What the heck is going on! Another dentist opening up the same time I am? Maybe Mrs. Seinfeld was right. Was I crazy? Did I just make the biggest mistake of my life and career?

As it turned out, it was the best decision I ever made. Despite these and other obstacles, I learned, studied and implemented a proven formula for success and grew my practice from a small fledging office in a rural community to a practice that is in the top 0.5% in the entire country.

STAIRWAY TO SUCCESS

Although this is a story about a dental office, these principles apply to every business. Basically, all service businesses are in the people business and without the fundamental understanding of basic human nature, it will be almost impossible to grow.

Step 1 – Show Your Client Appreciation and Respect
We all need to be somebody and be recognized for it. Every person we see is one thousand times more interested in himself than in anyone else. In our office, as far as we are concerned, he is the most important person in the world. If we don't follow this law of nature it will work against us. It is a basic human need to want to be loved and respected. Make that person feel special. Give him a big hello when they enter the door. Always greet them by their first name.

Step 2 - Listen
Our patients must like us before they will want what we have to offer. We can make more friends with our patients by genuinely being interested in them. Ask gentle probing questions about them or their interests and let them talk about it. You have to counteract your normal human behavior to share your experiences and talk about yourself. Let them talk and genuinely LISTEN! By following this principle, people will naturally like you and trust you because you care about them as a person. There will be no need to sell them. They will readily accept your recommendations, because people will trust us and feel secure that we know what is best for them. This principle needs to be followed by

every member of your staff.

Step 3 – Don't Sell, Help!

Find out what people want and give it to them. Scientific evidence has shown that people don't like to be sold. They like to buy, but they don't like for anyone to sell them anything. More and more people are interested in maintaining their health and youth. When we genuinely know and understand the needs of the client, all we have to do is meet their needs.

Selling consists of trying to convince someone they need a product or service, based on the seller's perspective of the benefits of the product. Helping someone consists of providing a solution that addresses his or her particular need.

Step 4 - The KISS Principle

When people become stressed they stop listening and learning. Pressure and stress will be the main reasons why people will leave your business. It could come from anyone in your office, and it should be mandatory policy that this principle is not violated. Let's face it. Most people are stressed out alone just coming to the dental office. We don't need to add to this and complicate their lives even further. We believe in the KISS principle (keep it simple s.....).

Don't complicate any part of their visit. From the initial phone call to every person they interact with, just keep it simple. Let them make the decisions. Try not to give them too many options. You will only confuse them. You are the expert. You know what is best.

Step 5 – VIP Status

We must inflate our patient's ego. A person's ego is one of the most sensitive things a person owns. It describes who he or she is and how they think about themselves. Once we learn how to boost a person's ego–genuinely–we will create a tremendous ally. Our egos have a large appetite and they need to be fed.

Make every person that comes in your office a VIP! Any business that is able to focus on this point and treat every person like a VIP will create ambassadors for your business that will readily recommend you to their friends and family.

Step 6 – Be Chameleon-like

You must be flexible and adapt to the needs and desires of every client. We see people everyday from different backgrounds with different cultural diversities. You and your staff need to act like a chameleon and blend in with the different types of people. When you can successfully get on their level, you will, once again, building on the likeability and trust factor.

Step 7 – Success!

You must be good at what you do! In our case we must be good dentists. Learning does not stop when we graduate. It is just the beginning of our education. When you get it in your head that you should be constantly learning and improving your lifelong craft, you will become more confident and deliver a better product to your customers.

Self-confidence in our abilities is extremely important. The well-seasoned practitioner knows full well how important our confidence level is in our treatment skills. Your patients want someone who is confident in their ability and will readily accept your recommendations if you are.

Here are the basics. These need to be established first and foremost:

(A). Becoming the best you!

> They say that your net worth is directly proportional to your self-esteem. Throughout my career, I was filled with doubt, anxiety, and other counter-productive messages that were holding me back. It was not until I began to program my sub-conscious mind with positive messages and, most important, believing that I deserved abundant success was when the real growth took place. Work on yourself. You need to constantly program your sub-conscious for success. The world is full of abundance. There is enough for everyone. Believe that you can accomplish great things! Do not look at the competition. It's up to you to take charge of your life and your business. You are the leader. You are the CEO. Once you believe in yourself, clearly define your goals, begin a plan of action and there will be no stopping you! All successful people took personal responsibility as a starting point before change really began to happen. What is holding you back? Are you not taking enough educated risks? Are you not looking at your business from your patient's point of view?

Once you get your head on straight, you will automatically begin to take new and powerful actions that will put you in the right direction. Where focus goes, energy flows!

(B). Putting it all Together

Nothing is done overnight. By applying the above principles and believing in yourself you are taking the steps to take your practice to new levels. Remember you own a business and that makes you an entrepreneur. An entrepreneur's job is to create value, market it and grow the business. In my mind, I think about ways to improve the business everyday. Now, no one was born a great businessperson or great dentist. We need to give equal time to learning and to improving both. Learning never ends. When you stop learning, you stop growing. Every step along the way of my career, I never said I was done. Every blockage that I encountered along the way, I sought out someone who was more successful than I was and modeled what they have done. Some of my biggest growth spurts came after spending a day in someone's mega successful office. There are plenty of experts out there that have paved the way for you. Learn from them and put your spin on it to make it work for you.

So what happened to our two dentists? I can only speak for one that, kept learning, modeled other successful dentists, took risks, and believed that in order for a business to grow you need to expand. This dentist did not stay in that original office. He knew that in order to grow he had to have the capacity to accommodate his growing practice. He built a 10,000 sq. ft. building in which as of this writing he has 26 chairs and 6 dentists working all in a single location. The other dentist that started at the same time remained in his small location and I am sure doing well but never grew. "A plant will only grow as large as the pot will allow."

You are reading this book because you want to achieve abundant success. It all starts with you. Change comes when you make that decision. Get out of your comfort zone. Take educated risks. Everyday you waste is a day you never get back. Become the best you, and you will realize as I do that the sky is the limit!

Entrepreneurship is living your life like most people won't,
so that you can spend the rest of your life like most people can't.

~ Unknown

About Dr. Bruce

Dr. Bruce Seidner, CEO of WOW Effect Seminars, LLC helps dentists around the country achieve their dream practice. He began his speaking career in 2010 as a guest speaker at some of the national dental meetings. He put together his own program in 2015, "Create the 'WOW' effect in your practice" – and is teaching his principles of success all across the United States. He has taken his knowledge of his thirty years in dentistry and teaches it to dentists in a program that not only transforms their practices, but also enriches their lives. His philosophy is simple: "Don't reinvent the wheel!" Learn from people that have been there and done it. What sets him apart is his amazing ability to sift through all the clutter and break it down for you in a very easy-to- understand simplified formula. Once implemented, he knows that you will be able to achieve abundant success.

Dr. Seidner is a graduate of Emory Dental School in Atlanta, Georgia in 1984. He earned his fellowship from The Academy of General Dentistry in 2001. He was selected as Chabad's "Man of the Year" in 2013.

Currently CEO of Seidner Dentistry & Associates, PC, he began his practice career in northwest New Jersey in 1986. Starting a small practice from scratch, he has grown it to a practice that is in the top 0.5% of the country and continues to grow every year. He believes you need to surround yourself with good people. Every business needs a leader. This is not a skill most people are born with and it is a process. When done correctly, you have the ability to empower your team and that's when true abundance will occur. His journey is truly a rags to riches story. He believes the American dream is still out there. You just need the correct knowledge to go out and get it.

He is a gifted communicator and a leading clinician in the All-on-4™ teeth in one-day procedure. He gives an over-the-shoulder program with his team in which dentists from around the country come to learn this revolutionary procedure hands-on in a live patient experience. He has also opened his office for a one-day program in which dentists can learn how his office runs and model after it. It is his way of giving back (or paying it forward) for the countless offices that he went to spend a day in and learn from them.

Bruce, besides building a mega-successful dental practice, has used his business skills and opened a real estate investing company in 2010. He is CEO of GTBS Properties LLC, which now controls over $7.5 million in residential rental properties. Applying his same success formula has his real estate venture growing profitably every year.

Contact:
Bruce@woweffectseminars.com
www.woweffectseminars.com
www.randolphnjdentist.com

CHAPTER 10

HOW CAN MY OFFLINE BUSINESS REALISTICALLY GENERATE AN ADDITIONAL SIX- OR SEVEN- FIGURES FROM THE WEB?

BY CHRISTOPHER ULRICH

There are millions of websites online today, and a special group of ordinary businesses watch their sales explode while their competition struggles to keep the doors open. Do you lose sleep, wondering how you will make payroll? Are you losing business to little-known or inferior competitors? There is a very good chance that the Internet is to blame – for one company's success and another company's struggles.

Over the last 20 years, I've been fortunate to help a wide range of clients, from small businesses to multi-billion dollar international brands. *While their bank accounts are significantly different, the fundamental approach to generating revenue is the same.* Whether a large or small law firm, medical practice, technology company, construction business, service company – or any other business – this process can drive real change and success.

WHICH BUSINESSES SUCCEED, AND WHY?

Most businesses fail because they don't "plan for success." Maybe they plan for today, possibly tomorrow, and that's if they plan at all.

Most businesses simply *do*. In Michael Gerber's highly respected book, *The E-Myth Revisited*, he describes the *technician* who believes that because he or she can do a task (accounting, law, programming, carpentry, baking, etc.) that he or she should own a business that does that task. They, of course, fail to recognize that they lack the knowledge of how to run a business, and that running a business is completely different than doing a task.

PLAN SALES AND MARKETING
TO PLAN FOR SUCCESS

A critical part of running a successful business is creating and implementing a plan for sales and marketing. Most businesses fail to do this, leaving them adrift. You can't use GPS to reach a destination without *choosing a destination*. Similarly, you can't attract customers and new business without a *plan to reach and connect with those people*.

In this chapter, we're going to focus on how to run a marketing strategy that accomplishes this goal and generates additional revenue for the business and its owners.

Let's develop that plan.

CREATE AND IMPLEMENT A PLAN TO ATTRACT
THE RIGHT PROSPECTS TO MEET YOUR GOALS

You need to build a marketing process that will attract and engage with the right customers, initially attracting them as a brand new contact. You need to convert them from a website visitor to an interested prospect, from a prospect to a hot lead and, ultimately, from a hot lead to a paying customer.

THE FIVE STEPS TO CONSISTENTLY GENERATE NEW AND REPEAT BUSINESS FROM THE WEB

Below is the exact marketing process we have used at Direct Response Group to help our clients generate over $600,000,000 in new revenue. This is part of a larger strategy we call **Selling Decision Makers** (www.SellingDecisionMakers.com).

1. Profile Your *Decision Maker*

2. Build a Compelling Website

3. Use SEO / PPC / Social Media to Reach True *Decision Makers*

4. Present the *Decision Maker* with Relevant Information and a Compelling Call to Action

5. Nurture Your List to Build Trusted Authority Status

These five steps define a very clear and repeatable process that can be adapted to any business, including yours.

The result?

Qualified prospects emotionally ready to buy from you.

Step 1: Profile Your Decision Maker

It is often said that you should know your target market. But before *selling decision makers*, you need to carefully define who that is for your business.

Is it a business or a consumer? What challenges do they face? Is the *decision maker* the owner of a business? An executive? What are his or her pain points? Goals and aspirations? What challenges have they faced?

*For our company, Direct Response Group, the decision maker we look to reach is a small business owner (a business with $300,000 - $30 million in revenue) that wants to generate new business originating from the web. It is typically an **offline** business, generating additional business using the Internet. The business has been successful and has challenges in growing. They are already using the web, but not to its fullest potential. They have spent money advertising on the web,* *but do not track results and lack any mechanism in place to nurture the leads they do find. They have confidence and trust in the process and do not want to micro-manage. The company is eager for success and willing to work with a team that can generate real results. The owner has 15-35 years of business experience and has seen professional and personal challenges in achieving financial growth and success.*

Sound specific? You bet. Unless you understand who your market is, how will you know the challenges they face? People want solutions relevant to them, not products and services important to a sales person.

Step 2: Build a Compelling Website that Attracts Response

This may seem obvious, but every business must have a website. The website can attract new business as well as validate you to prospects, existing customers and referrals.

Your website represents your business on the Internet. Even if you are an offline business (lawyer, doctor, contractor, restaurant, etc.), most of what people learn about you they learn online. Is your website sloppy? Incomplete? Out of date? Lacking in information? Unimpressive? A total disaster?

Since childhood we've heard about making a great first impression. Is your first impression an out-of-date website with sloppy content and poor spelling? What does that say about your business, the quality of your work and (by implication) the attention you give your clients?

Last year we signed a new client with a "dated" website. We worked with them to get current photos, a fresh layout and a clear message on their website. The site immediately began ranking well on Google, with more than one hundred keywords ranking at the #1 spot.

A clear and relevant website made engagement easy and attracted customers like never before.

The result? An increase in revenue of more than 35% for the year with no additional marketing.

You may have a great company, but do you show the world a horrible website? If you are giving the wrong impression, you are literally scaring away prospects and losing opportunities to your competition.

Step 3. Use SEO / PPC / Social Media to Drive Targeted Visitors

Virtually everyone searches online for the resources they need – both personally and in business. Google, Bing and Yahoo represent 97% of the search market in the United States, and as of 2015, more than half of that will be on mobile devices (which is why a mobile responsive website is so important). When not searching, they hang out on social media. You need to reach your audience where they already are, not just where you wish them to be.

Even for offline businesses that have existed by word-of-mouth and referrals, there is the additional opportunity to sign new business with people not referred to you.

Search engines, using SEO (search engine optimization) and PPC (pay-per-click advertising) are the best way to attract hand raisers – the people who are saying "me, over here … I have a need right now and need a solution." Social media, particularly Facebook, gives you unprecedented access to a highly targeted audience by age, geography, profession, income levels, areas of interest, as well as hundreds of data points from "big data" providers.

> *In a clinical trial recruitment campaign, we've seen cost reductions of up to 68% by better targeting ads to the right people. Keywords and ad copy focus on real needs and pain, while demographic targeting hones in on those who fit our criteria. We now get more inquiries with fewer visitors – and a lower budget!*

You can target anyone you want. Combined, they will attract the visitors you need to your website.

Step 4. Present Relevant Information with a Call to Action

Once you have your *decision maker* defined, have built your website and are reaching them via search and social media, what next? You need to send them somewhere – your website, a landing page, an opt-in page, a sign up page. Something.

That something will, of course, vary based on your business goals. For most companies, it will be (1) an opt-in with their email address, so you can market to them, and (2) a registration form to buy, get a quote or schedule an appointment. Far more people will choose #1, so it is critically important that you offer an opt-in opportunity.

Your landing page (where you send them from your advertisement) is designed for one purpose – lead generation. Connect with what your prospects want.

> *In one campaign, the target decision maker was the owner of a small business doing $500,000 to $2,000,000 in profitable revenue. She was successful, had a family, and little debt. She needed a business loan for growth, not a bailout. We presented offers for our client that touched upon her business needs and emotional triggers, and as a result, generated hundreds of fresh leads quickly.*

Valuable information, free reports, access to a free webinar, videos and other high value offerings are the carrot you dangle to get that opt-in. There is nothing deceptive about it… *they will freely give their information if you provide what they want.*

Ask Your Decision Makers What They Want

Think about your *decision maker* and what he or she wants and needs.

Just offer that.

It sounds simple, but the easiest thing to give away – and the easiest thing to sell – is what someone wants and needs.

> *We worked on a project for a solar energy company that focused on generating consumer leads. Their main advertising message was a tax break on solar equipment. Little response. We learned the motivating factor that caused people to buy was the ability to finance the purchase, where the monthly savings was greater than the cost. This company focused on the wrong issue.*

They were having disconnected conversations with their prospects. Once we brought the two into alignment, response rates immediately jumped.

Remember, you will never engage the interest of the other person if you are talking about a benefit that is of no concern to them. Without their interest, they will never inquire and never convert. Be sure you create compelling content that talks to their interests, their pain, their desires. That is where you will find success.

The Call to Action

Believe it or not, many people just don't know how to engage with you and will simply wander out of your website. They may be ready to start – *but now what?*

You must tell people how to engage with you.

Let's start with the basics.

Please put your phone number on the damned website.

If it is not there, in the top right corner of every page, send an email to your webmaster right now asking him to do so.

I know it infuriates you when you can't find the phone number of a company. Yet companies spend tens of thousands, hundreds of thousands, even millions of dollars on marketing and do not give their prospects an easy way to communicate.

Give them an online method to engage.

Attract them with a white paper, a newsletter, a webinar. Something of value. This, with a simple contact form, can do wonders.

Keep the lead or registration form simple.

Ask as little as you need to get a lead. Let the salesperson ask detailed questions later. The longer the form, the fewer responses you will get. Name, phone and email may be all you need. Consider a multi-part form that starts with the basics and, on the second screen, asks for additional information. If they stop, you have the essentials. If they continue, you have a more qualified lead.

We worked with one client providing a business-to-business service. Their "call to action" was an application form with more than 30 fields. It was completely over-the-top. By shortening the form to just eight fields, and then asking additional questions on the next screen, we more than doubled response rates in a day.

Ask just the essentials to get the lead or the order and ask the details later. Your response rates will soar.

Step 5. Nurture Your List to Build "Trusted Authority" Status

When people trust you by opting in, that is a great place to start a relationship. Don't ruin it by emailing them with a hard sales pitch that reeks of commission breath. No one wants to be sold to. They want to buy when they are ready to buy, on their terms, their timing.

This is the reason for a *nurturing campaign*.

A nurturing campaign is a series of connections and touches – email, phone calls, SMS messages, letters – whatever you choose.

> *In a campaign we recently developed using Infusionsoft, we created a sequence of twenty emails that spanned six months. In four of those we made an overt offer, in the other sixteen we shared information with links to pages on our client's site with even more detailed information. This enabled us to track who was reading emails, who was clicking through and at what frequency. Trusted authority status grows as more and more useful information is shared. In the end, they were far more successful when it came time to sell, than when they simply bombarded people with ads.*

These touches are designed to engage with people to deliver them value, information and resources. They serve the purpose of establishing you as an industry authority, not the hawkster who pitches them non-stop.

IMPLEMENT THIS PROCESS
TO GROW AND DEVELOP YOUR BUSINESS

Remember to think of this as a process in developing new business. Follow these steps consistently and you can achieve spectacular results:

Step 1. Define your *decision maker* to gain a greater understanding of your audience, who they are, what their needs are and why they might buy.

Step 2. Make your website more compelling so that it talks to the pains, issues and goals of that *decision maker*.

Step 3. Create campaigns that drive the right audience with the right message, consistent with the needs and desires of the *decision maker*.

Step 4. Present offers that share information, resources and services that can help them meet their needs, deal with their challenges and achieve a result.

Step 5. Continue to nurture your list in a way that gives away highly valuable information and builds your credibility. Remember, *people want to buy from people they trust*, and elevating yourself to a minor celebrity or trusted advisor status will make it far easier for you to close a deal.

Finally, remember, *people don't want to be sold*. Instead, *they will buy when they choose to buy*. Reach a targeted audience and build a relationship with the decision maker. Answer their needs and earn their trust.

Follow this process, and your prospects will engage with you and make the "sale" the easiest part of the process.

About Christopher

Christopher Ulrich helps his clients grow their business using proven strategies that have generated his clients hundreds of millions of dollars in extra revenue. Raised in an entrepreneurial technology family, Christopher grew up on computers, from early key punch machines at age 6, to the first PC's, Apple II+ and more.

After owning a retail store (age 19), a software company (age 21) and earning a securities license (Series 7 and 63), Christopher found his way to law school in 1992, expecting to work with Apple, Microsoft or IBM. While in law school, he started (and shuttered) an early search directory when others insisted the "Internet would never go commercial." After passing the bar exam, Christopher Ulrich practiced law for three years but was drawn back to the Internet and technology. He started one of the first ICANN accredited domain registrars. He then shifted his focus to online marketing, helping those early on the net grow their businesses quickly. For the past 17 years, his primary focus has been on profitable marketing and lead generation strategies, integrating his skills with real-world small business experience, technology know-how and deep strategic thinking.

While Christopher's early clients were some of the biggest online – Cingular, Buy. com, Register.com, Citibank, Computer Associates, NBTY and others, he gravitated to small- and mid-sized businesses. The thrill of working with a business owner/ decision maker in a non-corporate environment, who is able to quickly implement change, delivers the best experience for all.

Christopher lives on Long Island, New York, with his brilliant, lovely and younger wife Dina, and three wonderful children Charlie, Leia and Isabelle. When not working, you will find Christopher coaching basketball, inventing new technologies, searching for the best sushi chefs, and spending time with his family.

Christopher Ulrich is a graduate of Hofstra University in New York, and received his Juris Doctorate at St. John's University School of Law. He is the CEO of Direct Response Group, specializing in helping companies leverage the internet to grow revenue. His clients range from lawyers, doctors and engineers, to other professional, brick-and-mortar and financial services clients.

He is also the creator of Selling Decision Makers, helping businesses learn and master the complete revenue cycle, from lead generation to nurturing a relationship to completing the sale.

Christopher Ulrich is considered an expert in his industry, and has been invited to speak at many conferences, including those focused on the Internet, law and general business success.

If you have any questions, feel free to contact Christopher directly at: culrich@DirectResponseGroup.com

or www.DirectResponseGroup.com

CHAPTER 11

THE POWER OF LEARNING AND RELATIONSHIPS

BY GRANT DIGGLES

As I turned the last corner and drove my car into the parking lot at the airport, I took a deep breath at the sight of my new acquaintance's single prop Pilatus Airplane waiting for my arrival. Today was the first time my wife I would fly in a privately-owned aircraft. Looking for a place to park my car, I was waved onto the tarmac by a young gentlemen. Reluctantly, I drove through the parking lot, passed an iron gate and onto the runway next to the airplane. We were invited to fly to Seattle for a concert with a good friend of mine and his host, Michael, for a quick weekend trip and this plane was our ride.

Two other men came out of from behind the plane to greet us by taking our luggage and car keys and directed us towards the steps leading up to the cabin. I was shocked at the convenience and simplicity of the process. Up to this point, I'd been accustomed to commercial flights involving early arrivals, crowded terminals and TSA searches. This seemed too good to be true and admittedly, almost felt illegal.

As I entered the plane I was greeted by a spacious cabin, warm faces and a glass of Crown Royal XR on the rocks. I sat down, buckled up and thus began one of the most important milestone events in my life and my career.

As the plane taxied onto the runway, I stared outside the window wondering what Michael did for a living to achieve this level of success. At the invitation of my friend, I was a guest on this trip and I knew nothing about him. The plane began to climb and, as we leveled off my host offered to top off my glass of whisky. I graciously accepted and, in my eagerness to understand his situation began asking questions. The man I sat with that day didn't appear as a titan of industry as I would have expected. On the contrary Michael was mild mannered, soft spoken, unhurried and almost difficult to hear over the low drone of the Pilatus Turbo Prop engine.

What I learned that day helped to change the way I thought about business, success, and my approach to people in general. Specifically, it was at this time that I began to foster my own opinions and practices in the area of relationships and people.

As I sat in the Pilatus conversing with this Michael, he told me his story. As he explained his failures and successes, his challenges and victories, I was relieved to find out that his story was not unlike mine in many regards. Admittedly, I was waiting for his "secret" to success explanation, the insider information that the general public just didn't have access to… but it never came. Instead, he just ended his story with an unceremonious "…and here I am today." I looked at this man as if he'd just began explaining the greatest joke in the world only to tell me there was no punch line. Dumb-founded, I stared at the melting ice cubes in my whisky glass, searching for anything to say. I must have been staring at the my glass for awhile, for when I looked back up Michael was engaged in conversation with my wife and two other passengers. It would be another 30 minutes before I had his attention again.

Our plane slowly began to change direction and we entered our final approach. Eventually Michael and I made eye contact and, as he smiled at me I hastily asked, "What is the most important thing you did that contributed to your success?" His reply was so quick that I'm not even sure that he had time to think about his answer "People," he said. "I would not be where I'm at today without knowing and hiring the right people. I'm just one man, and without those people in my life, none of this would have been possible."

As our plane drifted towards the runway, I reflected on his answer. I began to think about all of the opportunities that came my way from others who believed in me. People who saw value in me before I could see it myself. Business coaches, mentors and even my upbringing were vital in my success as I can recall many times that I easily could have ended my enterprise if they hadn't supported me and come to my aid. I was ambitious and lack of introspection in my life caused me to believe I was a "self-made man." Over the years, the idea of a "self-made man" was a thrilling thought to me. A person who begins from humble beginnings to becoming a stunning success through hard work and effort is exciting and inspiring to many. But stories from successful business owners and even my own experiences suggest that self-made men simply do not exist.

As the plane slowly came to a stop I was reflecting on Michael's comment. I realized that my path to success, however that might be defined, was even more similar than I'd imagined. My thoughts went back to the most pronounced moment of my career at an interesting and unexpected time in my late twenties.

THE TEACHER AND THE STUDENT

I was 27 when I first became CEO of our thriving family business. The death of my mother necessitated an early succession plan and I found myself in the hot seat unprepared for what lay ahead. Only a year ago, I was starting a media and marketing company that, although was going well, involved me and only a few independent contractors I hired from time to time. It felt as if I had been playing little league baseball and was abruptly thrust into the Major Leagues overnight. I pretty much knew nothing.

It was at this time that I approached the business coach my mother had been using over the years to build her empire. Dr. Jones was a PhD who had coached thousands of businesses over the long life of his prestigious career. His knowledge of the many types of businesses, models, challenges and strategies would prove to be invaluable in the continued success of my company. For years, he was my teacher and I was his pupil, meeting each week and learning everything I possibly could about management, finances and planning. Looking back, I confess that we didn't do everything right, after all I was an ambitious young man with resources at my fingertips and was somewhat difficult to control at times. But the company did survive and thrive in the coming years.

I learned humility during my initial season with him. I learned that, more often than not, I didn't know what I was doing and the perspective of my coach was there to help me. It was during this season that I was expected to seek advice, to ask questions, and that it was okay that I didn't have the answers. This season was paramount in my development, and has laid a lasting foundation in the way I choose to run my business and build relationships with others.

YOUR PEOPLE ARE YOUR GREATEST ASSET

During this season, I also gathered the existing team that made up the players of my company. My mother was a titan in her industry. She was a strong, ambitious and charismatic woman who paved the way for her industry. Her unexpected passing shook our company to the core. Our people were scared, and I was young.

I remember addressing the whole group at a single meeting. With my business coach at my side, I mustered as much strength as I could manage to keep the team's spirits light and my confidence as high as could be expected. I wanted everyone to know that during this time of transition, nothing would be changing in the company, and that I would be relying heavily on each person to help guide and direct the future of our group. At the advice of my coach, I was trying to create an environment of safety for my team by extending an olive branch to those I had no relationship with as yet.

I then met with each team member individually over the next month. I used these individual meetings to learn as much as I could about each team member. Given the circumstances surrounding my entry into the company, I hardly knew anyone. These times were less of a conversation between the two of us and more of a monologue. They spoke and I mostly listened, asking questions about who they were, how they felt about our current situation and what I could do to serve them in the coming months. I wanted to ensure that they would stay and that they continued to work for a company that they could be proud of.

Over the course of the next several months, I had the opportunity to experience the quality of this incredible team that my mother had assembled. I believe it was their admiration and loyalty to my mother that caused them to support and encourage me in the beginning as I blossomed into a young CEO. Slowly over time, it was I they became loyal to, as I worked hard to earn their respect through repetitive efforts to connect with, learn from and lead each one of them.

SUCCESS REQUIRES COMMUNITY

The lessons I learned early in my career continue to affect the way I do business today. But it hasn't just been my personal experiences that have helped to guide me through the business gauntlet. It has also been the experience of others around me that enrich and direct decisions I make on a daily basis. In the spirit of continual learning, I make it a priority to network with those around me with the goal of building strong, lasting relationships. This has afforded me the opportunity to observe others fight their own battles and solve their own problems, influencing me to take similar actions in my own organization. In fact, most of my best ideas aren't mine at all, but great ideas from others who are just far enough ahead of me that I can "draft" behind their example.

Time and time again I've seen examples and listened to stories of successful entrepreneurs and business professionals who've leveraged the knowledge and relationships of those around them to catapult their own efforts. They asked questions, asked for help and effectively became experts at "getting out of their own way," so others might contribute their unique gifting and insights. I use this reciprocating relationship in areas of my own company, and the results have been fantastic. Outside of positive fiscal growth in the company, we've seen increased loyalty, improved teamwork and progress at an accelerated rate.

After that weekend in Seattle, I eventually had the opportunity to meet many of Michael's most trusted employees at one of his company events. Moving about the room I shook hands with each person asking what they did for Michael. Without exception, each of his employees spoke highly of him, volunteering their own explanations as to why they worked for him. Each story I heard built on the last, as they explained how they first met Michael. Although the stories were unique in their own right, there was a common chord that rung throughout. Michael was a teachable man who valued his people. He learned to step aside and let others thrive.

Driving home that night with my wife, I reflected on what I had experienced. It was clear to me:

> *If you want to find success, then find*
> *the right people and treat them well.*

About Grant

In business, Grant Diggles is passionate about three things: People, Possibilities and Profits. As a relational networker, Grant enjoys meeting new people and building networks that offer win-win situations for everyone. His charismatic attitude and intuitive nature has helped him sustain and launch several of his own ventures.

As the CEO of several businesses including, (1) The Cummings Group – a management and venture capital firm, (2) Outpatient Anesthesia Services – an anesthesia service provider to outpatient facilities in the Northwest and (3) Mediclarus – a web, print and branding development and automated communications platform to the healthcare market, Grant stays busy managing a wide array of services and solutions to a varied list of clientele.

With a background in media, marketing and coaching, Grant has also helped a variety of businesses and business owners think outside of their current circumstances to create new and exciting possibilities to increase revenue, solve stubborn problems and manage their business relationships. He has served as a guest speaker covering topics such as social media education and media and marketing strategies. He uses his experience as a business coach to help others create new possibilities and think outside-the-box of their current business strategies, client relations efforts and new venture launches.

In life, Grant is a husband to his wife, Sarah, and a father to their four kids. He enjoys spending time with his family on their farm in Oregon. He is actively involved in the development of his kids by teaching them a simplified version of the same principles he practices in business: "If you can be great at relationships and great at solving problems, you'll do well in the world."

You can connect with Grant at: www.grantdiggles.com

CHAPTER 12

TO GET, YOU MUST GIVE. TO OVERCOME, YOU MUST THINK BEYOND YOURSELF — HOW TO USE YOUR CHALLENGES TO CREATE A SUCCESSFUL AND HAPPY LIFE!

BY ELI DAFESH

I've been lucky.

I didn't always think so at the time, but looking back, I see it, though it didn't necessarily start out that way.

My father was a Christian living in the Middle-East who left to go to Jordan during the war, where he met my mother. Thankfully, love won out, and we immigrated to the USA when I was five.

So, in a nutshell, I was a Middle-Eastern immigrant who couldn't speak English, couldn't read English, and it turned out I had a learning disability, so I struggled in school. Obviously the road map to success, right?

So where was my luck? At home. I had a great family.

My mother was a living saint, and my father was a hardworking man who wanted us to have it better than he did. I was the oldest of six, and though we never had the newest clothes or a new car, we had love and music and food and family. Our little house was always open, and no one ever left hungry.

Despite my struggles in school, my parents always encouraged me and convinced me I was worthy, and that I could get far in life if I worked at it. Against the odds, I graduated high school and even took my solid D+ GPA to college (things were simpler then!), though I really didn't know what I wanted to do.

In one of those crazy-but-true moments, a friend came over with the answer: He'd just seen the movie "Shampoo" with Warren Beatty, and his suggestion of dropping out of college, going to beauty school, growing hair and meeting girls seemed to be the perfect career choice.

Fresh out of beauty school, I borrowed money from my father to buy an old salon with cheesy cedar paneling and some denim backed chairs, and opened my doors. As the real estate guy shook my hand, he congratulated me for going into business, but all I could think of was that it felt that I'd gone into debt!

I lacked so much, but I was young and enthusiastic, and I went for it, and had some pretty outstanding success. We went out to be different, and we were! When you came to us, you got the "Dafesh Experience," including shish-ka-bob on Saturdays – you were treated as if you were a guest in my home. Within a couple of years, we were cutting Frankie Avalon's hair, Fleetwood Mac's hair, and so many more.

There were plenty of ups and downs, but we'd "made it" in the high pressure Hollywood style world, and we'd done it our way. When Paul Mitchell was blaring loud music, we were spraying essential oils and focusing on the wellbeing of our guests.

Life was good!

. . . All that changed in an instant.

When my son, Wadia, was 3 years old, while looking out our bedroom window trying to see his little girl friend next door, he fell through the screen and plummeted two stories to the concrete below.

I'd just walked into the room as he fell, and within two seconds I'd literally followed him out the window, barely catching myself on the ledge as I fell. I picked up his limp body and kicked the screen door off its hinges, crying out at the top of my lungs. He wasn't breathing, and as I started mouth to mouth, I could think of nothing except that my beloved boy, my baby, was dead.

The next few minutes are a blur to this day. The rescue squad was able to revive him, but he was in the hospital in a coma for the next 10 days, and I was there every second with him. It was me there in that bed. It was me who had gone through the window. When your child is sick or hurt, it's the most helpless feeling in the world as a parent. You would give everything you have – including your life – to take their place.

The diagnosis was that he had suffered TBI, or Traumatic Brain Injury, and though he would recover on the surface, the effects of the injury to his pre-frontal lobe wouldn't be fully apparent for several years. He was always a good natured child, but the portion of his brain that controlled impulses was damaged, and when he was barely into adulthood, he fell in with the wrong crowd, made some bad choices and was incarcerated.

It was if I was reliving his fall through the window all over again. It was my life going down the tube. I was losing myself, despite my efforts to keep up the façade. Once again, I was willing to give everything I had to save my boy. I would have sold my soul. Soon, despite making a six-figure income, I was deep in credit card debt and unraveling as everything seemed to be going against us. Despite making a good income, I knew that in order to save my son, I needed to make an extraordinary income to be able to help him.

Until that moment, I thought I was doing alright. I was famous, I was popular, I was doing well financially, but...

...But there was always something missing. I was in the service business. I was doing the "brick-and-mortar" thing, paying my taxes, and FICA, and Workman's Comp. and training my staff, who would eventually leave and open their own places, sometimes right down the street. I realized that for 23 years, I'd been training my competition, and the more I chased success, the more I worked, it left me with less time for relationships, family, children, travel, my health, my life.

I'd spent so much time making a living I wasn't making a life! Despite owning the broom I was pushing, I had a J.O.B. I was giving every cent I made and more to help my boy. I was giving every second I could spare, but it wasn't enough. Standing at the edge of that precipice with my son, something changed in me.

A very rich client at the salon had told me more than once, "Eli, with a personality like yours, you could make a ton of money doing what I do." So I asked her "So, what do you do?" The next day I attended my first ever network marketing meeting at her house and my direction changed forever.

John D. Rockefeller and J. Paul Getty both had their own version of the famous quote: "I would rather have 1% of 100 people's efforts than 100% of my own," and suddenly it made sense.

Though I still struggled to read even as an adult, I'd bought all the audio tapes from all the great business leaders; Jack Canfield, Tony Robbins, Dr. Wayne Dyer, Bryan Tracy, Napoleon Hill, Jim Rohn, Zig Ziglar et al, and though I didn't read the books, I could for sure listen to the tapes! I devoured their wisdom, searching for a way to apply it to my personality and my situation, and then another seminal event occurred – I took a rare night off and went to see the movie "Pay It Forward," based on the great book by Catherine Ryan Hyde, and it solidified my direction. I didn't invent Pay It Forward, but I could live it!

My mother was perhaps the most selfless person I have ever met, and the lessons I had learned from her came flooding back. She had once told me that her greatest happiness was giving and forgiving, and I lived it on a daily basis in our home.

GIVE TILL IT HURTS, AND DO IT SELFLESSLY.

I sold my salon and entered the world of network marketing. I gave up 5-figures a month and bet it on myself and my wife Jillina in the hopes of earning six figures a month.

I started to work on "me," since early on I understood that I had to become a person worthy of the blessings I wanted. I listened to tapes, I went to seminars, I asked questions, I shadowed my mentors, I invited them to my home, hounded them for tidbits of knowledge, and even more importantly, wisdom.

What's the difference? As my friend and author David Adlard says, "Knowledge is knowing that a tomato is a fruit, but wisdom is knowing not to put it in a fruit salad."

LEARN TO CONNECT.

If you're going to be successful, you have to learn to connect to people, and learn to LISTEN. I talked to everyone, I listened more. I would pay them a compliment and then hit them with my favorite pitch:

"Hi! How are you?" (…and really mean it! LISTEN to their answers!) "What do you do? Great! May I have your card? Are you keeping your business options open?"

I have collected 12 fifty-page albums of business cards, and I use them.

BECOME A MASTER OF THE "FOLLOW UP."

The fortune is in the follow-up. I call it Social Entrepreneurship. I learned that "No," doesn't really mean No… it just means "No, Not Right Now." Follow up with people – you never know when their circumstances will change. Don't make judgments – we've all been down in one way or another. What I'm really hoping for is to help lead people to their potential.

When I meet people now, they are just my best friends in the making. We're not in the water business, or the health business or the supplement business of whatever your niche is. We are really in the CONNECTION business! This is Relationship Marketing.

How much do you really care about the other guy winning? Get the attention off yourself. Get out of your own way – get out of your box. When you start thinking about helping someone else, prosperity will follow – give and get back ten-fold. Compassion and empowering others are the keys to long-term success.

This philosophy will work in building your business, your prosperity and your happiness, because you're not putting all the attention to thoughts of what you lack, of your limitations, of why your life isn't working the way it's supposed to work and of why you are always broke. Of why you are always in debt, of why don't you have the love relationships you want and of how come you don't have the optimum health that you want.

All these things happen because in our society, we have been taught to think about me, me, me, and when you get away from that concept, and start thinking about unity, and thinking about working together, it ceases to be "I win/you lose" and becomes a "win-win" for everybody. Too often we live our lives in a state of poverty consciousness, no matter what our financial situation is, focused inward and on hoarding what we have, rather than from a security in knowing who we are, and being *thankful* for the life we have – essentially having an Attitude of Gratitude.

YOU CAN BE MORE AND HAVE MORE, NOT THROUGH GREED, BUT FROM GIVING VALUE.

As far as prosperity goes, money is not, contrary to popular opinion, the root of all evil. If anything, the LOVE of money is what causes the problems. "Money makes a good man better, and a bad man worse." It makes you more of who you already are.

As I searched for ways to help my son, I realized that money given with no thought of getting anything in return can feed the hungry, can help heal the sick, and when you give, abundance will flow to you!

What can you do? So many things! Help a child who has trouble learning. Take someone in for a few days when their circumstances leave them without a roof over their heads. Give a turkey dinner away and help at a soup kitchen or homeless shelter at Thanksgiving. Lend money to someone who needs it more than you. Help a non-profit... the list is endless. Be an example that others want to follow, and do it expecting nothing in return and the blessings will begin to flow your way!

Zig said "You don't get success by getting what you want, you get success from helping others get what THEY want!"

How can you help people find "Jiyuu?" it translates loosely to: "To Be Free." My passion now is to help people succeed in their health and their prosperity – their spirit, as it were.

Marlo Thomas perhaps said it best: *There are two kinds of people in the world: Takers and Givers. The Takers may eat better (at first!), but the Givers will sleep better.*

This, to me, is the Soul of Success.

FIND A CAUSE YOU ARE DRIVEN TO SUPPORT.

Paying It Forward is bigger than you, and that purpose will help to keep you motivated when you have the inevitable challenges. What is your desperate "why?" What's the why that makes you cry? What keeps you awake at night because you want to fix it so badly?

Powerful purpose is the best motivator to enable people to break through challenges: When your back is against the wall, you will find the strength to succeed if your "why" is big enough, and especially if it is bigger than yourself!

Mine started as my son, and grew into helping people with the desire to become independent, to help people escape from the rat race. If someone wanted to learn a way to make it in the "New Economy," I wanted to teach them.

Our greatest strengths and growth usually come from our greatest challenges, from being down in the dumps, and pushed beyond our limits. Without these challenges, we will never know how strong we can be, and as so often happens, years later, despite the struggles and tragedies, without them we would never have gotten to be the people we were meant to be. When you're at the end of your rope, you'd better hang on!

DON'T BE ASHAMED OF YOUR "SCARS"

I have learned to "own" my "bruises." These are the scars of our journey. These are the challenges that have molded us, that define us, temper us. They make us who we are. They make us human. Don't be afraid of your bruises – just focus on what you can do to rise above them.

I am thrilled to say that my son got out of prison and has stayed out. He is doing great health-wise, and has developed a six-figure income of his own. Once again, I am so happy to say that I am there with him. I have been blessed beyond measure.

My dear friend Grant Cardone asked me a question a few years ago: "Eli, you're successful, but are you TRULY fulfilled with your life?"

In answer, I look back at the changes that I made in the pursuit of my son's health, and I have seen the blessings it has wrought in myself and so many others, and I am very happy and proud to say that NOW I am fulfilled in my life, though there is so much more I want to do.

Treasure each day, my friends, and never let a day go by without doing something special for someone who can't pay you back.

Blessings, and may all your dreams come true.

Acknowledgments

I'd like the thank our Creator for the blessings in my life, especially my parents Wadie and Martha Dafesh, my wonderful wife Jillina, our children Wadia, Tiana, Scott and Chase, their spouses, our grandchildren Christian Elias, Noah and Jameson, my sisters and brother, Claudette, Rita, Laila, Shay and Isaum, my in-laws Tom and Berdine Orlando, extended family and friends who have been my rock along the way.

Thank you Celebrity Press, Evan Klassen and David Adlard for the opportunity.

Thank you to Mr. and Mrs. Hironari Ohshiro for their vision and compassion, and for teaching us the importance of "Jiyuu."

Thanks to my mentors and to everyone who has been a part of this great journey. Thank you for believing. Your examples are what I strive for daily.

About Eli

The Speed of the Team is determined by the Speed of its Leader!

One of the most sought-after and dynamic speakers and leaders in the world, Eli Dafesh's story of immigrant-to-entrepreneur inspires everyone he meets. Eli went from over $100,000 in credit card debt to developing over a billion dollars sales volume, and has helped hundreds of people reach six- and seven-figure incomes.

He rose to the top of the ultra-competitive California salon world, becoming one of the top platform artists, trainers and artistic directors in the world, alongside the likes of Paul Mitchell, Horst Rechelbacher (founder of Aveda), Farouk Shami (The Billionaire Hairdresser) and others. His three full-service salons were some of the most sought after destinations for the stars, and he appeared on shows such as Good Morning America.

In 1995, in the midst of a crisis in his own life, Eli was introduced to the world of Network marketing and gave up the salon world to serve others and help people develop financial independence, health and prosperity, and the importance of a grateful heart.

He is a leadership and business development expert, author, speaker and Entrepreneur who has inspired thousands of people around the world, and has developed multiple teams totaling over 500,000 leaders and partners. He has been the guest on many radio talk shows, TV shows and has spoken at numerous national and international conferences, sharing the stage with legends such as: Grant Cardone, the great Art Linkletter, Bob Proctor, Tom Hopkins, Mark Victor Hansen, Kevin Harrington, Les Brown, Paul Zane Pilzer, Dolvett Quince (from the Biggest Loser), Cynthia Kersey, and more…

Besides his family, his greatest love and passion is in paying it forward, and helping others. He was the founding partner of a Nasdaq-traded company, and was also co-founder of a coaching and training company, whose syllabus, "The System," has proven to be an invaluable tool for helping entrepreneurs and folks in the network marketing industry find hope, dream again and ultimately reach their goals and potential.

One of his proudest moments was being selected by Eric Worre, along with his wife Jillina, as two of the six members of the "Legends" panel at the 2014 Go Pro Recruiting Mastery event in Las Vegas as one of the top income earners in the network marketing industry world-wide.

He and his wife Jillina were introduced to Enagic in 2006, a top health and wellness company, founded in Japan, that has spread to more than 130 countries world-wide.

They have since dedicated their lives to helping people discover and master "Jiyuu," (To Be Free), and spreading awareness of TBI – Traumatic Brain Injury.

He lives in California with his wife and business partner, Jillina. They have four children and three grandchildren.

To learn more about Eli and Jillina, go to:
www.jiyuu.me
Twitter: @EliDafesh
Facebook: https://www.facebook.com/eli.dafesh
www.eliandjillina.com
www.elidafesh.com
eventiseli@yahoo.com

CHAPTER 13

PASSION HAS A NEW DOCTOR

BY DR. CATHY EMEWURA

Call me a physician on a mission.

My goal is simple – to improve sexual function in patients unaware they've been waylaid by the physiological and mental changes we undergo as we age. That's what was happening to Elizabeth, a divorcee who's blushing furiously and refusing to make eye contact in an examination room of one of my three Atlanta-based living and wellness centers.

The taboo that the world has built around sex is powerful enough to make a 47-year-old grandmother behave like a nervous schoolgirl. However, the tears shimmering in Elizabeth's brown eyes appear to indicate it's taboo-busting time.

Talk to me, Elizabeth – when my patients hurt, I hurt!

"D-d-doctor Cathy," she stammers in a voice I have to strain to hear, "Something's wrong with me. I, um . . ." She pauses. Inhales deeply. "Me and my boyfriend broke up five weeks ago. Since my divorce seven years ago, I haven't been able to have an orgasm."

When I try to get greater detail about her sex life, she silently crosses her legs and practically glowers at the brown linoleum floor.

During a previous visit, I learned that Elizabeth's daughter had a baby out of wedlock, and that event put Elizabeth under enormous psychological stress.

Unlike doctors who practice assembly-line medicine and shove patients out the door after a few minutes, my practice lavishes an hour on every patient. During our consultation, Elizabeth and I spend a fair amount of time putting together a detailed sexual history.

I need to understand in greater details the different events in her life that decreased her ability to orgasm or could jeopardize her future relationships with men. I have to ensure that my patients have a good chance of being able to reach, sustain and enjoy each climax in every sexual experience.

After getting Elizabeth's history, I give her a complete physical exam. Then I order a bevy of tests, to include an EKG, mammogram, PAP smear, and numerous blood tests of her cholesterol and hormone levels.

Insurance companies are not used to having a bunch of hormone tests done, but I refuse to cut corners when it comes to the mental and physical well-being of my patients. Why should I, when the state of medical technology offers physicians such a dizzying array of spectacular diagnostic tools?

I became a doctor to help my patients. So I painstakingly, methodically check off my patients' potential problem areas, until answers start to materialize. Turns out Elizabeth's sexual dysfunction is the result of low hormone levels, something that's fairly common, even though most patients – and most doctors – seldom anticipate it. Specifically, Elizabeth's testosterone is low. That'll probably surprise a lot of you, because most people associate testosterone with men. But women need it too, just at much lower levels than our male counterparts.

While I check a long list of my patients' hormones, the Big Three in terms of sexual dysfunction are testosterone, estrogen and progesterone. In the more than two decades I've worked as a physician, it's become obvious to me that as hormone levels go down, disease rates creep up. I have also observed that great health leads to great sex, and great sex brings about great health.

I wind up prescribing Elizabeth what I describe as the 'Passion Cocktail' that may include testosterone, progesterone and estrogen depending on the lab results and clinical evaluation. These hormones are produced by both the female and male reproductive organs. Recent studies show that replenishing low testosterone in women increases their orgasms and sex drive. I do this with their informed consent and after going over all the pros and cons.

When it comes to the health of my patients, and their sex lives in particular, it's crucial to maximize hormone balance to achieve increased energy and vitality. So Elizabeth and I also talk about the O-Shot, a new procedure that will enable her to have even more intense orgasms. I want Elizabeth to be aware that she has many more options than she realizes!

Pioneered by Dr. Charles Runels, the O-Shot is an injection that generates healthier and more functional tissue in the areas of the vagina associated with sexual response, allowing most recipients to enjoy especially strong orgasms.

On the male side of the equation, I also give P-Shots – penis enlargement injections containing platelet-rich plasma. Some people look at me skeptically when I tell them I've personally observed P-Shots enlarge penis circumference and length by one to two inches.

I'm often asked, 'Does the injections really work?' To which I invariably reply: "What man would get a penis injection, unless there was an undeniable benefit!"

And in case you're curious, no, I absolutely do not administer P-Shots in the absence of bona fide sexual dysfunction. The rich network of nerves and blood vessels in and around the penis isn't something to be trifled with merely to entertain thrill-seekers. I can't tell you how incredibly gratifying it is to have patients like Elizabeth hug me with a huge grin and a giggle, while exclaiming: "Doctor Cathy, you have ruined me forever!"

When I elevate a patient from someone who's just going through the motions, into a vibrant, passionate soul who can't drink deeply enough of life, it doesn't get any better than that. As I write this, millions of Americans are wandering around in a daze, clueless their sex problems are hormone-based. I'm not trying to get spiritual here, but when I encounter someone like that and am able to lead them out of darkness and into the light – wow!"

When someone's ovaries or testicles don't make enough testosterone, it's the job of the adrenal glands to come to the rescue. The problem is that the adrenals, which sit atop our kidneys like pale yellow, triangular hats, are mainly responsible for manufacturing a fight-or-flight hormone called epinephrine.

When I see patients in life-threatening, or high-stress fields like law enforcement, the military, abusive relationships and professional athletics, they're often suffering from adrenal-gland fatigue. The resulting lack of energy and sex drive results in a depressed patient like Stanley, who can no longer stomach his passionless, zombie-like existence.

A thirty-something workaholic who's in a committed relationship, Stanley can't get a good night's sleep and suffers from anxiety attacks. But at least he's finally taken the positive step of addressing his sexual woes, instead of continuing to use his sales job as a smokescreen to avoid intimacy with his partner.

Unlike Elizabeth, Stanley is able to discuss his sex life freely, without a scintilla of embarrassment or inhibition. Certainly makes my job easier! Although I do understand what it's like to have a Victorian outlook on sex, having been raised a good Christian girl in Canada and Nigeria.

It wasn't until college that I began to see sex for what it is – exquisitely beautiful, natural and one of God's great gifts to humanity. Stanley will vouch for that, in light of the way his body responds to the testosterone replacement therapy regimen I put him on. Among other things, he deals better with the stress generated by his high-powered sales job, and now sleeps through the night instead of grappling with insomnia.

Rather than hide behind work, now Stanley can't wait to come home and unleash his libido on his partner, who may be on the verge of building a shrine to `Stan the Man,' based on what I'm hearing! I won't say work is no longer hugely important to Stanley, because it definitely is. But thanks to getting his testosterone in balance, he now brings a focus that enables him to work smarter, not harder.

At this point, I need to address some very important aspects of Stanley's case. Along with testosterone, I also prescribed other supplements that will tends to calm men, and that supports his body's response to testosterone replacement therapy. When prescribing testosterone for Stanley or any male patient, I never replace estrogen because men's bodies automatically convert a percentage of testosterone into estrogen.

But here's the most important thing to know about replacing male testosterone: It's something I always approach very, very cautiously. That's because the potential side effects in men include strokes, heart attacks and unusually, blood clots. Most laymen think of hormonal imbalances as always resulting in diminished sexuality, but sometimes the exact opposite is true.

Regarding testosterone, before I subscribe it to a male or female patient, I'll give them some background material to read on the hormone's benefits and potential side effects. If a patient returns to me and it's clear they haven't done their testosterone homework assignment, I won't fill their prescription. Patients whose blood pressure is too high, are gaining weight, have diabetes or have a history of cancer in their family need to be managed properly before starting testosterone therapy.

None of these scenarios affect the Hendersons, a middle-age couple that drove from up North to be treated by me. Out-of-town patients who are drawn to me by word-of-mouth regularly come to my Georgia medical offices because they hear that I can get them off of their prescription medication, improve their quality of life and enhance their sexual relationship, enabling them to excel in every endeavor that they aspire to achieve.

Seems that Mrs. Henderson gained weight after childbirth and now loathes her body image. People who are appalled by their physical appearance tend not to be particularly sexual responsive to their partner. Mr. Henderson, who has taken his vows of `in sickness and in health' seriously, doesn't find his wife's weight gain off-putting in the least.

My screenings reveal the Hendersons are both on the low end of the testosterone scale, so I prescribe the 'Passion Rub' that included a testosterone cream for them to rub on their arms every day.

When I see the Hendersons again a few weeks later, their physical relationship is ablaze and Mrs. Henderson is playing tennis, losing weight and once again seeing her hairdresser on a regular basis. With his glowing spouse sitting beside him, Mr. Henderson looks me in the eye and thanks me profusely "for giving my wife back to me."

I tell you, people truly have no inkling of the indispensable roles testosterone, estrogen and progesterone play in their lives. Which is a bit startling, given that production of these dynamic hormones starts dipping as early as our 20s. I will try to replace using natural supplements and if that fails we will progress to the compounded hormones from Yams - which can be a cream, an injection, a pellet, patch, tablet or liquid troche.

Over time, these essential hormones are going to drop whether we like it or not. So why not do something about it? Why not stave off the inevitable, instead of waiting for it to happen and then suffering in silence?

Along with having their hormone levels adjusted by me, leading to intense sexual gratification, the Hendersons, Elizabeth and Stanley share another thread: They all eat better now than before I treated them. They did this at my direction, because I always take a holistic approach to what my patients need to enhance their quality of life. And one of the best ways of achieving that is with a diet, herbs, exercise, and lifestyle modifications. Vegetable juicing is one of the keys to long lasting healthy hormones.

Also, did I mention exercise? Hello!

I look at all aspects of a patient's life in my quest to restore sexual function to those with hormone imbalances. You have to be on an exercise regimen in order to be treated by my medical practice.

 I give my all to my patients, in their quest for wellness. I access each patient with their different situations, backgrounds and challenges and encourage them to sit in these changes as soon as possible. We then strive to achieve the best results possible which is ultimate happiness and joy for life.

Most family medicine doctors don't go over your hormones with a fine-tooth comb to make sure everything's okay. That's not a knock, mind you, because they're not trained to do that. I, on the other hand, do this as a matter of course.

Being a board-certified family medicine physician specializing in enhancing sexual functions, as well as a speaker and educator when it comes to that topic, my passion is to reignite passion by restoring intimacy.

This is how I assist my patients with being healthy, wealthy and successful forever!

About Dr. Cathy

Catherine C. Emeruwa, M.D., or "Dr. Cathy" as her patients affectionately call her, is a Board-Certified Family Medicine Physician whose passionate approach to medicine is applauded by her peers.

Currently operating three living and wellness centers in metropolitan Atlanta, Dr. Cathy focuses on holistic and alternative medicine, and is an expert on the treatment of sexual dysfunction brought on by hormonal imbalances. Specializing in sex therapy, she counsels couples dealing with marital-intimacy issues.

A hallmark of her medical practice is that she spends an hour with each of her patients. The hard-working mother of four is motivated to learn everything about her patients' lifestyles, diets, stressors and mental states, a quest she augments with exhaustive medical tests that take in everything from hair samples to hormone levels.

"Giving my patients my all matters to me," says Dr. Cathy, who's been practicing medicine more than two decades. "I'm not exaggerating when I say I treat them like family."

Born in Winnipeg, Canada, to a Jamaican-Canadian mother, a former nurse and a Nigerian father with a Ph.D. in microbiology, Dr. Cathy is one of five female siblings, including a twin sister who is Dr. Cathy's junior by 15 minutes.

When inquisitive, tomboyish Catherine Emeruwa was 12, her father, Dr. Augustin Emeruwa, got a position heading the University of Nigeria's microbiology department. The Emeruwa clan dutifully packed up and departed Winnipeg for Nsukka, Nigeria. Always an intellectually-rigorous student, Dr. Cathy eventually enrolled in the University of Nigeria's medical program and earned her medical degree in 1989.

After working as a physician for a year in Lagos, Nigeria, Dr. Cathy moved to London and Toronto, focused in both of those cities on being the best wife and mother she could be. And while excelling in those roles, Dr. Cathy was clearly put on earth to touch others with her healing skills. So it goes without saying that she found it incredibly gratifying to work as a family medicine physician in Brooklyn, New York, for three years.

In 2000 Dr. Cathy moved to Atlanta, where her gifts as a clinician and entrepreneur paved the way for a 7,000-patient medical practice, two nursing homes and a medical spa. Although prospering financially, Dr. Cathy recognized that money wasn't everything: She grew weary of healing people while ensconced in an insurance-driven, revolving-door practice model limiting her contact with patients to a few minutes.

So Dr. Cathy left her successful medical practice and started a new one designed to let her spend far more time with patients. As before, her medical practice is thriving largely due to Dr. Cathy's remarkable diagnostic acumen and her exemplary bedside manner.

An accomplished public speaker, Dr. Cathy is a contributor to bestselling author Jack Canfield's upcoming book, *The Soul of Success*.

Dr. Cathy also has a line of weight-loss supplements, sex enhancers and is certified to administer platelet-rich plasma injections that heighten sexual pleasure.

Catherine C. Emeruwa, M.D., is an extraordinary physician whose dedication to her patients is on par with her service to the metropolitan-Atlanta community, where her practice is located.

Connect with Dr. Cathy at:
www.twitter.com/drcathytweets
www.facebook.com/Dr.CathyMD
www.facebook.com/Dr.CathyMDAlpharetta

CHAPTER 14

CREDIT UNION AUTO LOAN INNOVATION WILDLY SUCCESSFUL — AUTO LOANS THAT BUILD FINANCIAL INDEPENDENCE! WHO KNEW?

BY JOHNNY GARLICH

I remember sitting across the desk from my friend and client. Eric was the CEO of a moderately-sized credit union with about 300 million in assets. He had been brought to the credit union several years earlier to lead it into a new era of banking. With financial directives from the board, he had led the company through dramatic changes in its operations and branding. Eric had transformed the credit union, but the financial results simply weren't where he needed them to be. Now he was forced to reduce expenses by firing a number of employees. Many of these people were friends.

He had taken over the company years ago, intent on giving his members the best experience possible. He had thought that the primary way to impress and retain his members was to dramatically shift services to the Internet. In this new vision of banking and financial services, members could serve themselves by taking advantage of services online. Labor costs would decline while revenues would rise. Technology would be the double-edged sword that solved profitability and member engagement.

"So what is the problem with the technology solutions you have implemented?" I asked.

"They have provided a lot of efficiencies. But the savings revolve around a lot of smaller transactional activities. On the revenue side they haven't added much," he lamented.

"The members don't have to come into the credit union to use a lot of our account services. But they also aren't coming in to buy our traditional financial services. We need more loans and more deposits. Plus our margins continue to shrink. To add insult to injury, the lawmakers keep slicing our revenue streams with new legislation. My technology savings are getting wiped out by legislation cutting my revenues."

"Our core strength has always been our ability to use our buying power to provide better rates and services to our members. Our traditional ability to offer lower rates has been minimized by the artificially low rates that result from the Federal Reserve's actions.

"We are being commoditized. Everyone is doing the same thing. I need to break away from what everyone else is doing and make more dramatic changes. Our products provider told me about your video conference auto loan delivery system. I need to bring something to the table that allows me to make more dramatic savings."

"I hear what you are saying: The market has whipsawed you. Your traditional competitive advantage of being a low-cost provider has been nullified by the Federal Reserve's focus on artificially holding down interest rates. The government has stepped in and removed revenue streams. Even though you have implemented a lot of technology, the down side of technology is that it isn't raising revenues; it is merely reducing expenses," I summarized. "May I make a suggestion?" I asked.

"Sure."

"Your problem stems from your perspective. You think that technology's role is to reduce expenses. You are interested in our service because you feel we can reduce your personnel costs. Am I reading you right?"

"Yes. If you can perform the functions of some of my people, then I can have lower labor costs. It's simple math," he asserted.

"Not really. I see a couple of problems. Number one, you need to focus your efforts on revenue, not expenses. Part of your revenue loss is coming from changes in the law. So you have to pivot. Those revenue streams are gone. You can offset those losses with cost cuts only so far."

"Aside from the changes in law, you have grown your auto loan portfolio by making a deal with the devil. In the past, a dealer wouldn't send you a loan. So you fought the dealer for your member's loan. Now the dealer will send you a loan if you pay him a fee. Like most credit unions, you hoped that paying a fee would net you more loans. But forfeiting your member loans to car dealers in the hope that the dealer will generate more net revenue is a strategic mistake."

"By being seduced with the hope of more volume from the dealer, you are sacrificing your relationship with your members on the single most expensive item they purchase. 90% of your members are now buying cars and doing their loans through car dealers because you told your members it was a good idea. Your walk-in direct auto loan volume pales in comparison to your dealer-generated indirect business. You are now at the mercy of whether the dealer will send you back your own members! Your profits on dealer indirect auto loans are the lowest of any loan in your portfolio."

"Car dealers want to sell cars and make money. They aren't interested in your member's financial health. You need to go back to your roots. Credit unions were started to bring together members and let their group buying power save money for all of the members. You aren't like a bank. You are not–for-profit. When you generate profits, you distribute it to your members."

"Your board's focus on return on assets is their way of measuring how good a CEO you are. But if you want to grow your return on assets, you need to provide what your members want. You took this job to help your members get financial independence. You are in a blue-collar area where people often live precariously close to the edge. One unlucky event can drive them to financial ruin."

"You need to help them achieve financial independence. That's why they joined a credit union. They trust you to help them make smart financial decisions. But helping them means you have to be able to represent their interests when they are making big economic decisions. Abdicating your member car loans to dealers removes you from helping your member."

"Because cars depreciate and homes tend to go up in value, a car is almost always the biggest household expense that your members experience. Helping them manage that ownership experience so that it delivers:

1. The greatest use and enjoyment

2. With the least amount of aggravation and

3. Lowest total cost is what you can provide—but only if you innovate."

"In fact, you are the only business that can fulfill that promise. No other business will have the member in focus. All other businesses will be motivated to sell something that violates one of those three principles."

"You cannot roll over and hand over one of the most important financial decisions of your member's life to car dealers and national banks. Only a credit union can provide the member with a financial package that will not only deliver automobile enjoyment, it will set the stage for the member to build a **protected savings account** and thus financial independence."

"Isn't that why you took this job? Weren't you focused on delivering financial independence to your members?"

My friend nodded his head in agreement. "Of course," he said.

"The first step is to put an auto loan package together that sets the foundation for your member's financial independence. We can help you create innovative products that provide benefits and services that members want and car dealers won't offer. Remember, your goal is to deliver the happiest ownership experience and set the stage for the member to build a protected savings account."

"How are we going to do that?" he asked.

"We will figure that out together. However, when you offer these new services, you have to mobilize a sales team that will educate the membership. That means that you want the member to come into the branch and build a personal relationship. The greatest single asset that a credit union has is its relationship with its members through its employees. Serving your members is your cornerstone. Banks and car dealers have no such inclination. They will always be looking to drive revenue even it means the member suffers in the long run."

"You are right. Only a credit union will take the long-term view of protecting the member. If I provide services that the member loves on car loans, he will reward me with all of his financial transactions: loans, credit cards, savings, checking and retirement funds! I get it!" he responded. "Since I am not-for profit, I can operate at margins banks cannot tolerate. We don't pay income taxes!"

"Now you are using your competitive strengths!" I said.

"Plus the credit union can use its cooperative buying power to negotiate insurance products that provide unique services and benefits that only a credit union would be interested in offering. By shifting my goal to providing financial security and independence to my members, I can provide the safety that my members want. I am not in the auto loan business. I am in the financial independence business!" he exclaimed.

I added, "Now you are getting it! Your goal is to help the member achieve financial independence. But convincing a blue-collar worker who has been living paycheck to paycheck to set aside money for savings is a difficult sale. Rather than convince them of saving with you, you need to create a repayment package that dramatically reduces expenses so the member can create a protected savings account with you. Take what they are spending now and convert it to a much smarter way of spending AND saving!"

"The most dramatic expense that you can provide safety and security on revolves around the car loan. You can deliver lower depreciation, lower sales tax, lower interest expense and freedom from repair costs based on how you structure your auto loan package. These expenses will save the member thousands of dollars, not hundreds. It is only through creating these savings that the member will be able to transfer that savings into deposits with your credit union. As you provide these huge cost savings, you can make your loan portfolio more profitable. It's a win-win for both you and the member."

About Johnny

After graduating from Stanford University in 1977, Johnny Garlich joined the family automobile business. Starting as the Used Car Manager and quickly moving to the General Manager, Johnny was able to become the leading Volkswagen dealer in the Mid-America territory.

His love of the nascent tech industry caused him to teach himself computer programming in the early 80s. He used his programming knowledge to write a leasing program that propelled his father's dealership into auto leasing of all makes and models. His success with leasing other makes and models allowed the dealership to participate in the Van Conversion business as it was being born. Soon the VW dealership was retailing van conversions and leasing high group imports and still retaining its lead in the VW zone.

By 1985, Johnny Garlich decided to leave the family business and start a dealership on his own. With almost no capital, he was able to acquire a VW and Subaru dealership and transform it into one of the top-producing dealerships in the zone.

By 1991, family responsibilities caused Johnny to move onto other ventures. He exited the retail automobile business with its long hours and moved into the insurance business with his former vendor where he used his automotive connections to provide aftermarket services to automobile dealers.

By 1994, Johnny once again decided he wanted to be his own boss and bought out his former vendor and opened an agency of his own. Within a few years, he was one of the top-producing aftermarket agencies in the country.

Always thirsty for innovation, Johnny developed a series of training and sales tools to help his dealer clients achieve previously unheard of profits in their finance departments.

In 2009, as Johnny Garlich was closing in on retirement, he used his successful agency to help fund a new concept: providing loan-closing services for car dealers via a video conference call center. He helped develop a unique sales delivery system encapsulated within a video conference call. He started a new company, called Deliveries on Demand, to provide loan-closing services for auto dealers. After several years of development, he introduced the first remote loan closing in the St. Louis market. Within a couple of years he was doing loan closings in several states.

But the technology kept changing, and when it did, Johnny decided in 2014 to teach himself the new programming and rewrite the majority of the code base himself! His IT Director thought Johnny was crazy. But a year and a half later, Johnny Garlich and his IT Director changed the course of financial services by introducing a remote auto loan program for credit unions that shifted the balance of power to the member and the credit union. At 60 years old, Johnny has written off a well-deserved retirement because he is having too much fun disrupting the financial services industry.

CHAPTER 15

TRANSFORM YOUR RESULTS THROUGH BLUE-IS-RED THINKING

BY JONATHAN WHISTMAN

I believe you believe that. I believe I believe that. Understanding the power of these two sentences and applying them in your interactions with others can do more to transform your success than just about any other thing. *It is the very soul of success.*

Yes, that's a bold statement. I make it because I've had a front-row seat to observe the power of belief both to empower good and to twist people for evil. I grew up in a religious cult that isolated and controlled the thought process of its members. The beliefs instilled within me from birth by my parents and every other adult I admired influenced almost every decision I made in my life up – until my late 20's. I believed that I believed that.

Once I broke free of the religion, I had to question even the fundamental assumptions I had accepted about life. I came to wonder how I ever believed and acted the way I had as part of that group. That journey provided me a platform for deeply understanding the power of belief and the path to change.

I've discovered how blind many of us are to the way we've developed our most fundamental beliefs about life, people and the way the world works. We readily assume that our view of the world is the most rational.

We become attached to how we feel and believe. To create real change in others, our businesses, our communities, or ourselves we must begin with understanding the 'why' and 'how' of belief. I call this skill, "Blue-is-Red Thinking."

To illustrate: imagine yourself as a child wearing a blue shirt. Your favorite color! Next, imagine that from birth everyone would, when they'd see you wearing this shirt say, "That's a beautiful red shirt! You look great in red."

When teaching you what color the sky was, "Isn't that a fantastic red sky? It matches your red shirt." Every time you saw the color that today you call blue, people called it red. What would you believe about that color?

If you can imagine this scenario you are starting to understand Blue-is-Red Thinking. It refers to how dramatically the belief a person has absorbed from their environment affects how they view and label things in their world.

Let's go back to our blue shirt that has always been labeled as red: would you consider yourself odd or crazy for calling blue, red? Would you even be aware that there was another way to see the color? Would you be open to the idea that you were wrong? Would it even occur to you to question the belief? Not likely.

Now imagine you travel to a new area. You put on your red shirt. While eating breakfast your waiter says to you, "That's a great looking blue shirt! It matches the blue in your eyes!"

What do you think? You'd likely think your waiter was a bit kooky or perhaps color blind. You've known for years red shirts always bring out the red in your eyes. Indeed who has ever heard of someone with blue eyes? You might chuckle to yourself as you consider the waiter's compliment. Would you for one second consider that you were the one with the wrong belief about the color of your shirt? What would happen as you travel throughout the city and people continued to call your red shirt blue and perhaps even poke fun at you when you call it red?

How tough would it be to finally accept that maybe it's you that is wrong? I would suggest that it would be nearly impossible. If you moved to this city, perhaps someday just to get along you would finally start calling your red shirt blue when around these silly people! You might chose to humor them, but would your fundamental belief change? Would you always hold on to the instinct to admire the red sky?

What level of effort would it take to finally get you to accept the sky as blue? Could you ever deeply believe it as blue? It's likely you would struggle to change your view of the color blue no matter how convincing the evidence.

This mental exercise can help you to understand the power and hold that people's beliefs have on them and the hold your beliefs have on you.

When we develop the ability to accept whatever viewpoint someone holds as an authentic belief – no matter how silly, crazy, warped or unrealistic we feel they are – then we have mastered Blue-is-Red Thinking. This isn't as simple as the age-old advice: "Walk a mile in someone else's shoes." This goes much deeper. It means getting as close to accepting their belief and the resulting thoughts, emotions and actions as stemming from a place of authenticity. Indeed, when you have a blue-is-red understanding of someone you realize the inevitability of how they are thinking, feeling and behaving in the moment. Anyone would be the same way. Can you see the power this has in removing judgment? Rather than losing energy in being at odds with someone else, we can start to develop a context of what is driving their behavior and their thought patterns. This simple act of understanding can be a powerful force for influencing change.

It is even more powerful when we look at ourselves. When you find yourself unhappy with the level of success in your life, try some blue-is-red thinking. What subconscious beliefs do you hold that drive your thoughts, emotions and actions and thus results?

Next time you find yourself feeling strongly about something, try asking yourself, "If I couldn't believe what I do right now about this because it's untrue, what might the alternate truth be?" As you try other viewpoints you'll discover that the intensity of your emotion changes.

Have you ever experienced the fun-house mirrors? The first one makes you look fat and short, the next impossibly thin, and the next a wavy figure. None of them are real, and neither are your beliefs. They are reflections. Visualize your beliefs changing just like walking down that row of mirrors. Laugh at the way it contorts you. Which mirrors do you like the best? Which beliefs serve you better? Which mirror do you usually use to reflect the world around you? In time you may start to recognize a pattern in how you initially feel or react. This is the perfect opportunity to uncover some foundational beliefs, some blue-is-red. You can see this with many childhood messages: "It's impolite to talk about money," "don't trust strangers," "behave like a lady," or "men don't cry." Each of these beliefs is unconsciously absorbed and acted on in our adult life. As a result, we see adults that have a tough time discussing money, even with their spouses. We see men who find it difficult to share their emotions. We find cycles of abuse or neglect based on the absorbed beliefs of the community or family that a person crafted their sense of identity in.

How does this thinking impact helping others? When a person believes that you believe them, they are more open to discussion and less defensive. Importantly, I am not suggesting that means you accept their belief as accurate. It simply means you accept that they came by that belief honestly, that they hold it authentically and that any emotions or actions stemming from this belief are likewise authentic. This is the key to unlock change.

Think about the terror of 911 when planes were flown into the World Trade Center. An act of terror. Insane. Crazy. Warped. If we adopt Blue-is-Red Thinking, we accept that these men acted out of honest belief and a place of authenticity. It doesn't make it less evil, but it does start to help unlock the key to change. These men by all accounts were family men that played soccer with their kids and many other activities that we would consider normal, and yet they committed an unspeakable evil. Why? Was it because they were evil? It is because they believed.

They'd been told since birth that blue-is-red. We may with pride and confidence say we'd never have acted in such a way, and I believe you believe that. When blue-is-red thinking is applied however, we are open to the thought that in similar situations of birth, we might have acted similarly. Only by understanding this root cause of belief can any nation hope to eventually eradicate terror. We must remove the root cause for belief, not attack the person or the current belief, which would be almost as difficult as telling them red-is-blue.

I can say this because I committed evil based on belief. I didn't feel evil at the time. I thought I was doing what was right and noble. I believed I was being faithful to my God. My son was born 4.5 months premature and we were told that he would require an immediate blood transfusion to save his life. There was just one problem: We were raised by a religion that told us blood was sacred and that transfusing blood under any circumstance was a sin. We believed that even if blood would save his life we'd be costing him his everlasting salvation. Focused on his everlasting salvation rather than his life right now, we refused him blood.

Thankfully a judge intervened and ordered that blood be administered. My son's life was saved. Today, I can't even imagine how I believed what I authentically believed then. And what I believed then I now see as evil. I do know with absolute certainty: I authentically believed what I believed.

I share this so you might ask yourself what beliefs you have and how you came to have them. Even the ones you like. The power of Blue-is-Red Thinking extends past things so dramatic as life-and-death into the ordinary.

In my work with leaders and managers of companies, I teach them how to accelerate success by mastering Blue-is-Red thinking. They are able to have change adopted more quickly by their team once they see things from the individual's belief. When I work with sales teams I find that they sell more, more quickly as they are able to switch into blue-is-red thinking. They sell more because as they approach their prospect from the right color (the color that their prospect sees the world from), they quickly become viewed as a trusted advisor. A powerful place to be when you need to influence a buying decision.

Consider a scenario: you've taken over leading an underperforming team. Your job is to get the very best from everyone to deliver what the team is responsible for.

Blue-is-Red Thinking will tell you this: Every individual *already believes* they are doing their best! No matter what the actual performance of a person is, *they believe* they are doing 100% of what they are capable of or they have what *they believe* is a valid reason for not giving 100%. This is true even of non-performers.

What might some of the beliefs they hold be?

- "Management is lazy or incompetent."
- "They don't pay me enough."
- "I already work harder than everyone else."

The toughest part is some of these beliefs are based on valid reasons and historically correct opinions. Until you understand them and overcome them, you'll be stuck. When you can come alongside them and truly believe that they believe whatever it is that allows them to perform less than 100%, then you can start to inspire the needed changes.

You can be gentle, inspiring, and servant-based in your approach, but you may be resented when you challenge people's belief about themselves. Hopefully the resentment is a temporary bridge to a more productive viewpoint and results. Much like a high school sports coach that you learned to love because he helped you see a better version of yourself.

What can enable you to have better success in transforming their belief into something that serves them and the company better? I would suggest it boils down to one thing: Mastering Blue-is-Red thinking.

It would be accurate to say that a leader "helps a person discover the truth" rather than "tells them." Sometimes before discovering a truth they must shift the foundational belief that truth is based on.

What people really need from a leader is authentic truth. They must believe you care about them and believe in them, but will only accept the best from them. You as a leader must believe that the "best from them" is much higher than what they currently believe. We follow people who make us want to be better and who harness our intrinsic belief that we can be. They must believe we believe that.

Sometimes beliefs are formed by comparison. For instance, things are only good or bad by comparison. So a manager might rate his management ability by comparing himself to those that have managed him. By this measure he believes he is a great manager. If you understand how he is framing his belief about what a great manager is, it becomes much easier to help him change.

People only know what great is by comparing themselves and others to what they have seen. Thus why I said earlier they believe they are doing their best and giving 100%.

I remember when I first started renting cars for travel. I loved renting cars for travel because they were always better than my car. It's different today. In fact it is completely opposite. Today I dread having to rent a car as it's always worse than my personal car. My belief about what constituted a great car was simply my point of comparison and it changed over time.

Why is this comparison belief important in leadership? Because your job is to understand *how* your team-member came up with what they define as great. Once you understand the foundation of their belief you can help them discover a better truth by helping them have a different point of comparison.

When you adopt Blue-Is-Red Thinking you'll spend less time struggling with your team and more time facilitating the changes needed. Many times you won't need to change a person's belief at all. By understanding the foundation of the belief, you can craft your requests to be in harmony with what they already believe.

Think about the sweeping power of blue-is-red thinking when applied on a grand scale. A blue-is-red thinker is comfortable challenging their own assumptions about the world around them and thus experiences success in relationships, health, finances, business and community. They seldom get trapped in unhealthy cycles, and when they do, they have the key to unstick themselves.

A blue-is-red thinker holds the power to influence and ignite change in others. The answers to political conflicts, racism, ageism, sexism and almost any "ism", is Blue-is-Red thinking. It is the *soul of success*. Please believe I believe that. My blue-is-red.

About Jonathan

Jonathan Whistman is a Partner at Elevate Human Potential. His work is centered on the belief that the greatest business results come from focusing on elevating the human potential within a business. When companies are able to tap into the imagination, talent and vision of their people, they see a dramatic increase in sales and a reduced level of workplace stress.

Best-selling author Malcolm Gladwell is famous for saying in his book, *Outlier,* that 10,000 hours makes someone an expert and so it is!

Jonathan was raised in a family with eight kids and his childhood was spent inside a religious cult where he devoted over 19,000 hours knocking on doors to create radical conversions in lifestyles and belief in the lives of those he called on. In addition he became a leader, regularly giving inspirational and instructional talks to audiences of up to 11,000 people.

This up-close look at how people form, change and develop beliefs became a foundation for understanding how to lead organizations and sales teams where success depends on getting the power of belief ignited in the people you lead or the customers you sell to. Leaving the beliefs of his childhood forced him to become familiar with the challenges that come from overcoming an ingrained way of thinking and being.

Using these insights, Jonathan has trained, hired, managed, observed and coached thousands of sales people through his work with leading sales organizations. He has been instrumental in molding the leadership talents of countless companies. His own companies have been featured on CNN Money, have won the GEW Top 50 High Growth companies' designation, and achieved the SXSW Top 5 Award.

When not working he enjoys long-distance backpacking, motorcycling and reading. He recently completed a 540-mile hike across Spain with Kellie Zimmet, the love of his life and business partner. His greatest business satisfaction comes from having a CEO client feel like they have their life back when the team is running well and achieving at a high level, and from seeing people overcome their own beliefs that restrict their potential. His greatest personal satisfaction comes in knowing he was able to change his own beliefs and thus create a better life for himself and his son.

CHAPTER 16

ALLOW FEAR TO FUEL YOUR DRIVE TO SUCCESS

BY MAX PICCININI

What if you had the power to transform any difficulties into your greatest assets ?

I was born of a French mother and an Italian father in Strasbourg, France. I had a rough time along with my brother and sisters.

My dad's dream was to play the violin. Believing he was too old for learning to play the violin, he transferred his dream onto me by forcing me to play the violin at age 3. Unfortunately, he used the hard way. I remember his big strong hand slapping me every time I made a mistake on the violin.

I was trained at a very early age that there was no room for mistakes. If I made them, I was going to be insulted, humiliated or physically abused.

We were fighting financially. I remember my dad using my green big scissors I used to cut paper in class in order to cut our hair – due to lack of money. Unfortunately, he was a French teacher, not a hairdresser. You should have seen our haircuts…

My self-esteem was low. I was leaving in constant fear. When I was 10 years old, my parents got divorced, and my dad got into relationship with a new woman.

This woman had more authority over my dad than my mum. Over the years he started to hold himself back from insulting me and hitting me for everything and nothing. I was finally getting a nicer version of my dad. I was meeting him on Saturdays every two weeks.

And finally when our relationship got better, something dramatic happened that shaped my life forever. It was November 11th 1997, I had just came back home from a basketball game that we won. I was only 14 years old.

We were watching TV on the sofa when my mum came into the room and asked me in a weird voice: "Max, please come with me, I got something to tell you." I wanted to continue to watch the movie, but she insisted and I could see on her face that this was serious.

I followed her and entered the main room. She closed the door, looked down and after hesitating a moment, she raised her head, looked at me with all her strength and told me: "Your dad just died this afternoon in a car accident." I didn't truly understand what happened at that moment, but my mother told me later that my face turned white instantly. I was in shock.

It took me a while to understand what this meant truly.

In the weeks and months that followed, I entered the greatest victim phase I ever did:

- Why is this happening to me?
- Why am I not lucky like others?
- You dad, you hurt me, you humiliated me, you took all your anger out on me, and now that I finally need you, you left like a thief in the night, leaving me alone. I was angry at him, at my mother, at myself and the whole world!
- What a crappy life I have, I simply don't have any luck! – I was telling myself.

One day when I was 15, my mother gave me a book that changed my life: *How To Win Friends and Influence People* by Dale Carnegie.

For me that was the first time I understood that I could influence things.

That was to me a revelation: It told me that we have the capacity to change and impact our lives as well as the lives of others. I became an addict to self-development books.

A few months later, I decided to go to the USA for an one-year exchange program and I ended up in Louisiana.

I did not speak a word of English. That's when I realized how lucky I was to have hands and a face to communicate! Two months later, I was fluent in English and discovered a new culture, a new way of thinking. It forced me to look at things from a different angle.

- What if my childhood and my dad's death were not a tragedy?
- What if they were an opportunity for me to learn and grow?
- What if all that prepared me for an extraordinary life?

After coming back to France from America, I kept asking new questions:

- What's my life about?
- What do I want to create?
- What's truly important and what do I want to accomplish?
- What do I truly want to experience?

One day, I took the most important decision in my life: There was NO WAY I was going to live with regrets. I was not going to settle for anything else other than an extraordinary life!

But…

Life was about to teach me a great lesson.

With no diploma, no network, no credibility and no money, at age 21, I started my own business in France in the distribution of wellness products with an American company.

I had to call people around to ask them to either buy the products or to join as a partner in the company.

That put me in front of my biggest fears:

1. Fear of rejection.
2. Fear of not being good enough.

3. Fear of judgment.

4. Fear of failure.

I was terrified of what people were going to think about me. Worse, I was scared to make a mistake! So the best choice was not to call. To wait until I was going to be perfect.

The problem is :

How can we become perfect if we don't do mistakes first?

By the way, who cares if we are perfect or not?

Easier said that done!

There is a difference between understanding something intellectually and feeling it emotionally.
– I *knew* I had to make these phone calls.
– I *knew* I had to stop procrastinating.
– I *knew* trying to be perfect was not the right way, and that it was okay to make a mistake.

But knowing was not enough, I had to feel it in my guts, feel the fear and do it anyway.

It took me many days, filled with stress and fear until I took the phone in my hand and told myself :

"Now Max, if you want to live your dreams, you've got to make that phone call. If you don't, you will face the consequences of wasting years of your life stuck in fear and distress."

My hand and my voice were trembling, but I made that phone call. It was horrible. I was stressed, I hesitated, I forgot everything I wanted to say, and of course, the person calmly told me he was too busy.

Out of this catastrophic call, a feeling of proudness and accomplishment filled me! I made that first phone call! I faced my fear and did it anyway! What could have appeared as a defeat was to me a victory. Life just taught me that in every defeat existed a seed of victory. What we just have to do is acknowledge it.

That day, I made eight phone calls. I had only one appointment, but that day I felt good.

I went to bed with a smile on my face, feeling proud of myself. What if just behind our fears was going to be joy and happiness?

The first thing they told me when I started my new business was: "If you want to succeed you need to set goals." So I did. And high ones. The problem was, as soon as I did that, a series of events and difficulties hit me right in my face! I was getting rejected day after day after day. It was tough. My business was not going anywhere.

So I did what most people do: find excuses! Some of them were:

- It's the crisis, people don't have money.
- I am unlucky.
- I am too young and don't have a diploma, they don't take me seriously.
- I don't have enough experience, I will never make it.
- French people are too closed, we can't do business here!

Was finding excuses going to help me reaching my goal? Surely not. But it was a good way not to take responsibility. :-)

So I was stagnating. After a while, I was about to abandon this business and go back to a normal job. But suddenly a little voice came to me. Something I read in a book one day:

Losers quit. Winners never quit.

For sure, I did not want to feel like a looser, so I had to find a better strategy.

Then I asked myself: What if difficulties were necessary in order for me to grow and reach the goal I set ? This made total sense!

Over the years, I set up higher and higher goals. And every time I was setting a new goal, new difficulties came along the way. It's as if they were working hand in hand…

Life was testing my determination to reach these new goals. But most importantly, I understood a very important principle: I had to proportionally grow as high as my goals were.

Every new goal we set will require us to build "new emotional muscles" and "new skills" in order for us to be able to reach that goal.

Now instead of fighting the difficulties, I was welcoming them. Instead of stressing about them, I was preparing for them, knowing that beating them was the only way I was going to succeed. Based on this simple philosophy, I started to grow personally exponentially, and so did my business and my entire life. I become more and more determined, positive and committed. My leadership, communication and speaking skills went through the the roof. I became more and more confident and happy.

In a few years, I was making over $10,000/month in residual income before I was 26 years old, and I became the top leader in the country. Before the age of 30, I became a millionnaire and I was invited all around the world in order to share my success story with thousands of people.

It's incredible what can happen to you when you change your perspective. . . when you choose to look at things differently.

Ask yourself these questions:

(a). What if everything was a gift in your life? I mean, *everything*.

(b). What if the difficulties you are meeting right now were your best opportunities to grow, learn and develop yourself in order to reach your goals ?

(c). What if that very thing that drives you crazy was the exact thing you needed right now in order to reach new heights of success and happiness?

Nothing happens by chance. Your heart is not beating by chance. The sunrise and the sunset don't happen by chance. You did not come to this earth by chance, nor are the difficulties you are experiencing right now.

I lost my mother when I was 26. She died of a cancer.

Again, was it easy? Absolutely not. I loved my mother and we had such a great connection. It was painful to live and difficult to accept. But did it make me grow? Absolutely! Did it give me perspective? Oh yes! Did it motivate me to become more healthy? Right on the spot. I am now a very healthy person and vitality is my one of my highest values.

I understood later that my tough upbringing and the death of my parents were the greatest gifts in my life.These painful experiences brought me now the exact opposite: joy, happiness and wiseness. They gave me perspective. They offered me an opportunity to grow and learn.

It's when you experience darkness that you can better appreciate the light.

Don't run away from the difficulties of your life! They are your life's gifts.

Face them and learn to acccpt and even appreciate them. Would you be the person you are without the difficulties you went through? Do you want it or not? You will experience difficulties in your life, and you will experience pain. They are part of life. Running away from them is like starting to play basketball believing you will never miss a shot or lose a game. It will never happen and it's not meant to be.

But you know what I found out? As soon as you acknowledge your difficulties, instead of stealing your energy, they give you energy. The reason is that you see them now as challenges instead of problems.

As soon as you accept that pain is part of life, it diminishes itself and gives you room inside for a much more beautiful feeling: GRATITUDE.

- Gratitude for learning.
- Gratitude for growing.
- Gratitude for who you are becoming because of these difficulties.

HERE ARE SOME STEPS I HAVE LEARNED TO HELP YOU BE SUCCESSFUL IN ANYTHING YOU DO :

1. Step up! Decide to go to reach your highest potential. You are meant for greatness.

2. Acknowledge your difficulties. If you try to run away from them, you will lose energy and end up making them even worse.

3. Face your difficulties, learn from them, grow like never before and change the world, one person at a time.

That's truly where you will find happiness and continuous success.

About Max

Max Piccinini, Success Catalyst, is one of the most influential transformational leaders in Europe. He is an Entrepreneur, Life, Business & Money Coach, Author and Speaker. He holds unique and dynamic seminars with attendance going up to 2000 people. His seminars focus on success, business, money, intimate relationships and vitality – welcoming thousands of people from all around the world.

Max is the founder of the program ItsMyTree™, a step-by-step approach to unlock your potential and go from where you are to where you want to go. His core philosophy is that there are laws and principles governing the world. First, you have to know them; then, you have to fully understand them, and finally, you have to own them fully in your core. That's when you are set for automatic success.

With his charisma and incredible energy, Max offers a very pragmatic and unique approach to help his clients create truly positive results. He regularly appears on TV, Radio and Magazines in Europe and Canada. Hundreds of thousands of people follow him over his online *Success Letter* on MaxPiccinini.com

Max is French-Italian, born in France, started from nothing, and despite a tough upbringing, became a very successful entrepreneur – a millionaire before 30 – and now lives the life of his dreams. He is now living in Switzerland, inspiring people all around the world.

You can connect with Max Piccinini, or learn more about his Success Educational Videos and his next seminars at:
MaxPiccinini.com
contact@maxpiccinini.com

CHAPTER 17

DEFINING SUCCESS THROUGH THE EYES OF A SELF-MADE MILLIONAIRE

BY VU TRUONG

Success is achieving what you desire. Money is just a way of keeping score! While many work towards success, few people reach their goals. Try this philosophy if what you're doing isn't working. When you understand this concept, you will change your own future and actually begin to listen to that little voice inside that tells you, "Yes, this is what I was born to do."

Many of the world's great personal success stories did not begin in the halls of private boarding schools, but on the streets of survival necessity, the homes where strong values were instilled, and at the elbows of wise mentors who recognized a potential entrepreneur who lacked experienced guidance. In some situations, obtaining an advanced degree is necessary; either to practice within your chosen field as certification, or perhaps because you prefer a more predictable future than entrepreneurship guarantees. However, if you fall into the entrepreneurial segment, the discipline of a structured education may even hinder your creativity and the inspiration it drives.

This is not to say that an advanced education is harmful or unnecessary; only that it may have a dilatory effect in allowing you to recognize your inspirational light that shines within. In fact, it is not unusual to seek specialized education to enhance what is already an entrepreneurial foundation.

WHAT SUCCESS THINKS LIKE

Imagine what it must have felt like to be Christopher Columbus; to have an idea, a belief . . . that was so compelling that he was willing to set sail across a sea everyone said would eventually fall off the edge of the Earth. Yet, he believed in himself; he believed in himself enough to recruit financial sponsorship and a crew of men who were willing to hoist sail. *That* is how successful people think. I graduated high school *summa cum laude* at the age of sixteen and one would think that plotted me to navigate university degrees with the same sort of attitude, but it didn't. Like Columbus, I wasn't content to sail familiar seas. I wanted to prove that I could become successful by choosing a different path.

The details of your background and what formed your core may vary. I grew up in a household with little money, but my father raised me to believe in myself; and it's my father who I have to thank for where I am today. He taught me discipline and gave me inspiration.

Sometimes your motivation lies in what you know best, and sometimes in what you know best you do *not* want. Whatever its core, it is within you and you alone. You are unique and therefore your path to success is simply a systematic series of choices that eventually land you where you flourish. Successful people realize that it does not happen overnight; ask anyone who has won the lottery only to find themselves destitute a year later.

You cannot maintain what you have not learned to handle; or know how to re-create. That is the element that removes fear of failure; the crippling, limiting, negative self-language that has stopped so many others from realizing their success. What you envision and what you actually see are totally different.

You may realize you have a particular aptitude for a pattern of thinking or delivery. For example, mine lay in real estate investments and I took a huge leap of faith. I quit my job cold turkey and used all my money to invest in residential real estate. My first pre-foreclosure property was very profitable and I'd found my calling. I can take a calculated risk and plan my future accordingly.

FINDING YOUR PATH

The first step in your process is to choose a direction that makes sense. It can come from an unanticipated source. My brother, Vinh, introduced me to real estate. He urged me to attend my first real estate seminar – which ended up being a great investment of my time as I look back.

If, upon awakening tomorrow morning, you could choose one thing that would be so inspiring as to make you roll out of bed and look forward to the day, what would that be? It may be something you've already been doing for a long time; perhaps it's something unrelated that you simply thought was where you belonged, or maybe it's something you've seen a need for and reasoned that if you need it, others do as well and therein lay inspiration.

CONTINUING TO LEARN

While an advanced education may not be your motivational fountain, continuing education is definitely a necessity for me, albeit more loosely defined. In this environment, though, the tuition is the desire to learn. Here is where the flavor of the education differs from that of the traditional sense. A truly successful entrepreneur *needs* to learn in order to feed that spirit of curiosity. Learning is like accumulating the ingredients for a new dish and the world is your kitchen.

Successful people are generally organically bright, often dropping out of school or graduating early because it's no longer of value to them. They have a desire to do more and they either have it or they don't. They will find some people or concepts extremely inspiring and are hungry to learn all they can about their focus. "You have to have it in your gut."

It's often a situation of being a hands-on person. You may not benefit as much by reading a textbook as you do simply sitting down and disassembling and reassembling—learning as you work, as I would call it.

I found attending seminars a great way to learn from those who have walked in the path I want to follow. They have made the mistakes, and paved the way for my success. After listening to some of their stories, I am able to understand I am not alone, and this isn't the first time someone has experienced what I am experiencing. They also help me avoid failing in some of the ways they already have. Hearing about those experiences makes the seminar or mentorship fee well worth the price of admission, and I save weeks or months in time, and thousands of dollars of investment because of what I learn from them.

SURROUND YOURSELF WITH WINNERS

Place yourself in the company of successful people. This is a truly pure-air environment where the members breathe enthusiasm and optimism. They do not fear the future for they feel in control of it and of their individual destinies. Often, it is not a case of *wanting* success, but realizing when you hold it in your hands. When you are in a locker room of winners, the confidence is contagious. Discouragement and critics are in the loser's locker room. Unless you surround yourself with the right people, you will never make it to that next level. Millionaires make millionaires.

You may remember the old adage that people judge you by the company you keep. It works both ways; you also judge yourself by the company you keep. When you work and socialize with successful people, you see yourself on their parallel, and at that point, you begin making decisions that will lead you down the success-paved path. This draws upon one of the most natural survival instincts; the herd mentality. While that seems fundamental, choose a successful herd. Success breeds success.

You may not know in advance where your success lies. For this reason, it is important to surround yourself with opportunity. Watch the pulse of the economy and look for opportunities that exist in this place and time simply because the world is as it is today. This is how you ride out the bad times; they aren't bad times for you because you know how to take advantage of what has value in the marketplace.

IDENTIFY YOUR GOAL

Be goal-driven. Goals can come in many visions and not the one that others might see. For example, your goal may be to give back in some sense – financially, educationally or otherwise. For you to be able to accomplish this, you must earn the funds to put in that collection plate. You cannot give what you do not have.

Sometimes, giving is not tangible. Other than making donations to charity, mentorship is another way I like to give back. I'm not always mentoring someone in commercial real estate, but sometimes more generally, although always for business. I have to remember, success is not absolutely defined the same way for everyone, and I want to help others achieve their idea of success, not mine. A personal goal is to use the concept of paying it forward. Someone helped me reach my goals, and now, it's my turn.

FOCUS ON YOUR PASSION

Goals are very important. Without having clear goals every day, I would have gotten easily distracted, and it would have been very difficult to accomplish much of anything. Distractions are everywhere, and I am easily distracted. Another way of staying focused on the prize is to be passionate about your goal. If you are not passionate, then change directions. Find something that will drive you to succeed, and get into driver's seat.

Here again, your passion may be just a piece of the puzzle that spells ultimate success. You may possess a particular skill set that while critical in your thinking, is only a portion of what is needed to accomplish the goal. When you surround yourself by successful people, you provide yourself, and them, with a pool of knowledge and talent. When confronted by what you perceive as an obstacle; and then presented to those with appropriate exposure, the obstacle becomes an opportunity to learn and to share what you have learned. Therefore, identify your goal and lend your abilities toward reaching it, even if you must delegate pieces of your dream to accomplish it.

Focusing on your passion also allows you to see back doors that others have missed. You are that chef in the kitchen who doesn't stick to the recipe, but likes to experiment with ingredients, amounts and combinations. The final product is unique and better than the original upon which it was based. Success is often defined as that better mousetrap; a need that has been filled with an improved product or concept. In order to come up with that mousetrap, you must use your passion to identify the potential improvements, which often come in the name of simplicity; combining two steps into one. They come with adjectives such as faster, cheaper, cleaner, richer, better, or healthier. We are a society of consumers and we love the idea of always moving forward.

Focus may require that you move out of your comfort zone. Choose instead to look at it as a means of developing perspective you may not have originally had. This is actually a variation of mentorship in that you defer to those who have expertise in some aspect you do not, even though they are not at your level of sophistication. The children who are your ultimate consumers best perform taste-testing a new cereal.

When you reach obstacles, don't hesitate to reach out to the people with whom you've surrounded yourself. Often you will give them the opportunity to "pay it forward" by helping you with mentorship. They may anticipate that which you do not yet see coming, and prepare you for it. In turn, you might offer an alternate perspective to them, or to those who come behind you when you assume the mentorship role. These are measurements of success that do not increase your bank balance; but the balance of your personal satisfaction.

FIND THE RIGHT MENTOR

When presented with a problem, you do not look for guidance in a room full of failures. Why repeat their mistakes? Instead, find the right mentor whose advice is valid and based on his personal success. I attended a real estate seminar that stood out from the rest. His material was consistent, very concise and completely honest. He did not try to oversell what he was offering and sincerely cared about the people in the seminar and how they could utilize what he had to teach. He later became my mentor – J. Scott Scheel, founder of the Commercial Academy.

Motivation can come from many vantages. It's important to focus on the positives and not the negatives that drain your enthusiasm and cloud your judgment, forcing you to make bad decisions. Entrepreneurs constantly face the decisions that must be guided not by want, but by need. At some point the vision takes on a life of its own and you are simply feeding it, nurturing its growth until it can stand alone.

I am a millionaire today because of the fruits of my labor. It did not come easily. I dealt with adversity and experienced many failures to get where I am. I certainly can't take full credit for my success because my wife Joy, family and my mentors had a lot to do with it. Money does not define me, and it does not dictate what I do from now on. I want to help make others successful, and if their lives benefit, then I feel rewarded.

Through the highs and the lows in my life, I have worked hard, and I hope I have been a good example for my son and daughter. I am passionate about real estate, and because of that, it is not just my career. This bridges who you were to whom you are capable of becoming, and along with honesty, are the key.

Some people I have encountered have diminished or even hidden their past. They're embarrassed; sometimes even a little disgraced by what they did to get where they are. Success doesn't depend on having the proverbial silver spoon. If you're willing to have solid values and to work hard, you will eventually shine.

I continue to invest in success; helping others to invest in real estate. We syndicate deals and find investors who understand what we do. I specialize in finding under-performing assets by forcing appreciation through back-filling vacancies and lowering expenses. By strategically applying this strategy, I am able to add tremendous value to an asset in a short period of time. There's nothing better than when all parties are happy with their return on investments (ROI).

There is no guaranteed formula for success. It is not based on economic background, ethnic origin, religion or even advanced education. It is based on passion, focus, and surrounding yourself with the right people who will help you make sound decisions. Ultimately, it is about giving back. You are successful when you have made a difference. Money has never been my goal, only a byproduct of my passion - investing in real estate.

About Vu

An achiever and a creative thinker at an early age, Vu was determined to succeed in life. He was raised in a household with traditional family values. As Vu matured, he naturally gravitated to become a successful entrepreneur.

Vu Truong is the founder and managing member of Trustone Capital, and has over 12 years of real estate experience. He has owned and managed millions of dollars of commercial real estate. Coming from owning and managing a large portfolio of single family, multi-family and retail properties, he brings over a decade of experience in investment analysis, real estate management, market analysis, and re-development.

Vu has created an amazing commercial real estate investing technique using his business aptitude and ingenuity to obtain a greater advantage in this industry. His true passion in Retail Shopping Centers and Multi-Family properties makes him a strategic investor that prides himself on building strong ethical values and relationships.

His primary focus is value-added investments, where he can drive value over a short investment horizon—whether it's Retail, Office, Industrial or Multi-Family. He actively seeks undervalued investments in the commercial real estate marketplace. His attention to detail, creative structuring and breadth of knowledge consistently exceeds expected results for his clients repeatedly.

Vu has extensive experience in analyzing and evaluating commercial properties. His research involves pinpointing investment opportunity through extensive analysis into market trends and conditions, projecting the future growth while carefully considering the company's competitive dynamics, as well as cash flow analysis. In addition, he has an extensive background in the construction platform including rehabilitation projects. Vu has valuable experience in assessing the risk involved in commercial real estate transactions from a management, financial, and mechanical perspective.

More importantly, Vu also belongs to a national exclusive members-only group that contains 30 key principals actively investing in commercial real estate. This elite group meets quarterly to discuss member deals, deal structure, market conditions, current financing trends and member's managing performance. This exclusive group currently has commercial real estate holdings that include but are not limited to Retail Shopping Centers, Hotels, Office Buildings, Self-Storages, Multi-Family and Medical Buildings.

PROFESSIONAL AFFILIATIONS/RECOGNITION

Vu is an active member of the International Council of Shopping Centers (ICSC), Commercial Real Estate Network (CREN), Houston Apartment Association (HAA), Local chapter of Certified Commercial Investment Member (CCIM), National Association of Realtors (NAR), Texas Association of Realtors (TAR), and the Houston Association of Realtors (HAR).

You can contact Vu at:
Vu@TrustoneCapital.com
www.TrustoneCapital.com

CHAPTER 18

CREATING PREDICTABLE, MONTHLY PASSIVE INCOME

BY TANISHA SOUZA

When was the last time you had something unexpected, traumatic, and shocking happen to you or your family? Was that a turning point in your life?

Many of the unexpected, traumatic and stressful events that happen in our lives have financial consequences. Use those seemingly negative events to help you realize that no matter what we do, where we work or how much money we make, we all need and can create passive income.

Growth is painful. Change is painful. But nothing is as painful as staying stuck somewhere you don't belong.

~ Mandy Hale

Most people who knew me assumed that I had the perfect life. I was a 27 year-old graduate of UC Berkeley, and I also had a law degree from USC law school. After doing a clerkship with a federal judge in Honolulu, I met my soul mate Chris, and got a dream job working as an attorney at the largest law firm in State of Hawaii. Shortly thereafter, we got married and moved into a rental unit owned by my father-in-law. It was perfect. Or was it really?

Here's what was actually happening behind the scenes. I had the same white 1989 Volkswagen Fox that my dad gave me in high school, but I was driving it with a broken gas gauge and without air conditioning. My car ran out of gas on the freeway because I couldn't afford to get the gas gauge fixed. I know my husband loves me because he married me despite my massive $100,000 student loan debt. Unfortunately, we were lucky to spend a half hour together each day due to my long hours at work. I had zero savings, and I had cashed out my meager mutual funds to pay for our wedding. My net worth was literally negative $100,000, and my monthly student loan expense was as fat as a mortgage payment. Tensions were high.

MY MOMENT OF TRUTH

One afternoon as I was buried in legal research at my desk, I stopped to consider the fate of my future. Without any quality time with my husband, I could see myself divorced, lonely and bitter. I would still be working 70+ hours a week in a job that I hated, launching lawsuits over insurance claims and evicting people from their homes. I could see myself working for 15 to 20 years to pay off student loans, driving my VW and just getting by on my self-imposed $15 weekly lunch allowance. I couldn't start a family. I didn't have time for kids. Lawyers 15 to 20 years older than me were miserably single because they didn't have time to date anyone, let alone have kids.

Massive stress caused me to lose 15 pounds because I just couldn't eat. At night, I got about 4 to 5 hours of sleep, and I regularly woke up with my head pounding and rings under my eyes. I found myself sleeping at my desk at work. Terrified that I might lose the very job I hated, I was on pins and needles thinking I would go bankrupt trying to pay my student loan bills.

That wasn't what I signed up for. I felt like I was trapped inside a burning building and the only way out was through the huge plate glass window on the 10th floor.

So I had two choices… I could either stay in the burning building and die a horrific, painful slow death, or I could bust out of the plate glass window and take my chances with whatever followed.

Sometimes, the best solution to escaping a burning building is to jump out of the nearest window. But I needed a safety net. I needed to pay off my loans and I needed reliable income that I didn't have to work for. I didn't want to be dependent on my job.

"Leap and the net will appear."

~ Zen Saying

Here's what happened next. I found out that a friend's home was in foreclosure over $5,000 in unpaid homeowner's association dues. The house had no mortgage and was worth $250,000. Just then I realized that if I bought that house for $5,000 and sold it at market value, I could pay off all of my student loans. That meant making more money on the property than I made in a year at my job. I asked my mom for books on foreclosure for Christmas. She bought me more than 10 books, and I read them all. Then Chris and I got to work.

We bought a foreclosure for $170,000, fixed it up and sold it for $375,000, clearing my $100,000 student loan debt in one year. After reading *Rich Dad, Poor Dad*, by bestselling author Robert Kiyosaki, I made the decision to create passive income so I wouldn't depend on a job for my survival ever again. We bought and sold a duplex, made $175,000 and then bought a strip mall for $1.125 million. After paying the mortgage and ground lease rent, we pocketed an extra $100,000 a year. We went on to buy other multi-million dollar properties. We went from a net worth of negative $100,000 to $5 million in real estate in three years. We achieved financial freedom by the time I was thirty.

REALIZING LIFE'S PURPOSE
THROUGH ADVERSITY

I've read many stories of people who discovered their life's purpose while overcoming adversity. The challenges we faced by flipping homes and changing careers, led me to my purpose in helping families create passive income.

I soon quit my job to start a wealth coaching business in Honolulu. Years later, I invented and patented the Income Snowball™, otherwise known as The Perfect Wealth System™. We helped people create predictable, recurring monthly income without investing money, time, risk, management or effort. Today we're an international wealth coaching firm helping families worldwide to retire early, rich and mortgage- (and student loan) free.

FAITH IS THE KEY TO SERENDIPITY

The happy ending? Because we took a leap of faith and took a risk, now I truly have a dream life. My husband and I work together to change people's lives while we raise our beautiful children and travel the world. My goal was just to pay off my student loan debt, it wasn't to become rich. Friends call us the accidental millionaires.

I challenge you not to wait until you're trapped in a burning building. Jump out of your window, face your fears and create passive income for your family. Follow these ten steps to start creating passive income now:

1. **Understand the difference between active and passive income.** Active income is income you work for. If you work a 9 to 5 job, you're a consultant, or you're self-employed, then your income depends on how long or how hard you work or even how many sales you make. Although there will always be some initial work involved in creating passive income, truly passive income is money that comes in month after month based on the initial work you did.

2. **Stop accumulating assets and start creating cash flow.** As American's we have been trained to accumulate assets that we hope will be worth more in the future. People try for decades to amass millions of dollars in their 401(k)s. Others buy real estate hoping it will double in value. Here's the problem: whether an asset appreciates is largely outside of your control. Remember what happened in the 2008 - 2011 real estate crash? What do you think is easier, saving $2 million or creating $5,000 a month in passive income?

3. **Decide exactly how much monthly income you want or need.** Take out a pen and paper and jot down your passive income goal. Do you want to leave your job, replace your income or stay home with the kids? If so, how much monthly income will you need to accomplish that? If your goal is financial freedom, you'll never have to work again once you have enough passive monthly income to cover your living expenses.

4. Start a passive income tracker.

Look at your income sources. Chart, on a spreadsheet, a list of your passive income and your active income sources. Passive income includes things like real estate, book royalties, licensing fees, etc. If 100% of your income relies on you or your spouse working, then start from zero.

5. Learn how to make money without money.

It takes creativity—not money—to make money. Banks borrow your savings, pay you less than 1% on it, and then loan it back out for 6% - 14% or more. They make money without (their own) money. The more creative you are, the more money you'll make.

6. Ditch the financial diet.

Don't make the mistake of living so far below your means that you can't live a happy life. If going to Starbucks a few times a week makes you happy, keep doing it. Otherwise, you'll spend money you don't have to make up for the weeks or months you felt deprived.

7. Build multiple streams of income.

When you have multiple streams of passive income, and one fails, you can still pay your bills. The other reason to have multiple streams of income is to diversify, so you don't have all of your eggs in one basket. We believe the ideal number of income streams is between six and eight.

8. Financial products and strategies are just tools.

Most people search for the "right" financial product to help them achieve financial independence, whether it's real estate, stocks or something else. The truth is, there is no magical financial product or strategy that can make you rich. Financial products and strategies are simply tools you can use to achieve financial independence. Knowing how to properly use financial products and strategies in changing circumstances can make you rich.

- Take the following example. Two people are given the same tools: a hammer, some lumber, and nails. They're told to build a tree house. Person A has studied as an apprentice under an accomplished carpenter for several years, successfully building small structures. On the other hand, Person B has only watched designers and builders remodel homes on TV. Both of them have access to the exact same tools: a hammer, some lumber and nails. However, who do you suppose will build the better tree house? Most likely, Person A because she has the education, skills and coaching on how to use the tools to build a better tree house.

- Likewise, in the 2008 - 2011 recession, most Americans had access to financial tools such as stocks, bonds and mutual funds in their 401(k)s, or even real estate. Millions of Americans lost their investments, retirement accounts, homes or investment properties. Other people prospered. Most people believed that the stocks, bonds, mutual funds and real estate would make them wealthy. The prosperous use their skills coupled with financial products and strategies to acquire wealth.

9. Separate your financial coaching from advising.

Financial advisors are like sports agents, and wealth coaches are like sports coaches. Financial advisors and brokerage firms get paid commissions on the sale of financial products, or they may earn a percentage of the value of your portfolio. Wealth coaches aren't paid commissions on the sale of financial products. They're paid to help you hone your financial skills so you can become the master of your own financial destiny. An average football player would benefit most from having a really good sports coach to help him improve his skills so he's drafted by the best football team. Once he's a top draft pick, every sports agent — and team — will want him. This is why hiring a skilled wealth coach, separate and apart from a financial advisor, is so important.

10. Systematize your passive income.

Michael Gerber, author of the E-Myth Revisited, teaches that entrepreneurs must create systems in their business in order to succeed. They must essentially "franchise" their businesses so they work with or without the owners' day-to-day operation. That is exactly what happens when you systematize passive income. Once you get it up and running, it should bring in income month after month without you constantly working on it. If there is significantly more to do than collect money, your passive income is actually another job. It's not truly passive income. A wealth coach can teach you how to systematize passive income like a money-printing machine. You set up the machine, get it working and let it make you lots of money.

You can't prevent life's pitfalls, detours and challenges. But you can do your part to prepare for them! I challenge you to follow the preceding steps to succeed in your passive income journey today!

About Tanisha

Tanisha Souza, J.D., is a best-selling author, professional keynote speaker, wealth and passive income coach, entrepreneur and CEO of Tardus Wealth Strategies. She has a passion for teaching people how to live their dreams by rapidly building passive income without risk. Tanisha quit the practice of law after replacing her income with passive income from real estate, and she launched Tardus Financial Services, a franchise of a larger mortgage-acceleration company. The company eventually evolved into Tardus Wealth Strategies, a full-service wealth and passive income-coaching firm.

Tanisha's passive income focus is the result of her strong belief that "everyone" needs multiple streams of stress-free, passive income. Tanisha invented and patented a systematic process for creating passive income without risk. She helps her clients set goals, then helps them to create additional cash flow and income from their existing income sources, a series of financial products and passive income investments. Tanisha's system helps families create income while simultaneously erasing mortgages and student loans. As a founder and co-owner of Tardus Wealth Strategies, she teaches, coaches and trains families worldwide to create enough passive income to pursue their passions. Tanisha's clientele ranges from working single parents with children to six-figure income doctors, lawyers and small business owners.

Tanisha studied and obtained her bachelor's degree at U.C. Berkeley, and she earned her Juris Doctorate from the U.S.C. Law School. She hosted a radio show "Your Money Matters" for four years, and she and her company have been featured on Fox News Las Vegas, Olelo, KHVH, KHBZ and numerous other radio and television appearances.

Tanisha and her husband Chris, reside in Diamond Head in the island of Oahu with their daughters, Christa and Jada. Additional information about Tanisha and her company can be found at www.tardus.com.

You can connect with Tanisha at:
tanisha.souza@tardus.com
www.facebook/tanisha.souza
TardusWealthCoach@TardusWealth

CHAPTER 19

AN EXPERT DISCUSSION ABOUT ELITE ATHLETE HABITS

BY DR. PAWEN DHOKAL

Growing up we all tend to have heroes or mentors we look up to. Sometimes these people can be our parents, our teachers, or our coaches. These "heroes" may even be fictional or someone that you have never even met. As a doctor, I try to make an impact upon my patients to make better health choices and become proactive for their wellbeing. What I have found though, is that the influence you have upon a person is often directly related to how much they value who you are or what you do. What I mean by this is, often times, I can suggest to a patient to do a specific set of exercises or change a habit that is having a negative impact on their health. The ironic part is that frequently I'll have the patients' parents or coaches say what I suggested had been previously instructed to the patient by someone else without any compliance. What this tells me is that the source of the suggestion wasn't trusted, or didn't have enough influence to make the necessary impact needed to make a change. This made me wonder: who do people look up to most and try to emulate?

To determine this, I asked several hundred people some simple questions. Who do you look up to? Who influences you to buy products? What industries or careers have an extraordinary amount of influence upon the public, especially youth?

I thought that people would say that their parents, doctors, teachers, clergy or friends have the most impact on their lives. And many people did say that these people have great influence upon them. However, I found that regardless of age, gender or profession, there was one segment of our population that has tremendous influence upon the general public, especially today's youth. A significant segment of those surveyed said that they look up to, would trade places with, purchase products that are endorsed by, and would listen to instructions or follow habits from Professional Athletes.

Sports are engrained in our society and we all are passionate about our favorite sports, teams, and players. We, as a society, have placed professional athletes on a pedestal for their abilities, income, and influence. With so many people tuning in to the latest game, athletes on covers of magazines and our 24/7 sports and news stations, it isn't hard to see how these athletes become influential. That's a lot of pressure and responsibility! Most of us wouldn't do well with that type of attention placed upon all of our statements or actions.

However, for the most part, our professional athletes represent their teams, cities, and sports very well. As I started to work with Elite Athletes when I was in Chiropractic school, it was my belief that the "best athletes" were the ones who "made it." I found that this was not entirely accurate. In fact there are many athletes that were more talented or gifted than the next person, but didn't make it to their ultimate goal of becoming a professional. Why is that? I wondered.

In my opinion from my research, the answer is habits . . . and personal beliefs. After almost 15 years of treating athletes, interviewing those who are super successful, and having overcome my own set of hurdles, I have found that those who achieve their goals and reach the top of their industries all have a few things in common. They have a strong self-belief system and have *developed* a set of habits that directly improve their skill set and mindset. I say "developed" because most of those professional athletes I spoke with said that they had to consciously integrate these habits into their daily lives. This wasn't something natural or innate that they were born with, but rather things that they recognized as being important to their success, and therefore learned to do these things frequently to increase their odds of success. I found these qualities were more consistent and magnified with professional athletes moreso than in other professions.

Here's the good news, you and I can do the same thing! I am going to teach you what habits Elite Athletes share in common, and how these actions and beliefs can lead to massive success regardless of your profession or current state of being.

What are these "secret" habits or rituals that elite athletes seem to have in common and why should one consider my suggestions? First, the success traits I describe below are things that anyone can incorporate into their daily lives. Secondly, they are compiled from several sources: years of reading and personal development, tips from centurions, and from many elite athletes.

I feel very blessed and grateful that my work has given me the opportunity to meet, talk to, or treat the likes of two-sport Star and Hall of Famer Deion Sanders, Super Bowl MVP Kurt Warner, legendary college basketball coach Steve Fisher, 5-time NBA Champion and Golden State Warriors Head Coach Steve Kerr, several Super Bowl winning coaches and NFL legends such as Takeo Spikes. It is from these conversations and interviews that I have been able to compile these habits that these and other successful people and athletes share.

TOP 10 TRAITS OF THE SUCCESSFUL

• *A morning routine*
Almost everyone I know has a morning routine that they follow. Think about it… I'm sure you do 90% of the same things every single morning, in the same order, in the same way. Most people don't give much thought as to how they start their day and what impact that has on it. The most successful people and athletes that I spoke with have a solid, purposeful way to start their days. I would suggest that you take a look at your own morning routine and make changes to best ensure you start your day out well and on a positive note. I've adapted mine to work for me and what I desire – which includes a positive mindset, clear daily intentions, nourishment, and some quiet time.

My morning routine starts by waking up and immediately thinking of as many things that I'm grateful for. I get up and drink a glass of water or have some tea with honey and lemon. I take a few minutes to pray and meditate, followed by a quick, healthy protein-rich breakfast. I then take an extended walk with my dog to get some fresh air, a bit of exercise and visualize my day. I end my morning routine and begin my day by checking my daily task list and trying to complete at least two important tasks before noon.That way I know that at least a couple of the most important (or at times annoying) tasks are sure to be addressed and not put off or potentially left undone.

• *Goal setting*
Set *clear* goals *with deadlines*. Write them down, preferably where you can see them every day.

• *Develop the ability to focus*
Start with short sessions or small tasks and be mindful of where your focus is. Is it 100% on the task at hand or is your mind wandering? With practice, you can be hyper-focused when you want and develop the ability to shut out outside distractions or pressures.

• *Ask for help*
Even experts consult other experts. Nobody knows everything or can do everything themselves. Humble yourself and ask for help. It's ok to do so and is actually a great way to learn.

• *Help others*
You know things that others don't. You have abilities and talents that come easy to you that are foreign to others. Help others when you can and don't wait for them to ask. Volunteer it. Everyone isn't as secure or confident enough to ask for the help they need. I really believe that when you give, you get.

• *Be prepared*
It isn't always realistic to be prepared for every situation. However for those things that you can prepare for, you should begin the practice of being as prepared as possible. Study. Think of possible scenarios. Have a plan B. And consider worst-case scenarios. I always remember the 6 P's:
    Proper Preparation Prevents Potential Poor Performance.

• *Follow your instinct*
I believe we all have a gut instinct and that usually that "feeling" is your subconscious' way of telling you something that you may not consciously realize. At times it's just a hunch or voice inside of you that tells you something. Listen to that voice. Can't hear that voice? Meditate to connect with your inner self and the world around you.

• *Take calculated risks*
Sometimes it takes great risk to obtain great rewards. At times all choices are risky. Calculate your odds of success and the potential rewards. The best athletes and businessmen calculate and assess any risks before taking chances to maximize success.

• *Be persistent*

> *Dripping water hollows out stone, not through*
> *force but through persistence.*

> ~ Ovid.

Persistence in most matters will overcome arguments, resistance, and obstacles.

• *Learn from your mistakes*
We all make them. The foolish make the same mistakes repeatedly. The wise will learn from their mistakes and grow from setbacks.

I'd like to conclude by sharing some of the most important things that Elite Athletes specifically do routinely to ensure their continued success. I have divided these habits into two categories: Body and Mind. Each exercise or activity has a specific purpose and when done regularly will have positive benefits upon your overall health and success.

FOR THE BODY

• *Stretch*
Most of us hardly ever stretch or do so only before activity. I need to share with you that stretching post activity is actually very necessary to make sure that your muscles don't cool down too quickly and stiffen up. Stretching your whole body helps to increase blood flow and range of motion of your joints. Yoga is great!

• *Hydrate*
Our muscles are approximately 80% water. We need our muscles hydrated for proper function. It is vital to digest food and get rid of toxins amongst many other vital body functions. By the way, hydration means drinking water . . . Not juice, tea or soda! I tell my Elite Athletes they should be drinking 2 ounces of water for every pound they weigh. For the average person, 1 oz. per pound is sufficient. Most people

do not drink nearly enough water daily. It's a critical and yet simple change that can have major health benefits.

• *Sweat*

Breaking a sweat daily in some manner is very important. It is good for your heart, lungs, mind, and body. Lifting weights is a great way to build strength and increase your bone density and lean muscle mass.

• *Nutrition*

The type of fuel you put into your body determines the quality of your output. What you eat not only obviously affects your waistline and health but also can zap or replenish your energy reserves. It is a proven fact that those with cleaner, healthier diets have a significantly reduced rate of illnesses and an increased lifespan. Fuel your body for success and give it what it needs to function optimally.

• *Chiropractic, Massage, Yoga*

Making time to get a massage and a chiropractic adjustment at least monthly will not only help you feel looser but will keep your nervous system functioning optimally and boost your immune system. Stretching after activity and integrating yoga are both great ways of keeping your body lean, limber and strong as well. Almost all elite athletes take these steps to keep on top of their game. There isn't any reason that everyone shouldn't benefit from such health care.

FOR THE MIND

• *Reduce stress*

Stress is one of the most underrated killers in America today! Often patients think that they manage their stresses well. However their internal body response to external stresses tells quite a different story. Be mindful of what is really important. After consideration, many people admit many things that were stressing them out aren't actually major issues when put in perspective. Check in with yourself regularly regarding your state of stress.

• *Meditate*

Meditation is one of the best ways to quiet the mind. Its health benefits are far reaching and include lowering of blood pressure, decreasing stress, decreasing respiration rate, and increasing quality of sleep. It isn't hard, it just takes some practice. As little as 5 minutes a day is enough to have body and mind benefits. I recommend Deepak Chopra and Oprah Winfrey's guided meditations as a way for beginners to get started.

- *Visualize / guided imagery*
"Begin with the end in mind." All of the best athletes visualize their success. You should as well. Visualize whatever it is that you want to achieve. Go further by using guided imagery to really engage all of your senses and heighten your attention to detail.

- *Set clear goals with deadlines*
Your mind works best to achieve your goals when they are set, specific, clear, and have a deadline. Reinforce these goals by reading them daily. There is nothing wrong with setting small achievable goals as well as large lofty goals. Achieving the small ones will build up confidence and momentum, while having huge goals will always keep you reaching for the stars and keep you from becoming complacent.

- *Belief in Self / Faith*
Pray if you're faithful. Be grateful for what you have if you're not of faith. But either way, have faith in yourself and your abilities... even in the difficult times that visit us all. Climbing out of these life ruts and overcoming obstacles will also build your confidence and strength.

- *Consistency in learning*
In this age with all the information at our fingertips, it would be a shame not to continually better ourselves, wouldn't it? The great ones weren't always great. They were once just good and improved to being great . . . by learning from mistakes, learning new things, and growing their perspective and relationships.

- *Affirmations*
We all have that little voice inside of us. Not only is it important to listen to that instinct, but it is also as important to guide that voice with positivity and self-love. Be kind to yourself. Life isn't always easy. Tell yourself good things like you deserve greatness, love and success. I encourage my athletes to write down a few affirmations or statements that they can repeat and read daily. This self-talk becomes self-belief, which is the foundation for action towards accomplishment of goals.

Remember, everyone goes through things . . . even those at the top. You're not alone, whatever you're going through, someone else has as well. Furthermore, oftentimes there are many people who would love to have your "bad days" because their reality is much worse than what you're going through. Remember that and strengthen your mind and take care of your body. Work to develop some of these habits that Elite Athletes and other successful people have. Lastly, be patient with yourself. Great things rarely occur right away and without effort. But you can make a small positive change today that will lead to greater things in the future!

About Dr. Pawen

Dr. Pawen Dhokal is the owner and the primary treating physician of ELITE Health, which is a Chiropractic and Prehabilitation Sports Medicine practice in downtown San Diego. His clients have included players in the NFL, NBA, Major League Baseball and U.S. Olympic athletes.

E.L.I.T.E. is an acronym for Every Life Is Treated Equally – five words that represent Dr. Dhokal's vision and belief that each person is entitled to the same high quality medical treatment despite age, status, profession, or physical talent and strength.

Dr. Dhokal also co-founded California Medical College. This college is a medical training school in California that specializes in getting students into the medical field sooner and better prepared.

He got his start in teaching at California College San Diego. Where he taught over 30 different college courses in his time there and was named "Instructor of the Year." He became the Dean of the Medical and Health Care Administration Programs at CCSD before he left to start California Medical College.

Knowing that helping others was one of his passions, Dr. Dhokal began teaching Exam Certification Seminars with Excel Medical and Image Radiology. These seminars outlined information that helped to increase test scores in state exams. At "TheTestDr. com", Dr. Dhokal has published medical and radiological information as a free online source for students.

Dr. Dhokal also worked as the team trainer for the SDJA High School football team. The next season he was promoted to be their quarterback coach, and then promoted as their offensive coordinator. In 2009, Dr. Pawen Dhokal became the head football coach for the varsity team and stepped away from coaching to pursue other interests after his 5th season in which the team played in the league championship game.

In 2012, Dr. Dhokal co-founded Sani-Screen Wipes, which are custom screen cleaning wipes for mobile electronic devices. These wipes are designed to clean screens streak-free and help control the spread of germs on cell phones and tablets.

Though Dr. Dhokal is very active in the community and has the pulse of education due to his involvement in teaching medical seminars and through his college, his passion remains healing others and turning people on to the power of chiropractic.

Dr. Dhokal graduated from the University of the Pacific with a Bachelor's degree in Sports

Medicine and received his Doctorate in Chiropractic at Palmer College Chiropractic-West. In his spare time, Dr. Dhokal enjoys hiking, paddleboarding, reading, traveling, and learning more about health, wellness, and personal development.

CHAPTER 20

IS YOUR LIVING TRUST A TICKING TIME BOMB?

BY BRADFORD D. CREGER

It is estimated that 95% or more of all living trusts drafted in the U. S. today include major drafting errors which could cause significant problems, or worse, unintentionally disinherit your children and/or grandchildren.

We should start with the assumption an attorney drafted your living trust, but how do you know it was done correctly? Did a third party with the proper estate planning expertise confirm that your living trust was properly drafted to meet your needs? If your living trust isn't done correctly and one spouse (or both) dies, the potential mess left behind can be catastrophic. Before we dig deeper into some common mistakes… let's first discuss how you, as a consumer of legal services, can best get a second opinion to determine if your living trust is properly drafted.

REVIEWING YOUR EXISTING DOCUMENTS

It makes absolutely no sense to return to the attorney who originally drafted your estate documents to ask him or her if they were done correctly. Why? This is akin to letting students grade their own work. Moreover, do you honestly believe anyone would actually admit to not knowing what they were doing the first time around? Probably not. So you can't go back to the original attorney to get a second opinion – as this obviously doesn't count as a "second" opinion.

You could try to find another attorney on your own but you run the risk of either using someone else who also lacks the appropriate expertise; or perhaps you'll find someone who may blindly recommend the unnecessary replacement of your existing documents. If you can find an attorney that specializes in estate planning, they should be able to tell you if your trust documents are properly drafted. Curiously, even a new attorney, with no prior experience, can claim they specialize in estate planning. It is inherently difficult to measure professional competence, but especially so in the area of legal services which makes it difficult to find a competent estate attorney on your own.

Interestingly, your financial advisor may be the best choice to provide you with an unbiased review of your existing estate planning documents. Why? <u>Your living trust and other estate planning documents are the foundation of your financial planning</u>. Your living trust should hold and control the majority of your assets. Your durable powers of attorney will be necessary for a spouse (or another) to access your retirement accounts (and other investments not held inside the living trust) in the event of your disability. It is extremely important for your estate planning documents to be done correctly, and a quality financial advisor should be able to read and understand the documents which govern and control the investment assets they are managing on your behalf.

THE TRUTH ABOUT COMPREHENSIVE WEALTH MANAGEMENT

Did your current financial advisor promise to provide you with "comprehensive wealth management" services? Proper estate planning is the foundation of comprehensive wealth management, so a financial advisor who claims to offer these services should be able to read and understand your estate documents. A <u>true</u> comprehensive wealth manager acts like a <u>financial architect</u> and will need to understand the legal and tax issues - hopefully just as well your estate attorney and/or CPA.

Designations are just the first step in the education process and only scratch the surface by providing a general overview and teaching buzzwords and power-phrases. Unfortunately, too many financial advisors then use this introductory information to claim estate-planning expertise which they don't actually possess.

Rather than further developing their estate planning knowledge and the experience necessary to deliver on the comprehensive wealth management promise, many advisors will address this incredibly necessary and important skill set by bringing in-house, or affiliating with, an estate attorney to evaluate their clients' trust documents. Is this an incorrect approach? Not necessarily, but if you hired an architect to draft blueprints for your dream home and they didn't understand basic home construction… would you have any confidence in their ability to deliver that which they have promised? Probably not.

So how does one test their financial advisor's estate planning competence? Print your trust documents and take them to your next portfolio review meeting. During the meeting, place your trust documents on your advisor's desk and ask for them to be reviewed. If this has already been done, ask for a "refresher" to remind you of how your estate planning documents affect your investment assets. Your advisor should be able to scan through the documents (and in about 5 to 10 minutes - while you wait); they should be able to diagram and discuss how the trust is structured and how it affects your investment assets they are managing. This is what I call the "Trust Challenge."

Specifically, they should be able to tell you how the living trust provides income and principal while both you and your spouse are alive, what happens if one of you dies, and what happens when the surviving spouse ultimately dies. They should be able to tell you who receives your assets, what assets they receive, when they receive your assets and how they receive your assets. They should be able to calculate the estate taxes due, if any, and approximate the after-tax amounts received by each of your named heirs.

If they can't do this, or worse, refuse to do this, then you know that they do not possess the necessary skills to provide the "comprehensive wealth management" services which they have promised. Is this a reason to terminate a long-term relationship with your financial advisor? That's not for me to say, but if they have falsely claimed to possess expertise in estate planning, what else might your current financial advisor be claiming to provide yet failing to deliver?

Keep in mind a competent architect would never need to consult with an electrician to complete and deliver the electrical plans within your blueprints. Similarly, a true comprehensive wealth manager shouldn't need to rely on an attorney to read and understand your estate planning documents.

Now that we understand who might best be able to assist you in reviewing your estate planning documents, let's discuss some of the more common drafting errors which are easy to detect (even for the layman).[1]

COMMON TRUST MISTAKES

Although every situation is inherently different, and your estate planning documents can be as individualized as you and your family are, there are a few basic guidelines which govern the proper drafting of these documents.

The most common mistake is passing assets outright and free-of-trust to your children (and/or grandchildren). It is easy to understand why this is considered a mistake. When you pass assets outright to your heirs they are deprived of both significant asset protection as well as potential tax benefits that, if properly understood, would be utilized by nearly everyone. First, when passing assets "free-of-trust" the inheritance will unnecessarily be subject to your heir's creditors, a bankruptcy and/or potential loss in a divorce. Why not just keep the assets in trust to preserve the benefits of asset protection? The trust can still provide your heirs with the full use and enjoyment of the assets.

---

1. No matter how competent your financial advisor may be, this will not eliminate the need to consult with an estate planning attorney – to both confirm your advisor's findings and draft new documents, when necessary.

Additionally, when passing assets outright to children, you are losing a potential significant tax advantage. As of 2015, the estate tax exemption is $5,430,000 and this same amount may also be exempted from the generation skipping tax (or GST). When you pass assets to your heirs free-of-trust, you're also sacrificing this potentially significant tax exemption. You aren't "skipping over your kids" but rather "skipping a tax" when the money eventually passes to your grandchildren. In order to take advantage of your GST exemption, you must keep the assets in trust. When your children die, the GST exempt assets (if not spent) will pass transfer-tax free to your grandchildren.

UNINTENTIONALLY DISINHERITING YOUR HEIRS

So what's the "drafting error" that could unintentionally disinherit your children and/or grandchildren? To understand this problem one must first understand how a living trust is used. Other than avoiding probate, the living trust is primarily designed to control the distribution of your assets; back to yourself in the event of your own disability, and to your intended heirs upon your death.

Once both you and your spouse have died, your entire living trust document and all the language therein becomes irrevocable (i.e., permanent), and cannot be changed by anyone. This makes it incredibly important to "get it right" before it is too late to correct. When your living trust becomes irrevocable, the language which governs access to income and principal is the most important to your family.

Almost every living trust drafted today uses what is referred to as an "ascertainable standard" to govern access for both the income generated by the assets and/or the assets themselves (i.e., principal). The ascertainable standard language allows access to trust assets to provide for the "health, education, maintenance and support" of a beneficiary.

Remember, this language becomes permanent when mom and dad (i.e., the "Grantors") die. So if a beneficiary later develops an illness or has an injury, then these provisions will allow the trust to provide for their healthcare needs. This broad access to the trust's assets sounds "OK" to most people – and early in my financial planning career, this sounded OK to me too. So what happened to change my perspective?

About 17 years ago, I was working on an estate and financial plan for a client whose only child was hit by a drunk driver and paralyzed from the neck down. I quickly recognized that had her mother died prior to this tragic accident, her mother's trust (for her daughter's sole benefit) would have been irrevocable. At the very time when this child would have needed her inheritance (to raise her standard of living beyond the minimal level of subsistence provided by public aid), the ascertainable standard language would have forced her to spend the trust's assets down to zero (on her own healthcare) before government assistance would've been made available.

This got me thinking about how unpredictable life can be. No matter how well we can think things through and try to plan for all conceivable contingencies, we cannot rule out an accident, illness or even a birth defect that could potentially change everything in an instant.

I had "discovered" a major drafting error which is still prevalent today and included in nearly every trust drafted in the United States. That drafting error? When mom and dad die, the language governing an heir's access to income and principal becomes irrevocable. If, after the trust becomes irrevocable, a child (or grandchild) suffers a devastating injury in an accident or if a grandchild is born with a birth defect... the ascertainable standard language will potentially force that child (or grandchild) to "burn through" their inheritance paying for their own healthcare costs. Losing the ability to earn an income (or in the case of a significant birth defect, never having the opportunity to earn an income) makes these trusts, and the language governing income and principal, incredibly important. Surprisingly, no one had previously recognized that this drafting error existed – and worse, no one had figured out a viable solution. So what can one do?

A NEW ERA IN ESTATE PLANNING

As soon as I realized the magnitude of this potential problem, I challenged the estate attorney I was working with and suggested to him that every trust I had previously designed (and he had drafted) for our joint clients was significantly flawed. His response: "There is nothing we can do." I didn't accept this and in a few days I came back to him with an idea. The solution I came up with is now referred to as "contingent ascertainable standard language" or "springing special needs provisions." What are these provisions and what do they do?

I asked him to draft ascertainable standard language "contingent" upon certain triggering events. More specifically, I asked him to combine the "springing" feature similar to what is used in many durable powers of attorney with "special needs" provisions which limit access to income and principal. If the beneficiary (of a trust) had a qualifying "trigger" event, then his/her trust could be "converted" into a "special needs trust." This protects the assets while at the same time potentially allows access to both state and federal aid, if available. This ensures that this beneficiary does not "lose everything" paying for their own medical care, in a situation where preserving these assets could have meant the difference between having only the lowest level of subsistence (provided by the government), and a chance at a more normal lifestyle (with access to the additional funds provided by their special needs trust).

The attorney loved my idea and quickly delivered his first draft to me for review. I then proceeded to "poke holes" in what he had drafted. This back-and-forth process went on for several months until we finally agreed the language could not be improved upon. Working together, he and I created "contingent ascertainable standard language" or more commonly "springing special needs provisions" and with this, the first significant change in decades to the standard trust language governing access to income and principal. From that point forward, this new language was incorporated into all of his trusts as well as every estate plan I designed, no matter which estate attorney was selected to draft documents.

MORE COMPLEX DRAFTING ERRORS

Some mistakes are more difficult to find. These drafting errors are mostly related to language that unnecessarily limits flexibility and eliminates a beneficiary's ability to properly adapt to their circumstances and/or unforeseen needs at some future point in time. Over the last 22-plus years, I have found numerous mistakes including the unintentional forced liquidation of assets (including a primary residence), unnecessary income taxation, and limits on the ability to equalize or adjust an inheritance among children or grandchildren, to name just a few. How do you detect these subtle mistakes when they're difficult for the untrained reader to locate? Simple. Question every provision in your estate documents which requires a specific action, rather than allowing a choice among several options, and have the reasoning for the limitation explained.

I ask… are you sure your current estate planning documents adequately and appropriately protect and preserve the wealth you have worked a lifetime to obtain? If you haven't already done so, take your trust(s) to your financial advisor and get their valuable insight and feedback.

The vast majority of the hiring decisions in financial services are driven by personality assessments, and not based on an unbiased comparison of relative professional competence. I trust (no pun intended) I have provided you with a simple method to determine if your financial advisor understands estate planning well enough to help you and continue claiming that they provide comprehensive wealth management services.

About Brad

Brad Creger is passionate about his work - he does this because he never wants anyone to go through what his parents did. His father was diagnosed with Parkinson's in his late forties and he was forced to retire at 51. Although his father was an investment advisor, they didn't have their financial or estate planning done correctly and his mom lost everything caring for his dad. Because his father focused solely on investments, he did not have the right disability insurance or any life insurance. Their estate attorney didn't insist on anything other than a simple will and the result was disastrous when his dad was disabled. Their accountant didn't pay attention to his mom's business, and instead of selling and living off the proceeds, her business bled dry. This was a very tough life lesson for Brad, and he was committed - when he became a financial advisor - that he would not only focus on the things he could be paid on, but also his client's entire financial picture.

He first acts as a financial architect, and does a comprehensive wealth management assessment and then a complete written plan. He then acts as a general contractor and coordinates the services of other experts and professionals – such as the client's CPA, attorney, TPA, banker, etc. He also will assist when it comes to the insurance and investment needs of his clients.

Early in his career Brad took a comprehensive look at his brother's finances, so that there would not be another financial tragedy in his family. Among other things, he made sure that his brother had proper disability insurance, and eight months later his brother was disabled. Because he had the right policy, his brother has been receiving payments for the past 19 years, and will continue to draw on it for 15 more.

Brad is currently the President/CEO of Total Financial Resource Group, Inc. (TFRG), an independent diversified financial services firm with their main offices located in Pasadena, CA. Brad began his financial services career with Cigna Financial Advisors in 1993. During his first three years, through Cigna, he clocked over 2000 classroom training hours – which was 20 times more than the industry standard.

Brad has delivered estate and business succession planning services through numerous investment brokers at PaineWebber, AG Edwards, Morgan Stanley, Dean Witter, Prudential and Crowell Weedon for their Southern California VIP clients, and has created a body of estate planning law known as Contingent Ascertainable Standard Language (aka – Springing Special Needs Provisions).

Brad has been featured in *Forbes, Financial Planning Magazine, Pasadena Magazine* and *Outposts Magazine* and has been seen on ABC, CBS, NBC and Fox affiliates as well as *The Wall Street Journal's* Marketwatch.com, CNBC.com, Morningstar.com, Moneywatch.com, Yahoofinance.com, TheBostonGlobe.com and TheMiamiHerald.com.

Brad obtained a BA in Economics from UCLA, and has the designations of:
AAMS® – Accredited Asset Management Specialist
AIFA® – Accredited Investment Fiduciary Analyst™
CFS® – Certified Fund Specialist®
CLTC – Certified in Long-Term Care

Brad is a Registered Principal with First Allied Securities, Inc. , a registered broker/dealer (Member FINRA/SIPC) and an Investment Advisory Rep for both Total Financial Resource Advisory, Inc., a Registered Investment Advisor and First Allied Advisory Services, Inc., a Registered Investment Advisor. California Insurance License # 0B22199.

CHAPTER 21

WHAT CAN MAKE OR BREAK AN INJURY CASE

BY W. WEST SEEGMILLER

Research shows that if a person represents him/herself in an injury case, she will receive on average 1/3 of the amount her outcome would've been, had she been represented by a lawyer.

Many injured victims grumble about the fee lawyers take from a verdict or settlement, which can be as high as 33 to 40% or even 45 to 50%. Here is a simple calculation to illustrate the fallacy of this thinking. Which is a better outcome for an injured person: a net to him of $7500 after a fee of 25% for a $10,000 settlement, or a net to him of $180,000 after a fee of 40% for a $300,000 settlement? By the way that's a net to the injured client of $7500 versus $180,000. The case value is the key here, not the fee percentage. A good lawyer can enhance case value. Although an injured victim may choose to ignore these facts, it is important to take them into account when deciding whether or not to hire a lawyer.

There is a Chinese fable about a young man and a snake, which serves to describe the relationship between an injured victim and the defendant's insurance company. It was a freezing cold winter and it was snowing heavily. A young man walking along a road came upon a snake who was weak and dying. Seeing the young man approaching, the desperate and hungry snake begged the young man, "Please help me get warmth and food! It's too cold to survive. Please carry me with you or otherwise I'll die." At first the young man refused, "No, no, no." He replied, "I'm not going to carry you. You'll bite me and *I* will die." But the crafty snake promised, "Oh, I won't bite you. Just carry me for a little while and once I get my temperature back you can let me go." The man hesitated, but then agreed, "Ok I'll carry you over but don't bite me." He then picked the snake up and tucked him into his clothes. However, when they arrived at the destination, the snake immediately bit the young man without mercy. While dying, the young man exclaimed, "But you told me you wouldn't bite me!" The snake replied, "I know and I am truly sorry but that is what *I am created to do*."

It is sad but true that the snake in the story and most insurance companies share the same nature. Each is predisposed to function in a way that may harm an injured victim's interests. Many times this comes down to a corporate culture. These companies don't employ mean-spirited or angry people to work for them. They have really nice, friendly people; and you believe that they will be very helpful people, but, they have a job to do—and they will do it.

Having been in the personal injury business as a trial lawyer for 35 years, I want to share with you a few tips that can make or break a case for those seeking redress after an injury accident.

1. CREDIBILITY AND A TRUSTED GUIDE

Credibility is a theme that runs through an entire injury case – credibility of the lawyer, credibility of the treating doctors, the experts and the client's own story and life. Credibility affects all aspects of an injury case. For example, if a client has a history of other injuries he has suffered, but doesn't disclose that history, it later will be revealed as a part of the trial, or in his deposition under oath. When the opposition finds out, his credibility will be irreparably damaged and his case may be over right there.

Our law firm makes extensive use of focus groups. We gather together a group of people and present cases and issues. They tell us without exception that credibility is the primary concern relative to the client first, the doctor second, and surprisingly, the lawyer last. In fact, studies have shown that the lawyer only has about 15 percent impact on a case. Lawyers like to think they have much more influence than that, but the jury data are clear. Lawyers don't have that much impact on the case itself. The client's credibility and the type of case are the factors that give value to a case. Focus groups tell us that a lawyer's performance could actually harm a case. For that reason, we even focus group our lawyers. Many are surprised if they receive a negative review and question the authenticity of the group. However, the lawyer now has a choice. He can dispute the findings of the group and not change anything, or he can humbly consider the information as a gift and a path to growth. Many times this can be a life-changing event for a willing attorney.

Following the integrity of the client, comes that of the doctors and experts. You cannot have doctors or experts who testify for a living or who do unnecessary surgeries; who have a history themselves of either medical board discipline or of having been sued multiple times. It destroys credibility. It also casts a pall over all the other medical providers and expert credibility. It is vital to have clean doctors and good, credible e x p e r t s . The doctors and experts must be convincing, medical treatment has to be realistic, and the client, of course, has to be credible.

Studies have also shown that plaintiff lawyers within our culture are already under a cloud of suspicion. They walk into the courtroom and without even opening their mouths jurors are prone to distrust them. They can be the most honest and amazing people on earth, and jurors will still see them as pariahs, not to be trusted. The public generally believes lawyers are going to lie, withhold information and attempt to manipulate them.

A good lawyer has to show the jury that he or she is not the stereotypical lawyer and is "off code."

"The Code" is the public's perception that a lawyer is a master manipulator. Our culture, and consequently our juries, tend to have this predisposition. Therefore, it is important for an effective lawyer to show the jury that he's not "on code"; he is "not one of those." The jury must be shown, not convinced.

There are various ways for a lawyer to separate himself from the stereotype. One way is to show his vulnerability. He can do this by demonstrating his awareness of the weaknesses in his case. Every case has them. In a sense it is a confession to the jury that he understands there are weaknesses and a revelation that he himself is worried and concerned about it. He can go so far as to express that he is afraid the jurors are going to have preconceptions about him, and about his client, that are not necessarily correct. If a lawyer exposes his real feelings, he then will reveal his own weaknesses and fears. This engenders trust and creates a bond. From that position, the lawyer can then more effectively lead the jury through the discovery process of the case. He becomes a trusted guide. This is much different than an orator standing at a podium attempting to convince the jury with words and bravado.

Credibility, genuine compassion and lawyer vulnerability are the keys to a great case outcome.

2. REASONABLE EXPECTATIONS

A client needs to maintain reasonable expectations at all times. "Reasonable expectations" means he has to be sensible in his anticipation of what his lawyer can do and realistic in his expectations for the outcome of his injury case. Many times injured clients will never get well. They'll always have a disability remaining. So sometimes a client will say, "Just put me on the stand and I'll tell the jury how much I hurt and just how much my case is worth. They'll believe me. I'll convince them. Put me up there." That kind of overconfidence can be death to a case. The jury will immediately sense this and punish the client for it. Juries are smart. They are good consumers and they know a bad product when they see one.

3. STORY PROTECTION

Social media is a huge part of our social consciousness right now. There are many different sources of social media and this content is all retrievable by your adversaries. They can and will access all that you post. If you are online saying, "I got in an accident and boy did I win the lottery! I'm going to make a lot of money on this," that will get back to them. They are very astute on the other side. They have teams of people sitting in their offices who scour through all the social media. Any communication you make after an injury is subject to discovery. They can find it.

For example, if you tell your best friend, "Hey listen, don't tell anybody but…" and then the insurance company asks you (and they will) who your best friend is, you have to tell them. When they take his deposition under oath, he will tell the truth and he is going to say, "Yeah. He told me this was his lottery win." You must protect your story and you therefore just have to assume any communication you make after an accident is going to become fodder for the defense on the other side. So be safe in your communications, and that includes social media.

4. MISPLACED LOYALTY

Many plaintiffs are loyal to their own insurance company and it's often misplaced. Insurance companies run commercials that demonstrate how they appreciate your business, care for you and save you when you are in trouble. Their agents will call on special occasions, send you Christmas and birthday cards, and will have done this for years. But when there's a claim, they turn a different color.

There is a longer version of the Chinese story I was telling you earlier. In this version, the young man and the snake became friends along the way. They laughed and sang songs together, and even talked about their families. But all these good memories abruptly faded the moment the snake bit the poor young man. Similarly, you may have been paying your premiums over decades, receiving Christmas and birthday cards every year, and even visiting your agent occasionally, but when it comes down to collecting on a claim, they will do what they were "created to do."

5. JUSTICE VERSUS MONEY

Another way your case can be damaged is when you're asking for too much, or if the jury perceives you are just after the money rather than what's fair. That's on code. That's what the jurors expect you to do. And so you have to dispel that by telling them you're not there to ask only for money. You are asking for justice and in our legal system that can only be done with money. You're simply asking for compensation so that your life can be "made whole" and put back on track where it was before you were injured.

Consequently, a good lawyer that goes "off code" will show how the client's *life* has changed as a result of the injury other than just how much financial loss he has occurred. There was one time when our client, an older man, injured his back and had to have a surgery. As a result, he later became impotent. He simply could no longer perform. We convened a focus group consisting of both males and females who discussed the impotence issue and we then observed them deliberate. To the male respondents, the fact that our client couldn't have sex ever again was devastating. They claimed that the case value range was between 50 to 100 million dollars. In contrast, female respondents estimated this loss at absolutely zero. Perhaps one female's response illustrated what most of the women felt when she said, "Well look, this sex stuff, you men have it all wrong. It's not about sex at all. It's about relationships. We didn't see any evidence that his relationships have changed, or that his life has changed. From what we can see, his relationship with his wife, children and grandchildren has not changed."

Because of the apparent disparity between the two groups in this first focus group, we attempted another approach with a new group. We showed that when this man got up in the morning and looked in the mirror, he thought of himself as less of a man than he was before. We proved that he was reluctant to play soccer with his grandkids because he didn't feel like he was a man anymore. We explained that intimacy with his wife was very minimal now as he was embarrassed and ashamed. We showed that it affected his self-esteem. This time the focus group, whether female or male, were on the same page. When we showed the film clips of this new focus group to our adversaries at a subsequent mediation, the case concluded with a seven figure settlement.

6. CLIENT RELATIONSHIPS MATTER

It will never be easy for me to visit a cemetery, and this is also true especially for parents who have lost a beloved child. But my clients, a couple whose adult son was the victim of a stabbing assault, had been visiting the cemetery bi-weekly ever since their son's death six years prior. I was beyond speechless and will never forget the day I went to the cemetery with them. The tranquility of this cemetery was as excruciating as stabbing a knife into my own heart, and I remember that their son's shining headstone was brighter than almost all others. It reminded me of how many sleepless nights and lonely days the couple has spent remembering their son. The more time I spent with this family, whether in my office or dining with them in their home or attending their community's memorial event for victims of crime, the more strength and compassion I felt. It was their gift to me. I was emotionally compelled to do my best to help them go through those painful yet unavoidable days as we prepared for trial. We prevailed and justice was done with an eight figure verdict.

Many of my colleagues say that an attorney should not let his sentiment or emotion affect his judgment. That is true but only in part. Emotional involvement in a case will engender commitment to the case and compassion for the client. Objectivity will not be lost. So I say to my colleagues, "Build solid relationships with your clients, become emotionally involved and deepen your compassion for them." Without knowing your clients and earning their trust in you, you may win your case but you won't win it well. After all, what matters at the end of the line is not your wealth, education or title, but the relationships that you have built throughout your entire life. Humble yourself to understand your clients, listen to their hearts and place yourself into their lives, and serve them with compassion and commitment.

I hope this guide will hclp you if you have the misfortune of being injured in some way. You will likely need a seasoned lawyer as a trusted guide who understands the importance of these principles.

About West

William West Seegmiller is the founder of one of Southern California's most distinguished personal injury law firms. More than 30 years ago, Seegmiller began his practice because he wanted to help people who like himself had been injured in an accident.

Reputation for Doing the Right Thing:

West Seegmiller earned a stellar reputation for being a straight shooter and a zealous advocate for his injured clients. As founder of the West Seegmiller Law Firm, Mr. Seegmiller fights vigorously as he does his best to settle cases and win verdicts for each and every individual and family he represents.

Compassion for Victims:

Mr. Seegmiller knows first-hand what it is like to suffer serious injuries in a traffic accident. As a young man in his 20s, Seegmiller was in a motorcycle accident and underwent painful treatments to recover from his injuries. Indeed, he knows how important it is to treat his injured clients with first-class service.

Mr. Seegmiller is proud of the fact that he has handled thousands of cases resulting in verdicts and settlements of more than One Hundred Fifty Million Dollars ($150,000,000). Mr. Seegmiller has the experience, and confidence to stand up to the most powerful insurance companies, trucking companies, and government agencies. A warrior committed to the fight, he will not back down until his clients receive the justice they deserve from those responsible for their painful injuries.

Education:

Mr. Seegmiller earned a Bachelor's degree in Political Science at the University of California - Davis and his Master's degree from the University of Southern California. Additionally, Mr. Seegmiller earned his Juris Doctorate from the McGeorge School of Law University of the Pacific in Sacramento, where he was selected to compete in the highly competitive Traynor National Moot Court Team and was a member of the prestigious Pacific Law Review.

Since establishing his own firm in 1981, Mr. Seegmiller continues to educate himself and expand his knowledge in the legal field. He has refined his skills in the practice by attending both the Harvard Law School Program of Instruction for Lawyers, as well as The Jerry Spence Trial Lawyers College.

CHAPTER 22

USING YOUR SUPERPOWERS IN SALES AND ENTREPRENEURISM

BY MATT CURRY

My name is Matt, but some people have called me HazMat, which is short for "hazardous material." My wife, Judy, says she's the Tasmanian Devil Whisperer. That's because I have a condition called Attention Deficit Disorder, commonly known as A.D.D. or A.D.H.D. This condition makes it really hard (OK, impossible…) for me to sit still and focus on anything for more than a few minutes. I'm like a pinball, bouncing off the walls, switching gears on a dime. My mind and body go full tilt from the moment I wake up in the morning until I finally fall asleep at night. Life is kind of crazy for me sometimes.

I was diagnosed with A.D.D. back in the 1970s, when I was eleven years old. We did not have the understanding of what it was and how to treat it like we do now. I struggled in school and could not concentrate unless it was something I was interested in. I didn't think there was anything wrong with me. I was happy. I was involved in sports, and I had lots of friends. Life was good from my perspective.

I was one of the first "Ritalin Babies" to take that prescription drug, and it really did change my life. I was able to achieve better grades because I could sit through an entire class and not be disruptive. I liked the way I felt, and I loved getting good grades. I was eventually taken off the medication because the trials were still early and the doctors were cautious. As a result, though, I discovered something important – I was able to function and make good grades without the drug. The ability was inside me, but without the medication to help, I had to figure out how to get back to that state of success.

We all have weaknesses. We all have flaws. I believe that for most of us, these defects or weaknesses – when channeled properly and perhaps even celebrated – can become our greatest strengths.

Yes, your flaw may actually be your superpower! That's been my experience. A.D.D. is my superpower, no doubt about it. It gives me an incredible amount of energy, which allows me to multi-task and get a lot of stuff done. My A.D.D. also makes me intense, impulsive, fidgety, anxious, and impatient sometimes. It makes me controlling, scattered, and extremely blunt. But it also helps me get people pumped up and headed in the direction I want them to go. It makes me unafraid of chaos and assertive in the face of conflict. I'm decisive. I take action. I execute. My A.D.D. allows me to be creative while going a million miles an hour.

I've never viewed A.D.D. as a negative. Instead, I've embraced it. I've channeled my A.D.D. onto a positive track and used it to build businesses that have not only made a lot of money but have also made a lot of money for other people and improved their lives.

I've created numerous profitable companies – including the number one automotive repair chain in North America, a thriving nonprofit youth sports league, and one of the fastest growing franchises in North America (Curry's Auto Service – 10 stores) – by making the most of my A.D.D. using these principles. I've won numerous awards, grown my net worth to multiple millions, given back to my community, and most importantly, built a great life for myself, my family, and others. I believe all that great stuff happened, not *despite* my diagnosis, but *because* of it. I didn't conquer A.D.D., I leveraged it! And you can leverage your perceived weaknesses, too.

Look, everybody's got some type of disorder . . . or two, or four. Find out what yours is, acknowledge it, and use it to help. Don't be ashamed of your adversity; wear it as a badge of honor. Treat it as an asset, not a deficit. Let it guide you toward living your personal truth.

It is my belief that many successful entrepreneurs/salespeople, even if they have not been diagnosed with A.D.D., have tendencies that mirror it. These seeming flaws can become superpowers when recognized and properly channeled. You, too, can learn what you are good at and what doesn't work for you. I have learned that there are certain things I do not do well, and so I surround myself with others who have superpowers that can help me where I need it.

Adult Coach Pete Quily has a list of *151 Positives of A.D.D.* which demonstrates how this otherwise "negative" condition is full of positives. When I'm feeling down or otherwise need a shot of self-assurance, I can scroll through his list and check off some of the helpful characteristics I possess – characteristics that have served me very well professionally. Here are a few of my favorites:

- Ability to find alternate paths to overcome obstacles
- Adventurous, courageous, lives outside of boundaries
- Able to see the big picture
- Intuitive towards others' difficulties
- Can create order from chaos
- Energetic
- Fun person to be around
- Good at motivating self and others
- Has the gift of gab
- Impulsive (in a good way) not afraid to act
- Not afraid to speak mind
- Visionary

(http://www.addcoach4u.com/positivesofadd.html, accessed September 2, 2014.)

Focusing on my strengths helps me put my "weaknesses" into their proper place. My deficits don't define me. . . and neither do yours. Take a few minutes to make a list of what you consider weaknesses, and then consider how you can use them productively as a source of strength.

USING THOSE SUPERPOWERS

Everybody is in sales. As an entrepreneur or salesperson, it's important to figure out how to use your superpowers to achieve your goals. It is difficult enough to make a sale in a perfect situation, but if you compound that with distractions and nervous energy, it can be a bit challenging – unless you know how to channel that energy in the right direction.

Wouldn't it be great if there were a button you could push in the human brain that made people say "yes?" What if you could push that button with practically anybody, anytime, anywhere, and get them to buy your product or service? How awesome would that be?

Well, I'm here to tell you that there is such a button. There are certain words and phrases that are emotional triggers, and when people hear these words and phrases at the right time and under the right circumstances, it actually causes a chemical reaction in their brains that makes them more agreeable. Since our goal in sales is to direct people into agreeing with us and getting them to say "yes" to us as quickly as possible, understanding how to trip these triggers is important. If we can figure out what each individual customer's prime motivators are, we can use the emotional triggers to get them to decide to say "yes."

We have to keep things simple, though. Too much information slows down the decision-making process. When you start trying to dazzle a customer with bullshit, you are on your way to losing them. You have to make your sales pitch so straightforward that even a 12-year-old can understand it. This is one of those times when having A.D.D. is a real superpower. Those of us with A.D.D. are blunt; we are concise; and we're intuitive. We're able to get a quick read on what makes people tick, which makes it relatively easy for us to stop confusing and start convincing. This is channeling that superpower to achieving your goal.

What superpower can you begin to channel in your business? How can you begin using it today?

QUICK EXPERIMENT

Let's start with a quick experiment. Take a moment to look at yourself in the mirror right now. Then say aloud, "No." "Sorry." "We don't do that." "I can't help you." "That's impossible."

How did it look and feel when you said those words?

Now go back in front of the mirror and say, "Great!" "Super!" "Yes!" "Excellent!" "Awesome!" "No problem!" "I can do that!" "Love it!" "You 'da man!"

How did it look and feel when you said THOSE words? You couldn't help but smile by the time you were done, right? What a difference!

Just as it pained you to say the negative words and phrases, it also pains your customers to hear them. Those kinds of words and phrases do not inspire and motivate. They obstruct and deflate.

SALES SUPERPOWERS!

A top superpower for a successful salesperson is a great attitude. Attitude is everything! The best salespeople are a blast to talk to. They know how to establish a rapport without being sleazy. They leave all their problems or worries at home and become like an actor on a stage when they're selling. They're not phony, though. In fact, it's just the opposite. They are the real deal. They're genuine, happy, positive, straightforward, and informative. They love what they do.

Customers are drawn to salespeople like this. That's because they know how to forge a real connection with their customers on a person-to-person level.

The second thing a great salesperson has is confidence. Effective salespeople believe in themselves and what they're selling. That kind of confidence comes from having product knowledge. You need to be an expert in your field and a master of the product or service you're selling, whether you're selling auto repair, stereo equipment, cars, carpeting, IT services, shoes, barbequed ribs, pet supplies, or anything else. You need to know your product inside and out. People want to buy from someone who knows what they're talking about: someone who can show them the value of whatever it is they're buying.

So how do you get that kind of confidence? In the world of car racing, we call it seat time. The only way you can get familiar with a new racetrack is by spending time in the driver's seat, rolling around that track. The more you drive, the more you learn – about your car, the track, the conditions, the other drivers. . . and perhaps most importantly, about yourself. Confidence in racing comes from racking up real world driving experience. The same is true in sales. It's a fact that some of us are born with superpowers that make us great salespeople, but it's also a fact that anyone's salesmanship skills can be improved with study and regular practice. Make learning one of your life's goals. Make the investment of your time, energy, and resources in your particular field of expertise so that you can learn to solve other people's problems within that context. You just have to climb into the driver's seat every day and practice your pitches, because the more pitches you give, the more confident you become.

Lastly, to grow into a sales leader extraordinaire, you need to enter each sales situation prepared. Not only do you need to prepare yourself emotionally, mentally (with a positive attitude), and intellectually (with thorough knowledge of your products and the sales process), but also physically by having the proper tools and knowing how to use them. What props must you have on hand in your line of work? Is your paperwork within easy reach? Do you know how to use all of your company's technology, such as the software, the calculator, and the cash register? You don't want your momentum broken by having to hunt for a pen or figure out the adding machine at the pivotal moment when you're trying to close a sale. Be a good scout, and be fully prepared to pitch and close a sale at a moment's notice. You have to be prepared for success!

MATCHING YOUR VISION TO YOUR SUPERPOWER

Many companies, CEO's, salespeople, and employees try too hard by having an elaborate message that works against their brand, confusing potential customers about the value of their products or services instead of convincing their customers of what makes their brand great. It is important to have a clearly-defined vision for your company, and then turn your vision into a clear, succinct mission statement that you communicate to your customers and that you also train your employees to effectively deliver. The message you send to your employees, customers, and shareholders is vital to the success of your company and your brand. What many don't realize is that you can actually harness and transfer your superpower to your employees, and even pass it on to your customers, through the power of your mission statement and the vision you have for the business.

There is no more effective way to release your superpower on the world than through your vision and mission statements. They are at the core of every successful business plan. All skilled entrepreneurs know that the careful process of conceiving and writing these elements must never be skipped. But how many understand that they can actually pass the powers they possess on to others through the science of defining and writing these statements? Since I have never read or heard this instruction in a business training event, I suspect it is an element of business planning which is rarely considered.

In order to create your mission and vision to both reflect and employ your superpowers, you must first understand what your powers are (hopefully the exercise earlier will have helped you with that step), and then you need to give them words. . . life on paper. For example, if you are driven by energy and passion, put it in your mission. . . does your company exist to meet need A, B, and C, or does your company passionately bring A, B, and C into the world through a tireless commitment to your customers. The words, and meaning behind them, matter. Every single word you use in your mission and vision has depth, value, and emotion. In this simple example, the words "Passionately," "Tireless," and "Commitment" are key points you use to train your employees. They can be analyzed, role-played, and adopted. They vibrate with positivity which can be felt by your customers as well as your employees. A great variety of words can be used to reflect your particular superpower. It is the way in which you use them in your mission statement that infuses them with your special power. Words are superpowers in themselves!

When your mission statements reflect the core of who you are, the powers you possess, and the method by which you want to change the world, then you have material to use in each and every training meeting you ever conduct with your employees. As they understand fully what you are about, and are energized by the strength of your connection to that vision, they will embrace and become that mission and vision themselves.

About Matt

Matt Curry has worked in the automotive aftermarket business for over 30 years. He started changing tires when he was 15 and worked his way into management, overseeing seven automotive stores for several different companies, doubling and tripling sales and profits at every store he managed.

In 1997, Matt and his wife, Judy Curry, started Curry's Auto Service with one shop in Chantilly, Virginia. Curry's Auto Service ultimately became one of the largest independent auto repair chains in the Washington, DC metro area, with nine shops across Northern Virginia and one in Maryland. Matt and Judy succeeded in differentiating Curry's from its competitors by offering strong value propositions that highlighted under-represented demographics within the auto repair industry. By instituting prominent ecofriendly, green-focused programs and community outreach, and earning female-friendly accreditation from AskPatty.com, Curry's actively contributed to the economic, social, and environmental development of the communities in which it operated.

In 2010, Curry's was chosen by the readers of *Northern Virginia Magazine* as the "Best Auto Repair Shop" in Northern Virginia. That same year, Curry's was named *Motor Age* magazine's Top Shop in North America. In 2011, the company was awarded the prestigious Angie's List Super Service Award and voted Top Shop Finalist by *Tire Review* magazine. Matt was also recognized as a "Home Grown Hero, Entrepreneur of the Year" by The Network for Teaching Entrepreneurship.

During the recession in 2008 and through 2011, Matt launched a major expansion, growing from four stores in 2008 to nine in 2011. In recognition of this growth, Curry's was named to the Inc. 5000 list for 2009, 2010 and 2011, moving up about 1000 spots each year. Curry's opened its tenth store in March 2013.

In addition to being an Inc. 5000 company for three consecutive years, Curry's was ranked the 126th fastest-growing business in Consumer Products and Services Industries by *Inc.* last year. Curry's was also recognized as one of the 50 fastest-growing companies in the DC region by both the *Washington Business Journal* and *Washington Smart CEO.*

In early 2013, Matt expanded his business model, investing in two vertical companies: a computer development company and a technology company called **The Hybrid Shop**, which specializes in electric vehicle propulsion systems. After only 12 months, in November of 2014 The Hybrid Shop successfully raised $2.5 million through a Private Equity raise.

Matt and Judy made a successful exit from Curry's Auto Service by selling to a publicly-traded, $1 billion corporation in August 2013. They now concentrate full time on The Hybrid Shop, the world's leader in training and education in the diagnosis, maintenance, and repair of hybrid vehicle technology and battery conditioning and repair.

COMMUNITY SERVICE AND AWARDS

In 2004, Matt raised $209,000 and launched the Dulles South Youth Sports (DSYS) league in August of 2006. More than 1,600 area children and teens now participate in the DSYS leagues each year. The Currys continue to advise the organization and help fund DSYS needs, including starting a scholarship and field fund in the hope that DSYS will have its own private playing field someday.

In 2012, Curry's Auto Service was a finalist for the Washington Area Jefferson Awards for Public Service. Matt and Judy have donated their time and money, totaling over $500,000, to 57 national and regional charitable groups, churches, parent/teacher associations, and youth athletic clubs since they started their company in 1997 and were recognized by *The Washington Business Journal* in 2012 as among the region's Top 50 Corporate Philanthropists.

CHAPTER 23

ANSWERING THE WAKE UP CALL

BY CINDY ERTMAN

*"Life is a series of choices. Intentional choices create impact,
so you can find fulfillment, serve others and influence
change in the world."*

~ Cindy Ertman

As I walked into the room, I felt instant discomfort. It was clear that I did not fit in. I was dressed in a fitted pair of designer jeans, a crisp white blouse, a great pair of heels, a smart blazer and a stunning diamond necklace that I had worked very hard to acquire. As I sat with over 100 trainers from around the globe on the first day of a year-long *Train the Trainer* program led by the legendary Jack Canfield, I thought I had made a huge mistake. No one looked like me. I felt like I had just walked into a spiritual tribe meeting and I was clearly not part of the clan. As part of me considered my exit plan, the curious part of me did not allow me to flee.

As a mortgage executive, I expected the training to teach me to be a better leader, focus more on smart business techniques, and help me better train my mortgage troops. However, I got more than I bargained for.

Little did I know that just three short days later, my life would change forever and in ways I could have never imagined had I stayed in my comfort zone. The choice to stay in that training was the single greatest decision of my life.

Sometimes, we're really ready for a big change and we simply don't know it.

I seemed to be close to achieving my perfect picture of success. I had married the perfect guy, the star quarterback, while still in college. I had three beautiful children, two boys and a girl. I had an enviable career. I had broken through the glass ceiling and was earning an income that would impress most top executives. But something was "off."

As the primary breadwinner in the family, I had taken on the serious commitment of maintaining my family's comfortable standard of living. However, my income fluctuated greatly and I lived in constant fear that my success would not last. I put tremendous pressure on myself to be the best at everything. I was constantly exhausted trying to be the perfect mom, businesswoman, wife, friend, sister, lover, and so forth. Balance was not a word in my vocabulary. I also felt my husband beginning to resent my success, and the health of my marriage became a growing concern. I secretly yearned to leave the high pressured life of a successful businesswoman to raise my kids and be a stay-at-home mom. When I realized that I would never be able to step back in time and play that role, I cried for hours, feeling scared and trapped. I was in serious need of a wake-up call.

I knew that I needed to make changes and that I wanted to invite new opportunities into my life. I was seeking "something more," yet the clarity of the "what" still felt elusive to me.

I had already been coached by numerous leaders in the personal and professional development industry. I had mastered certain practices, including daily disciplines such as my 60-minute morning practice, with 20 minutes of meditation to ground me and calm my overactive mind, 20 minutes of exercise to strengthen my body, and 20 minutes of education on best business practices. In addition, my personal development work had helped me build a very successful mortgage business. I had been a "Top 100 Mortgage Originators" in the U.S. for over 10 years, and more recently, I had been named one of "The Top 100 Most Influential Mortgage Executives in America" by *Mortgage Executive Magazine.*

In fact, it was the "influential" award that became the catalyst that led to my transition. As I opened the blue satin box that had been delivered to my desk, I had no idea what was inside. To my surprise, it was a beautiful crystal award honoring me as one of "The Top 100 Most Influential Mortgage Executives in America." In all honesty, my first thought was that it may have made its way to me by mistake. I think it is interesting that I immediately went to self-doubt instead of excitement.

Yet quickly, I transitioned to my "ego driven" happy dance. I was wowed at the magnitude of this award and, for a moment, allowed myself to completely drop into my ego and relish in the accomplishment.

So, as I allowed myself to truly receive the award in the spirit in which it was given, I began to think about how I could utilize my influence, my revived passion and my newly-found clarity about my gifts, talents, and abilities to instigate positive change - not just in the mortgage industry, but also in the world. As I so profoundly learned, sometimes the life we think we want, isn't that fulfilling when we actually achieve it. Financial achievement, acclaim, and popular success may feed our egos, but it may not truly feed our soul - and deep down we know it. So, I began to lean in to my dream and vision of launching my own coaching and training company, *The Defining Difference.*

The imagined ideal seems to be wearing off for a lot of people these days. In the groups I lead, and with clients that I coach, people are seeking more meaning and purpose in their lives. They seem to be asking more questions about how to get clarity on the "something more" they need to fuel their souls. Moreover, people seem to want to make a difference in the world and serve a greater purpose with their lives. This inspires me because it was precisely this conversation that I had in Jack Canfield's seminar that turned my life around. And now I have the opportunity to support others in their awakenings and on their journeys.

When you begin to pay attention to that little voice inside your head that wants to give and contribute more to the world, you instigate a powerful shift; from success to significance and from intention to impact. You shift your personal and professional orientation to living on purpose. And that shift changes everything.

We all have the ability to rewrite our stories and to create our lives by design; we just need a roadmap to follow, along with the courage and support to make the change. As we all know, change is hard and many of us resist it. In fact, many people resist it with such fierce intent that they spend much of their lives living in regret for what "could" be. But to have an impact in the world and to achieve true fulfillment in our lives, change is required. We need to consciously shake up our lives and take deliberate risk for the sake of our growth and expansion.

If I was going to teach and train *The Defining Difference,* I knew that I needed to jump off my personal cliff and shake up my own life. It was time for me to transition from who I had been to who I might become, and give voice to my dream.

So, it was time to resign from my corporate leadership role to create the space in which I could live my purpose. As I approached the office of the president of the region within which I had become a superstar woman executive, I could feel my heart racing. As I began to share my vision with my business partner, a surprising calm came over me. When I confided in him that I was feeling scared and uncertain, he was remarkably kind and understanding. He realized that I had longed for this for many years. In fact, we both realized how committed I was to the new and inspired path that stood before me. My business partner expressed how grateful he was for my long term commitment to his team, and offered me his genuine support for my new endeavor.

The Defining Difference began to take form as a success-based training and coaching company devoted to helping people master the power of intentional choice to create a defining difference in their own lives.

Many of us live our day-to-day existence on autopilot. We go robotically from place to place because we think that we have to…not because we choose to. What I have found is that when we turn off the autopilot and take hold of the controls of our lives, we are fueled by an infinite source of energy that has been there all along (we just didn't tap into it).

It is important to wake up, take stock and inventory of where we are in our lives, and more importantly to consider where our soul wants us to go. It can be scary when we consciously remove the filters through which we view the world, but it can also be profound, and ultimately liberating!

We all make choices in everything we do, each and every moment of every day. Not making a choice IS A CHOICE! We all fall into habits, in our interactions with others, in the planning of our days (or lack of it), in our health habits, in how we "show up," and how we relate to others.

It is an accumulation of all of these choices that we consistently make that creates our current reality. Changing our lives begins with shifting our choices.

Sometimes just a few small SHIFTS in our day-to-day choices, mental attitudes, and daily routines can have a profound effect on the way we experience life. If we begin to consider the barriers that prevent us from getting what we want out of life, the things that are holding us back, we can easily see that the walls that confine us are self-constructed.

What if you took a risk and imagined new possibilities for your life? What would happen if you asked, "Who am I here to serve?" What would happen if you moved out of your comfort zone and removed that invisible barrier that holds you back from achieving the things that you really want in life?

When you focus on creating your Defining Difference and creating an intentional life, you start to play a new game. Think about the next year, 5 years, 10 years, and 20 years. What would you like to achieve over this period of time? What does SUCCESS look like for you? What intentional choices would you have to make to achieve the outcomes you desire? If your life today is not how you envision or desire it to be 10 years from now…the choice is yours to create a new vision for your future, NOW!

I don't just preach living a life by design and intentional choice – I live it. One of my greatest life challenges, one that put *The Defining Difference* to the test, was the collapse of my 30-year marriage. It was not something I expected, and it forced me to make choices quickly. The old part of me wanted to lead with anger, blame, and shame – to discredit my soon-to-be ex-husband. But if I was committed to living life with intention, and I understood that I could choose how I wanted to respond to this event, then I was bound by my commitment to do divorce differently – by design. I chose to look through my pain and imagine possibilities on the other side of my hurt feelings and broken promises. I worked to imagine an expanded life, with new and rewarding opportunities. This practice of envisioning positive possibility in the face of heart-wrenching crisis is one of the single greatest accomplishments of my life.

I made a choice to have a friendly divorce and I made every decision from the perspective of the outcome that I wanted to generate for my family and myself. This was not an easy commitment. Some days it seemed almost impossible. But I was deliberate in my choices and committed to a positive outcome. I'm proud to announce that, today, my ex-husband and I are friends. We act as a team in making decisions that affect our children and we sincerely want the best for each other. I firmly believe that I intentionally chose and influenced that outcome.

My life is a living testament to what can be created when we live life by design.

Whether you are fed up with your career path, the state of your personal relationships, or the current condition of your health, you too are a series of deliberate choices away from shifting your reality. At this very moment, you can begin to create a different life by making different choices. With a little support and guidance, you can create a vision and start on a new path for a destiny that is self-chosen.

When we use the power of intentional choice to make decisions that align with our ultimate purpose or the outcomes we truly desire, we create a powerful filter. Our choices are either in alignment with our intention, or they are not. If they are not, and we are committed to our intention (or vision) then we must make a different choice – it is that simple.

We can supercharge our intention and expand our vision by becoming a generous offer in the world. This step is about focusing on a greater good – not just our own fulfillment. When I shifted from thinking that I was in a service industry to a mindset where I asked each day, "who am I here to serve?" my life changed. Suddenly, my choices became more generous and inclusive, and the floodgates began to open.

And when the call comes in – ANSWER IT! Answer the call to "wake up" in your own life and lean in to your true calling to live your life on purpose. My mission is to help and support you on your journey to create a defining difference in your own life. When you transform your own life, it gives others permission to do the same. Are you ready to answer the call? I did, and it opened up a whole new world of possibilities in my life. I'm certain that when I come to the end of my road, I will look back and smile, knowing that I played full out and lived in full expression of myself - with no regrets. I am grateful for taking risks for the sake of growth in my own life and now serve as a role model for others along their journeys.

About Cindy

Cindy Ertman is CEO and Founder of *The Defining Difference*, a success-based coaching and training company devoted to helping people master the power of intentional choice to create a defining difference in their own lives. She is a dynamic speaker, author, coach, TV host, and success strategist.

After being acknowledged as one of "The Top 100 Most Influential Mortgage Executives in America" by *Mortgage Executive Magazine* and years of inspiring growth in her industry, Cindy has now dedicated her life to empower the growth of others. She has developed a track record of helping high achievers *shift* the way they see the world and expand their vision of possibility by teaching them her personal success approach called *The Defining Difference®*.

Cindy Ertman's coaching and training programs help her clients get more out of life by making powerful, intentional choices to propel their income and achieve their peak performance, nurture their health and wellness, build connected relationships, and reduce stress by removing the blocks that limit their potential.

Cindy is a catalyst for transformation. Her passion is teaching men and women alike – who have achieved a certain level of success, but are now searching for their "something more" – how to make intentional choices that inspire an increase in commitment, motivations and success habits to drastically shift results. She supports them in bridging their GAP (Goals Aligned with Purpose) so that they can positively impact the course of their future.

In early 2015, Cindy joined three other amazing hosts for the conscious-edge, thought-leading Talk Show called *Wake Up!* The show is focused on supporting and empowering women to lean into a bigger conversation in order to wake up their minds, wake up their bodies, and wake up their souls.

She is a founding and active member of the *Association of Transformational Leaders* (ATL) which is a forum for individuals of significant influence in artistic, academic, social, political, corporate, and humanitarian endeavors, devoted to doing transformational work in their respective fields.

Cindy graduated from the University of the Pacific in Northern California, but is a native of Southern California. Cindy's #1 priority is her three adult children, and she also enjoys spending time with close friends and family and time enjoying the beach in her local community.

Cindy's soon to be released on-line training course, 'How to Wake Up Your Life in 6 Weeks' and her groundbreaking new book, *The Defining Difference®*, **to be released in late 2015, teaches her proven success formula that she used to catapult her achievements throughout her life – both personally and professionally.** To learn more about Cindy's Coaching, Training or Speaker Services, please email Cindy at: Cindy@TheDefiningDifference.com or visit: www.TheDefiningDifference.com.

CHAPTER 24

SLEEP - YOUR BRAIN'S OWN RESET BUTTON

BY DR. BEVERLY YATES, ND

Do you want to be an effective business leader?

Do you want to be a business leader who gets things that matter done, is well paid, and has the good health to really enjoy it all?

Go to sleep.

Want to hit your goals? See profits soar, productivity increase and personal satisfaction grow?

Go to sleep.

For a surprising number of people, especially business people and entrepreneurs, poor sleep keeps them from achieving their goals and leading the life of their dreams. Chronic problems with remaining alert, relaxed and focused tend to plague people who don't sleep well. For some people with persistent sleep problems, there are basic things they can do to get a good night's sleep on a regular basis.

A lack of good quality sleep can lead to:

- Poor decision-making
- Depression

- Anxiety
- Exhaustion

Crummy sleep can also lead to potentially serious chronic health problems like sleep apnea, obesity, severe food cravings, memory disorders, and more. Many people are very surprised to learn that a lack of sleep affects a person's short-term memory, and can lead to persistent issues with memory.

Poor sleep also affects a person's mood, making them much more irritable and difficult to be around. This can have a negative impact on professional and business relationships, damage job performance, affect promotions at work, shrink pay raises and bonuses, and impair work team morale and camaraderie.

And guess what?

This lack of quality sleep also affects personal relationships, too. Poor sleep can destroy family and intimate relationships in ways that might not be obvious to the person who sleeps poorly. The irritability, anger, depression and acting out caused by poor sleep are a real stress on everyone around the person who has poor sleep. The mood swings affect all the people closest to the one having the sleep issue. The changed, altered behavior of the poor sleeper can be rough on family members, lovers and friends, as well as being rough on the person with the lousy sleep.

So, what should you do? Throw your hands up in surrender, as if there is nothing you can do about it and accept perpetual poor sleep? Act as if you are doomed to suffer from poor sleep for forever?

No.

There is a lot you can do to help yourself improve your sleep, with safe, effective, natural means. Much of it includes lifestyle shifts that can support you getting a good night's sleep on a regular basis.

Good sleep is a *requirement* for leading a life that feels good. Good sleep has two parts, both the quality of sleep you experience and the quantity of sleep you get. To really sleep well on a regular basis, you need to **both** sleep long enough **and** sleep deeply enough, getting what is called *restorative sleep*, too.

This dynamic duo of deep sleep and long sleep lets your body and mind do its critically important work of repairing the body and refreshing the mind. Without this necessary downtime called sleep, the needed repairs, restoration and refresh work don't happen. This leads to illness, exhaustion, burnout, frustration, memory problems, poor decisions, mood problems and much more.

If you don't think long-term poor sleep can affect *you* negatively, consider this: what would it be like if you had a factory that you ran, 24/7/365? That's right, a factory you ran 24 hours a day, 7 days a week, 365 days of the year, without adequate downtime, maintenance and repairs?

You wouldn't be surprised if the factory had problems with maintaining its production, would you? And you wouldn't be surprised if the factory struggled to turn in a good performance over time, would you? In fact, it is likely you would *expect* the factory to have problems at some point if you ran it this way. So, in the spirit of prevention, it is likely you would schedule maintenance, set up regular repairs, and from time to time you would turn everything off so it did not wear out prematurely. This just makes sense, because you would want to get everything you could from the factory, right?

If this makes sense to you, then ask yourself: Am I giving myself enough time to rest? Am I respecting my needs for fun and relaxation? As I push hard to reach my goals, am I doing it in a way that *honors my needs* or am I destroying myself and others in the process of pursuing what I consider to be success? Take a moment to be honest with yourself, this is truly important.

So let's look at some triggers for poor sleep habits. Since lousy sleep affects personal performance in the business world and outside of work, it is really good to know what some triggers are for poor sleep. Once you know what these triggers are, you can dodge them and make any needed changes so you can improve the likelihood you enjoy a good night's sleep, night after night. You want sleep to be your friend, not an elusive thing you rarely get to experience.

TRIGGERS FOR POOR SLEEP HABITS

- Alcohol – more than one glass of alcohol is likely to lead to a poor night's sleep – alcohol affects sleep quality, making sleep too light to be restorative

- Depression
- Anxiety
- Stress
- Changing your sleep schedule on weekends and holidays from your weekday sleep schedule
- Not having a sleep schedule at all
- Going to bed at wildly different times
- Getting up at very different times
- Going to sleep too late to get enough sleep
- If you wake up in the middle of the night, doing "one more thing" and then have trouble getting back to sleep
- Trying to fall asleep with the TV or radio on
- Watching scary movies or TV shows right before bedtime
- Watching violent movies or TV shows before bedtime

TIPS FOR GOOD SLEEP ON A REGULAR BASIS

These are tips meant to remind you of good habits that can lead to deep, restorative sleep:

Timing Your Sleep for Success

- Go to bed at the same time each night.
- Get up at the same time each morning.
- Have a regular bedtime routine for yourself; if you are a parent, you know how difficult it becomes if you let your children have a chaotic bedtime; why do that to yourself?

Don't Do This

- Don't check emails right before bedtime; allow at least two hours between your last peek at email and bedtime.
- Don't check social media right before bedtime; allow at least two hours between your last look at social media and bedtime.
- Don't let your sleep be interrupted by gadgets. Turn **off** your cell phone, tablet, computer and any other digital device that can interrupt you at least 2 hours before bedtime so you are not

disturbed and have a peaceful transition to your sleep world.

Your Sleep Environment

- Make sure your bedroom is completely dark when you go to bed.

- Make sure your bedroom is completely quiet when you go to bed.

- Make sure your bedroom is cool when you go to bed; if the room is hot and the air is stuffy, it may be harder to sleep well.

Mind Management for Sleep

- Meditate and/or pray just before bedtime, this can calm and soothe the mind.

- Do any preparation for the next day in the late afternoon or evening so you get it done and it isn't on your mind.

- If you awaken in the middle of the night, it's OK to stay in bed; don't get up and start doing things, just lie peacefully until you fall back asleep.

- If you can't sleep and do get out of bed, do something that is peaceful and non-stimulating, like knitting or read an enjoyable book.

Body Management for Sleep

- Finish drinking all beverages at least 2 hours before bedtime so you don't have to get up during the night to pee.

- Finish eating all food at least 3 hours, and preferably 4 to 5 hours before bedtime.

- Monitor how much caffeine you are getting (including all beverages, supplements, over-the-counter drugs like some pain relievers, and other sources) and figure out if it harms your ability to sleep.

- Avoid alcohol. Drinking alcohol can make you feel sleepier at first, but as your body breaks down the alcohol, it can keep you from resting deeply enough to get full benefits from the restorative phases of your sleep.

Exercise and Stress Management

- Don't do anything you find stressful right before bed; tackle it the next day or do it in the early part of the day.

- Exercise 5 to 6 days of the week. Even a little exercise, 20 minutes or more each day, helps improve sleep quality and sleep quantity.

- Be sure to allow at least 3 hours between your exercise and your bedtime, so you get the best benefits of both exercise and getting to sleep at the same time each night.

A NOTE ABOUT SHIFT WORK

Avoid shift work whenever possible. It's really hard to yank your body and mind all around the clock. Your performance at work and level of alertness will suffer with shift work where you work varying times around the clock. And it's highly likely your weight will suffer too, as shift workers tend to gain weight more easily than others. The nature of shift work disrupts your body's rhythms, including hormonal balance and neurotransmitters that help to keep you healthy. Long-term shift work is a strong interfering factor for getting good sleep.

TIPS FOR LONG DISTANCE TRAVEL ACROSS TIME ZONES

If you find you need to travel frequently across 3 hours or more worth of time zones, you may find that jet lag really affects your in-person performance when you arrive at your destination and when you return home. Here are some tips for making this kind of transition a bit easier.

1. About 3 days before your travel, start taking 1 – 3 milligrams of melatonin at the time it would be bedtime in the time zone you are traveling to.

2. If possible, take a short nap at what would be bedtime in the time zone you are traveling to.

3. Once you arrive at your destination, get outside in the fresh air and sunlight as quickly as you can. Stay in the sun and bright light for at least 10 minutes outdoors. This simple maneuver helps to reset your inner body clock and speed adjustment to the new time zone.

4. For most travelers, meals are the hardest part of trying to adjust to the new time zone. Don't force yourself to eat if you really don't want to. Bring healthy snack bars, protein powders, etc. to help you deal with this issue if needed.

Please know that change can be hard. If you find that you have lots of habits that don't serve you well, make a plan for what you can change and take it in phases so you aren't overwhelmed. There's no point feeling bad about yourself, it isn't helpful on your way to creating great sleep night after night. And you are not alone, as many people struggle to get a good night's sleep.

Once you've identified where the issues are, you can make needed changes and see how your sleep responds. Some people find that 3 or 4 specific changes are enough to make the difference for their needs for rest. Others find that a more extensive lifestyle overhaul is needed in order to get good habits in place and then reap the rewards that great sleep can bring to the quality of a person's life.

Keep chipping away until you claim restorative sleep as your permanent prize! It's worth whatever it takes to make this happen.

About Dr. Beverly

Dr. Beverly Yates, ND is a California licensed doctor of Naturopathic Medicine and a 1994 graduate of the National College of Natural Medicine in Portland, OR. She is also a graduate of the Massachusetts Institute of Technology (MIT), where she earned her undergraduate degree in electrical engineering and minored in bio-electrical engineering.

As a MIT-trained Naturopathic physician, Dr. Yates is a prolific content creator in multiple health and medicine sectors, both online and offline. She is focusing on online marketing and digital collaboration in specific niches.

Dr. Yates served as the lead supervising doctor for the first-ever fully-accredited Naturopathic and Integrative medical residency in the state of California. She was a governor appointee to California's Naturopathic Medicine Committee, which regulates the Naturopathic medical profession on a state level.

Dr. Yates serves as a National Media Representative for the American Association of Naturopathic Physicians, appearing as an expert in natural medicine on TV shows in select metropolitan areas. She is a member of the Medical Advisory Board for Gaia Herbs, Inc., Schwabe North America, and other companies.

In response to Dr. Yates' contributions to community health, she provided testimony for the Tri-Caucus of the California legislature concerning the growing impact of obesity and diabetes in communities of color around the state and the country.

A popular author, public speaker, and teacher, Dr. Yates shares her knowledge with audiences comprised of both the general public and other health professionals. Sought after for her ability to provide concise, clear explanations about complex medical processes and natural medicine, Dr. Yates appears regularly on numerous TV broadcast networks including ABC, CBS, CNN, CW, Fox, NBC, and PBS; her radio interviews include NPR, CNN Radio, Sirius International Satellite; and her print interviews include *Essence Magazine, Good Housekeeping Magazine* and *Women's World.* She has collaborated with Rodale Press on numerous books for over two decades as a medical consultant, sharing her expertise on herbal remedies, botanical medicines, vitamins and supplements for chronic illnesses.

Areas of Expertise:
Weight Loss, Cardiovascular Health, Diabetes, Hypertension, Sleep Problems and Sleep Apnea, Mood Disorders, Stress Resilience.

Publications:

Dr. Yates is the author of *Heart Health for Black Women: A Natural Approach to Healing and Preventing Heart Disease,* Marlowe & Co., 2000. Dr. Yates is also a contributing author to: *Maternal, Newborn and Child Nursing: A Family Centered Approach,* Pearson Education, Inc., 2003, which is a textbook used in nursing and medical schools. She has self-published the *Ultimate PCOS Weight Loss Herbs and Supplements Guide,* along with other materials about PCOS (PolyCystic Ovarian Syndrome) and is writing a number of other books.

Dr. Yates can be reached at: Info@DrBeverlyYates.com.

If you'd like to sign up for her email list, please go to:
http://www.DrBeverlyYates.com/Soul-Of-Success

Phone: 415.381.4600, x101

CHAPTER 25

THE AMERICAN DREAM

BY DAVID DELGADO

At a very early age in the late 1970s, I was sitting in my grandfather's black Lincoln Town Car jumping up and down asking my grandfather, "Is that a phone in your car?" Back then they didn't have cell phones, and this phone was big, black and almost the size of a public phone squeezed in between the front leather seats. I could not believe seeing the size of this phone, and car phones were not in everyone's budget. My grandfather was successful, as you can assume anyone who had a phone in their car was. In those days, a car phone was not common and cell phones didn't exist. I was inspired at an early age by my grandfather's success.

Our family didn't grow up with a silver spoon in our mouth; we were average middle class folks. My dad worked in construction with his dad, my other grandfather. My mom was a housewife and I had two siblings and a golden retriever. I enjoyed playing baseball at the local park while my father was the baseball coach. I enjoy thinking back on those years, thinking of all those great days. As time went on, my parents could not get along and they eventually got divorced when I was 8. I felt lost without my father, my soul was sucked out of me. I stopped playing baseball, I didn't want to talk to anyone or go to any social events, and all I wanted to do was to stay at home.

During this time, 8 more years had passed with no sight of grandpa. Out of site out of mind is true. My mom was forced to take a job to support the three of us and our dad was in and out of our lives as he started a new family. During my early childhood years my mom struggled, so I would always be thinking of ways to entertain myself with my cars or playing in my backyard. My mom hardly made much money, and she would cry herself to sleep in her bedroom.

Then one day we were out to dinner, and this was a spectacular beach restaurant. With the yachts I saw in the distance, this was not just any ordinary dinner we were at. My mom had enough gas money to get us there and back, but not enough to feed her three children at this beachfront restaurant. Then as we walked through the restaurant, my mom received a kiss from this tall older man. I was shocked. I didn't know who this person was. But this man had a lot of charm, charisma and was full of life. I asked my mom who was that person that just kissed her and she said, that's your grandfather. I said to myself, my grandfather, who is that? I knew my dad's father, who was extremely close to me, but now I had two grandfathers!

At the time, I never realized I had two grandfathers and then it all hit me at once. All the memories, sitting and bouncing in his black Lincoln, at his home looking up to him, my mentor was standing right in front of me. We were definitely out of place at this restaurant. Keep in mind for the past ten years, we didn't eat out, we didn't have any money and my mom would cry on her bed, because she could not pay her bills because she had no money. Our house was disorganized; my mom had a tough time raising two boys and a daughter. Going from private school to public school because of the divorce was inevitable.

I remember one day with my mom we sat at the table, having dinner, at a renewed meeting with aunts and uncles at a Christmas dinner. I knew this is what I wanted and had been missing. Throughout my life my grandfather did not know this, but he had been instrumental in my life. I had no relationship with him. It was over the next ten years and a dozen or so times meeting him, from our poor dysfunctional family to the next ten Christmas dinners, which gave me insight that there are two kinds of people.

My grandfather built one of the largest real estate investment firms in Los Angeles County. He was an only child who was raised by his mother and did not attend high school in order to work and help support his mom. He was a mover and a shaker. When he would arrive at the Christmas dinners, he was the most important person in the room. Then we would return back home, where my mom suffered to make ends meet. At the age of twelve I wanted my own newspaper route. This led me to other ventures to support my desires. My desire was money, but it was more than money. I didn't want to ask my mom for money if I wanted to buy an ice cream bar from the ice cream truck. After all, the night before I saw her in tears because she didn't have enough to pay the bills. That's one thing, that having this knowledge of my mom's dad and how successful he was, which shaped and inspired who I am today.

Also, at the age of 12 years, I started my flower business. Selling flowers on the weekends at local street corners taught me to work for my money, to be disciplined and to set goals. I would set goals to make $80 in my pocket after all expenses and every weekend it was like clockwork. I had a big breakthrough at an early age, and one weekend I made $425! It was insane, being only twelve years old with $425 in my pocket. I remember seeing my mom driving by checking up on me while I was out running around going from car to car showing flowers, and each time they would buy them. I never realized how many people buy flowers!

Ten years later, 1-800-flowers was born. This became the largest publicly-traded flower shop. If a flower shop can go public, then just about anything can. If you are considering starting a business or if you are in business, there are many people that can help you with business start-ups, but one thing I learned was that the first steps are critical. I would highly recommend doing a little research and do it right. It does take planning, creating a business plan and some advice. The advice I tend to recommend is to find a role model. Role modelling will get you to your dreams the quickest.

Throughout life, we will always have challenges or what I call 'a fork in the road.' It is really how we deal with these forks that will shape who we become tomorrow. I was working at UPS at the time. I was on the late shift and attending college. I was always trying to figure out a way to start a business. I didn't care for the shipping business, and by this time, I was no longer selling flowers, I decided to study real estate. I just turned 18 and the job at UPS served me well. Going to school and working the late shift was perfect for me.

One day after work, my brother's friend was shot in the head on the porch of our house. It was a case of mistaken identity. This was a fork in the road in my life. I heard the gun shots and walked out the front door, and there he was laying face down on our driveway, right next to my car. I didn't know him that well, but that day changed my life. That day I discovered that life is short and you should live each day like it's your last. I would suggest going after what you want in life and don't look back . . . and that's what I did. My upbringing was not only limited, but I learned to appreciate life.

Life has its ups and downs. I also believe success does too. I don't think there is one person I know that lived a life that was super-successful who never experienced both. I believe in order to achieve success you must weather adversity. This is exactly how we learn, achieve more and do more. As you start a new goal or business, find someone who you can lean on to speed up the learning curve and to mitigate any financial risk.

In the real estate industry, there is my mentor Craig Proctor, who I lean on, so it would be good for you to find someone in your industry who has already had the success you want that you can use as a role model. With the Internet, in less than a few seconds you can find these individuals. This is what I call a short cut to success. Many of these successful business leaders have been interviewed or may even have a publication that we can learn from. Reading about them and researching their business can leave you with some golden nuggets for your business. My grandpa was also my mentor. He told me in order for you to be successful, you must eat, sleep and dream your business. We see it all too often where a successful business went out of business in a very short time. If you do the research, you will find out that the CEO of that business lost the desire.

My real estate team consists of Buyers' Agents, Outside Sales Agents, an Inside Sales Team, a Transaction Coordinator, an Office Manager and a Field Coordinator. When I started selling real estate, I needed leads. The more leads I had, the more opportunities I had, and this meant more sales. The Internet makes it a lot easier to start a business and many times you do not have to reinvent the wheel with your business. I suggest you study a really good business and that business may not have to be in your same field. For me it was easy, I found Craig Proctor. He is my coach and I am also a real estate coach for Craig Proctor Productions, where I coach agents throughout North America.

Here's what I learned from Craig Proctor. I didn't have to reinvent a real estate selling machine like his team. Craig Proctor was named #1 REMAX agent worldwide, selling on average 500 homes per year. When I discovered this about Craig, I knew this was a person I could learn from. That's what I did in 2008, and in 2009, I was named inaugural rookie of year. Today, Craig pays me to coach his members. I am certainly not coaching other real estate agents for the income, what's more satisfying is the way I feel from helping others succeed.

Many of my marketing strategies and systems I have developed have not come from the real estate industry. My best ones come from outside the industry. So if you can't find a mentor in your industry, don't give up, find someone who is outside your industry. Study what they do – such as: Where do their prospects come from? How and from where do they generate leads? What's their Unique Selling Proposition (USP)? Develop your marketing system around those specifics. Once I had enough leads, I found myself leveraging them with a highly-trained team. Each person is separately responsible for individual tasks or what I call a checklist to work from.

To sum it up, if you are looking to start a new business or expand your sales, you need to do three things:

Develop a strong Unique Selling Proposition. This is the question your prospects are asking themselves: Why should I do business with you? For me, my Unique Selling Proposition is, "Your Home Sold Guaranteed or I Will Buy It for CASH!" My USP is my brand. I understand what home sellers really want and they want buyers and I have over 300 approved buyers, and if one of these buyers doesn't buy their home, I will step in and buy their home.

Find ways to dominate Internet lead generation. There are many companies that will show you how to generate leads online.

When you develop and implement a lead generation system, calling your leads back quickly will result in higher conversion ratios that will make your sales explode.

About David

David Delgado was first introduced to real estate at an early age. His grandfather, a mover and a shaker, built one of the largest real estate investment firms in Los Angeles County. Despite his grandfather's wishes for him to pursue business outside of real estate, David followed his dreams. In 1996, pursuant to his dreams from early childhood, David stepped foot into the mortgage industry and in 1998 was schooled by the most successful mortgage bankers in the country. In 2003, David became a real estate broker, helping run a successful nationwide mortgage company and soon after became the broker of record of Delgado Realty and Loans.

In 2006, David was the creator and founder of DreamLoan, a mortgage banking advocate company for homeowners. During this time, David discovered a conflict of interest between Mortgage Lenders and Loan Officers vs. homebuyers and refinancers. As a result of his discovery, David submitted ideas and suggestions to Congress to protect Consumers and to eliminate the conflict of interest that existed in the home loan market. For the past 50 years, this was a conflict that had been unknown to the average consumer. As of today, there are no further conflicts of interest between the mortgage loan officer and homebuyers and loan borrowers as the U.S Government has enacted several mortgage reforms to eliminate any conflict of interest.

David and his family's legacy in life is helping others. David's mission is to build up others by creating wealth for his clients through buying and selling Real Estate. His clientele ranges from local first time buyers and international investors to relocators and home sellers. David continues to innovate new marketing concepts, new systems, programs and technologies for the real estate industry to create investment strategies for seasoned real estate investors, move up buyers and to provide specialized knowledge and support to first time buyers.

In October 2009, David received the Quantum Leap Award from Craig Proctor at a real estate super conference in Orlando, Florida. Craig Proctor is the creator of the Quantum Leap System - which innovatively applies the concept of leverage, specialization and systemization to provide superior real estate service.

David's insight into lending, helping people and service-first-before-sales has shed the light of hope to other fellow Realtors® throughout the country. His remarkable comeback story has been featured throughout the real estate industry, local training events and when he is asked why does he share his story, he says, "It's because when you have hope, anything is possible."

Contact Information:
David Delgado
Delgado Realty Group
Phone: (562) 201-7449
Fax: (714) 763-4378
Email:david@daviddelgadorealty.com
www.daviddelgadorealty.com

CHAPTER 26

THE TRUE DEFINITION OF SUCCESS IN LIFE

BY JUSTIN F. SHAW, RFC

DEFINING SUCCESS

Achieving personal success stands at the crux of the American Dream. Whether it's the dream of a large house or an early retirement, many people chase financial success with the same vigor as those that previously sought the proverbial "fountain of youth." I used to be one of those people. Once I tasted financial success, it totally consumed me. My professional success was a mere reflection of my clients' financial success. Within the first 10 years of my career, I had achieved levels of professional and financial success that would have taken most others 20 years to accomplish. I was driven, regardless of the ultimate price, to prove to my family that I *was* going to be professionally successful.

It wasn't long before a vicious cycle formed whereby my perverted version of success became correlated to the material possessions I owned. Success was measured by material wealth and not by the understanding that money was but a mere *tool* to be *used* to achieve personal growth and success. Interestingly, the more I bought, the larger the void within me became. My troubles manifested themselves when I foolishly spent money on things to fill that emptiness within me. The more work consumed me, the less time I had to devote to those I loved. I had put work first, family second, and my relationship with God third. Soon it became apparent that this "lifestyle" was having a detrimental effect on my family life. My marriage suffered. Little time was dedicated to my kids during their formative years and at only thirty-five, I was the quintessential example of having more money than wisdom. While I was quick to dispense advice to my clients, I hesitated to apply said wisdom to myself.

A CHANGE IN FOCUS

Regardless of how hard I worked, I wasn't insulated from economic downturns. The sudden downturn of 2008 forced my hand. Suddenly, my clients' priorities and more defensive financial posturing severely impacted the growth of my business practice. People didn't want to talk about their finances even if they needed my help. Many acted as though, if they avoided the subject matter, it would simply not impact them! They avoided opening their investment statements for several months, if not years! These devastating events were to become the very same that would ultimately save my personal life while redirecting my professional career.

This was a great time for personal and professional growth. These unwelcomed experiences forced me to reassess myself. I could no longer base my self-worth on the money I generated or the possessions that I owned. I began to realize that I *had* value *without* extreme material wealth. My excess became moderated and I began to focus on my marriage, my children and my relationship with God.

Soon the discordance within me began to subside. My internal void started to fill up with meaningfulness and purpose from the very familial and spiritual relationships I had once casually taken for granted. I began to feel happier and more fulfilled in both my personal life and within my professional arena. Clients seemed to notice a greater resolve in me to meet their goals. I shifted my focus to helping my clients prepare for retirement in what were then unconventional ways. If I were to change, then I would have to reinvent my practice and marry it to these newly reacquainted values.

THE REALITY OF RETIREMENT

It's no secret that Americans spend more time planning their vacations than they do planning their retirement. When they do take the time to plan, they often don't have all the knowledge or understanding of the economic workings around them to plan effectively. This truth often leads to financial disaster.

Most people will retire with a false sense of security, often developed from the financial industry itself. The industry's focus is to tell their clients what they *want* to hear instead of what they actually *need* to hear. As sad as it may be, this is the *prevailing* approach to today's planning.

Free online self-help tools often misrepresent the analysis of one's financial health. Clients fail to realize that financial calculators are an oversimplification of future financial needs. They offer an easy answer, and fail to take a myriad of economic fluctuations into consideration.

These variables are purposefully designed to make an individual's financial outlook appear better than it actually is. Such tools can actually do more harm than good! The fact that their decisions become predicated on falsehood may lead to an unfortunate reality. False assumptions may include low rates of inflation and high rates of return on their assets during their retirement years. Their poor decisions are predicated on a general lack of insight into the complex inner workings of our financial system, combined with a stubborn and misguided certainty about the decisions they are about to undertake.

A much different picture begins to present itself when I enlighten them of a more realistic inflation rate of 5% instead of their 2.5%, and a rate of return at 7% instead of their 10%. Taxes fluctuate, so one year you might pay 20%, and the next, 25%. This more realistic scenario means that the money that was going to last until age 100 will now only last until age eighty-five. What a shock this must be to any unprepared centenarian. The reality is that most people are, in fact, totally unprepared for the future.

Wisdom dictates that it's better to realize this five years before, rather than five years after, a person retires. Consider that the two most common ways people run out of money during retirement include having an unrealistic budget and exposure to "unexpected market losses" while taking withdrawals from their retirement accounts.

LIFE AFTER RETIREMENT

If you truly look at "lifestyle" during retirement, the numbers become even hazier. Most people are going to retire around sixty-five years of age, and then could live to be ninety. That means that retirement funds need to last approximately thirty years. But if you look at how life is now lived, people are more active, with travel and costly activities, in those first ten years. One should consider what their "retired lifestyle" will look like long before reaching that day.

It is a well-known fact that people who proactively plan tend to be more successful than those that merely react. People need a realistic income plan for retirement. It needs to cover their healthcare costs, and their costs of living, as well as any unforeseen incidental expense. Part of the problem is that people assume that they can grow money in their retirement years at the same rate as they did during their working years. This is simply not the case. Consider that people in their seventies tend to travel and spend less than in their sixties, but they might still have a lot of money tied up in the market. That's great if the market is bullish, but it's not! That introduces a lot of risk into the equation that must be managed appropriately to avoid a precarious situation as they age further. So thanks to medical science, people have the ability to live longer. However, this only works to increase the already incalculable unfunded liabilities of the government. History reflects that at least one of their measured responses will most definitely include an increase in the tax rates.

After eighty, there is another spike in spending associated with healthcare expenses. A person should be prepared to assume the lion's share of these expenses in the latter part of their life or the life of their loved ones. Many loving couples can become strapped with unmanageable healthcare-related costs, which further erode their distressed lifestyle. People need to realize that if they want to be successful, they need to be focused on accumulating wealth in their younger years, and then preserving it in their older years. This proactive approach to retiring ensures that they will have enough money to survive.

Taxes! Nobody wants to talk about them but they are applicable to most financial situations. Everyone is in the dark about them and how they affect their retirement income. I suppose that they foolishly think that if you don't mention them, then they will not be impacted by them? When the IRA was introduced in 1973, the highest marginal tax bracket was 70%. The idea was to defer taxes when the rates were high, and then take money out later when the tax rate was lower. Unfortunately, but not surprisingly, those very rates fell as when we saw them drop to 50% in the early 1980's and then, more recently, to 39.6%. This resulted in a phenomenon whereby people invested money at a lower tax rate than they would ultimately withdraw it at. It is a situation that is completely opposite to the one that was prophesied in 1973.

Unforeseen economic downturns may also negatively impact the best-intentioned retirement plans. Case in point, I learned that a close friend enjoying his much deserved retirement in his sixties was managing his own accounts. I soon learned that all his funds were heavily leveraged in the market. I strongly suggested he move the money someplace where it would be more protected. In the end, he shifted over 10% of his funds, but managed the other 90% himself. Just moving the 10% was difficult as it was returning a much lower rate than his other money. I reiterated to him that it would best to: "plan for the worst; hope for the best." The unthinkable happened in 2008, when the market "fell off" the proverbial cliff. This same person ended up losing almost all of the money that they had been self-managing. The only funds left were those very funds, which amounted to a mere ten percent of his retirement assets. This person was forced to return to work after only ten years of retirement. Sometimes, you need to keep people from being their own worst enemy.

MAKING THE CONNECTION

The sudden downturn of 2008 *forced* me to downsize and restructure my growing "empire." It became apparent that all of the success I had, thus far, achieved, suddenly became untenable and meaningless dead weight that just had to be shed. I divested myself of unneeded expensive cars, properties, and other "symbols" of success. It was the shedding of an entire way of life; a radical readjustment to how I viewed everything around me. No longer would I judge myself by the goods I owned but rather by a more meaningful relationship to family, faith and myself. I don't miss it one bit! Now, while enjoying time with my family, I am learning to appreciate how I am able to touch the lives of those around me. Downsizing ultimately made more room for the things that mattered.

That experience also really underscored the importance of financial planning. I realized that if I could be caught off guard as a professional at the top of my game, then anyone could. This economic turmoil became the catalyst for my self-awareness and for the implementation of unconventional planning strategies that worked to mitigate retirees' losses.

The way to ensure success for your future is to take a measured look at what money will be needed to "live", while appreciating that the demands for those future assets will change as a person moves closer to their nineties.

It is often said that, "A goal without a plan is just a wish" (Saint-Exupéry), so the key is to have a *measured* and *planned* approach to budgeting for a more comfortable retirement. The comfort of knowing that your financial affairs and family are taken care of will provide immeasurable peace of mind when you seek it most. In short, it is best to assume the worst – plan for a rainy day – and hope for the best.

There's no day like today to plan for tomorrow!

About Justin

Justin F. Shaw, RFC founded Advanced Financial Concepts in 1998 and has been providing long-term financial and retirement planning for a large client base. An industry leader in financial and retirement planning, he graduated with a Bachelor's degree in Finance from the University of Houston. Justin went on to develop strategies that increase wealth for his clients and sets them up for financial comfort in the retirement years.

With a unique and personalized approach, Justin works closely with clients to develop wealth strategies that meet their needs and set them up for success. He knows there is no such thing as a one-size-fits-all solution, and tailors his proven strategies to each client's needs and goals. It's not about personal success, but about sharing his success. Justin is a leader, and a committed community member before anything else.

As the president of Advanced Financial Concepts, Justin sets himself apart as leader. He earned his designation as a Certified Funds Specialist from the Institute of Finance and Business, as well as becoming a member of the National Ethics Association. He is ranked in the top 2% of financial professionals in the city of Houston, and has been awarded numerous honors, including those for client satisfaction. In 2010 and 2011, he was featured in *Texas Monthly Magazine* for his success in the financial services industry.

Focused on growth, Justin took his knowledge and has developed a reputation as a public speaker – reaching a larger audience with his message of financial empowerment. In 2003, he founded the Houston Center for Financial Education, with the goal of introducing his revolutionary wealth management strategies to the community. Conducting these workshops over the years have helped Justin develop a unique ability to understand and analyze his client's situations and needs.

He has reached millions through his two radio shows, *The Financial Road Map* on 1070 AM KNTH and *The Financial Truth with Justin Shaw* on Business 1110 AM KETK. On the radio, his goal is to dispel some of the rampant and incorrect myths around financial planning and personal wealth. By interacting with the public through broadcasting, he reaches more people with his message of financial freedom.

Justin's involvement in the community around him is paramount to his mission of spreading his proven success. The knowledge, experience, and strategy he has gained over the years is only valuable if he is out there sharing it with people and helping them in their own lives. His innovative ideas and proven methods have allowed him to develop a road map to personal financial security, and that road map offers something for everyone.

CHAPTER 27

THE ART OF SPONSORING

BY ZBIGNIEW "ZBYSZEK" KABATA

Just imagine . . .

You can do what you want . . .

Live where you want . . .

Work when you want . . .

When you go for vacation, you just go where you want, for how long you want . . .

. . . No boss, No stress, No money problems.

FREEDOM

I was born in a country where the word "freedom" was only in a dictionary. My father flew on planes as a mechanic for an airline company. He was a very hard-working man. His free time he spent with my mother building our house and taking care of our garden, so that we always had fresh fruits and vegetables. He built a very nice house surrounded with many pine trees. My mother had to take care of four children, so she had more than enough to do every day.

After I had completed my secondary schooling, I decided to go to a maritime academy to follow my older brother Krzysiek. I liked travelling and at the same time earning more money than average, so working on a vessel suited exactly what I wanted. My studies were full of opportunities to travel. My first trip was on the famous sailing vessel - "Dar Pomorza."

Before I completed my studies at the age of 24, I had already been on every continent including Antarctica, and to many countries where lots of people could only dream of being. In my last year of studies, I decided to follow my father and work as a navigator on a plane. Before that, I needed one year of practice as a navigator, so I sailed on a ship to the Far East. There, I met my "Japanese brother" – Miki. Due to the political problems in my home country, I decided to stay abroad. My dream about flying on planes was over. As a refugee, I could not get any jobs in my chosen occupation.

After three years, I got my vessel and we sailed. I did not know that the captain was a real drunkard. We were lucky not to sink due to his negligence. In the last harbor, Cardiff, just before coming home, I had to lock the captain in his cabin as the situation became dangerous. The owner of the vessel promised to pay me extra money for bringing the vessel safely to Rotterdam. I kept watch for 80 hours non-stop without sleeping. But when we came home, the owner did not wish to pay me and I had to arrange for arresting the vessel.

Similar situations were happening often, so that is why I really didn't like that job. A hundred hours of work weekly and owners not playing fair made the work unpleasant. I did that job only for money. Then I knew that I had to change something. I started thinking about something else that could bring me money and pleasure.

In 1992, I saw an advertisement that a nutrition company was looking for some people to work with. I signed on as a distributor. My sponsor, an Australian guy, was a good teacher. He knew what was important in the business and how to show where the money was. I did what he told me and signed-up many people. When it turned out that the company was not officially on the market, I lost my team. Two years later, I joined the same nutrition company under a new sponsor, Gerrit, after it had been officially opened. I built my team very fast. I knew the marketing plan and products perfectly well, so it was easy to explain the business.

I've worked with the nutrition company for 18 years. I participated in hundreds of meetings in different countries around the world. I built teams in 24 countries. When the company announced the opening of

Malaysia, I decided to go there. My very good Chinese friend, Jian, helped me to find a five star apartment in Time Square located in the heart of Kuala Lumpur. I rented it from an excellent agent – Paul. On the top there was a beautiful, sixty-meter-long swimming-pool surrounded with palms. Every morning, I swam 1500 meters. While I was swimming, I was talking to myself: "Now, it is time to clear my brain from all problems and negative thoughts." I felt I was free as a bird. After swimming, I went back to my apartment, got dressed in a T-shirt and went into the city. I was full of positive energy. When I was walking, everybody could see that I was a very happy person with an abundance mentality. A big smile was on my face all the time. I spent two to three hours a day doing my business, but I had super results thanks to my mindset on abundance. Every time I handed a flyer out, I just talked to the person and invited them to the next meeting, then signed them up. I signed up people during the days as well as the nights. Once I signed six people at 3:00 am. I became the master of sponsoring.

During my stay in Kuala Lumpur, I flew to the Philippines just for two to three days, but ended up staying for two years instead. With my fiancée Jossie, we opened a nutrition club and a restaurant. I was living a truly happy life. I visited many places there and travelled like a cowboy.

Even though I signed up so many people in my business, nothing much really happened. They were quitting fast. I just didn't know what to do with the new people. What the company taught us was not working at all. After traveling and living in Asian countries including China, Malaysia,Thailand, Philippines, Korea, Macao and Singapore for almost five years, I decided to go back home for a while.

Then I had a dilemma as to what to do next. I liked Asia very much – nice people, good food, nice beaches, smiling faces. An excellent Korean martial arts master was my personal trainer - Mr. Lee. All that made me really happy. I decided to look for a solution how to create income from any place on earth, especially from nice tropical beaches. I started searching the different possibilities on the Internet. I bought several Internet courses. Over four years, I spent over $45,000 on courses and affiliate programs hoping they would help me earn enough money to live where I wanted. Nothing worked. I didn't earn a dime!

Four years ago, my sister took my mother out of her home against her will and moved her to another country. I lost all contact with my mother – even up to now. I decided to stay at my mother's home in case she ever made her way back. I began ignoring things. As a result, I got my water and electricity cut off which meant no Internet. This continued for ten months including over the winter. I had to change course. So I decided to go back to work on vessels. My captain's license had already expired, so it took me several months to make it valid again and it required a lot of money too, which I had to borrow from my brother Janusz.

While I was studying to get myself up-to-date again, my friend sent me an email about a new Internet advertising company. I signed in and started to study how that business worked. It was very simple, so I was happy that I could do it too! It took me only ten minutes a day and I could do it from anywhere on earth. I started to build my team with the best people I knew. I connected some other Internet businesses together and started earning money fast. I also applied for the one-year *Success Principles Personal Coaching Program* with Jack Canfield. I was accepted. After a week or two, my "personal power" was reborn. I made a decision to earn $100,000 in the next 8 months – from scratch and dead broke. My fiancée Jossie took a loan in a bank to support the business. I didn't make $100,000. I made over $87,000 in all my Internet businesses in just eight months. Now I'm on the way to make my first million dollars in the coming year. Before I retire, I will make all my 101 dreams come true.

MY POWERFUL STRATEGIES FOR EFFORTLESS SPONSORING

Many people ask me what I'm really doing to sponsor people so easily. First of all, I love people and I love to help them and make them happy. I like them smiling. That's my biggest secret. My attitude always was, "How can I help somebody?" instead of "What can I get from them?"

I have built my business on a solid foundation. When I meet somebody whom I find is an interesting person, I make an appointment and I decide if this person's dreams are worth my time. I approach people only once. I' m not begging them to join my business. When I talk to people they will join me sooner or later. I just put them on my "no" list and send them a copy of my earnings every Sunday afternoon. I show them my progress. My motto is that I have everything they want and they have nothing that I want. I look for the best people. Treat your business seriously. Explain your business to ten people daily. Employ yourself. Develop and master your skills. Read books every day. Work on your working habits. Your team will do what you do.

Know the numbers and the compensation plan. Control progress every day. I teach my people another way of thinking by showing them exactly where the money is. Keep your business simple. Don't talk too much. Keep people interested it in. Find out what the person really wants and what you can do for them, not what they can do for you. If they are happy, you will be happy as well.

Remember: people do not join your company or your business, they join you. They join you because they see that you can help them solve their problems and make their dreams come true. Don't forget that the fastest way to get rich in life is to solve other people's problems. Before I sign somebody onto my team, I like to meet them personally. I like to know what they are doing, what they like, if they earn enough and if they are happy. If they don't meet my expectations, I just disqualify them.

I also like to bring people to the meetings. The bigger the meeting, the bigger the picture. But before an event, I like to meet them personally. I want to know my business partners. I like to see them, listen to them and know what they are really like. I ask people to write 101 dreams and goals in their lives – without any limitations. While they are doing it, their imagination wakes up and thrives.

You have to develop your own techniques on how to approach people. Remember, you attract people as you are. Do your business honestly and good-heartedly and then people will trust you and join you. You don't need to educate people when you talk about business. What you have to do is to show them your business.

I make it very easy, after asking some "essential" questions, I decide if they qualify or not. If they do, I show them my business and my earnings, and then they ask me to sign them up. Most times, they even don't know the name of the company. They have to trust me first and then join my business.

I'm looking for business partners. I never sign up for a good deal. People don't buy things for price, they buy things for value. If you are dying in the desert – how much will you pay for a bottle of water? Remember! If the value is big, then the price looks small.

You need to find out how to talk to people. Sooner or later, your warm market will run out. The easiest way to get their telephone numbers is to offer them something they need. Learn how to master referrals. Ask people if they know somebody who wants to double their income in the next two months or earn an extra few hundred bucks. You have to focus on getting referrals. You need to learn how to package the story. Show what is most important in your offer for them.

Some people run some advertising and wait for results. I like to go out and meet people. Even in these Internet days, people like to join people, not Internet sites. Become a professional. Don't be upset with failures. They're just a part of every business. Just say, today is another day in the office. It's fun and I love to do what I'm doing and smile!

Have an abundance mentality. It will allow you to let your fears and emotions go away. It will allow you to leave a potential prospect without any fear that you are losing something. There are unlimited prospects around you, so don't worry if anybody joins your business. Such a mindset is critical. People will respect you when they see that you have more than you need. Work for pleasure.

Find a way to get invited into other people's world as a welcomed guest instead of a pest. The best way to do that is to increase your value in the market so that people would like to contact you. You must position yourself as an expert. The best way to increase your value to other people is to educate yourself and learn from experience. People need to know that you can teach them and show them the way to be successful. Become an expert at sponsoring people.

Demonstrate a higher value. If you do not do it, then people will not join you. You must show that you are attractive and that you have something to offer: what they don't have – but would like to have. Stay fit and healthy. Dress clean and fashionably. Relax. Feel comfortable in any situation. Don't forget that people like to see your smile. Show them your positive energy but don't try to impress them. People have to see you as a leader, so speak with confidence. Be the one who leads the conversation.

Follow-up is the real fortune. You are paid for taking orders. You should spend most of your time on follow-up and take as many orders as you can. Become an Alpha leader. They live in an abundance state of mind. They sponsor people effortlessly.

You can put me in different locations and I will do the same thing – even if I have to start from scratch. I can sponsor people anywhere and anytime. I show them how to earn money. When I sponsor one person in my primary business, I will then also sponsor them into another business of mine. I teach them how to earn and how to work as one team. Don't pump your team with motivational calls. Remember, the best motivation is money in the pocket !!

About Zbigniew

Zbigniew "Zbyszek" Kabata was born in 1956 in Warsaw, Poland. He is an entrepreneur, marketing expert, consultant, international coach and mentor, professional speaker and founder of NetWealthTeam, building an empire of multiple income streams.

His father flew in Polish Airlines PLL LOT, the biggest airline company in Poland. He was a World War II veteran, flying on bombers. After the war, he worked with Polish Airlines PLL "LOT" for 38 years. At that time, flying planes in PLL "LOT" was a very privileged job. His mother is a World War II veteran who took very good care of four children. The family earned more than average income, which ensured the children had a good education.

In 1975, Zbyszek attended the Maritime Academy in Gdynia. After his exams, he sailed on the famous sailing vessel "Dar Pomorza." In 1979, he placed 4th in Poland in Judo in student competitions. In 1981, he graduated from the Maritime Academy in Szczecin with the title of M.Sc.Eng. in Maritime Navigation, but decided to stay abroad after graduation due to the introduction of Martial Law in his home country. During Martial Law in Poland, the only option was to stay abroad, so he lived in Holland for 30 years. At the age of 24, he had traveled to all the continents, including Antarctica.

From 1992 to 2011, Zbyszek worked with an American nutrition company as a distributor – building an international team in 24 countries on four continents. Between 2004 and 2008, he spent most of his time in Asia, living mostly in China, Malaysia and the Philippines. One of his happy memories in Asia was that he met his great friend, Mr. Lee – master of Korean martial arts and his personal trainer. Thanks to Mr. Lee, he learned Korean martial arts. In those days, he spent all the money which he had earned on vessels, but learnt a lot. The saying that best describes his experiences at that moment: "If you mess up, then mess up BIG – so you can learn a lot!"

He has a Dutch and Polish Captain's license for sea-going vessels and speaks four languages fluently. Up to this point, he has visited 86 countries around the world.

His MISSION/VISION is to help as many people as possible around the world get what they want. At present, he is planning to go back to Asia while earning multiple income streams from any location on earth and live an abundant life. The biggest reason and inspiration for his need to earn a million dollars this year is to bring his mother back home. He believes in his heart that this book will open the doors of great possibility to help find his mother.

Zbigniew "Zbyszek" can show you: *How you can easily build the wealth and success you desire.* He said, "Your whole experience of living and working will never be the same again after I help you find your inner warrior and liberate the power hidden within you."

If you want to 'SKYROCKET' YOUR BUSINESS, read his easy-to-read book and visit him online at:

www.NetWealthTeam.com
www.ZbyszekKabata.com
Find out more about him at: www.ZbigniewKabata.com

CHAPTER 28

GENIUS IS BORN OF THE NIGHT

BY NOSH MARZBANI

THE PRODUCTIVE HOURS

We underestimate the enormous energy and potential of our properly formatted, sleeping brain. This internal environment is the seedbed for all that we accomplish during waking hours. The magic comes in learning to how to prepare and fertilize that precious soil.

A negative thought invalidates your power, stealing your energy and leaving you vulnerable. That negativity translates all your thoughts, actions and weaknesses into a palpable reality. As Paulo Coelho put it, *"You are what you believe yourself to be."*

So, it becomes all the more crucial that you manage the imagery of your mind, learning how to control not only your present, but also your future, a future that accurately utilizes your potential. Your mind is like a projector into your future; a guidepost that points the way and influences the decisions you make each day. Align yourself with the productive, healthy generator and your future will take care of itself.

How does one generate this healthy thinking? It begins in a space of your brain where old programming is not permitted to exist. You must learn to be present with your breath, in the moment, and able to access that brain space at will. This is where you plant your pre-thought, which yields the fruit referred to as vibration. This vibration sets the rules of the game for your every waking moment, leading you to the inevitability of your desired personal success and maximization of happiness.

We can use the modem of meditation to develop healthy vibration. It permits you to access the deeper states of yourself; answering questions of who you are and what you are born to do. It is here that ultimate success lies, and that pre-thought will sprout, not only to guide your potential energy, but to release you from former negative energy. This is how to establish a new "norm"—a healthy consistency that improves your quality of thought.

What does qualitative thought feel like? It will change the course of your life; your posture, values, thought process and your perspective of anything and everyone who crosses your path. You will no longer use others to assess your value, for it will emanate naturally from within. Remember... you form your own reality, thus when your perception originates from the healthy part of your mind, you will only see success. Think of this as experiencing a wonderful dream, a custom-tailored magical playground that allows each of your dreams to come true. The true wonder is, that it is not relegated to the sleeping you, but the waking, ever-present life you lead. You will only acknowledge the best, in yourself and all that surrounds you.

Action creates vibration and must necessarily be of high quality. Thus, you place yourself in an enviable position; one that has a very high value others will wish to emulate. They will love your energy; it will encourage them to seek the same. You will develop your soul; that indefinable quality that gives you magnetic attraction to people of a like-caliber.

You will learn to value your solitude because your vibration emanates from an authentic place that reflects happiness. This strengthens your resolve in the face of challenge, giving direction to your energy. Your energy will essentially return to you, recharging your soul via the responses of others. You will experience a sense of well-being and positive thinking that fertilizes that birthplace of effective thought, allowing it to flourish and replenish itself. You will feel the essence of true peace of mind.

THE TOOL OF MEDITATION

Sleep is not just hours spent in the non-waking state, but healthy, refreshing and productive sleep allows one to meditate in a way that broadcasts a positive vibration to every cell and organ. You will awaken with a smile on your face and a vibrant energy that brings vitality to your every act during the day.

Learn how to develop pre-thought by meditation; begin with a journal. At bedtime, write everything in your journal that you've thought, done, heard, felt…a complete mind-dump onto its vacant pages. There lies no judgment here, no censorship. It's as if you are taking out the *thought garbage*. Just as you sort through the dated items in your refrigerator and throw them away, sift through the thoughts and events of the day and put anything that doesn't fall into your new thinking pattern on that page. Once you're done, destroy it; by fire, the trash, the garbage disposal; any iconic act that allows you to dispense with it once and for all.

Just as you clean out the refrigerator by wiping the shelves, neutralize the negative whiffs that still ghost your brain by taking a walk. This is a time for appreciation of the simple things and good people in your life, of the things you have to be grateful for. Breathe and tune into your heart, walking joyfully as if on your way to an appointment with a very important person: your best self. Let your excited heart rate push energy throughout your body; recognize and embrace this. Your energy has been purified; you are ready for the next step.

A DOSE OF GRATITUDE

This is when you return to take a warm shower or bath. It is a time where you can reflect on the positive feeling you created while on your walk. What made you feel happy? Was it the stretching, fresh air, breathing, music from your MP3 player? Did you pet the neighbor's dog, admire a blooming rose, look up at the sky and actually *see* it?

Prepare your bed, wear comfortable clothing or nothing at all; and clear your room of all distractions. Spend 3 to 5 minutes meditating on the life you would love to create. This is where you are communicating with your subconscious mind.

Now that you've planted those seeds of gratitude for the beauty and natural peace about you, go to bed and sleep.

Upon waking, you will remember the pleasant aspects that carried you into sleep. Transfer that positive energy into action - start by smiling, stretching, exercising, and nourishing yourself with an awesome breakfast. Improving the quality of your sleep acts as a small lifestyle change, but (it) will redefine your life. Your breathing, level of thinking, health, speech; every vibration within you will change and reflect the positivity you're manifesting.

Do not overlook the need for regulated sleep. You should have an established bedtime and begin preparing for that at least one hour in advance. This is a time for relaxation, embracing your sense of well-being, letting go and reflecting on the abundance that you truly desire. You are thereby establishing healthy vibrations. Use this hour in segments, following these suggestions.

During the first 15 minutes write down everything you wish to dump; all things that could be considered waste. The next 15 minutes should be dedicated to a walk of happiness. This is the time when you generate positive thoughts and upon your return, take a warm shower, and clear the room. Make your bedroom space feel very safe, warm and comfortable. Now invest about 5 to 10 minutes in meditation.

The act of nightly meditation is well supported with conscious visualization, and is a time for simply being, as you would like to be and with the intent to see and feel the life you desire. The goal is to enter into your heart space where you can feel certain and excited, about all the good that is coming to you. It is here that you open up and let every part of your being know that you deserve the life you desire and that you are ready to start living the life of your dreams. Now lie down to sleep. Your sleep will not only be more refreshing, but will exude the vibration you need to propel you to higher enjoyment and achievement during the following day.

Keep in mind that this hour prior to sleep is an hour of preparing to live your best life ever. This will be when you consistently distill the negativity out of your life and focus on the success vibration; your moments of joy, peace, acceptance of yourself, and the life of your dreams.

Many, many people, even those who may appear to be highly successful, are actually leading frantic, stressed lives. They are perpetually dissatisfied; driven to exceed today's reality with tomorrow's possibilities. They use building blocks composed of stress and dissatisfaction, though; thus the outcome can never be enough. The concept of completeness and happiness is an elusive commodity reserved for someone else; they are always looking for different and more.

This hour spent before sleep removes that craving; that competitive poison that always leaves you feeling dissatisfied and inadequate. Now you can enter a state of complete relaxation where you can be at peace and one with yourself.

The key here is consistency as it supports a gradual, but eventually dramatic shift in how you see yourself and how others see you. They will notice, and envy you the sense of self you display. You will be confident, happier, relaxed; you will be at peace and you will feel the stillness behind the action that is taking place constantly in your waking state. This balance and harmony will underscore your every move, bringing new relationships and opportunities into your life. People are attracted to confidence and happiness; that magnetic personality you so often hear attributed to well-known people like John F. Kennedy and Mahatma Gandhi. You will be propelled into a natural state of leadership and influence; not because you manipulated or negotiated your way into it—but simply because it is who you are, or more to the point, who you always were and finally permitted yourself to be.

You will sense that not everyone feels as you do; there will be disturbances in the energy emitted from those about you. The more regularly and effectively you meditate, the less that negativity will be able to affect you. Of all the relationships that are newly added to your life, the one you have with yourself will be the most powerful. Cherish it and spend time with it, drawing from that space. It will be of high value in that you will have come to value yourself. You are unique, precious and valuable. You are important and you have capacities that the world needs. Your abilities can and will make a difference; not only in yourself, but also in those around you. Others will be motivated by your personal celebration of life and your life will consequently become magnificent. You will attract and thus share in the environment of people who most closely share your ideals and strengths; and naturally, there is strength in numbers. You will achieve more than you could possibly imagine.

THE NEW YOU

Developing a relationship with your future self is an important key to success. It will feel like floating in silky warm water; familiar and secure in its supportive atmosphere. Here you may celebrate your gifts and know, as well as love, who you are. When you can see into your future with stillness, calm, absent of judgment or opinion, you will begin to recognize the potential you have previously overlooked. Anything now, is possible. The relationship you are developing with yourself is a space that will allow you to rest and just be present. You can relinquish pretense, lies and prejudice that previously kept you unstable and constantly jockeying for the socially acceptable demeanor you felt you should display. You will lose your own preoccupation with being judgmental, meaning that you can appreciate the people around you, their strengths and contributive potentials.

Perhaps even more uniquely, you will find yourself suspended in your own sense of time. It stretches to permit that which you allow in and shrinks to disregard the wasteful, destructive elements you have been working so hard to banish from your life. It becomes self-perpetuating and you will find as you continue consciously, the gestures of disregarding the negatives will become your automatic response. You will realize that you have reached that space where you always wanted to be; within yourself. It becomes so recognizable that it fills the cells of your body, your eyes; it becomes the newly altered use of your senses.

Success attracts success, but these vibrations of success must be legitimately embedded from within. You cannot pretend your way into this feeling; you cannot understand its power unless you have done the work to achieve it. There is no more room for fear—it has already been vanquished and you need not fear its return. You considered the obstacles and dealt with them in a way that was organic and in time with your inner vibration. Fear and doubt can no longer find a foundation from which to grow in this cleansed, valid inner space you have created.

You are no longer affected by the past; you have set the course of your future and it is based on your heart's desire. As a magnetic pull, it attracts all the good things you have always wanted in your life.

You have become your "best" self; filled with purpose and the light of making the right decisions the first time without hesitancy. You will simply recognize the difference between your personal right and wrong because you are aligned with virtue. Your confidence and your ability to attract the life you love will be based on your own self.

You have created an atmosphere of healing from within. This is a unique energy that you may call upon in times of stress. When you respond to people, situations, stresses in your life, you will respond with power because you will know how to relax. As you relax, the energy will flow outward easily and comfortably; almost as if you are throwing a punch with amazing speed and accuracy, delivering power while being at ease.

THE WARRIOR WITHIN

The heart, mind and body need to be at ease for the warrior spirit inside you to come forth and reveal its true power. As it does so, every ounce of you is filled with confidence and strength. Your entire being will feel well rested, aware and capable of handling whatever challenges you may face. But the warrior must train and develop a healthy productive sleep routine. He does not worry because he expects success and has already prepared the stage thusly. He understands the consistent formula of preparation before sleep that gives him the superior strength needed for massive success.

When you are that best warrior, you are calm, confident, and capable. You understand there are problems and difficulties, but you can now see the solutions that escaped you before. You have prepared well enough to have lightened your emotional step and be calmly responsive in your defense. You now have the routine, and consequently the intent and drive of a true warrior… a warrior worthy of leadership.

About Nosh

Nosh Marzbani is a celebrity expert known for integrating the mind and body. He is a guide to highly creative people that desire deeper levels of balance, harmony and physical energy. He takes his clients on a journey through the unexplored realms of consciousness where he assists them to actualize the dream of their greatest life. Nosh is known for patiently providing holistic systems and tools for inner peace and personal power. By accessing the wellspring of innate intelligence, Nosh openly shares the secrets to effectively maximize the healing potential of the human heart. .

Nosh teaches his patients not only to move towards their dreams, but to go further, faster. He uses the mind body connection in very specific ways, addressing the vital role a healthy, tuned body plays in the journey of both the spiritual and physical.

Nosh teaches that much of the communication and connection which happens in life is translated through body language. How we talk, move, look and the degree of our self confidence, often reflected in our posture, affects the levels of success we can achieve.

Nosh helps people understand their bodies and how achieving their physical potential can directly bring about their highest self. In the process of developing both physical and inner greatness, Nosh Marzbani has been identified and sought out as a Life Improvement coach by celebrities and business executives alike.

Nosh believes that when our bodies perform well; we have the highest amounts of energy to accomplish life goals, while negative self-image destroys progress because, as Nosh states, "You're only hurting yourself."

Nosh Marzbani regularly receives good reviews written by those who have benefitted from his expertise. Nosh's coaching style focuses on addressing the whole person. He gives people the positivity and the encouragement they need to go out and live a life that is truly meaningful – one which is in alignment with making meaningful contributions that are personally fulfilling and valuable to society.

Nosh instructs that serving others is part of being your best self; and the more you give, the more you get in return. Nosh Marzbani's mission is creating powerful people who can go out and make a real difference in the world.

Nosh loves adventure and action sports. He has traveled the world to learn about human nature, music, art and culture. He is a serial entrepreneur and real estate investor who became a millionaire before the age of 30. He graduated with honors as a Master in Asian Medicine. During his educational journey, Nosh became the youngest Assistant

Academic Dean at SAMRA University of Oriental Medicine, as well as the youngest Admissions and Regional Director for Acupuncture Students. He has also won multiple gold medals in martial arts.

To learn more about Nosh, please visit: www.noshmarzbani.com

CHAPTER 29

ENTREPRENEURISM: THE NEW ECONOMY — FEED YOUR POCKETBOOK AND YOUR SOUL

BY NIKKI NITZ

The two biggest issues most people face in life are related to time and money. Most seem to not have enough of either. What if I were to tell you there is one solution to both problems? It is called Entrepreneurism!

How often do you dream of living a better life than you live now? Have you been in a job or owned a business that provides you an income but makes you miserable? How many times have you missed important family events because you spend so many of your hours working? When you do eventually get home from work, you find you have no energy left to spend quality time with your spouse and your children. Hobbies? Who has time for hobbies, right?!?!

For much of my life, I've certainly experienced this. I've learned there is a better way and I want to share it with you! By discovering my passions and my life's purpose, I have been able to design a business that provides me with freedom, fulfills me, supports me financially, and most of all, is fun! It has taken me years to figure this out, and I'm sharing with you so you can achieve the same results more quickly and easily.

For the first 15 years of my career, I job-hopped. I looked at my resume and saw there was a pattern where I changed jobs about every two years. Once I noticed the pattern, I asked myself why? Why was I continually changing employment? For me, it was because the job became boring and mundane. It lost the excitement and the challenge. I also wanted to make a bigger difference but I wasn't in a position of control to make positive changes. Therefore, I'd go searching for the next opportunity. Eventually I discovered I was never going to be happy being an employee because I have entrepreneurship in my blood.

I quit my job at a time when I was living paycheck to paycheck. I started my own consulting business helping entrepreneurs be more profitable in their businesses. A few years later, I was approached by a colleague nearing retirement and was asked if I was interested in purchasing his business that was synergistic with my consulting business. Now I owned two successful businesses but I wasn't fulfilled. I had businesses that were feeding my pocketbook, but not my soul.

A couple of years prior to purchasing my second business, I was introduced to Jack Canfield who many of you will recognize as the co-author of this book as well as all the *Chicken Soup for the Soul*™ books. He is deemed America's Success Coach authoring the book, *The Success Principles*™. For those of us who invest in reading, we all have that **one** book that changed our lives. For me *The Success Principles*™ is this book and my life will forever be better.

Jack has become one of my greatest mentors and I owe him an enormous amount of gratitude. Jack showed me that I could create the business and life of my dreams and this is exactly what I set out to do. You can do it too!

THREE SIMPLE STEPS TO CREATING THE BUSINESS AND LIFE OF YOUR DREAMS

(1). Develop Your MINDSET

Operating a successful business and living your ultimate lifestyle begins with having the right mindset. Many business owners overlook this extremely important step and jump right into step number two –

Motion. This overlook may work in the short-term but will come back to bite you in the long run.

People often get into business doing something they love but do not invest in learning the art of business. This eventually catches up to them and they become so overwhelmed with operating the business they want to throw in the towel and quit. There is hiring and firing to be done, employee conflict to resolve, equipment to repair, and bills continually needing to be paid. They begin working more and more hours yet aren't getting any further ahead. Often times they are getting further and further behind! They don't own a business, they own an expensive J.O.B. This isn't going to be you!

We all have the same 24 hours in the day. How we choose to spend this time makes the difference between a successful person and a non-successful person. It also makes the difference between someone being fulfilled living their ideal life and someone dreading their work and living a disgruntled life.

To own the business of your dreams and to live your ultimate lifestyle, you need to be passionate with what you are spending your time on. If you aren't you will eventually become miserable and your business will likely fail.

How do you know what you are passionate about? Time flies when you are passionate about what you are doing. Hours can go by yet it seems like minutes. When you are not passionate, time drags on. It seems as though the clock is not ticking. When you are passionate you have an excitement within you. It makes you want to jump out of bed every day because you "get to" versus you "have to". Your passion lights a fire within you.

Spend time discovering your life's purpose and clearly understanding the purpose of your business. The two purposes are different. However, to reach the most fulfillment and happiness in life the two need to be in alignment. Your career and business should support the lifestyle you desire. Most people have this backwards. Most make their lifestyle fit around their career instead of determining the life they want to live and having their career support this lifestyle.

We all have a purpose in life. Unfortunately most people are wandering through life aimlessly not knowing what they were brought into this world to do. To discover your life's purpose, identify your unique gifts and talents. What makes you special? What skills do you have that most people don't? What can you do better than most? What motivates and inspires you? Sometimes you can reverse it and look at if from the perspective of what you hate. For example, if you hate seeing abused women then maybe your life's purpose has to do with helping abused women or preventing abuse.

Your business has a purpose of it's own. What is your business set up to accomplish? Why does it function?

In *Start with Why,* Simon Sinek explains that people don't buy *what* you do they buy *why* you do it. People buy what you believe in. In my experience, very few business owners know why they are in business. They know what they do and how they do it, but they don't know the meaning behind their business. To be successful it is your responsibility as the business owner to clearly understand the *why* of your business and communicate it with your team.

To feed your soul you need to be clear on where you want to live and work. Many people sacrifice their desired geographical location for their career. If you do this you will not reach your full potential of happiness because you will always have this desire to have a life somewhere other than where you are.

When looking at it from a business perspective, you need to ask yourself from where do you want to work? For some, a brick and mortar building close to their home is desired. Personally I set the goal for myself several years ago to have my career flexible and mobile. I wanted to be able to work from wherever I choose and have a flexible schedule versus the typical eight-to-five job. I have achieved this goal and essentially my laptop computer is my place of business. My business can go with me wherever I choose to live. It may not be for everyone, but for me this is my ultimate lifestyle.

The final piece to getting your mindset right is to have a plan. Setting out without a plan is a sure way to get lost! As Benjamin Franklin said, "If you fail to plan, you are planning to fail!" Be clear on your destination in life and in your business. What are you ultimately trying to achieve? Once you know this then you can identify the steps you need to take to get you there. You accomplish these steps and this leads you to owning the business you want to own and living the life you want to live. Most importantly enjoy the journey!!

(2). Get into MOTION

Now that you have a clear mindset, you can get into motion. You know what you are after and it's time to go get it! You aren't going to be able to do it alone. You are going to need people to help you. Who makes up your internal team (administrators, managers, staff members)? Who do you want on your external team (attorney, accountant, insurance agent, coaches, mentors, etc.)? The key to having a dream team is for everyone to believe in the purpose of your business and to be motivated and inspired to collectively strive to achieve the mission.

Your business needs to have systems in place so that it can operate with or without you as the owner. Many business owners get trapped in their businesses because their business cannot function without them. This is when you own an expensive job versus a valuable business. When systems are in place and people are properly trained, the systems operate the business versus the owner. This is what frees up your time and allows you to spend time away from your business enjoying other important parts of your life such as your family, friends, travel, and hobbies.

You have your team and systems in place so now you can produce. Your business needs to produce products, services, or both. You need to have something to sell and it can't be just anything. It must be something your market wants. Often, business owners recognize things people *need*, but if they don't *want* them your business will fail. When making purchases, people do not make logical decisions they make emotional decisions.

Now that you have something to sell, you need to promote it. Your market needs to know how valuable your product or service is to them. If people don't know what you have to offer, you aren't going to sell anything!

(3). Manage the MONEY

You've taken the time to work on your mindset and you've gotten into motion. You are passionate about your business and know its purpose. Your business is operating with a motivated team and properly functioning systems; both are producing, people are buying, and this is when the money flows.

Revenues are essential to every successful business. But I need to warn you. The power is in the profit! It is not about how much you earn it is about how much you keep!

Profit is what allows you to reinvest back into your business and repay your debts. Profit is what drives the value of your business and makes it more valuable and salable. When your business is generating profit this is when you can do amazing things philanthropically with your money, and make an even bigger difference in the lives of others.

One of the typical reasons people become business owners is to increase their personal wealth. Yet in my experience this is one of the things many business owners do not achieve. Quite often they are the last ones to get paid and sometimes they have to forego their paycheck all together because there isn't enough money to keep the bills paid. It doesn't have to be, and shouldn't be this way! Once you realize *The Power of Profit*™ and start focusing on generating more of it, you will begin increasing your personal net worth.

By following these three simple steps I am living my ultimate lifestyle. I live in the amazingly beautiful Virgin Islands. I have a business providing education and inspiration to people so they can live an enriched and abundant life full of freedom, finances, fulfillment, and fun! I have a very flexible schedule allowing me to spend my time as I choose. I enjoy what I do for income so much that I spend much of my time on it. The goal is to be so passionate with your income source that it doesn't even feel like "work" and I've achieved this goal. The result is generating inspired income and living an inspired life.

You too can live your ultimate lifestyle through entrepreneurship. First discover what you are passionate about. What would you do for free because you enjoy it so much? Know the purpose of your business. Fill the needs of others while also fulfilling yourself. As my mentor Zig Ziglar says: *You can have everything in life that you want if you will just help enough people get what they want.*

About Nikki

Are you feeling Broke and Busy and wish you were Rich and Relaxed?

Nikki Nitz is committed to helping people create profitable businesses that provide the owners the freedom to live their ultimate lifestyle. Her education and inspiration are helping people live enriched and abundant lives full of freedom, finances, fulfillment, and fun!

Nikki's passion is teaching you the business skills you need to be successful without having to work all those hours. Successful entrepreneurs learn how to get out of the traps that keep most people chained to their business so they spend more time on their family, passions, and hobbies, while efficient systems keep their business running smoothly.

Nikki knows the challenges small business owners and entrepreneurs face and she knows how to turn things around. She teaches *The Power of Profit*™ and how to generate more of it. Profit is what drives the value of your business, increases your personal wealth, and provides you the freedom you are craving.

In her 20+ years as a Certified Public Accountant and business consultant, Nikki has witnessed too many business owners pour years of blood, sweat, and tears into their businesses only to find that when they are ready to sell, they don't own a valuable business. Nikki will guide your business through a re-design that will take you from wondering how you're going to pay next month's bills or cover payroll to efficiently and profitably managing your business.

Through her products and programs, Nikki takes you from *Broke & Busy* to *Rich & Relaxed.*

Invest in your business, your life, your happiness and your future. You deserve to live your ideal life. Nikki will help you take your business to the next level and put you in control of your business and life.

www.NikkiNitz.com

CHAPTER 30

TRANSFORMATIONS FROM THE INSIDE OUT — INSPIRING OTHERS THROUGH YOUR PASSIONS

BY NEEL KANASE, M.D.

Each day we are given the opportunity to impact someone else's life. It may be through the job that we do or the words we say as we go about our busy, chaotic days. For me, I've found that I have the ability to help more people recognize how beautiful they are through a most unexpected way, *which is by building confidence through helping them feel better outwardly*. When I purchased a single laser clinic in 2005, which is now known as American Laser Med Spa, I had no idea how much my passionate desire to help people could be used. Today, I help people with laser-based treatments so they can achieve true confidence and vigorously pursue their pathways to happiness. **This motivated me each and every day**. My work is more than a physical transformation; it is a tool to help people improve their lives.

At times, people underestimate why it is so important to feel good about yourself aesthetically, and to seek out what it takes to increase your confidence so you can give your best to this world. Through my experiences in medicine, I have been able to become a contributor to some of the most beautiful success stories ever—real life transformations that have helped people feel younger, more beautiful, and confident to make the changes they wish to see. The joy that comes from helping the busy mother who wants to spend more time with her children is so rewarding. Seeing how my team and I can assist the busy professional who has big ideas that are being held back by something that can be eliminated is wonderful. Getting to work with someone who has an actual medical condition that stops them from realizing their inner beauty is amazing. These things are the catalysts that keep me remembering how fortunate I am to do what I do, each and every day. *There is no more beautiful transformation than the one that helps peoples' hearts and souls shine through in the life they live.*

THE JOY OF CONTRIBUTING TO LIFE

Born and raised in India, I worked quite hard to become a doctor, something that I had desired to become for quite a long time. Neither the long hours of studying nor the intense schedule were things that held me back, because I realized the value of what a doctor could bring to people's lives and it fit so well with my personality. *I always wanted to be a person who contributed to my environment and the community I lived in through the skills I developed.*

I moved from India, where I ended up in the Texas panhandle, making the old saying true—I wasn't born in Texas, but I got here as soon as I could! It was here that I built my practice in rural medicine, becoming a part of a small community in which I was honored to have the first- hand experience of seeing how much I could help others' lives. Unlike most doctors that you'll find in urban areas, a rural doctor is like a 'country doc', doing quite a bit more. I was the one who worked in ER, dealing with traumas as they came in. When a woman found out she was going to have a child, I was their doctor during that time, working closely with them from prenatal up to delivery and beyond. The connection to other peoples' lives that I felt – when I had the privilege of seeing the same child I helped bring in to the world go from infant to toddler to five-year-old – was incredible.

There were all these wonderful and meaningful things happening around me all the time and each one confirmed why I loved medicine. However, there was also something else happening at the same time, and it was slowly sucking away the joy out of what I had to offer others. I'm talking about paperwork. It's a huge part of the medical profession and someone cannot be a doctor without having a lot of paperwork. This involved more than just completing patients' charts and documenting their files; it also meant that I had to deal with insurance, coding and billing, and a variety of other things—we all understand the tedious nature of bureaucracy and paperwork in our lives. *I quickly realized that I was spending more hours on all that paperwork than helping those I wanted to serve, which was unacceptable to me.* It burnt me out and I knew that I had to create a new plan that would better fit my desires, one that still gave me a medical avenue to bring joy to peoples' lives without having to deal with all the cumbersome details that a rural doctor has to address alone. Basically, *I knew that I was committed to not spending the next thirty to forty years doing more paperwork than people work.*

Through a bit of looking and some good fortune, I came across a wonderful opportunity that had the potential to give me what I was looking for— more people work and less paperwork. A doctor in the area had decided to sell her practice and move to Dallas. It was a laser hair removal clinic and I was immediately drawn to the concept and purchased it. To those who knew me at the time, it seemed like quite an odd jump, but I instantly saw how I could continue to bring value to people through my work, but on terms that would keep me happier, too. From that day on, *my life has been a whirlwind of discovery, helping communities become stronger through building clinics in them* and helping those who want cosmetic adjustments in their outward appearances receive that care – so they have the confidence to do more in their communities, as well as with their personal goals. *Confidence always has been and always will be what people need in order to contribute to life in a joyful and meaningful manner.*

BUILDING COMMUNITIES ONE PERSON AT A TIME

Through purchasing a single clinic to help me transition into a line of medicine that would rejuvenate me and take away the burn-out I'd experienced, an entire world of opportunity opened up for me, all based on this one mission:

I want to make people happy.

When I think about how I will reflect on what I've done in this world fifty years down the road, I know one thing for certain: *I want to evaluate my life and actions and know, without a doubt, that I made a contribution to society and a genuine effort to make things better*. I realize that this is a tall order, but not as daunting as you might believe. **When ideas stem from passion, they are truly easier to bring to life**. Will there be obstacles? Most certainly, but those obstacles never deter you for long. And for me, before long, my single laser hair removal practice became six facilities, which offered more services in cosmetic medicine to help meet the needs of the people in the communities I was working in.

INCREDIBLE STAFF TO OFFER INCREDIBLE CARE

Owning and operating six clinics requires having staff, of course. I take a lot of time ensuring that I find the right people to work for my clinics, not only individuals that have the specific qualifications they may need for their job, but also that carry the same desire that I have to make people happy through what they do. *When I hire someone, it's my first chance to give back to the community that the clinic is in*. I'm providing employment for a person who is looking for it. But this is just the start with that employee. I am also focused on:

- **Giving this employee a chance to support themselves and their family**. I may own the clinics, but running them is a team endeavor. All of our successes are dependent on our combined efforts and my hopes that everyone will deliver the same high results that I do. That's done through training, interaction, and creating a team environment.

- **My employees' financial health**. I have a trust fund set up for financial improvement and credit correction, and retirement, plus a goal that they learn about retirement strategies. This includes a program that I've purchased from Dave Ramsey, a renowned American financial author and educator. I want every one of my employees to retire as a millionaire and I'm thrilled to offer them sources of information. I want to inspire them at a deeper level than just boss to employee.

- **Supporting local charities**. As a person and business man, this is fundamentally important to my practices. The American Med Spa team, as well as me individually, find great rewards in reaching out to organizations in need and supporting them.

During trying times…

Like in all businesses, there are times when there are challenges that must be addressed. In order to keep offering my personal best and never surrendering to my goals regardless of economy or loss of good employees, I think of our 16th President, Abraham Lincoln. He tried many ambitious things many times over and didn't always have success immediately, including failing in two attempts to run a successful business, failing at running for Senate two times, and failing at a Vice Presidential election once. Then he ran for President…and what a difference it made! Thankfully, he never gave up. *It's this type of determination that I like to cultivate in the clinics. Everyone who walks in, whether an employee or client, should walk away a better person.*

It's the heart of the **Seven Core Values** that I am firmly rooted in, which are:

1. Tell the truth.
2. Obsess over customers by being passionate, delivering results, and remembering that "retail is detail."
3. Always educate and learn.
4. Focus on doing one thing and doing it well.
5. Innovate.
6. Think long-term.
7. Be humble.

HELPING CLIENTS FEEL BEAUTIFUL
IS REWARDING WORK

My employees, clients, and I all have a relationship that is dependent upon each other. I have this breadth of knowledge that I use to conduct my business, but I am not the only person that is with a client from beginning to end through their process. Staff is pivotal! However, it is the client transformations that really warm my heart and bring me joy. You truly cannot imagine how powerful it is to see someone's confidence blossom and explode when they feel good about themselves physically. *At times, the seemingly littlest things can deliver the biggest results.*

1. We help clients through a journey.
   Whether it is for six months or two years, we take a journey with our clients through this transformational experience they are undertaking.

It's important that they know we have not only compassion for their situation, but also knowledge and medical expertise to help with their success. Our ability to do this is what helps us retain clients and hear the gratitude about their success stories and the role they feel we played in them.

2. We have a long term relationship with our clients.

By genuinely caring about our clients' lives, we get to know them personally, as well. They become friends. We know when their children are getting married, if they are up for promotions, their charitable work, and are witness to their increasing confidence as their cosmetic procedures are completed. It's an honor for me to walk out into the community that I live in and find friends, not just former clients.

Most of us love a good success story, but from my perspective, there is no more powerful success story than an emotional success story.

I've had several clients in the past that have had Polycystic Ovarian Syndrome (PCOS). The symptoms of this syndrome are male pattern hair, especially on the face; including ears chin line, and upper lip. A condition of this nature can clearly cause self-esteem issues in women and PCOS is a process that is challenging to treat because it stems from high testosterone production in females. For these ladies, even a 40%-50% improvement within six to eight sessions is transformational, compared to 90%-95% for someone without PCOS. This emotional healing is so impactful and it's hard to even attach the proper amount of emotion to it through words. It's the joy in a woman's voice when she says, "This helps make me feel like a woman again; I don't have to use a razor blade or shaving cream on my face. I feel so good!" **These expressions create wonderful memories, reminding me of the power that my staff and I have to help people out in a pretty big way**.

Although rare, the opportunity to work with children is always something that is special and **a reminder of how fragile the developing mind and body is**. Through these opportunities, it's a wonderful way to help build up the emotional strength of a child through some simple procedures that will take a relatively short amount of time, but create the type of confidence and increased self esteem that will last a lifetime.

And equally joyful is the chance to meet people who have already gone through an entire career of caring for, nurturing, and tending to everyone else's needs by giving of themselves endlessly as a teacher, parent, or professional of some sort. They are finally willing to take the time to do something for themselves, often saying, "I've lived for everybody else, but now it's time to do something just for me." They're happy and excited, and it's contagious—not just in the office, but in the community that they go out into with a refreshed, rejuvenated attitude.

EACH OPPORTUNITY IS A SPECIAL CHANCE

There is not a person that I could meet in this world that I don't feel needs help of some sort. I'm not just talking about offering a service through the clinic. Rather, I am referring to relaying what I stand for and what I want to represent in this world. I'm constantly inspired and driven by the challenge to help people think of themselves more positively, because that is where the most amazing transformations can take place.

I may be helping someone deal with what concerns him or her externally, but its true value comes from what happens when they realize that they can walk confidently into any situation. That's when someone can become a contributor to their community and world.

About Dr. Neel

Since 2005, Neel Kanase, M.D. has been the owner of American Laser Med Spa. He started out with one clinic and now has six clinics total, five located throughout Texas and one in New Mexico, with over twenty-five employees. It's through this exciting avenue of cosmetic medicine that he's found his home and calling, helping clients find more self-confidence to do what they love to do best.

After moving from India in 1995 with his degree in Medicine and Surgery (M.D.), which he received from the University of Bombay, Grant Medical College, Neel moved to Texas and made his home in the panhandle. There he attended Texas Tech University to receive his Master of Science Degree in Food and Nutrition, and then completed his Residency in Family Medicine at Texas Tech University, and was given prestigious recognition by his colleagues as:

- Outstanding First Year Resident (1998-1999)
- Outstanding Resident Teacher (1999-2000)
- Resident's Choice Award (2000-2001)
- Resident Teacher Award (2000-2001)
- Outstanding Resident of the Year Award (2000-2001)

. . . as well as being named Chief Resident for the Texas Tech University Health Sciences Centers Family Medicine Residency Program.

Neel has always placed great value on education and constant improvement, which is why he has attended Harvard Medical School annually for Laser and Aesthetic Skin Therapy CME training since 2009. He is licensed to practice medicine in Texas and New Mexico. His professional affiliations for cosmetic medicine are:

- Fellow with the American Society of Laser Medicine and Surgery (ASLMS)
- Founding Member of Goldman Circle American Society of Laser Medicine and Surgery (ASLMS)
- Member of the American Medical Association and the Texas Medical Association
- Member of the Botox Cosmetic Physician Network

Neel's family in India was from the middle class, but he was always inspired by his parents desire to sacrifice whatever they could to help him and his two siblings achieve more. From early on, this type of attention to creating a better child, and therefore a better world, has been a concept that Neel has embraced in everything he has pursued. It also taught him the value of never backing away from a goal, even if it's driven from fear. One of these fears was of heights. He started steps to conquer it by making several attempts to sky dive, but the weather never got him off the ground. Eventually, Neel sought out a different route to overcome this fear and received his pilot's license, and also found an exciting opportunity by becoming an Aviation Medical Examiner for the FAA from 2003-2008.

Aside from his family, education is another thing that has always inspired Neel and he's known to make the annual trek to Warren Buffet's shareholders meeting so he can learn from him about both business and fortune.

For inspiration, Neel is passionate about the inspirational teachings of Mahatma Gandhi. It's this mindset that has really guided Neel in his passions for creating stronger communities with involved, caring citizens.

If you'd like more information about Dr. Neel Kanase, you may contact him at:
Tel. (806) 333-7878
Email him at: neel@americanlaser-medspa.com
Or visit his website: www.AmericanLaserMedSpa.com.

CHAPTER 31

YOUR LIFE IN THE HEADLINES —EVERY HUMAN'S POWER TO CREATE

BY SHIRLEY RICHARD

For my parents, Julienne and François, who gave me wings.

In the spring of 1959, my mother, Julienne, gave birth to me at home following several hours of labour. After all, something so beautiful takes a bit of time, one must apply herself.

And *voila!* The doctor held in his arms her latest bundle of joy, hot off the press:

"Congratulations Mrs. Richard, it's a girl..." To which, my mother replied: "YUCK! She's an ugly little thing!"

I'm guessing this reaction was fueled by not only surprise, but also fatigue.

Nonetheless, those were her exact words upon seeing me. It scarred me.... for life... Kidding! I completely understand why my mother was a tad disappointed after my birth.

Apparently I was covered in birthmarks: one smack dab on my lip, a large red birthmark on my right arm, another huge marking on my thigh which, to this day, has left a scar, and a final one, on my *derrière*. For those of you who wonder about that final one, we'll have to leave it up to your imagination and move along.

Following this momentous event, the entire brood, dutiful Catholics that they were, attended my baptism:

"Have you chosen a name for the child?" Let's just say that my mom had to do a little finagling to get her way. According to our priest, since there were no saints named Shirley, she couldn't possibly give me that name. Even so, my mother had the final word. She told our priest that I would not disappoint and that I would become the first ever: "Saint-Shirley-of-Portneuf, pray for us...."

So here I am, with you in all of my sainthood and modesty, to bestow upon you, dear readers, the Good News. Here it is: we are all potential Creators. WE control our lives. We are the primary stakeholder, the executive producer of our very own movie.

In life, much like on stage, you can create your own scenario, along with whatever role you wish to play. Your life in the headlines. If you enjoy what you do, if you love who you are, that's fantastic, job well done!

I have faith in life and that's how I've learned to have confidence in ME. I believe that I am worthy and that I deserve the very best. We ALL deserve the best.

We are all worthy of the most pleasant, beautiful and rewarding scenarios. What does it mean necessarily? . . . Your life in the headlines.

First and foremost, it means that you have a life! Thank goodness, that's a relief. Secondly, you have a head and your very own mind. That's even better! Because as much as having a life is fantastic, what good is it if we can't be in command of our own minds. It's not the best scenario that's for sure! We'd be on cruise control, moving along haphazardly, like zombies.

Add your name to that headline, be part of the main program, YOU in big bold letters, just like in children's drawings. Have you ever noticed that children always draw larger than life versions of themselves and if there's any space left on the page, they'll add mom or dad, the family dog, maybe even a kid brother. But as we get older, we seem to shrink that image, almost to the point of disappearing. Let's face it, as we grow older we're already shriveling, do we really need to disappear all together?

As of now, as of this very moment, take up as much space as you can. After all, this is your script, your headline, your life!

Not only are YOU the headliner, but you are living and breathing in YOUR scenario, no one else's. And the great news is that you have a choice, as of right now, to reinvent or re-adjust that scenario – any way you want. Isn't that great? You can even edit everything yourself. Periods of your life that were dull, un-enjoyable, those you would rather forget – cut them out! Go ahead, live it up! PRESS DELETE. You're in charge. Think about it! At any moment, we can choose what we create.

After numerous years of working as an actress and an entertainer, I suddenly wanted to make changes in my life. I wanted to reprise my role as a businesswoman and jump back into the pharmaceutical industry. And taking on a role means putting on a costume, becoming a character; it's an entire production. As for the script, we can improvise.

The same things apply to your life. Summertime, it is mid-July and 30 degrees outside. I am on holiday, but I'm donning my corporate attire. I'm not wearing shorts and a t-shirt. Even in this sweltering heat, I'm putting all of the odds on my side in order to get that coveted corporate position. I head out to the employment center and polish up my CV.

Before interviews I practice a little self-coaching in front of the mirror and, of course, I bring my wardrobe up to date: goodbye practical Crocs, hello fashionable heels! I acted and dressed like I already had the job I wanted. I was fully committed, I had signed a contract with myself! That's commitment, and it makes a world of difference in getting what you actually want. Simply put, by playing the game, I got the job I wanted and in very little time. I attracted it like a magnet. Then, after I had worked for the same company for a few years - and without any heads-up - I was asked to attend a conference call. The mood was as intense as my boss's tone when he announced that two of my colleagues had been let go, and that I . . . I was being assigned a new territory.

I took a deep breath and thought myself lucky to have survived the company's downsizing. If they kept me on, then it meant that I was good at my job. I had a choice: either cry over spilled milk and complain about these changes or welcome this new challenge with enthusiasm and a renewed sense of confidence. I chose option two.

A new sales territory! I was starting over; this was a beginning instead of an ending. It's as though I was rejuvenated. A new world was opening up to me! How lucky was I? I had a brand new playground with which I rediscovered my vitality, my creativity, instead of being on auto-pilot like I was before. The next day, I met with my Director and told him: You know what? Not only do I embrace this change, but I'm going to meet my biggest challenge yet: I will be named the best sales representative of the year !

WOW!

I had three paramount motivations. The first: show my boss that he had made the right choice in keeping me on; the second: I was going to increase sales in my new territory; and the third: I was going to prove that the author of my latest bedside read was correct. To have an opportunity to be the principal actor in my own scenario, to be the headliner! I was reading a book by Jack Canfield, who wrote about success, intentions, and visualization.

Never before had I aspired to receive the title of best sales rep. I was happy just moving along and working, period. But now, I wanted to test something out.

I had written this affirmation in my notebook:
> "Get up on stage and receive a trophy for best sales representative of the year."

Throughout the year, I made a few adjustments to my affirmation. Being up on stage wasn't a crucial factor. What I wanted the most was that trophy. That's all! So I scratched out 'Get up on stage' and my sentence metamorphosed into:
> "I am holding the trophy for best sales rep in my hands, I can feel its weight, my hands are sweaty and I am both moved and extremely proud."

What I did was add emotions and feelings so that my affirmation wasn't just words, but also feelings and a sense of accomplishment. Every time I read that intention or said it out loud, the law of attraction seemed to work a little bit more, because I was living that moment as though

I was already there, with a great deal of emotions and all five senses. Although I was convinced and determined to live that moment, my body, unfortunately, didn't get the memo. That very same year I had some serious health issues. Come Christmas, the only gift I asked for was that everything be resolved quickly. Yep! I place daily orders with the Universe! So, I was operated on January 24th. Exactly one month after my request. Now THAT is service!

Nonetheless, I was unable to attend our annual meeting being held in Dublin. Nothing against the Irish, but when you get a surgery date, you don't hesitate, you go! Three days after leaving the hospital, I was home, catching up on some emails: and what do we have here? It's an email from the company President.

He informed me that I had won the award for best sales rep of the year... with everything that had been going on health-wise, I had completely forgotten my affirmation.

A few weeks later, I received my trophy at home. You see, I wasn't able to go to Dublin, I wasn't able to get up on that stage, but that trophy was in my hands.

I felt its weight, my hands were sweaty. I was moved and, most importantly, I was proud of myself! When I read my notes following that tiny but mighty edit, I understood the importance of choosing the right words when writing down my dreams and my goals.

It also dawned on me that visualization works. You were right Jack! Following this, I had to travel to Berlin for work.

I had sworn that I would never set foot in Germany. Why you ask? Well, because I associated Germany with the Second World War. Where did this fear come from? My mother. Yep, the truth is exposed, Julienne was not perfect. Before putting us to bed, she would read us the same stories over and over. There was: Uncle Percy. That's the story of my mom's real-life uncle who, as a soldier, was held as a prisoner by the Japanese for four years. ''Cute'' story, isn't it? A bit of a change-up from Snow White. She would tell us about all of the horrible details and misery that he lived through in those work camps.

But the icing on the cake was *das Sahnehäubchen*, which was Anne Frank's diary. Are you familiar with this story? It tells the story of a young Jewish girl that hid with her entire family in order to escape the Nazis during the Second World War. After this, Julienne would always say: OK, good night! Sweet dreams! I must have been 4 or 5 years old. My imagination was so strong, almost realistic. I lived through every scene in my mind.

All of this was enough to be scared stiff about Germany and Japan. Finally, I took control, faced my fear and I traveled to Berlin.

But I didn't take any chances. I dyed my hair blond just before leaving. True story, no joke. I even visited the Holocaust museum – which was my Fort Boyard. I ended up enjoying a beautiful trip meeting with great people. If what we experience in our imagination: feelings and fears that are the same as in real life, then we might as well create beautiful scenarios in our heads.

Imagine a day when you're not feeling super positive, to put it bluntly, everything sucks...here is a simple exercise that you can do first thing in the morning.

Just commit to being happy, even if it seems difficult. Visualize your perfect day, even if it's off to a rough start. Bottom line: all you need to do is want it to change. Sometimes it seems easier to stay miserable, we prefer staying in our little cozy spot, sitting on our sofa and stewing. Basically, you're asking the Universe for things to go well.

Think about it. When a child wakes up in the morning, all he wants to do is be happy and play! That's his game plan. He's setting his GPS to FUN. Why couldn't it be the same for us? Can we have some fun? Every morning I ask for a gift and I receive one every day. Santa Claus is part of my life 365 days a year. You have to be open in order to receive...Ask yourselves these questions? Do I accept happiness? Do I accept gifts? Or promotions? Yes? The Universe will bring these to you. The people that I meet are there for a reason, to help me reach my goals and to put my life in the headlines. I love it. Every single person I meet is there for me! They're all part of the movie of my life, either as lead characters, silent roles or even extras. . . And, you too, dear readers, are now a part of my scenario, the movie of my life, and you are playing a beautiful supporting role.

Take home message:

I often get asked about my daily routine:

- I work at controlling my thoughts.
- I am thankful and I appreciate everything I have, everything that is on my path.
- I create affirmations, my intentions, and my objectives.
- I ask, I ask and I ask: Never be afraid to ask. Ask until you get what you want, just like kids do!
- I sincerely believe that I will receive.

Guess what?

- I receive, I receive, and I receive!
- I am thankful, and . . . I try my best to be in the moment.

I can tell you that my life is beautiful: full of great wonders.

You are creators, loving beings, passionate beings. Everything that surrounds you is part of your production and is there for your ultimate good and that of those closest to you. You can be who you truly want to be and offer your most precious gift to the world: YOU. Write your name in the headlines: You . . . on the main program.

About Shirley

Shirley Richard is a leadership and life coach, speaker and author. She has always been driven by a strong desire for self-realization and has always felt this constant need to challenge and push herself beyond her limits. Nourished by extensive reading on personal growth literature, she starts listening to her own intuitions and finds the power to make her dreams become a reality.

She holds a Bachelor's degree in Administration with honors in Marketing from Bishop's University, and as a new graduate, she first worked as a representative in the pharmaceutical industry in which she was very successful.

A few years later, she feels an urgent need to express her own creativity even more. One of her most cherished dreams has to be fulfilled. She decides to become an actress. Leaving behind the pharmaceutical industry, she then flies to New York City and gets enrolled at the famous Lee Strasberg Theatre Institute.

Back to Montreal, and for the next fifteen years, she successfully finds work as an actress.

She gets involved in hosting more than 600 special events (comedy shows, conferences, award ceremonies, annual meetings) for major companies. She gets cast in many TV commercials and corporate videos .

Shirley then founded her own theatre company. Inspired by the utmost importance of building self-esteem, she produces and write her first solo show to be performed in schools and cultural centers to thousands of children across the province of Quebec.

After the birth of her first son, she gets back to the pharmaceutical industry but in a different way. She coaches new representatives and uses her facilitating and motivational skills in order to create trustful and constructive links with them. All her regional and national incentive meetings lectures create a major impact. Her charisma, her passion and *"joie de vivre"* push her to motivate her colleagues. She then discovers herself having that special gift for making people feel good about themselves.

Shirley is passionate about inspiring others to uncover their purpose, stretch beyond their self-imposed limits and experience the greatness that is within them. She wants to share her experiences so that others can join her in this wonderful adventure called our life . . . so they can become the creator, author, and STAR of their own life.

She then takes coaching classes in the States and becomes an accredited leadership and life coach from Coach For Life, Orlando. She founded her own company "Cré/Action" that offers personalized coaching services.

Votre Vie en Tête D'affiche (Your life in the headlines) is the title of her new conference on the utmost importance of creating and living one's own life to its fullest.

Shirley Richard is a member of the International Coaching Federation and a member of l'Union des Artistes.

She now lives north-east of Montreal.

For more information : www.shirleyrichard.com

CHAPTER 32

THE TRUTH IN CREDIT CARD PROCESSING!

BY KEVIN HODES

Ok, you have done your research and you think you have the best deal for accepting credit cards. You have signed up, you are processing for a few months and you realize when you look over your statement that it's not what you were told, or thought it would be. Well, let me tell you, you are not alone.

There are a few factors to look for when considering credit card processing. But first please stop doing the following:

- Stop taking the calls from telemarketers! There is no such thing as wholesale pricing and none of these people are with Visa or MasterCard. But it sure does sound good, doesn't it?

- Stop signing up with anyone that just walks in off the street! Cold calling representatives typically are still new to the industry. They most likely don't have the knowledge and or experience to possibly set you up correctly. Ever hear, let me call my manager to see if we can get you a better deal? They are calling in to get advice on what to do next. Next thing you know, you are speaking with the hard closing manager.

- Stop calling organizations that send you post cards and letters in the mail! These are your typical bait and switch teaser rates. And where are these companies anyway?

Now that we covered the slimy part of credit card processing, and I have your attention, there are two components of credit card processing, price and service. It is hard to get both, but when you do, latch onto that company or salesperson because they are few and far between. Anyone can undercut another organization for a penny here or there, but if there is no service, who are you calling when you have a problem. Or you can have the best service but the worst price. Have you ever heard the saying "Price, Quality, or Service? Choose Two"? What if I told you that you can have all three? With the knowledge you are about to gain and a little research, you can get Price, Quality, and Service.

So, how do you get the best deal? First, look for an organization that has been referred to you from another business owner that you know. Companies that have been around a long time and have built their clientele from mostly all referrals, probably means that they are doing something right. If you have been in business for a few years, you most likely have been burned already with promises from shady salespeople. Remember this, just like you, there are experts in all fields of business and not all organizations are the same even though they may offer the same product.

Find a Certified Payment Professional. Yes, there is such a person. There is a registry and you can search for someone in your area. Or, work with a credit card processor that has been endorsed by an association that you pay dues to. That organization has done extensive research to make sure you are getting the best deal and won't be taken advantage of.

FYI, banks don't process credit cards anymore. They have contracts with processors and can have as much as a 40% markup. Banks are great at offering a checking account, maybe a mortgage, or giving a bank loan every once in a while, but they just don't process credit cards anymore. Why would you work with your bank anyway? Do you think they are going to give you great service because you deposit monies in their bank? They will refer you to the 800 number when you need help. They can't even see your merchant account at the branch, so how are they going to help you? They will be happy to take your deposit if you have one or pay that mortgage. Did you know that when you are sitting with the banker that they receive points or bonuses that can equal as much as $500 just for referring you to other services within the bank, specifically the credit card processing. So who are they helping, you or themselves? It's really not the bankers' fault; it's what the big banks teach them to do.

Beware of software providers or distributors that say they have a preferred vendor. Or they will give you a discounted price on the product you are buying if you use their preferred vendor to process your credit cards. Ever wonder why they do that? The software organization or distributor will then make a piece of the action. Typically, it's a sizable markup. 40% more than you would pay if you were with a company that is thinking about your profit instead of their own. This is now a source of income and they have locked you in so you can never switch, although they always guarantee you have the best deal.

But, I am not sure how paying 40% more is the best deal? Work with an organization that doesn't lock you into using their preferred vendor! It opens the door for competition and it keeps everyone honest. You should be able to do your research, negotiate, and switch when you want. Yes, research the company that you are considering. Preferred doesn't always mean it's in your best interest. In this case, preferred really means what is in their best interest.

Another important factor, PCI DSS is real! Or better known as, The Payment Card Industry Data Security Standard. And, if you don't get compliant, the processors will charge you a monthly noncompliance fee. You should be leery of your current, or any future processor, if they say that they won't charge you or say you don't have to become compliant. Everyone has to get compliant and there are systems in place that cost money to be there to help you with this process. You can Google PCI DSS and see for yourself how important it is to get complaint. Remember you're a consumer as well and this is to help stop fraud.

A few years ago, a long-time customer called me and told me to get down there right away. I was happy to show up as I always do and he and his wife proceeded with letting me know that we had been charging them more than they should have been paying for years. I was shocked, because we are aggressively priced so our customers aren't paying more than they should. They stated that this very nice person had just left and was from Visa and MasterCard and said they needed new credit card equipment for $59 per month and they would save thousands of dollars the moment they switched to this wholesale pricing through the company represented. They handed me the new offer to review. First of all, I stated, you don't need new equipment and if you do, we would upgrade it at our cost, not yours. Spending $59 per month for a 48-month, non-cancelable lease is not necessary. Never lease a credit card machine. Companies that care about you and not themselves will offer you equipment to use for as long as you are a customer. If your current processor doesn't do that, find one that does.

I continued to review and stated, "The new rates being offered would also increase your fees 40%. You will now be leasing a credit card machine that we have always provided at our cost, and you will pay more in processing fees every month." They said that they have it in writing that there will be a guarantee of savings from this nice person and they said we need this new equipment because it's out of compliance. Fast forward 2 years, I received a call and they said they made a terrible mistake and needed help. They realized several months after moving away from us, that they were paying 50% more in fees and called the company that signed them up. The nice person that had signed them up was no longer with the company, and they cannot return the non-cancelable 48-month leased credit card machine. Several months pass and they were called upon by another company on the phone that said they can fix all their issues and just happened to be in the area. This new nice person also offered lower rates and said they needed a new credit card machine that would work with a special system that no one else offered. I figured out that these new rates didn't change and the new credit card machine was proprietary and was another 48 month non-cancelable lease. At this point they were frantic and that's why they called me.

I gave them some advice and they are back working with us. This is a true story of one of our customers being taken advantage of. I was so disappointed that someone in my industry had taken advantage of a business owner in this way that I drove to the address on the business card of the second company. It was a fictitious address. This happens every day to business owners all over the country looking for a better deal. It is important to know that most processors will meet or beat any deal you receive as long as it's not a bait and switch. There are professionals in all fields of business. Some are better than others. If you don't have your very own professional credit card person, you may be paying more than you should and may not be receiving the service you deserve. Or worse, you may think all of the people in credit card processing are all the same. I can honestly say there are good people in credit card processing; they are just harder to find.

Now, for the part you have been really waiting for. How do I get the best rates? First, stop shopping by rate! That sounds crazy doesn't it? Well, when you shop by rate, you may get a lower rate but other fees will be charged elsewhere to make up the difference. It's a numbers game and you will always lose with this buying technique. Ok, here is a secret I want you to know. Take your total fees deducted and divide that into your total credit cards processed. This will give you your aggregate rate. The factors of your aggregate increasing and decreasing monthly will depend on how you accept and process credit cards: Swiped, over the phone, Internet, average ticket and what type of cards you receive. Swiped will be the most cost effective. Internet and hand keyed are typically the most expensive. To keep your aggregate low, you need to work with a company that agrees to the interchange pricing model. Interchange is the cost the card issuer has established for that exact credit card.

There are 100's of these different rates and they range from .05% to 2.95%. But, if you have interchange it will hit the network and you will always get the best price for that exact card type no matter if you swipe, hand key or it is processed on your web site. Stay clear of tiered or bundled rate structures. Tiered and bundled rates may make it easier for you to understand the fees, but is not cost effective for you. In this debit card rate scenario, a tiered rate was 1.59% and the interchange rate was .05%, so why would you want to be on tiered? If your bundled rate was 2.75% and the interchange rate was .05%, why would you want a bundled rate?

In the past, the Interchange pricing model has been reserved for large national merchants. It is now available to you and is by far the fairest pricing model. In this pricing model, interchange and assessments are passed directly to the merchant, with a separate fee added for profit. The merchant always knows where the actual profit is. There are no hidden fees or surprises. Interchange is always the way to go, you don't want to be on the tiered or bundled rates.

After you have met or spoken with that new individual and/or new company, get on the Internet and do a Google search of that company.

Go to the BBB and find out if they have complaints. Seriously, when it comes to your money, DO YOUR RESEARCH!!

About Kevin

As owner and founder of Swypit, Kevin Hodes prides himself on bringing honesty and integrity to what he considers, the "slimy world of credit card processing." A former chef aboard luxury yachts, his craft brought him into contact with business professionals, dignitaries and politicians, enabling him to develop "street smarts of business super highways." Intrigued, Hodes turned from the galley to launching a business consulting firm; a move that eventually led him to the world of credit card processing.

Hodes is quoted as saying, "I got into sales, but I brought my food service savviness of making things incredibly awesome all the time," he said. "I found myself a little niche in the business—taking care of customers."

The end result has melded his expertise and personal integrity. Hodes' company, Swypit, offers next generation electronic payment processing solutions, combined with world-class service, price and leading edge technology. Swypit is the endorsed merchant services provider for the Southwest Carwash Association, Texas Tire Dealers Association and numerous nationwide franchises and Chambers of Commerce. In addition to card acceptance services, Swypit offers businesses free credit card terminals and discounted point of sale systems capable of managing inventory and payroll, gift cards as well as cash advance services. Kevin's company focuses on providing exemplary customer support in an industry that is rife with third party providers, who are often more intent upon selling equipment than providing an effective solution for businesses, small to large.

As a Certified Payment Professional, Kevin Hodes has demonstrated the necessary knowledge and skills required to perform competently in today's complex electronic payments environment. This ETA Certified Payments Professional Program (ETA CPP) recognizes that effective merchant service providers must provide not only a broad range of knowledge of the industry, but demonstrate mastery of sales, pricing and interchange, business process, operations and workflow, products and solutions, risk and regulatory compliance and security matters. The ETA is an international trade association representing more than 500 companies that offer electronic transaction processing products and services. Their mission is to advance the payments industry profession by providing leadership through education, advocacy and the exchange of information.

As an individual, Kevin is a Planning and Zoning Commissioner in one of the fastest growing cities in America. He is a board member of the Frisco Chamber of Commerce and The American Fallen Soldiers Project. He is active in community foundations and events including the Boy Scouts of America, Eagle Gymnastics Academy, Donnie Nelson's Texas Legends Military Night Sponsor, Frisco Citizen's Fire and Police Academies, Wipe Out Kids Cancer, Young Entrepreneurs Academy and an alumni of Leadership Frisco. With regard to his impressive dedication to the community, Hodes says, "I believe that you need to give back. If you don't give to the community, then you shouldn't even be in business." Kevin's attitude has proven to be a cornerstone philosophy of his character and is ultimately responsible for the enormous success of his company.

You may obtain further information about Frisco, Texas-based Swypit by visiting the website: www.swypit.com
or by calling: 1-877-379-9748.

CHAPTER 33

OUT OF THE BOX, INTO THE LIGHT

BY LIZ SHARTEL

"Hey, I'll go with you," I heard myself saying to a few college friends as we walked out of our favorite restaurant. [That spur-of-the-moment choice I made would prove to be pivotal in my life.]

We jumped into an old VW van and embarked on the mission of collecting aluminum cans for a campus philanthropy project. The endeavor took us many miles away from town, and by the time the back of the vehicle was loaded down with our accumulation, it was quite late.

While traveling back, the driver fell asleep at the wheel, the van went shooting off the side of the road, increasing in speed as it barreled down a large hill, and ultimately smacked into a cement wall/culvert.

Needless to say, the crash was devastating. My two friends in the front were killed on impact and the three of us in the back barely survived, as the vehicle caught on fire and burst into flames just moments after we were able to exit. I remember the panic I felt when my coat began to burn, and when I fully believed I was not going to survive.

For weeks after, lying in a hospital bed unable to move from the severe blow my back incurred, I had plenty of time to think, grieve the loss of my friends, thank God I was still alive, and reflect on my life's direction, in general.

In the ensuing months of rehab and physical therapy in order to walk again, something within me started to take hold — a desire to live my life with clarity around what I truly wanted to do. I felt I had been given a second chance at life, and I was rooted in gratitude.

When I returned to school, I changed my major immediately. A newfound love for photography and writing sprang from me, and I spent countless hours in the darkroom developing film, and writing for the school paper.

When I was in elementary school and painfully shy (with a substantial stutter to go along with it), my Mom would push me to go outside my comfort zone....way outside! I could barely get up the nerve to say hello to a stranger, and yet found myself coerced onto a large stage at a local talent show – dressed up like a nun, playing the ukulele, and singing "Dominique, nique, nique!" She made me take diving and tennis lessons, French tutoring, a LOT more ukulele lessons and, of course, speech therapy for my stutter. Although uncomfortable at the time, I realize now what a gift she was giving me!

After the car accident, early conditioning kicking in, I found I consistently pushed myself out of my current comfort zone. I decided to run for Student Senate, and I remember being physically sick on the day the election tallies were to be publicized in the school paper, fearing I would only get a handful of votes, for all the (my) world to see. To my surprise, I got it! I was appointed to the Commission for the Status of Women also, and I was totally in my element.

I made myself take a horseback riding class to get over my fear of horses (which didn't happen), but I did pass the course (barely). I joined a competitive diving team, and played short-stop on the All-University Championship softball team. (Thanks Dad, for all the hours you played catch with me in the backyard!)

One day while strolling through the Student Union I happened to notice a bulletin board flyer, offering a workshop on interviewing techniques. Bingo! Just what I needed before graduation, I thought. Albeit painful to watch (I was videotaped during mock interviews), it was hands-down one of the best things I did for myself during my college career. This was a life-skill I could take out of the classroom, and into real life. It served me greatly, and I really enjoyed seeing how many job offers I could get.

I started in a management training program with Southwestern Bell/ AT&T in Dallas, Texas, in the old "Plant" Department, and found myself climbing 30 foot poles (with only a belt and gavs strapped to my boots) when my position at the time was Installation Foreman.

More challenging than that, however, I subsequently worked for Dale Carnegie, and was stretching my comfort zone with public speaking, memory techniques, and sales. I've heard it said before that when you go out on a limb, where the branches are thin, it's scary – but that is where the fruit is. To this day I use the practical skills I acquired at Dale Carnegie – logging into memory a variety of lists, bullet points to a presentation, and name recall.

The value of learning specific life-skills outside of the mainstream, educational box was made obvious to me.

What wasn't so obvious to me, as it turned out some years later, was the fact that I was in a box when it came to my marriage and family life. Having been raised in a very traditional home, with traditional values, I was surprised one morning when I heard the front door slam – right after my husband left the house – and right before he called out, "Grow up!" Ouch! He was leaving me for another woman, about which I was clueless.

The divorce was very difficult and drawn out. I found it to be especially hard because I loved being a stay-at-home Mom, and always tried to create the most fun, happy childhood possible for the kids. I struggled greatly when I saw them hurting, and I felt like everything I worked for, over the course of 17 years of marriage and 13 years of parenting, blew up in my face.

Then one day, during the worst part of my divorce, I was walking aimlessly around a bookstore when, for some reason, I was completely drawn to a book called *A Thousand Names for Joy*. I had never heard of it but was so led to read the book that I remember looking up and saying to the universe, "Ok, I'll buy it!" Once home, I could not put it down. . . could not stop absorbing it. The author was Byron Katie, and it was her commentary on the 81 chapters of the Tao de Chang, which I also had never heard of before.

It was mentioned in the back of Byron Katie's book that she offered a "School for the Work." I immediately decided to attend the nine-day program, and it proved to be life-changing for me. Now, over ten years later, I consistently use her simple, powerful inquiry process she calls "The Work." It is one of the most impacting tools I have, and when seemingly bad things happen now, I can see the good, the silver linings, and the blessings in them. I can accept reality and "love what is," allowing people and situations their freedom to experience their journeys without judgment.

Looking back on it now, I see that, before my divorce, I had been very rigid in my thinking that our family life needed to look a very certain way: much like the Ozzie and Harriet Show, or a Norman Rockwell painting.

And by doing The Work, I discovered that not only was it OK that my kids did not have a cookie-cutter, "normal," ordinary life – but it was EXTRAordinary; in fact, my kids ARE extraordinary as a result of trying, challenging times. They orchestrated and then embarked on their own paths – one going to a boarding school, one leaving high school early to start college, and one going to Lockheed Martin every week after school. My daughter had an interesting observation when she once said, "I think the crack in the family let the light in." I greatly admire Libby, Shelby, and Luke for their individual uniqueness, intellect, and creativity.

As I started to climb out of the stiff, tightly-contained box I had been in, I became hungry to seek out and learn from enlightened souls, and so started my quest. I enrolled in Jack Canfield's *Breakthrough to Success* (which was amazing!), and interestingly, it was there that I was exposed to *The Passion Test*, by Janet and Chris Attwood. The test almost effortlessly brings to light each individual's top five passions, with the contention that to live a full-out, vibrant life, all five passions ideally are present and playing out. What I discovered from that easy process surprised me, and what surfaced as my #1 passion in life planted the seed for the business I would start a few years later, and for becoming a Certified Facilitator for The Passion Test.

In addition to Byron Katie, Jack Canfield, and the Attwoods, I have been blessed to have participated in training seminars with Patty Aubery, Sean Gallagher, Louise Hay, Cheryl Richardson, Marci Shimoff, Master Stephen Co, Paul Wong, Caroline Sutherland, Cynthia James, and The Landmark instructors.

My encouragement is that others will seek out these life-altering opportunities. Having learned from these beacons of hope over the years, "bringing good into light" is my intention for my business today. By definition, "beacons" are people, places, or things that illuminate, guide, and inspire. Beacons Community Space is a warm, welcoming environment for those wanting to personally engage with others, adding meaning and joy to their lives. Through life-skill classes (i.e., communication, conflict resolution, and preparation before passing), along with interactive workshops, networking events, celebrations, charity functions, and on-going support groups… Beacons' commitment is to be a center for life-enrichment.

The foundational idea behind forming a community space was basically to combat loneliness. I believe that "no man is an island," and "it takes a village…." Whatever one is going through there is strength and buoyancy in connecting with others around the issue.

I have noticed this to be particularly true with young people. We formed a group called "Expression Lab – a Space to Create for Teenagers," where teens take complete responsibility/ownership of their creative endeavor – from formation of the idea, installation, and marketing – to hosting and manning the event. Through art exhibits, music jams, and poetry slams, getting together with their peers in-person, off-line, and collaborating in a creative, artistic way is supportive, inspiring, and uplifting.

How powerful it is to witness young, emerging artists of all types being given a platform and a voice! People of all ages have been showcased, as well. The works of seasoned, local creators are highlighted and the intimate setting allows active interaction and discussions between guests and artists, authors, and musicians.

I am also extremely impassioned about our "Living-Life Tribute" project. It encompasses a life-celebration party before someone passes: wonderful, heartfelt speeches and toasts can be made face-to-face in front of the person and their loved ones before it's too late to be appreciated here on earth. Immense healing occurs, and regrets by the person passing and by those left remaining are minimized. No need to think, "I wish I had told so-and-so how I felt while I still had the chance."

I think soulful success is being able to handle life's challenges and difficulties as gracefully (and full of grace) as possible. It is being able to reach into your toolbox of life-skills and know there will be something there to help you. It's being able to strengthen relationships, resolve conflict through authentic communication, and live a life filled with peace, purpose, and passion. Practical skills not only impact and increase your own happiness but also the happiness and well-being of all those around you. And don't we owe that to ourselves, and others?

To me, the *soul of success* is being willing to go out on a limb, outside the box, definitely outside one's comfort zone... and into the bright light of possibilities!

About Liz

Liz Shartel is a personal growth, education advocate and charity sponsor. She is the founder of Beacons Community Space located in Denver's Cherry Creek North, and started The Women's Exchange of Colorado.

By creating a gathering place for a wide array of educational, cultural, and social events, Liz connects people through a love of camaraderie, learning, and making a difference through community collaboration. From morning workshops, support groups, and networking events… to evening book signings, fundraisers, and speakers…Beacons' focus is on life-enrichment.

Liz Shartel began her journey of life-learning when she discovered and attended the Byron Katie "School for the Work" during a difficult time in her life. She subsequently participated in workshops with Janet and Chris Attwood, Jack Canfield, Louise Hay, Cheryl Richardson, and Master Stephen Co. She is a Certified Facilitator for The Passion Test. Her mission is to bring good into light, and to be a light of hope to those needing support.

Liz graduated from Kansas State University, and is the daughter of Betty and Shelby Smith of Wichita, Kansas. She divides her time between Colorado and New York, where her three young-adult children reside.

CHAPTER 34

THE FITNESS REVOLUTION — ONE COMMITTED PROFESSIONAL AT A TIME

BY DWAYNE WIMMER

FIT FOR LIFE: This is an ideal that I've always been driven and inspired by. As a kid, there were two things that I was really drawn to—teaching and sports. This became the driving force that got me through college and helped me realize my career goals, which were to be a football coach and a physical education teacher. I succeeded, and then I realized fairly quickly that I had bigger fish to fry.

In order to find what would fulfill me, I started by getting a part-time job at a fitness facility in the late 80's as a floor fitness instructor. During this time, I realized something huge: I could teach people one-on-one. This really inspired me and I was always thinking of ways to help clients' make the most of the experience, and for me to offer them the most. My first step toward this was helping to facilitate a weight-loss program that included one-on-one training. It was a way to help people achieve something important—weight management—and the experience taught me so much about one-on-one training, which is where I felt I could offer the most to those people that came to train with me.

Realizing the power I had to help people achieve some pretty incredible things was amazing, and I wasn't about to squander it. I kept learning and being a student, going to conferences and seminars to learn the science and business of exercise, and network with people who thought

317

more like I did. These are the very same people that are a part of who I am today.

CREATING AN EXERCISE "THINK TANK"

Exercise is the heart of my career because I am so excited about inspiring and helping others to develop healthy lifestyles through realizing their body's natural potential. Most peoples' stories are quite similar at the beginning of a fitness goal. I've seen and experienced this so much through my career, whether it was training a high-end athlete or someone who was just getting started on their journey to get fit. One thing that we all have in common when we strive for a certain level of fitness is that **we want more out of our bodies because that will bring more to our lives**. Then we meet an obstacle of some sort and we're surprised by it.

Why do obstacles always catch us off guard? From everything I've seen and experienced, obstacles are created by two primary things. The first is a lack of knowledge about the science of the body. The second is a false perception of what we view as "being fit." What happens next is that people begin to reach out to someone in the fitness industry that has something to offer them to help with their goal. They easily believe that going to this fitness source will make all the difference between their success and failure.

People seek out the best ideas that will deliver them the best results with the least effort.

After the research is done, it's action time. They are ready to buy that program, whether it's for at home or at a fitness club. What happens next? Unfortunately, failure is often what happens next. These people are instantly deflated as they realize that they are the "typical results," not the "atypical results" that are noted in the fine (very fine) print. **Getting fit is not easy work, but it is rewarding work**.

It's at this point where you are going to have to make a choice—are you committed to the process to become more fit or are you going to give up because it's too hard? I hope that you never give up, but I do understand. That's why I'm so committed to lifting up the game of people in the fitness industry by showing the distinct difference between a personal trainer by title and a personal trainer who is a professional. Most of us need a hand, so why not have a knowledgeable hand to help us along?

When people think of personal trainers, their ideas usually evolve around these two principles:

1. Receiving help to learn the techniques to use for exercise that will take care of a problem area, or possibly provide that body transformation that is always seen on television commercials and in online advertising.

2. They want a personal trainer to provide them with the motivation to keep going and working at fitness every day. There's a perception that if someone is there to motivate and inspire us that we cannot fail.

I can guarantee you that a majority of personal trainers are going to tell you they can be those two things to you. And, you are going to end up disappointed. Consider this:

The fitness industry is a huge money machine, having generated over 70 billion in income in the US alone in 2013—this doesn't include programs you can purchase online. Another interesting statistic is that less the 20% of the population in the US workout on a regular basis. These numbers are staggering, aren't they? These numbers say something very important, which is: *there are too many snake oil salesmen and far too few true professionals in the fitness industry.*

Since I love the fitness industry and want it to be better than what it is in its current state, I'm inspired by everything that can be done to bring the fitness industry up to a higher level of professionalism, where the people who want to have healthier, more productive lives are receiving better information and direction; not just being sold by the next "easy fix."

FITNESS LEADERS ALLIANCE

I'd always suspected the change that needed to take place in the mindset of people in the fitness industry, but it was really brought to the forefront of my mind when I opened up my fitness facility, Vertex Fitness Personal Training Studio. At this point, it was about more than me being the best trainer I could be for my clients, it was about me finding and teaching other trainers to have that similar passion and approach.

Over the years, as the studio has grown, I have sought out other fitness professionals to work at Vertex who are committed to being fitness professionals, not "yes people" to clients—those people who will tell them what they want to hear, even if they know it isn't going to be effective. It has been a major struggle. It's so frustrating because it's a huge clash with my passion for exercise and the belief that everyone needs to have good information before they can have good results.

Through my maddening efforts to find the right type of personal trainers to hire, I did learn some very important things, and these are all a part of what it takes to be a professional fitness trainer. I wanted to find:

- Individuals who want to help others by sharing real information based on science.
- Individuals who are not going to say or do whatever it takes just to earn that paycheck.
- And, individuals who are willing to learn the science about the body and how it works.

Imagine my surprise when I realized that the numbers of people out there who fit my stringent criteria were pretty minute, practically non-existent. But then it came to me and I realized what I needed to do. My mission became this:

I was going to create fitness professionals by creating a system to help them meet all the proven information and results that I had access to.

This realization was so powerful and it was the birth of the Fitness Leaders Alliance. I was done trying to find that needle in the haystack. It was much smarter to set up a mechanism to train people the proper way and then hire the cream of the crop.

MARKETING VS. MINDSET

Fitness Leaders Alliance is still young, but it's growing by leaps and bounds as I've journeyed out to find others who do think like I do in regards to fitness. They are out there, and like me, they have realized that when you are sharing real information that doesn't come with the bells, whistles and gimmicks of marketing, it's a lot harder to show someone that you are offering them the "real deal." Imagine this scenario:

I'm talking with a client and they've done a lot of research on programs by this time and each one has promised them something amazing in exchange for their efforts and money. The premise behind these programs is this simple thought: how can I get people to pay me for what I have without any real research supporting it? Most programs do not have science backing them up and they are not required to in order to be offered to consumers. There are no boundaries, at all. That's what professionals like me are competing against. I'm telling them that it is hard work and why. **That means that it suddenly becomes more difficult for people and that scares them, but that is the truth**. However, I can help them handle the truth and explode to a new level of fitness in their lives because *I understand how it all works—scientifically, not just emotionally.*

If you ask ten different people, "What's the definition of exercise?" you'll probably get ten different answers. There is no standard exercise definition that people know as being the truth. Some people think walking their dog is exercise. Unfortunately, for the average person, it's not. This individual definition about exercise creates a huge challenge for everyone. **How do fitness professionals start speaking the same language and talking the same talk**? It's tough, but with enough results, I believe that it is not impossible. Results can be proven and if you take something proven to the general public, using marketing the right way, I feel that we can revolutionize the fitness industry. Those who don't want to put in the effort and time will fade away, leaving those who are truly serious about exercise as a lifestyle for the long haul. We'll be the ones building clients for life.

This process has already begun, which is very exciting. Through Fitness Leaders Alliance and a network of highly committed professionals in the fitness industry, we have begun to get together and talk about the science of exercise. There is so much research out there that shows what works based on how our bodies perform or are meant to perform. Basically, before any trainer can possibly hope to help a client, they need to be trained themselves so they are bringing something of value to the table, not to mention something that is sustainable, part of a lifelong process, not just a short term goal.

WHAT YOU KNOW MAKES ALL THE DIFFERENCE

Whether your goal is to get more fit or to become a fitness professional, there are four starting points that you can learn right now. I'm excited to share them with you because understanding them will make it a less frustrating process for you. If you are working toward being more fit, you will understand your body just a bit better. If you are working in the fitness industry, you'll reduce your chances of a client telling you, "Nothing is working. Goodbye."

1. If it sounds too good to be true, it probably is.

There is no easy way to get in better shape, or get more fit. *Basically speaking, exercise is an overload to the body that gives your body a reason to change.* So yes, exercise is going to be difficult.

2. If you're just going through the motions of exercise you will not get much out of it.

With life and exercise, going through the motions hardly ever brings the rewards. You've got to work hard to get results. *Exercise is not busy work, it is a focused effort.* You can get much more out of a planned and focused half hour workout than you can get from mindlessly hopping around for an hour and a half.

3. Disassociate exercise and weight loss.

Weight loss involves eating differently, consuming fewer calories by eating low calorie-dense foods that are also higher in nutritional value to reduce body fat. Exercise is an overload to provide a stimulus for positive physiological changes in the body, which unfortunately doesn't spend many calories. There is a cross over, but less than one may expect. Focus on eating differently to lose weight, exercise to change the bodies ability to do work and become a better functioning unit. *The largest similarity between the two is that it isn't easy and the process is slow.* You didn't get to where you are now overnight, which means changing your habits and regime slowly will yield the best results.

4. Strength training, not cardio, is the biggest bang for your time.

When you perform a well-designed, total body strength-training program you will get more from working out two times a week for thirty minutes than you would doing an hour a day of cardio. Your body will adapt and you'll get stronger and be more productive. *Doing a total body strength-training workout with enough intensity will provide you a cardiovascular workout, as well. As a result, you'll be able to do more, be more productive, and spend less time getting better results.*

These four things that I've shared with you are only the start of making a huge difference in how you approach exercise, regardless of which end you are approaching it from.

THE JOURNEY ALWAYS CONTINUES

With the formation of Fitness Leaders Alliance and the various umbrellas that fall under the organization that are geared toward fundamental education and on-going education, a system has been set up in which the fitness industry can be revolutionized in a positive, impactful way. To be the best at your profession, you must embrace constant learning. You'll never know it all.

Through teaching, I learn and my clients' learn through what I teach. It's an amazing relationship and a long-lasting one. With the practices that I have implemented, I've been able to watch incredible journeys kick-off and see the difference that a commitment to exercise makes in peoples' personal and professional lives. **With a more fit body, everything in life is better**. I'm changing lives one person at a time and looking forward to create fitness professionals one person at a time, too.

About Dwayne

Dwayne Wimmer founded Vertex Fitness Personal Training Studio in 2001, excited to bring a new concept of personal training to the people of Philadelphia's Main Line in Pennsylvania. Driven by knowledge and results both, while a strength coach at Villanova University, he worked closely with world class athletes such as Brian Westbrook, formerly of the Philadelphia Eagles, on strength training and conditioning for optimal performance. Dwayne's client base extends much further than world class athletes. Along with athletes, he works with adolescents to seniors, and he's a highly acclaimed and sought-out personal trainer who has received numerous awards, such as Best of the Main Line Personal Training Studio and Best Main Line Personal Trainer.

Through efforts and a driving passion to bring the "professional" to the fitness industry, Dwayne co-founded the Fitness Leaders Alliance in 2013, which is an organization dedicated to the training of more highly qualified fitness professionals. Its focus is on ethical business practices, scientifically proven methods, and the realization that continuous learning is important in the fitness industry.

A graduate of Missouri Western State University, Dwayne has a Bachelor of Science degree in Physical Education, with an emphasis in Coaching. Aside from personal training, he's spent time as a physical education teacher, strength and conditioning coach, and a football coach, but has found his passion and home in the fitness industry, inspiring and reaching out to others. As a strong believer in continuing to learn, Dwayne has also taken classes at East Stroudsburg University toward a Masters Degree in Sports Management.

Since June of 2013, Dwayne has co-hosted the podcast, "The Fitness Professional Show." This provides a wonderful platform to help with his goals of creating a more professional fitness industry. And now, he can add author to his list of accomplishments, having created a chapter in the upcoming book *The Soul of Success* with Jack Canfield (renowned for the Chicken Soup series).

To get to the point where he is now, Dwayne has always been thankful for the support of his father, a man who always believed in his mission and saw the need for what it was that Dwayne envisioned. During his free time, Dwayne is an avid motorcyclist who enjoys viewing the amazing landscapes and finding good restaurants to enjoy – that are off the beaten path. He also takes advantage of opportunities to travel and experience many other cities while attending fitness seminars and giving presentations about the industry he is so passionate about. As a way to give back to the community that has been a part of his entire life, Dwayne has created Vertex Fitness PUMPED (People United

Making Progress through Education and Donations), which provides support to area non-profits through a community-wide outreach effort. At this time, they help three non-profits per year in the Philadelphia area.

For more information from Dwayne, you may contact him at:
Tel. (610) 525-6604
dwayne@FitnessLeadersAlliance.com
Or visit: www.FitnessLeadersAlliance.com.

CHAPTER 35

WILL YOU HAVE PEACE OF MIND IN RETIREMENT?

BY JACE T. (JT) MCDONALD

When asked about writing and co-authoring a book with legendary business professionals and entrepreneurs, it's a great honor to realize that years of being self-employed and having the same and different challenges as so many others, that you are successful and have reached a level of success so many strive to attain in their businesses over their careers. It's a true blessing.

So why do we do what we do? Because it matters!!

If there was a better way to do something – would you rather know the first day or the last? For those we get to meet and help, it's their first day in learning better ways.

In starting to write this chapter, I am reminded of a call that I received early Saturday morning, from a young lady whose father died. I returned the call not knowing this and she stated her dad had my business card and had spoken highly of what I do. She stated her dad had passed away at a healthy 71, and she wondered if her Dad had taken the time to do what I had recommended. . . I'll touch on this at the end of this chapter. . .

I often reflect back on those early years of running one business and then even more businesses. Actually to be truthful, they ran me. I can say I ran them, but that would be a lie, they truly ran me, day and night, 24/7.

I am reminded by a little sign that stated, "Don't get so busy running a business that you forget to make a life." Well, as I reflect back on those early 17 years and my first marriage, I was that man. Obsessed with a concept of a dream that really wasn't the concept I wanted.

In life we have choices. However, if you're a business owner or successful person, often we have things occurring in our lives that take time from thinking clearly.

How we cope and move forward daily I am reminded of the accident on my mother's birthday that forever changed my nights and mornings. Remembering seeing the snow-covered road and the fatality that my business was involved in. We need to step back more and see our businesses and lives and see how we are dealing with situations and are we doing truly what's best for our wellbeing. Are we evaluating what others are doing for us as the best things out there, or do we need more second opinions.

In my early forties, with a wonderful son, Ryder, almost 2 years old, and a wonderful wife Jessica, who also oversees my dream, I started two State-licensed 24/7 Assisted-Care Homes for individuals with high needs, my days are never quite long enough.

Why? After working over 17 years running a contracting service business with over one hundred employees, a day never passed that I thought there must be a better way. Guess what I found! Really, I found what I was looking for. It was expensive to find it, it cost me my first wonderful wife (yes, she really was an angel), lots of free time with friends and family, and yes, it was more expensive than I ever dreamed. You see, it was never about the money, but it was peace of mind. The mental cost to me was very high, and downright hard on me – there were many sleepless nights.

Most business owners and entrepreneurs just don't have financial peace of mind, not because they are not working hard enough, they just have the wrong vehicles to earn properly. Most of America is stuck in the stock market and not aware they may qualify for using programs banks use to make money.

Do you think Warren Buffet goes to his bank and says, "Great! Less than 1% earnings again this month, I'll place more money with you."

NO. He wants three things from his investments, just like you should:

1. Target gains that you can count on and plan on.
2. Costs that you truly know upfront.
3. Simple exit strategies with no fees.

I found this so true when I learned about the fractional settlement industry, and thanks to my father who worked for the Public Service commission of Wisconsin for nearly 40 years.

Why not you? You too can learn about new strategies, I knew my business had to change, so did my life. After losing the love of my life at that time, and yes, it got worse, I had experienced a fatal auto accident at my company and the dog also was put down, I was done, I thought. I didn't want to learn a new industry and why should I now start afresh again. Boy! I am sure glad I did, for so, so many reasons.

This leads me to a story of a man who never really asked for help, a lot like me. He was a navy man who knew he wanted to be a farmer. He became a successful farmer owning thousands of acres of Iowa land, and after reaching his late fifties he could have retired and enjoyed life more. Instead, he decided to start a ranch in Wyoming – outside of Casper to be exact. He wanted to take on a new challenge. He did so when most people went on to retire, but he was ready for another career as a rancher.

However, he was not one to ask for help. As he got older, our paths crossed. Well, they had to. You see, I married his granddaughter and his youngest daughter was my mother-in-law. He came into my office one morning and said, "I want to understand what you do and how you could help me." Wow! That was really an honor for me; you see, to have someone who doesn't usually ask for help ask you to help. . . that is really an honor!

After meeting with him many times, I saw his drive and passion and, as some say, his hard, stubborn ways. It was his way or the highway, as I saw myself in a much later version in life, pushing my 80s. So I was a bit stunned and asked why? Why me? He stated they saw and heard a bit of what I did, and he also felt there must be a better way for him, and he wondered about our main services of Asset Growth and Protection.

He didn't feel he was correctly set up to avoid probate costs for his family, or pass on his legacy without nursing homes getting the assets someday. Also, he actually stated that he felt the bank's wealth management department was making too much off him, and he could be earning better with his funds, and what would a comparison look like?

So he was correct, he did not have the proper trust structured to protect his assets. We did the proper paperwork to save the assets and pass them on – so his family would not have to come up with thousands of dollars when he passed on. When asked if he felt it was ok for their kids to come up with 10 to 15% or if it would be a burden they wanted to avoid, they agreed.

He also asked us to compare bank options he was using with ours. I stated, "Yes, let's sit down with them and see what they have to say." And we did. What a shocker it was for me to learn that the bankers were unable to read some of their own statements. After additional staff review, we saw he was earning, after fees, a very small amount of $54.80 on funds in excess of thousands of dollars, and that was the six month interest on that money, after fees of course.

With any investments you need to know three simple things, especially from your advisors, and if you don't know this, you may really want to get another opinion:

1. What is your target for earnings or gains; our fraction platform target is 11%.

2. What are your total costs? $125 a year seem fair? I think so, even with about a million dollars.

3. What is your key exit strategy? You need a really good one, how about the max earnings at maturity with no guesswork. I really like that one. I call it sleep-easy investing.

So the moral of this story is that even an old dog can learn new tricks, or better yet, even a hard-working, stubborn old rancher who knows his money is not working as hard as he is, can learn that there is a better way to do something. Do you want to know the first day or the last day? And yes, the first day maybe when you're 80, but thank God you learned it before 90.

Do you know why I tell you I enjoy Thanksgiving meals with family and other family events? Well, to go and enjoy yourself with family for whom you oversee their dollars, if you lose a dollar you will not enjoy your meal, I promise. . . especially if they are four rancher's daughters.

To have some tax-free income plans in place for them is also important. Well, it is if you think as I do that taxes are going up, not down. Do you think taxes are heading down? If so, I want to move to your neighborhood, sounds like a fairytale dream world. I'd like to come visit. I bet there are no parking tickets and no speed limits when you drive, ha,ha! Taxes are going up more than ever soon, because the baby boomers are retiring and with not enough people working to pay taxes, they have one way to go — UP!

Ever feel your money is not working as hard as you are? I too felt that way, I needed a new sense of direction and I found it with the fractional settlement industry and learning about other tools such as IULs. Asset Protection Trusts and Self-directed IRAs. These are all things you need to know so you can have your money working harder for you and start getting you on track for a faster, brighter future.

Our clients want three things:

1. Safety and protection
2. Tax benefits
3. Maximum earnings without risking #1

This is what we show business owners and independent agents to help their customers with each day. What if you didn't have to worry about the market's ups and downs, how would that benefit your life? What if your children's kids would benefit from your new planning options?

What is new peace of mind worth? Truly, it has been worth more than money for me, more peace of mind than I could have ever dreamed. Like many business owners I speak with, your business dream that you have, is it still a dream? Some say it turned into a nightmare out of control, it's controlling them.

I will now continue with the story from the beginning of chapter. It was hard for me to inform the daughter that her dad was a great man I got to meet and speak with. But "No," he did not protect his assets, and they will have a large probate expense to deal with, Also, "No" – her dad was not using our safe asset growth tool, and "Yes" – the markets did affect her dad. He had lost over $500k when I spoke to him months earlier, and I am afraid that what he hoped to leave after the market losses and fees, he had just lost even more this month before he passed. That stress I think killed him.

I hope you're the lucky one reading this before it's too late to check into better options and at least learn about them. Do you think taxes are going up or down? Yes. I think so too – UP. The concept of Asset Growth and Protection for business owners, retirees, tribes and government use, is to grow the funds and protect your assets for your loved ones.

Would it be helpful to have a TAX-Free retirement? Yes we can do that also! I look forward to our next time together.

Enjoy the day, God bless!

Acknowledgement

I know each day that my wonderful son and wife are here and when I am gone, I want them to keep enjoying the life we had created. Hopefully your life can have less stress over financial worries and business issues with our easy turn key affordable solutions that so many have found and thank us for each day.

My writing of this information I share is dedicated to my parents Thomas and Deborah McDonald who always believed in me and encouraged my efforts when others did not.

To my first wife Stefanie, I cherished our time together and current wife Jessica who also inspires me to drive on and continue helping others achieve success.

My dear friends and family you know who you are and of course my greatest gift, Ryder my son, you will never know just how much you changed my passion for being a entrepreneur to wanting to be your dad forever. The days I am gone not seeing you, are my hardest away from you.

My dear clients and agents who I am blessed to assist, thank you for allowing me to do so each day, it truly has been a gift to me to work with you and share my passion.

About Jace

Jace T. McDonald (aka JT) had a passion for business since he was a child. For almost 25 years he continues to educate business owners on tools to help their families, and have peace of mind financially with Asset Growth and Protection tools not used by the main stream.

JT is currently married to Jessica Baumler from Iowa, who is an inspiring Olympian horseback rider and who currently oversees both of the State of WI Assisted-Care home facilities (in Marquette and Adams counties) that JT started – to assist those near and dear to him.

By establishing the tribalinitiative.com, JT helps tribes create revenue and jobs with a focus on children's programs, ending poverty with financial programs that banks use to help them earn money, and create entrepreneurs and opportunities in Indian country.

JT enjoys taking time with hundreds of representatives that he and his team help to assist nationally. He also enjoys spending time with family, friends and clients fishing throughout WI and Canada.

His son Ryder is keeping dad very busy with bike rides, walks with the dog and playing on the new swing set and slide. Ryder also enjoys talking on the phone, so don't be surprised if you get a call from JT and Ryder will have lots to say. JT thinks he gets that from Jessica??

You can reach JT by calling: (608) 516-1956

Or visiting:
bfitrusts.com
tribalinitiative.com
Or by emailing: support@bfitrusts.com

CHAPTER 36

THE ART OF SELLING WELL

BY JOHN-MARK MITCHELL, CRS, GRI

Life was good and I had big plans that involved becoming an attorney and really paving my way in this world, helping people with their legal needs and loving the life I lived. Then I decided to take a year off before I entered law school. When deciding what to do during my break, I decided to get my real estate license. I can't even say I fully understand why I went that route, but I did. *I had short-term expectations* and thought it was a means to an end—a law school graduation end. **However, I was wrong**.

Within six months of being in real estate, I fully realized that I had stumbled upon the place I was meant to be. It wasn't simply because I found myself becoming the top agent in my office. It wasn't because it was nice to earn a paycheck. Rather, *I knew that real estate was right for me because of the intense joy that I felt inside me when I was working with clients*, either buying or selling, and helping them achieve their goals for that time. **I couldn't ask for more!**

Before I knew it, ten years passed me by. I was busy, productive, and enjoying this amazing life and still loved what I was doing. **I had no doubts or regrets**…something that most of us can see the value in. One day, someone asked me, "John-Mark, what makes you successful?" I had never come across a question that sounded so easy to answer, but was so difficult to respond to. *Honestly, I'd never really thought of myself as successful—kid you not!* I was just feeling fortunate to be doing what I did and delivering something of value to the greater Triad area of North Carolina. Well, I had to answer that question and I couldn't just say, "I work smart and hard," although I definitely did work smart and hard. I had some serious introspection to do.

WE CANNOT SHOW OTHERS SOMETHING THAT ISN'T INSIDE OF US

We're here for a short amount of time; we have to always think about what we can do to benefit others and cause them to succeed in their world. This is our reward.

This process of evaluating a question about your success is an interesting way to do some internal reflecting and figure out what matters most to you. **It's what truly matters to you that will make your business flourish or flounder**. I recalled a comment that I'd made some twenty years ago when I'd first ended up in real estate. I had an unintentional "shock and awe" moment for the agents around me when I stated, "I wish that 50% of the agents would get out of the business." It was brazen and I never had the chance to explain just what I meant by it, but I did mean it—just not for the reasons that most people may think. I wasn't saying it because I was afraid of the competition. I was saying it because I wanted to be respected as a professional and desired to have real estate agents as a group looked upon favorably. I wanted a higher standard! I knew that if I took care of customers the rest would fall into place, which meant that I didn't have to worry about it. **What we give to others will return to us tenfold**. I still believe this today, both the statement and the philosophy.

That leaves the next question: *how do we make sure we are taking care of our customers? It's a privilege to serve them*, after all. It's also important to keep in mind that *it's never about the money*. It's about the effort and not being lackadaisical. Customers need the best realtor with the best insight and no one, me included, can achieve success without embracing the following points:

1. **Education**.
   The real estate industry has an abundance of mandatory and optional continuing education classes. Taking advantage of this is smart

because it will help you grow and it also helps you become the expert that your clients need, and expect. Take those certification classes, study hard for them, and master them if you want to become a master. Get those credentials behind your name and explain what they mean. This carries over into everything in life, not just real estate. As a rule of thumb, you should spend 20% of all your work time making yourself better.

2. **Knowledge of your product**.
There are many different areas that fall under real estate and you have to know your product that you are selling. For example, if you want to sell a million dollar home you had better know that market. What you surround yourself with is who you become. That's why you must always be prepared so you can have an intelligent conversation with your customer. Make it a goal to know your product better than all your competitors combined.

3. **Volunteering for your heart, not the recognition**.
To keep your heart in a good place, use it often by volunteering "just because it feels great!" Don't look to boast about it because it should never be for your glory, but rather someone else's benefit. When we do things from the heart and don't worry about recognition, the right people will notice.

These three things are a part of what I emphasize that my agents focus on, and I lead by example in these areas, taking great care in ensuring that I already am what I suggest they become. *Doing this is my statement in business, and there is no room for doubt about how serious I am about taking care of my clients and being a positive force in their lives while I am in it.*

THERE IS NO W.I.I.N. WITHOUT INTEGRITY

We are given little tests all the time that we have to either pass or fail. What you do with these tests determines everything. The right thing is always positive, even if you don't win.

Integrity is the driving force that keeps my soul aligned with my passions for real estate. If I always remain in a position where I am approaching everyone from a genuine place, a place where the customer is my primary focus and I am doing my best to serve their needs, everything else will fall into place, and in the end things will be good. *We cannot control everything in life, but we can always control using our integrity in every situation.*

To become a part of a successful team or be a successful leader, you must first become successful as an individual. It doesn't work any other way. Many people say that you should brush up against success. Sure, it's nice to meet successful people, but I look at it all a bit differently. I say, "Erase the idea that standing next to Michael Phelps in a pool makes you a better swimmer." You have to put in the time to become better; it doesn't just rub off on you.

W.I.I.N. is my personal acronym of how I work every day and it helps me to stay on track. There is something in this that everyone can take away, whether they are interested in a career in real estate or in just achieving personal excellence through a more authentic channel. W.I.I.N. is the actual result of my thoughts about that tough question: why are you successful? It's a combination of what I've found was masterful wisdom out of all the books on success and selling that I've studied, and its personalized to my business. Plus, it is effective!

W: <u>Watch your competition</u>. Know what the people you are up against are doing and commit to doing it better, or don't do it at all. Study them the way a professional football player studies his opposition on film and paper before playing in the Super Bowl. Pretend that every day is the Super Bowl of selling and you're determined to end it as the champion.

I: <u>Imagine you are the customer</u>. Focus on the pros and cons of your product or what you are selling. Ask questions such as:

- What would make this easier or better to understand?

- What do you wish was different?

- Or ask the client: What did you like or dislike about your last broker experience? (Never use this to talk negatively about that broker, as it sets a bad tone and *will* tarnish your soul of success.)

By keeping your perspective as that of the customers, you will deliver them the results that they want and secure a loyal customer. Customers want to know that you are there for them and focused on their experience at that moment. Learn how you can help. This has always worked for me, and as a result, I haven't had to worry about where my next customer is coming from because I know—it is likely to be the friends or family of those I've worked with in the past.

I: Institute a plan of action. Set up a plan for the product or service that you are selling and consistently stick to it; especially if it is advertising! Not all plans have to be complicatcd. Ycars ago, I received a great strategy from a marketing genius. He said to always pass out ten of my business cards every day. I have always done this and when I started, it forced me to go out and meet people. In fact, I wouldn't return home until I'd handed ten cards out. And guess what? I still love to meet people. If you are ever working in a people industry and stop liking to help people, you'd better have a Plan B, because things are going to be changing quickly.

N: Notice all the positive things along the way. This is something that takes internal action—a warning to yourself on how you view everything that comes our way. None of us should ever be so driven by our goals that we do not realize all the good experiences that happen along the way. Even the bad experiences can be good if they help us see how to be a better person in business and better for our customers.

When you W.I.I.N., everyone wins. It is that simple. Are there ever going to be challenges that force you to maintain your integrity and a winning perspective? Yes, there are, and I'm going to share one with you to help you demonstrate this point:

A few years ago, I had a transaction where I was a dual agent. This is something that many agents don't like to do because they feel they will represent one party in the transaction more favorably than the other, or they are fearful of a lawsuit from poor representation. For me, this logic doesn't work because I sell many of my own listings and I actually find it to be very good for the parties I represent. In this one transaction I'm sharing, I represented a client and showed them a property that I had listed three times before they were willing to submit an offer. At the last minute, I also received a call from another agent who had some customers who wanted to submit an offer, too. I covered my bases by:

- Making everyone aware of what was going on.
- Not revealing any information about what the offers would

include.

- Encouraging everyone to submit their best offer.

Everyone did this and my buyer clients ended up losing out on the property because the other realtor's client made a full offer. *There were several people shocked*—the sellers, the other agent, and my buyers who did not get the accepted offer—but I was not shocked at all. I conducted the entire situation with fairness and integrity, making it so I was doing what was best by everyone and making certain it was done by the rules. That was more important than sacrificing a larger commission, and again, doing what was right paid off. Although they lost the offer, my buyers realized something important: I would work for them over money.

When we put people ahead of ourselves it makes a world of difference. This is the way that everyone in sales should be.

Integrity lifts you up for success and nourishes your soul. Stories like what I shared are too unique and that's why amazing results due to high levels of integrity are not as common to come across as we believe they should be. We must always remember that business has the potential to impact someone else's life in a meaningful way. Often times, what may seem negative at first can end up being a blessing. Without integrity there is no winning.

SALES AND THE SOUL ARE A DYNAMIC TEAM THAT DELIVERS BIG RESULTS

When it comes to real estate, people also remember the positive experiences.

Through the years, there have been agents that have come and gone in my life, clients that have come and stayed, and opportunities to learn each and every day. Through my awareness of all these things, I've kept my passion and purpose for real estate. My formula may not be the one that works for everybody and that's okay, but for customers who want more out of their realtors and realtors who celebrate any chance they can to use their talents to serve people, great things can happen. **These are memorable moments that leave an impression on us, a brighter spot in our hearts as we think about what role real estate does play in our lives**. And, as with all big decisions, customers want to work with people who are the best. That's why I will always remain passionate about my soul purpose, which is giving my real estate customers my very best—*NO EXCUSES!*

About John-Mark

In April 2014, John-Mark Mitchell, CRS, GRI took his twenty-plus years of real estate experience and became the owner/broker for his own luxury real estate firm—Mitchell Prime Properties. He recognized that it was time to take this bold step and branch out into his area of expertise, which is high-end real estate. Driven by a strong desire to create a real estate culture based on his proven success strategies, John-Mark has blazed a distinct trail in his market.

John-Mark graduated from Campbell University with a Bachelor of Arts degree in Government Pre-Law and was always active on his campus with the Student Government. He's also been featured in *Who's Who* and *Outstanding Young Men of America.* The experiences and skills gained from these experiences have been fundamental for John-Mark in building his real estate career and becoming known for his tagline, "The Art of Selling Well."

Choosing real estate over law school, John-Mark entered into the business early on, becoming a top producer within a short amount of time and gaining recognition as the top agent for twelve consecutive years for the largest real estate company in Winston-Salem. He later became a partner with Yost and Little Realty in 2007, a high-end property company and was a member of Christies Great Estates. In 2008, he received a Movers and Shakers Award. The company was sold in 2010 and John-Mark joined a company out of Seattle, Washington, called eXp Realty International, where he launched their luxury division and continued his success as a top producer, receiving Top Agent International acknowledgement for 2011, 2012, and 2013. He remains a shareholder in the company. As of 2012, he also serves as First Broker in Charge for Concierge Auctions for the state of North Carolina.

In 1998, John-Mark started a high-end home magazine for the Triad area, which is known as *Fine Homes Magazine* today. A firm believer in giving back, John-Mark co-founded a local charity for the homeless in the Winston-Salem area, known as B.R.A.C.E., which stands for Builders and Realtors Active in Community Efforts and received the Governor's Award for his efforts. John-Mark is also a co-author with Jack Canfield for the book, *The Soul of Success*, and is the featured realtor in the May 2015 issue of *Top Agent.*

John-Mark credits his parents, family, and friends for their continued guidance and support in his life. He's particularly grateful to his mother Mabelline Mitchell, who has always inspired him to give his best efforts in business, even when it was not easy to do. A fun claim to fame for John-Mark is that he won the title of Mr. Winston-Salem in the 1990s. He is also published in poetry and is an avid reader, plus enjoys playing the piano—especially Beethoven and Mozart.

Contact John-Mark Mitchell at:
Office: (336)722-9911 or Cell: (336)682-2552
Email: Johnmark@GoMitch.com
Or visit: www.JohnMarkMitchell.com.

CHAPTER 37

THE DEFINITION OF INSANITY

BY DEBRA KAY SMITH

I'm sure you've heard the latest definition of insanity: It's repeating the same habitual behavior but expecting a different outcome. I might also put it this way: You've been going around in circles long enough. Does that describe you?

Are you running faster and working harder than ever before, trying to realize your dreams or simply trying to keep the wolf from the door? How's that working out for you? Perhaps you've been putting in more and longer hours at work because cutbacks have left you holding the bag, doing the work of several with no greater reward than before. Maybe you make *lists* of Things-To-Do, and rush to chalk them off the list, multi-tasking like nobody's business, but even that is no longer working for you. You rarely ever pause long enough to take a deep breath, let alone stop to smell the roses, and you seldom sleep more than five hours a night. Your health and concentration are suffering, and you've run out of options. Do you feel like, no matter how hard you work, you just can't get ahead? Does it seem as if you're going down for the third time and you may, never again, get your head above water? Does the word "desperate" describe you better than any other word? Well, take heart, because I've been there and done that, and I've discovered a way out of this exhausting downward cycle.

After taking time to re-access why my plans were no longer working, I finally came to this conclusion: maybe it was time for a change. That was the turning point for me. It took a purposeful decision on my part to do things in a new way, focusing on a different goal, making better use of limited resources and turning my energies in a new direction. Here's the take-away: important changes always require a conscious decision – a change of mind – to stop spinning our wheels and start moving with the flow of our hearts. That's the key.

At that point I had to begin to re-define myself and get to know who I really was and what I really wanted. That meant sitting down and spending time alone to re-evaluate my priorities, and that can be a tall order in the fast-paced society in which we live. Most of us have trouble shifting into low gear, and find that as much as we hate our lives, we've become addicted to the frenetic pace we've set.

So don't be surprised if it's a challenge to slow down. Even if you've done it before, take time to shut out the world long enough to stop and take an inventory of your gifts and talents, as well as your preferences and dislikes. Have you been living someone else's dream? Perhaps your parents paid for your education, requiring you to go into a field that didn't trip your trigger, and now it's time to move on.

Sit back and contemplate this question: What do I love? What kind of dreams did I have as a child? Now that may sound like nonsense, but the sad truth is that things often go wrong when we lose sight of the child inside us, and end up doing the logical thing instead of what motivates us deep inside.

Who are you really, at your core? What gets you so excited that you can't wait to jump out of bed to face another day? What are you passionate about? What motivates you? Do you love helping others, or serving your community? What would you do if the sky was the limit and you could do whatever your heart desires? Would you rescue those held captive by human traffickers? Would you save the whales? If you sit down and meditate on these things, answering these questions on paper, you may discover treasure you've never seen before. Find your passion, and you'll find what you're called to do.

Once you discover your true identity and what you love, I guarantee that your confidence will go through the roof! There's absolutely nothing like it! You'll feel like a kid again, actually having fun; you'll discover a new clarity regarding your life's mission—your destiny. It's never too late to make an about-face, and move in the direction of your dreams! No doubt you've heard of Grandma Moses, an artist whose paintings have become renowned the world over. Well, consider this: she didn't begin to paint until she was what most would consider "over the hill." And if she could do it, so can you.

At that point I had to decide whether I was ready to risk changing my course. I knew it wouldn›t be easy. It would require concerted effort as well as education and training – though education doesn't always mean formal schooling – the truth was that I would be starting all over again. But I was inspired by a glimmer of hope for a better, more exciting future, and I just couldn't pass up the chance to realize my dreams. I had to decide what I wanted to be when I grew up, and move in that direction.

My new goal was to live out my destiny, becoming an expert in my field. To that end, I began to read a book a month on my topic of interest. I made a habit of studying that topic for thirty minutes every day, 365 days a year. I also threw caution to the wind, and signed up for college courses online, attended seminars and webinars, went to conferences and made a point to join conference calls, in order to live out my dream.

Then I had to make a list of both my short and long term goals and how I would achieve them. I had to map out a plan and then work that plan. I realized that when embarking on a new endeavor, I had to ask myself this vital question: Where am I going, and how am I going to get there? During this process I also learned not to skip this step, because our goals are the vehicles that carry us to our destination!

I also discovered something else I hadn't realized before. Enthusiasm could only take me so far. Without diligent effort – that never-give-up attitude – I would lose my momentum and give up before reaching my destination. So I had to be persistent and stay the course, never taking my eyes off the goal, no matter what else happened. It was important to understand that not every race is a sprint. In fact, most are long distance events, run over time, and require a high level of training, determination and endurance.

So what are you waiting for? What's holding you back? Fear of failure? Feelings of inadequacy? If that's the case, perhaps you would benefit by hiring someone to coach you, every step of the way, holding you accountable and cheering you on, if you need more motivation than you can muster on your own. But don't let this precious opportunity pass you by to turn your life around. It's an investment that will reap great rewards. If I could do it, so can you!

If you'd like to learn more, feel free to contact me. I'm here to help.

Debra Kay Smith

About Debra

Debra Kay Smith is taking the world by storm. She is a woman of many talents – a motivational speaker, entrepreneur, author, a success coach and the CEO of Driven 4 Elite Success, Inc. With a focus on powerful short term goals and rewards, she has a gift for helping clients see the big picture and focus on long-term success. She loves coming in with fresh, witty ideas and a unique spin, to propel her clients toward success in every area of their lives. She uses humor, fun, and creative ideas to mentor you, the client, from idea conception to the fulfillment of your ultimate goal.

Debra Smith's areas of expertise include: marketing, branding and networking, and to her colleagues she is known as a seasoned marketer with finely-honed networking skills. She is also a proud member of Toastmasters International.

Debra's education includes a Bachelor's degree in Education, and she is working on her Master's in Leadership. She's an unstoppable motivator and a veritable dream to work with.

Check out her websites at:
www.driven4elitesuccess.com
www.driven4elitesuccess.net

Contact her at: driven4elitesuccess@gmail.com

CHAPTER 38

MAKING THE MOST OF YOUR LIFE

BY DAN JANJIGIAN

It was summer, and Nevart was running in the fields of Eastern Anatolia. Playing in the grassy knolls that overlooked the nearby sea was a great distraction from the chores that she'd have to do if she were in the house. Her Mom, as usual, was cooking, and her siblings were nowhere to be seen. Knowing that her father was working nearby, she ran to his shop where she often went to duck out of the sun. That afternoon was particularly hot.

Slamming the door against the wall as she walked in, her father looked up quietly and smiled. He was a short man, but strong with the hands of a man twice his size. He had a dark mustache that ran to his jawline, and as usual he as sitting squat on his stool next to several buckets with different colors of stain. Nevart would watch as he would grab a roll of yarn, dunk it into one of the buckets, and then slap the yarn against a flat pan that he'd laid on the ground. He'd repeat this process again and again until the yarn kept the color of the stain. Nevart was always mesmerized by this process, and it relaxed her to watch her father work.

Walking back to the house, she nearly fell as her brother and one of his friends came running from behind the house. Melkon was built like their father and was the oldest of the boys in the family. Escaping back into the kitchen, she watched as her mother finished the pastries that she was working on. On the stove the milk was boiling for the yogurt, and Nevart blurted out, "Grandpa is coming!"

"What?" her mother cried, "Is he here? Do you see him?"

"No," said Nevart, "but whenever you make yogurt, Grandpa comes."

Mariam, the oldest of her siblings, just laughed and said, "Grandpa won't be coming until the baklava is coming out of the oven!" Although baklava was all of their favorite desserts, Grandpa, ironically, did come, just an hour later.

Back in those days, when Grandpa came, it was from a distance. The walk, since he didn't have a horse or a mule, took nearly 7 hours, so visits were infrequent. He lived in an inland village up in the hills outside of Trabzon, and on this particular trip, he was coming down to get some of the pieces of a stove that he would strap to his back to carry home.

Life was simple for the Narlian family and it was wonderful. The kids went to school, just minutes from their home. The seaside was just down the hill from where they lived, and there you could find the freshest tomatoes, fish and meats, and there was always a game of backgammon to be played along the pier. Heading west of their home was a hill and park that gave a full view of both ends of the village, and you could sit for hours just watching the boats come in with all of their merchandise. Trabzon was a bustling port, and from Bostepe, the name that the hill was called, all the men looked like ants as they moved crates on and off the boats that came into port.

This was life as Nevart knew it. Family came first, and everything was simple, until it wasn't.

In April of 1915, when Nevart was nearly 8 years old, her father was required to attend a meeting with all the other Armenian businessmen in the area. As he was escorted from their house in the middle of dinner, he tried to give her that smile that he always saved for her when she sat in his shop, but the smile was empty. That was the last time she saw him. 1915 marked the beginning of the Armenian Genocide, which saw the eradication of 1.5 million Armenians.

In the course of just a few months, Nevart bore witness to the drowning of her mother and sister when a Gendarme (Turkish soldier) walked between her and her sister Mariam as they were hand in hand, and separated them by walking between them and leading Nevart to a holding area where she'd wait to be put in an orphanage. Her mother and sister were taken with the rest of the women and older children, had their hands bound and were forced off a bridge to be drowned by the sea. At the time, she had no idea what happened to her other siblings, and survival became her first priority.

The orphanage was not a pleasant place. It smelled of stale milk and was always dark. The children were not allowed outside except for a few minutes every few days, and even then, they were restricted in what they could do and where they could go. Children that became sick or "out of control" were moved into a different part of the orphanage that the other children were forbidden to enter. Nevart and her curious personality put her in the position of always trying to peek through the door when someone went in or left, but she could never see beyond just a few feet. At one point, a Turkish worker, fed up with Nevart's insistence on seeing what was inside, pushed her in for a minute, before pulling her back out abruptly. In that instant, Nevart was changed. The room was filled with death and decay, and in that moment, she saw the bodies of dead children that had been with her in the orphanage just days before.

After months of being moved from sleeping quarters to eating areas, Nevart was pulled into an office where she was told that she'd been adopted by a local Turkish family. From the second that she was introduced to the family, she knew that she would not stay with them. Within days of being at their home, the family had made plans to send her back.

A neighbor, hearing of the failed adoption, asked to meet Nevart, as they were looking to adopt a young Armenian girl as a playmate for their daughter. The match worked, and Nevart started the next phase of her life with them. As a Muslim-Turkish family, with a father who was a known political figure, life could have been very difficult for Nevart, but the opposite was true. The family took care of her as an extension of their own family, and made sure that she retained all of her knowledge of her religion, even baptism, and her language. The girls also got along like the best of friends, and throughout her life, Nevart would always recall her times with them as some of the best of her life.

There's so much more to this story, but I'll summarize some of the high points. As the genocide came to an end, the Armenians that were left scoured the country to find the children, like Nevart, that had survived.

Those children were then sent back to their original home towns to try and reconnect with family members. At that time, Melkon, Nevart's brother, was the only survivor of her family, and they found each other at the town well. Together, they made their way, via Greece, to Ellis Island, where they were initially split up for a time, and then later reunited in Fresno, California, where she lived until she moved in with her daughter (Florence) and son-in-law (Aram), my parents, in the mid 70's. Over a half century after the genocide, she and her brother were finally reunited with their younger brother, Baghdasar, who had escaped the Genocide into Russia. Grandma Nevart, who was one of the greatest inspirations for me and my siblings, lived with our family until she finally passed away at over 100 years old, just seven years ago. She's the toughest woman I've ever met, and hands down, my idol.

LIVING FOR THE DAY

Growing up with a genocide survivor is a unique experience. There are so many stories that will never be told, so many memories that have been covered up, and so much pain that has been locked away. There's also so much appreciation for LIFE, so much value in the power of the human spirit, and so much joy to be shared. My Grandmother was one of the funniest people you'd ever meet, and one of the toughest. The last time I measured her, she was 4'7" tall (age 95, when I had her put her hands on the counter and, "stand as straight as you can!"), and she had a laugh that was incredibly infectious. My Mom and sister would constantly laugh so hard they'd come to tears.

The question I'm often asked is what's given me the confidence since I was young to take the "chances" that I've taken in life and business. The answer is simple, I got it from my Grandmother! From her, I've learned the three keys that you need to get what you want out of life. Let's face it, you only get one go-around, so why not make it extraordinary?

Lesson 1: Crack your Skull
Since we're discussing Armenian history, let's talk about the Armenian national fruit, the Pomegranate. If you've never had one, it's called the "fertility fruit," because basically it's nothing inside the skin but seeds. The secret to getting to the good stuff is cracking the shell open, holding half of the pomegranate in your hand, and then paddling the outside with a wooden spoon. (Look it up on YouTube, it's amazing!) Now, I'm

not saying that you should literally crack your skull open to get the ideas out, but let's be honest, you have great ideas that go nowhere but the six inches between your ears. Try this exercise:

Write down five LIFE-CHANGING things that you've been wanting to do for over a year. I'm not talking about "putting an addition on a house," or even "seeing New York," I'm talking about items like:

- Write your biography
- Record an album
- Travel Europe
- Have a family reunion
- Learn to fly a plane

What are some of the things that you've always wanted to do? They're always nagging at the back of your mind, and you tend to keep pushing them back, over and over again. The issue is your skull! Figuratively BREAK IT, and let that idea start to move into reality. Put a plan in place of how you can start to move towards accomplishing that goal.

Look at the first example we listed: "Write your biography." Ready? Then set out a time in the next seven days that you can dedicate an hour to getting started. Put it in your calendar, and start typing. Now, you may find lots of obstacles:

- You're not a professional writer: Great! Start writing and let someone clean it up later.
- You can't type: Perfect! Get a pen and paper.
- You can't spell: Fantastic! Download an audio app and start speaking into it.

The point is, there will always be reasons you can't do it. If it's important, then get it started!

Lesson 2: Seize the Day
Remember the Dead Poets Society? If you haven't seen it, see it now! *Carpe Diem* – Seize the Day - Grandma understood that life is fleeting. There may be no tomorrow, and even today isn't guaranteed for all of us. If you had a dream of being a professional athlete, and now you're 60, that pro-baseball career may have passed you up because you didn't

seize the opportunity to pursue that dream when your body was more capable to make that happen.

There are so many things that we can lose and replace in this world: Money, power, and fame. However, there's one commodity that can never be replaced, and that's TIME. Think about that. I can replace nearly anything else, but once I've lost a minute of time, that's gone FOREVER. Now I wish I could tell you that I've never wasted time, but I'd be lying. What I can tell you with great confidence though, is that I've taken nearly every opportunity to go after the things that were on my "bucket list," so that I'd never feel a moment's regret that I'd waited too long if those opportunities were taken from me. Remember, death isn't the only thing that can take opportunity, although it is the most final!

Look at the list of items that you wrote down in Exercise 1 from earlier. Now shuffle them so that anything that is "time restrictive" is at the top of the list and work your way down from there. After time restrictive, list the items that you're most passionate about from top to bottom. Put checkboxes next to each item, copy the list, and put it on your bathroom mirror. Remind yourself at the beginning and end of every day, what's most important for you to accomplish, and get started on doing it TODAY!

Lesson 3: Embrace Negativity
When I graduated high school, I moved to San Luis Obispo, California, just days later. I wanted to embrace my future, and not wait for it. My friends told me I was crazy, and I should stay.

"Enjoy a few more months of free rent and expenses!" I'd hear. "You'll probably be broke by the time school starts..."

After my freshman year, I took a job with the Southwestern Company to sell books door-to-door on the East Coast, and it was for commission only. Not only did my friends think I was nuts, but my parents basically forbade me from going. Two years later, when I took the Fall quarter off to travel Europe for three months, they nearly disowned me (btw, YES, I was paying for my own college and expenses at the time!). When I left Microsoft to start my own start up, one of my best friends told me I'd fail. When I went back into direct sales 10 years later, I was told I'd fail again.

It's in the nature of all people to try and "protect" you from things that aren't the norm. There's a reason that 5% of the world's population controls 95% of the resources. They took the routes that weren't normal. They took the chances that their counterparts told them were "stupid," or "reckless" to take. Now that I'm approaching my mid 40's, I can tell you that there's very few regrets that I have in my life, and anything that might feel like a regret can easily translate into valuable lessons that have helped me get to where I am today.

Life is a journey, and we get to choose the people that we take along with us. My Grandmother's journey is what's allowed me and my family to walk this Earth, and helped pave the path that we've all taken. That has translated into whatever measure of success we've found. These three lessons are the most valuable that I know in not just living a great life, but living a life of substance.

About Dan

Dan Janjigian is a national speaker to sales agents and managers regarding the art of the Cycle of Sales and leadership training. He's been featured on ABC, NBC, CBS and Fox, plus CNN and the BBC, and has appeared nationally on Dan Rather, and World News with Peter Jennings. He's a National Sales Director for Family Heritage Life, and owns the Gridiron Financial insurance brokerage, based in Austin, Texas. Operating in eight states, Gridiron finished 2014 (last year) as the highest producing brokerage of over 400 organizations that sold the Family Heritage products, and also boasted 4 of the top 15 salespeople in all of the Family Heritage companies. As a manager, Dan has directly worked with and trained the top two current agents in FHL, and he also continues to personally sell, breaking the record for the most premium sold in the 26-year history of the company in April of 2014. He also owns the record for the most individual policies ever written in one week, at 94 policies.

Online, Dan has a training site at: www.danjan.com, and is active in working with upcoming and veteran sales professionals and managers through coaching and social media.

Sales is not his singular skill. Dan was a professional bobsledder for nearly 10 years, competing from the US and Canada to all over Europe. In 2002, he raced in the Salt Lake City Olympic Games, and in 2004 was a Silver Medalist in the America's Cup series. At the beginning of the millennium, Dan moved into acting, being accepted into the Howard Fine Acting School in Los Angeles. That led to roles in films such as *Seabiscuit* and *The Longest Yard*, as well as several indie films, but no film brought more notoriety than *The Room*, which turned into a major cult classic, was made into a top selling book, and now has been optioned to be remade by James Franco and Seth Rogin in 2015.

As a restaurateur, he was involved with the widely-popular Geisha House in Hollywood, California, partnering with Ashton Kutcher, Tara Reid and others, as well as running The Parish Room in Austin, Texas, highly regarded as one of the best music venues in the country. Other notable items were several appearances on Home Shopping Network and America's Store, including appearances with Suzanne Summers, showing the power of WebTV, as well as being a winner on Wheel of Fortune in 2013.

Dan regularly speaks and coaches sales agents and managers on the Cycle of Selling, and how to increase sales and build cohesiveness within organizations. He's also regularly spoken to schools on the power of pursuing dreams and how to go after your goals.

Dan is married to his wonderful wife Beca, and has three children, Jenica, Landon and Nevi. They live in the Austin area of Texas, where he still works directly in recruiting and training his personal sales teams around the United States.

CHAPTER 39

PUTTING THE HUMAN IN TECHNOLOGY

BY DARIN SCHOUMAKER

It's an interesting position in which an IT guy like me stands. More often than not, the first introduction I get to people goes something like this: "Our server crashed!" Then I get to say, "Hi, my name is Darin and let's see what I can do to help you out." That's what I do, as the owner of ManagedNet Technology Solutions, I am the human face that goes with the technology that businesses become increasingly dependent on every day. We are in a fast-paced, technology and information-driven society, and it is here to stay.

Successful businesses utilize Information Technology (IT) to gain a competitive edge every single day and there will come a point in every businesses life when they need the help of an expert IT professional. They say that death and taxes are inevitable, but having an IT disaster is also inevitable *if* you don't have safeguards in place. Someone will try to attack your system in some way and there is <u>never</u> a preferred time for something like this to take place. It's always going to be inconvenient and costly. According to FEMA:

- 70% of small firms that experience a major data loss go out of business within a year.
- 43% of these companies never even re-open.

I am driven by not wanting anyone to be a FEMA statistic due to a catastrophic data loss, or other technology event. I can and do help, knowing that unless you have someone working on your side that knows how to be your protector in the vast virtual world, you're going to have a technology problem at some point. I like to think of myself as that guy who helps, and it excites me to hear comments about how there has never been an IT issue that I couldn't resolve. It's a testament to the spirit that I have as an individual, and the ManagedNet team has, when it comes to working with clients on their issues—or better yet, preventing them!

HOW DOES AN ELECTRICAL ENGINEER BECOME THE GO-TO IT GUY?

- You have to be connected to a clients business in a genuine way.

By chance, I graduated college with a degree in Electrical Engineering, but it was at a time where the economy wasn't offering many opportunities. As I evaluated all the factors out there, I did see a growing trend for businesses that needed someone with networking experience, which I did have. It seemed perfect! I got a job at a bank's corporate office in their networking department.

It was at this time that technology was really starting to be infused with business, which meant that there was:

- Lots of anxiety about how it all worked.

- A lack of knowledge about what IT was, exactly.

- And, a misunderstanding about how technology could be a great thing—a tool to take a business to the next level.

These challenges excited me instantly and my very analytical mind dove into the entire process, basically from its onset, and **I realized that I had found my calling**. What made me distinct was that I was also a people person, not just a guy who talked to technology like it was the human being. To this day, I realize something very important: *the real value I bring to my clients is that I am as vested in their success at a level similar to that of their own*. I want them to focus on their passion of building their business and I'll focus on my passion of making IT manageable and less daunting, something that my clients know is being taken care of to the "highest standards available."

And life goes on… As technology grew, I ran with it and embraced it, which led to some pretty amazing things in my life, including helping banks go from no networking at all to fully networked, as well as providing this same type of service for healthcare companies. One of the most *exciting challenges* I experienced, as technology and computers boomed in the business world, was being able to help a healthcare company go from just sixty to six hundred employees, all utilizing technology in just two years, while, at the same time, overseeing a new corporate data center. Each of these experiences were successful for me and it was my passion for those long, crazy days that kept it going forward in a positive direction, regardless of challenges that came my way.

Before long, my specialized and specific experiences put me in the position where I could become a sought-out consultant for many businesses, mostly mid-sized—large enough to afford IT but small enough that they couldn't have their own IT department. It was exciting, but I quickly realized that consulting, just like Electrical Engineering, was a highly saturated market, filled with both unqualified and fully-competent individuals. I didn't let this affect me, though, because I knew that I had an advantage because of my ability to connect with humans as much as technology. Understanding this has been pivotal in creating a dynamic distinction between the services that are offered through ManagedNet Technology Solutions and what other IT companies offer.

I ONLY NEED AN "IT GUY" WHEN THINGS GO WRONG, RIGHT?

- Your IT professional is as necessary to your success as your CPA.

There are many small to mid-size businesses that cannot afford to have their own IT department and are resistant to invest in things such as IT over marketing and other profit-building tools within their company. They don't believe that IT gives them a good value for its cost. *This is a huge misperception that I work on daily to overcome, every chance I get.* Here are three possible risks that happen when you toss aside IT for something else:

1. **You are not giving clients the protection they deserve for giving you their business.** Most businesses truly appreciate and value their clients. This means that they'll do an awful lot to please them. They send cards, coupons, and answer the telephone with a friendly voice, but what happens when a business owner has to

contact them and say there was a data breach, or that all of their information is gone because the computer system was somehow compromised? Will those cards, coupons, and friendly voices be enough to keep and maintain their trust after news like that? The odds are not in that business's favor.

2. **You will end up with a large, unexpected, and often unable-to-manage expense.** I assure you, this is not a fear tactic. The chances of you having some individual or entity or malware infiltrate your system is quite high—almost guaranteed to happen. That's when my business gets that frantic call I mentioned earlier and we are forced into a reactive situation that has a fairly huge price tag. Preventative IT can keep your operations running smoothly and it's my job and joy to stay ahead of people with ill intents on the Internet. Heed this warning: *Hackers are indiscriminate; your data is a valid target and is subject to constant exposure any time you are on the Internet, or uploading unsecured files, even from trusted sources.*

3. **You risk losing your entire business.** This has happened, and sadly, despite the emphasis on solid IT, it happens daily. Somewhere in this world, someone either avoided IT or used a novice (for example: the nephew who loves computers) and they ended up taking a detrimental hit for it. There are some businesses that will never recover from a breach of their system, and in an instant all that you've put your heart and soul into can be taken away.

The thought of people losing what they've worked so hard to build up, or having serious tension and nerves from IT obstacles that could have been circumvented, is hard for me to take because it is unnecessary. This is what I share with all my clients and it is part of the reason that my consulting company keeps clients:

If you think "cheap" when it comes to IT, you will most likely get exactly what you pay for. Using unqualified IT people with no understanding of the industry or your business is a recipe for trouble. *The reward of short term savings by using unqualified IT resources evaporates quickly when your business is adversely exposed to the perils inherent in today's IT environment.* **A prosperous business thinks long term and plans accordingly by setting up a valid IT management system that is sustainable.**

As a business owner, it's easy to become complacent with IT because it always seems like it can be "put off" until another day. However, **a system needs to be monitored regularly and kept up to date to be truly effective;** *that's what we do at ManagedNet.* Our passion is in getting to know and understand the business and business owner. We operate as part of their business with honesty and integrity, working with their technology as if we were working with our own. It's our job to make sure that there is no open door invitation for breaches of any sort in your virtual environment.

LEARN THE TOUGH LESSONS THROUGH EXAMPLE, NOT BY EXPERIENCING THEM.

- Never leave any "if only" moments in your business.

With the passion that I have for being the master of technology, I have a profound appreciation for all of my clients' businesses, because their businesses are what enable me to do what I love. That's why I will always try to get clients' on IT management plans that fit their needs and are based off knowledge of what it is that they do and how they go about it in their day to day operations. Sometimes, however, despite my best efforts and approaching clients from a place of genuine interest for their business, they take a pass. The scenario below is based on a real life situation that I was involved in:

A new client had a staff CPA named Joe (fictional name). Joe understood certain software that pertained to his job quite well, including how to back it up. That was great and he was very capable of doing that; however, he felt that his knowledge encompassed all forms of system back-up. He felt that he was "trained." The company President took him at his word because he owned 25% of the business, turning me down when I offered a service plan for back-up. I asked, "Are you sure?" and they responded confidently—"Yes."

Fast forward one year… This business had a catastrophic failure with their primary server, which required the need to recover data from back-up. We went in to try and rectify their problem and asked Joe for the back-up data and he couldn't provide it to me. The back-up plan he'd put into place hadn't worked for over six months and the initial set-up wasn't properly executed. <u>Improper execution of back-up = no back-up</u>!

The result of this was that this business temporarily lost:

a. Production Website facilitating all business internationally

b. Project Development work for new business

c. CRM system, which is client information and all emails sent and received

d. SQL Databases, which held all unique data to their thousands of customers world-wide

This was a huge problem and a costly one. It ended up costing this company over $25,000 to outsource their data recovery and reconstruct their internal IT infrastructure. It took three weeks to get this problem solved and nearly made the business go under. What makes it really bad is that it **all could have been avoided with a proper data back-up system and practices in place**. They would have had daily monitoring and maintenance to assure everything is working properly, as well as offsite data storage to protect it in case of fire, flooding, theft, or some other disaster. One of the main purposes of a business relationship with a thorough IT professional is to take care of these details proactively, leaving business owners and employees time to do what it necessary to make their business profitable and proficient.

Can you guess what happened when I approached the President of the company about handling their data back-up after that event? You guessed it! They understood the value and importance of this service and ever since that day, which was quite awhile go, they have been an appreciative and thankful client, knowing that **ManagedNet has their back—not to mention their future**.

The desire to spend money wisely in business is understandable, even expected. However, conservative financial wisdom needs to be tempered with today's IT realities; I'm not a fan of working through those "I told you so" moments; it's not fun for anyone and it is almost guaranteed to be far more expensive than a prudent IT management approach. Proper back-up and system management is something that I have a firm belief in; I want to be the guy to help create more success stories than comeback stories. My clients all see that in me, too, and even when I may not be able to get their agreement immediately, *I remain patient and passionate in my diligence with them because I realize how hard it is to be only human in a technical world.*

ARE YOU READY FOR A TECHNOLOGY DISASTER?

- I will always be passionate about being prepared.

Helping businesses understand if they are properly prepared for a technology disaster if one strikes is at the heart of what I do in the IT consulting and management field. My commitment to educating business owners who cannot afford to have their own in-house IT departments is exciting for me, because I get to learn about their business, their goals, and what I can do to contribute to their success. These types of partnerships have proven to be strong and dependable because clients know that I genuinely care about their results and that we're a team when it comes to their technology needs. I'm not going to let them down, and in turn, they become committed clients for life. This is powerful and it fuels my passions for what I do. To me, there is nothing more human than helping someone out with the technology that helps drive them toward a more successful business.

About Darin

In 2004, Darin Schoumaker founded ManagedNet Technology Solutions, an IT consulting and management firm that offers high-end Information Technology knowledge that is geared specifically toward individual business needs. Darin and the ManagedNet staff serve a national client base, but the company is located in Orange County, California.

Darin graduated from California State University, Fullerton, with a degree in Electrical Engineering and entered into the networking industry, working primarily for banks and healthcare companies, helping them to set up the proper systems to take advantage of technology that was in demand in the rapidly-changing business culture. All of these challenges and opportunities to help businesses assimilate to these changes sparked an immediate passion in Darin. He discovered that he had a distinct edge because of his ability to be able to relay highly technical concepts in a way that technology resistant businesses or individuals could grasp, and even embrace.

For over twenty-five years, Darin has effectively worked with companies and industries, taking the time to understand their specific needs. This is how he formulates plans for businesses regarding which technology they need and ensures that it'll keep working securely for the business and be able to manage its future growth. Darin is also known as the man who can step into any technology-related business disaster and help put the pieces back together again. He creates plans that help ensure that a business is never made vulnerable again by a compromise in their technology, whether it is via the Internet or data that is downloaded. Once Darin gains a client, they are most always a client-for-life.

Darin and his wife Mary, along with his children Chase and Cady, make their home in the sunny Southern California area. Their two terrier mix dogs, Joey and Lucy, were adopted from a local animal rescue organization and bring much joy to their family. When Darin's not working, he's actively involved in his community, serving for ten years on his HOA board, setting up community events, and enjoying his affiliation with Boy Scouts of America, where he has finished Wood Badge Training and is now staff for BSA Wood Badge Courses, which is an advanced leadership training course. He also serves as Advancement Chairman for his son's Boy Scout troop, having personally helped mentor over thirty young men on their journey to become an Eagle Scout. He's inspired to provide quality experiences and leadership opportunities to the youth in his community.

When it comes to causes, Darin is passionate about helping find a cure for Diabetes, a disease that hit home when his son was diagnosed with it in 2011. Doing what he can to give hope of a cure to those who suffer from this disease is important to him. For the other adventures in Darin's life, he always welcomes an opportunity for hiking or kayaking, as well as other outdoor activities.

You can reach Darin at: (800) 808-0638, ext. 810.

Visit: www.ManagedNet.com or email him at: Darin.Schoumaker@ManagedNet.com.

CHAPTER 40

DISCOVERING MY PURPOSE

BY DEBORAH SIMS

April of 2005 is a month I will never forget. The series of events and circumstances that led up to that Spring created the most rewarding and challenging chapter of my life, being a Foster Parent.

In 2005, my three daughters and I were living in a small suburb in Southern California. Coming into their teenage years, they had packed schedules with school, sports, church, and of course, their social lives. All three were extremely dedicated to their sports, and as a family, we spent most weekends juggling various tournaments and games all over the country.

In 2004, a family moved in next door to us. One of the four sisters happened to play on my youngest daughter's soccer team. It wasn't long before the two of them grew extremely close and were spending most waking moments together. As their relationship grew, our families got to know one another. They had four daughters between the ages of nine and fourteen. At the time, my girls ranged from twelve to eighteen years of age. They became somewhat of a neighborhood pack.

In the early months of 2005, my youngest daughter came home with very strange news. In the middle of the night, our neighbors' father was arrested. A few weeks later, he endured a trial and was sentenced to one year in prison. In a scary and confusing period of time, we tried to help our neighbors in every way we could.

It wasn't long before I recognized another issue. The girls' mother was a recovering addict and had appeared to have relapsed with the sadness and pressure associated with her husband's sentence. As the days went on, I became progressively concerned about the girls. Not only were they poorly fed and wearing dirty clothes, but their house had become filthy and their mom was sleeping most hours of the day. By April, the girls had begun to share what they had witnessed their mom using, and they were extremely concerned for her health and safety.

On the way to a bat mitzvah on a beautiful Saturday afternoon, my daughter and I received a phone call from the oldest girl. Their mom had left the house inebriated and was driving under the influence. She expressed that she and her sisters did not feel safe and asked if we could come get them. In minutes, we arrived at their home. With some tremendous courage from the four sisters, they evacuated their house. That evening, we shared a deeply emotional experience and together we decided to join our clans so their mom could get the help she needed. My three daughters and the four neighbor sisters became the 'Seven Sisters.'

The girls moved in that night, and we began to make accommodations for our family's newest members. We bought portable closets and new clothes for each of the girls. My daughters made space for a roommate in each of their rooms. We began to organize the shuttling of bodies to and from school, sports practice and their other activities. Meanwhile, their mother was placed in a rehabilitation center and had begun her road to recovery.

Three weeks later, we seemed to have figured out somewhat of a routine. Right then, a disaster struck! Child Protective Services ordered the Sheriff to go to the girls' school and retain them as 'wardens of the court.' I was heartbroken as I watched them escorted to the patrol car, their eyes full of tears, sobbing in humiliation and sadness. As wardens of the court, it is nearly impossible to gain approval as a Foster Parent through Child Protective Services. If I was to get them back as their legal guardian and prevent separating them into four different homes, I had an extremely difficult task ahead of me. In the following days, I worked all day and all night, reaching out to every contact I had and investigating any hoops and loopholes I could find to keep CPS from splitting up the sisters. Through determination and with nothing short of a miracle, CPS approved me as the girls legal guardian; I was now officially a Foster Mother.

In the subsequent nine months, our families joined as one and we rode a roller coaster of highs and lows, growing together along the way.

As a Foster Mother, I took on a lot of responsibilities that proved to be much more challenging than I could have anticipated. Every evening, I supervised phone calls between the girls and their parents. Once a month, I supervised their visitation with their mom. Although my sole goal was to help these young ladies through this dark time, I couldn't help but feel like a villain. The girls' parents did not see me as the person who kept their family together temporarily, but rather as the person who tore them apart. Neither parent would speak to me nor look at me, as they felt nothing but hatred towards me. Although this hurt deeply, I had no time to dwell in my sadness while the girls at my home were enduring extreme emotional hardship and psychological trauma. In addition, a psychologist from CPS would visit our home monthly to help the girls converse and cope; however, there is no knowing how they were really feeling during that time in their young lives.

All we could do was to try to make the best out of a crumby situation, and we did! The seven sisters played in their tournaments and among themselves in our backyard. They hosted dance competitions that lasted for hours and had movie nights that resembled the living room of the 'Brady Bunch.'

In addition, 2005 was a year of firsts. I took the girls to their first dentist and doctor's appointments. We taught them how to clean their rooms, keep their closets neat, and how to do household chores in an organized rotation. In such a crucial period of their lives and in such a dire situation, I watched them grow in so many ways both as individuals and together as a group.

With our newly acquired family members, our budget was very tight. As someone who is self-employed and who had recently started a new business, time was very limited. Friends came with open arms of support. Although there were countless acts of kindness, the most memorable acts involved helping with cooking and driving. Several days a week, various friends would drop off abundant and beautiful baskets of food for us to have for dinner. In addition, several moms volunteered themselves to drive girls from our clan to and from various sports fields for each of their practices and games. One dear friend even provided a financial donation to help us continue helping the girls. Although they may feel that these were simply small gestures, their help made it all possible.

Our journey came to an end around Christmas time. Since the girls were not able to be with their parents, I felt it was important for them to be with family. With financial help from our community church, they were able to spend time with extended family members in Oregon. In the weeks following the holidays, their mother completed all of the steps required by CPS to retain the foursome. Their father was released from prison, rehabilitated, in early 2006. As expected, almost all contact with the girls ceased, per the request from their parents. From time to time, however, I would see the girls at games and we would embrace, reminisce, and catch up on any new updates. Although our communication became limited, my love for each of them remained the same.

The unsung heroes from those nine months are my three daughters. My eighteen year old gave up her entire summer following high school graduation to act as a driver and baby sitter for all the girls. Meanwhile, my twelve and fourteen year olds took on these very adult issues with immense amounts of maturity and compassion. They all forfeited their social lives and had opened their private space to help their newfound sisters. Many days were hard, but overtime we all learned how fortunate we were. Our family had experienced divorce among other things, but the foursome opened our eyes to the bountiful blessings we shared.

I share this story because this experience changed my life, my perspective, and my purpose. I witnessed four young girls go through an unpredictable series of tragic events where they had no say or control in what was going to happen to them.

As a Wealth Advisor for decades, I have witnessed woman after woman experience monumental financial and emotional tragedies due to unanticipated incidents. I have also witnessed common fears shared between many of my clients.

These are the top fears of most women:
- Health and Health Care
- Running out of Money

- Being a Burden on their Children
- Establishing and Committing to a Budget

It is important to be honest with yourself and to recognize what your fears are. It is normal to have fears. Identifying them and having a plan to overcome them is what is important. This is what we help our clients with in our planning process; I call it their 'Financial Future.'

The key to taking control of your Financial Future is simply to get started! It may be scary at first, but I have seen this transformation in my Clients. Once their confidence begins to outweigh their fears, many of them become passionate about being involved in every step of planning for their Financial Future.

Following 2005, I've made it the purpose of my career to help women take charge of their financial future. Over the years, I have helped many women who have experienced unanticipated hardships, both financially and emotionally. Experiencing the strength of those four sisters and their willingness to adapt under unfair circumstances completely changed me personally and as a Wealth Advisor. I made it the purpose of my career to help women take charge of their finances. Through workshops, events and social media; I challenge ladies to reach deep inside and discover their passions, their wants and their fears. We help women feel confident in all aspects of their Financial Future – from planning a wedding to preparing for a loved one's funeral.

April of 2005 is a month I will never forget. Those nine months pushed me emotionally and financially to places I had never been before. By taking these risks, this experience gave me purpose for the rest of my life. As the Seven Sisters have transformed into women before my eyes, they continue to inspire and drive me every day; whether they know it or not.

No matter what situation you find yourself in, below are my recommendations for everyone who wants to begin to gain their confidence and take back control of their Financial Future!

- Get organized! Begin to complete one task at a time. This is an important step and may seem overwhelming at first but you can make it fun! Treat yourself to a new purse or briefcase. Organize your financial and personal subjects with folders or labels in matching colors. Make a checklist and treat yourself at each task's completion. Remember this is for you!

- Educate yourself. One of the biggest challenges is knowing the questions to ask. Use the Internet and books to explore subjects interesting to you. Share what you have found with your friends and associates. I congratulate you for reading this book and this chapter to help start you on your journey.

- Surround yourself with a trustworthy team of experts. The people on your team should be there to plan and protect you, first. We partner with Estate Planning Attorneys and tax professionals to help simplify our clients' lives. With our expertise on Wealth Management, Clients come to us because we focus on what is important to them to initiate their financial strategy. We identify their fears and aspirations. With compassion and empathy, we consult our clients on how to achieve their desires. The final step is implementing a financial plan that gives them confidence for today and a secure future for tomorrow.

At the end of the day, unpredictable events occur. However, with a little guidance, every woman can be confident in her financial decision making and can adapt to life's circumstances, just like the Seven Sisters.

About Deborah

Deborah Sims began her career with Dean Witter twenty-five years ago in Downtown Los Angeles. Within five years, Deborah was named Vice President of Great Western Financial Services, an acclaimed Wall Street firm. For the last fifteen years, Deborah Sims has been practicing as a Wealth Advisor. Today, her office is located in the heart of Historic Rancho Santa Fe, California. While using her unique approach, founded on providing personal service, her mission has been to educate her Clients with the knowledge to simplify a complicated subject.

The Estate Management Group provides financial guidance to Clients of Wealth, Business Owners, and Foundations, to help them plan their Financial Future and to protect their Family Legacy. Deborah Sims works closely with a network of locally renowned Estate Planning Attorneys and Certified Public Accountants. By structuring a team with outside specialists, Deborah is able to provide her Clients with access to a variety of services. This original method has simplified her Clients' needs and has distinguished Deborah in the Financial Service Industry.

In addition to Estate Management Group, Deborah Sims has established Engaging Women in Wealth for means of empowering women about their financial futures. As a woman on Wall Street, Deborah believes it is important that every individual feels confident about their personal finances. By creating a series of interactive workshops, Deborah's focus is to create a friendly environment where women feel excited and engaged about their wealth.

Estate Management Group and Engaging Women in Wealth were founded on loyalty, traditional values, dedication, uncompromising quality, and exceptional personal service. By creating a personalized relationship with each one of her Clients, Deborah is able to strategize and create plans designed to help all of her Clients achieve financial freedom. This is accomplished by identifying her Clients' passions that often include: Charitable Giving, Collectibles, and establishing a Family Legacy.

As Principal of Estate Management Group and Engaging Women in Wealth, it is Deborah's mission to be her Clients' most trusted Wealth Advisor through professional knowledge, integrity, and personalized wealth management services.

Additional Services Offered:

- Fee Based Asset Portfolio Management
- Estate and Charitable Planning

- Tax Efficiency
- Creating Wealth Plans for Family Legacy

Affiliated Organizations:

- Rancho Santa Fe Foundation Women's Fund
- Rancho Santa Fe Rotary
- USC Trojan League Associates of San Diego County

Estate Management Group ~ Engaging Women in Wealth
16906 Via de Santa Fe
Rancho Santa Fe, CA 92067
Mailing: PO BOX 926
Rancho Santa Fe, CA 92067

866.434.4500 or 858.756.0004
www.estatemanagementgroup.com
www.engagingwomeninwealth.com

CHAPTER 41

THE SECRET TO MULTIPLYING YOUR INCOME EXPONENTIALLY, GUARANTEED!

BY CHI LEUNG CHAN

HOW I MULTIPLIED MY INCOME EXPONENTIALLY

Who doesn't want their income to double, triple or multiply any multitude of times? I mean, imagine what you could do with all these "extras" in your life. Take trips with loved ones, buy things you want and help others in need.

I know I wanted to make a lot of money badly. This is why – after taking the shortest possible route to getting my Masters – I went straight to work for a big company, and then another, and another, and yet another . . . until I got stuck in yet another mediocre job with another mediocre salary.

And you know what the worst part of this was? People I know who worked less hard than I did and who studied less than I did, were all getting ahead of me and making more money than I did.

This feeling of knowing you can and want to do more, but are unable to, went on for years. Then, by accident (or perhaps I was unconsciously searching for it), I stumbled upon a book that taught people how to make a lot of money.

I tell you, this changed everything! All this time I have been looking for someone to teach me how to make money, and yet the answer could be found simply in books.

There are literally several thousands of extremely successful and wealthy people out there, who have written their life's worth of experience and knowledge into a single book – all with the intention to help others become successful and wealthy as well.

So the question for me was not, "How can I make a lot of money?", but rather, "Am I committed to making a lot of money?"

Since then, I have started studying different (audio)books, attended seminars, watched videos of speakers and followed different courses. The result was that I have multiplied my income exponentially since I picked up that first book in 2010, literally! My gross income in 2010 was €50,000 and in 2014, €182,500! And the way things are going, it looks like I will be doubling my income in 2015 again.

SO WHAT IS THE SECRET TO MULTIPLYING YOUR INCOME?

"Change is Inevitable, Progress is an Option."

~ Anthony Robbins

The world around us is changing every single day. Just a few years ago, we used email, laptops and USB sticks. Now we are using Instant Messaging, Tablets and the Cloud instead. The pace of change is incredible.

The same holds for what you know. You could have been the best of your class and graduated *magna cum laude*, but if you do not continuously improve yourself, what you know will eventually become obsolete.

This is what I realized when reading that first book in 2010. It was not that I was failure, not good enough or not smart enough, it was simply that I was not progressing myself everyday. Like Tony Robbins points out, once I decided that progress is a must and not an option for me, everything changed.

And that is *the* secret that will multiply your income exponentially, guaranteed!

THREE SIMPLE STEPS TO CHANGE YOUR FINANCIAL FUTURE

Now that you know what the secret is to multiplying your income, it is time to reveal the three simple steps you must take to change your financial future.

Let us review each step in more detail:

Step 1: Research your field of interest

"Success leaves clues."

~ Anthony Robbins

- Do you want to get better in the field in which you are active?
- Do you want to change over to another profession?
- Do you want to start your own business?
- Do you want to earn a lot more money?
- Do you want to improve your social skills?
- Do you want to gain more confidence?

Whatever it is that you want or would like to achieve, you can be certain that someone else has done it before, successfully. My advice to you (and Tony's as well), is that in order for you to gain the knowledge you seek, the quickest and probably also the most economical way is to buy a book (or books) written by the people who have successfully done what you want to do.

Consider what books actually are. A person who is extremely successful at the thing you want to do and/or has spent a good deal of his/her life extensively researching the subject about which you want to know more, has written all those years and years worth of knowledge and experience down in a book. And all of this can be purchased for a few dollars. Just imagine, if you were to read three or four books about a particular subject, that would surely save you at least fifty years or more of your time, since if you needed to discover all of this information yourself, this would be the time you would need.

You must be thinking, who in the world has time to read books all the time! I know, I thought exactly the same thing. I mean, most people – between sleeping, eating, working and relaxing – have to divide their time among their spouse, boy/girlfriend(s), kid(s), friends and family, right?

Then I discovered something called audiobooks!

Whether you want to or not, the average person will spend at least one hour commuting to work, from work, to a client or to a supplier each day. And on bad days this could be even longer. Normally you would spend this time listening to music, watching videos, browsing the Internet, basically finding ways to spend your time to make it go faster.

Now imagine using this "spare time" to listen to an audiobook in the area you want to progress in! What do you think would happen?

"If you read one hour per day in your field, that will translate into about one book per week. One book per week translates into about 50 books per year. 50 books per year will translate into about 500 books over the next ten years."

~ Brian Tracy

I am pretty sure I have not read 500 books during my entire study period. I am actually not even sure I have even read 500 books before 2010 at all! How valuable do you think YOU could become by doing this one simple step? The possibilities are limitless.

Now comes the million dollar question: how do I know what books to read or what field to study? I am sure you have heard people say that you have to find your passion and then put all your focus and energy into it, then you will become successful, right?

Fantastic! If you know what your passion is. But what about the rest of us who might have a hunch, but certainly do not know for sure? I, for one, cannot say with certainty what my passion is, then what?

I have struggled with this "finding your passion" topic for quite some time until I heard someone explain this as someone who goes to a top-notch buffet restaurant for the first time. This buffet consists of over 1000 different dishes that you can choose from. But wait, there is catch. You can only choose one dish. How on earth are we going to pick one if we never tasted most of the dishes to begin with? This is the dilemma

90% of us are confronted with when trying to find our passion. Then I figured, why not try out a couple of dishes to see what type of dishes you like and then move from there.

A good place to start exploring are in the areas you are good at, since most of us tend to like to do things we are good at.

Step 2: Take informed action

Have you ever seen the movie or read the book *The Secret,* which discusses the law of attraction? Very informative book; however, the information both informed and confused me. It just did not sound like it was the complete story and indeed it was not. You also need to actually take action as well.

The same holds for **Step 1** mentioned above, as watching videos or gathering information alone will not make you any richer. If anything, it might actually make you poorer if buying books is the only thing you do!

If it was that simple, anyone who has ever read a book on how to become wealthy would be wealthy, right? You actually need to apply what you have learned in practice to see what works and what does not.

"Information is not Knowledge."

~ Les Brown

You need to make sure that you persist and practice. You know the saying "practice makes perfect," right? Not completely true though....

After speaking with different people from different walks of life and also having done a brutally honest personal review, I found out that you can distinguish five different types of persons who want to succeed (financially).

1) **Not believing, thus not trying:** You have people who believe they will never be able to make more money, so they do not even try at all.

2) **Trying, but not believing:** You have people who feel they should be making more money and they will try. But they do not actually believe that they can actually achieve this, hence as a result they will not.

3) **Believing, but not persisting:** You have people who believe they can be making more money, but at the first sign of challenge they get discouraged and stop.

4) **Persisting, but not knowing:** You have people who believe they can make more money and persist despite all the challenges, but still fail every single time.

5) **Knowing and succeeding:** Then you have people who believe they will make more money, and they study, do research and get advice from experts before they start, and eventually they will become wealthy.

The saying should actually be correct – *practice makes perfect*. There are times that you will need to gather additional information or have an expert explain to you "how to do it."

Be aware though, not to make the mistake many others (including myself) have made, by asking people *you know* for advice instead of asking the expert *who knows* for advice. Although I know it feels right to do so, because they know you, you trust them and they sincerely want to help you. The simple matter of fact is that you would not ask your butcher to teach you how to bake bread, right? And you would not ask your electrician to fix your car, right? So why would you ask your friend, who happens to own a few stocks, for advice on what stock to buy?

Same applies here, if you want to progress in your field, make sure you ask the person who has done it successfully consistently for advice!

Step 3: Do more than asked
You are having a nice dinner at a restaurant and suddenly you get a complimentary drink from your waiter. How would you feel? Most of us would feel pretty good since it was something that was not required and also something we did not expect. So, the waiter's tip would surely be bigger than usual. Now if you were to apply this in your business life, what do you think would happen?

> *"We are all self-employed irrespective of whether we work for ourselves or work for someone else, as essentially everything we do has our name card on it."*
>
> ~ Brian Tracy

Once you realize that you are your own business card, then what do you think would work best for the internal/external clients you are serving? You are right, by doing more for them than they have asked for.

"You do not get paid for the hour. You get paid for the value you bring to the hour."

~ Jim Rohn

If you consistently do more than you are asked to do, then you will become more valuable and you will multiply your income exponentially.

IS IT REALLY THIS SIMPLE?

There you have it, this is the secret including the three simple steps that will guarantee you multiplying your income exponentially. But I hear you thinking, is it really this simple?

"Success is Simple, but not Easy."

~ Jim Rohn

Indeed it is this simple, but I never said it is actually easy to do, since the simplest things to do are even simpler not to do. However, if you stick with this, I guarantee you will make more money, a lot more!

Be sure to watch out for the two biggest and most common pitfalls on your journey:

1) **Stopping too soon:** Sometimes it could feel as if you are doing all the right things, but still nothing seems to change. Then you give up…. and just before you are about to get what you want.

   Compare this with nine months of pregnancy; the first few months are nothing special; then in the sixth month, the back pains and nausea start, and it gradually gets worse; until the ninth month where everything is swollen and everything hurts (we guys know instinctively not to argue at that moment); then the water breaks, the labor pains start and all before seems like a piece of cake. I am pretty sure if the mom had a choice, she would say "this is not worth it, lets quit," then when the child is born she would know it was all worth it.

Achieving anything is exactly the same, when things are getting really tough you know that you are nearly there!

2) **Hoping someone else changes instead of you:** Ah, the memories. Have we not all experienced this before. Why doesn't my manager, client, colleague or supplier change so they can see just how valuable I am to them. The thing is, not everybody will see just how valuable you are. And trust me, wishing they will change is *just not going to happen*.

The only one you have control over is YOU. So stop hoping or trying to change someone else. Instead, if you keep changing, enhancing and progressing yourself, someone will eventually come along and see just how valuable you are and you will be rewarded according to the value you have created for yourself.

Finally, a question I get asked quite often, when I am speaking with people about this secret. "Didn't you just get lucky?" In a sense, yes, however, let me answer this question using a quote I really liked from a movie I have recently seen that is called Fifty Shades of Grey:

"The harder I work, the luckier I seem to get."

~ Mr. Grey

About Chi Leung

Chi Leung is a continuous improvement enthusiast who constantly searches for new boundaries to explore. This exploration drive has resulted in him trying out a multitude of different disciplines and roles throughout his professional career – ranging from finance professional, consultant, entrepreneur, sales staff and recruitment director to personal development trainer and author. His personal development career has pushed him to follow courses in human psychology and obtain professional *Train The Trainer* training from Jack Canfield (the World's 1# Success Coach).

Chi Leung received his Master's in International Business in 2001. And like most graduates, he thought that he would conquer the (business) world. The reality was quite different though, as he struggled for nearly 10 years, where he made extremely little progress professionally and financially. It was not until he learned. . . "the secret to multiplying your income, guaranteed" that his professional and financial future changed. In merely a couple of years, his income has increased by **500%!**

The secret to 'multiply your income, guaranteed' is centered around the philosophy of continuous improvement. The essence is that the world around you is ever-changing and to get ahead and stay ahead, one will need to improve oneself everyday or risk becoming obsolete. Having visited over 24 different countries to date, Chi Leung is certain that this simple secret is effective in any part of the world.

Chi Leung, having personally experienced the "pain" of not knowing, has since been exploring different ways to share this valuable knowledge. For this reason, he is co-authoring this book, giving seminars to groups and organizations, and is setting up a 'howtoliveyourrichlife' blog.

Chi Leung currently lives in a small country called Holland that is world famous for its .... ehhh .... tulips .... of course, and is still looking for new opportunities to explore and challenges to conquer.

You can connect with Chi Leung at:
www.linkedin.com/in/chileungchan

CHAPTER 42

THE CLIENT COMES FIRST

BY RUDY L. KUSUMA

Buying or selling a home can be a complicated process, and people are looking for an agent that they can trust to guide them through what can be a milestone in their life. Many real estate agents work as a solo agent – they're a one-man show. Working alone means handling all of the paper work and the processes behind the transaction, the contract, and arranging access to the home. The responsibilities are many, and they can lead to a real downturn in customer service. Often, solo agents are just too busy to provide a 'client first' experience.

The most effective way to achieve that experience for the client is through a team approach. A real estate sales team allows for each person to be focused on one thing in the process. It takes the juggling and multi-tasking away and allows everyone to really make sure the client is being taken care of. Our agents just focus on finding deals and negotiating contracts, while our tech and support staff work to handle everything else. What sets us apart is that we provide an entire team for our clients when they come to us to buy or sell a home.

LEARNING ALONE

When I first got started in 2007, I worked by myself as a solo agent. It started out good enough, but as business grew, I got busier. Soon I had so many clients that I was constantly busy and always on the phone. My personal approach to the customer began to fall by the wayside as I took on more and more customers.

In 2009, I realized what was happening, and that it needed to change. I was overwhelmed, overworked, and looking for a new approach to serve the consumers. My clients were suffering, and I knew that would lead to less business, and things would get even worse. There was a finite amount of time I could spend on work, and I needed to develop a system for sustainable success.

WORKING AS A TEAM

Traditionally, a solo agent spends 75% of their time looking for leads and prospecting for new business. That includes door knocking, cold calling, networking, and following up on referrals. Here, we have an inside sales team that work solely on leads and potential customers. Each month, there are about five hundred people in the area considering buying or selling a home. The inside sales team works on connecting with them and getting appointments made for them with my selling partners (a.k.a. the outside sales agents).

The agents in my team also don't have to worry about generating leads – that is left up to our advertising and marketing departments. That part of our team is responsible for creating campaigns that generate those leads, prospecting buyers and home owners who are considering of making a move. At the same time, our database manager ensures that our database is up to date so that we can follow up with potential clients who might not have been ready when we first connected with them. When someone goes to sell their home, we already have a database of over 5,700 potential buyers looking for homes in the area.

After the leads are generated and the inside sales team has reached out and found people who want to work with the team, our outside sales team takes over. Our outside sales team will work on actually negotiating the deals with the clients. They get to focus entirely on working with the client and guiding them through the negotiation and contract process. Without having to worry about the other parts of the job, they can provide a level of customer service that sets us apart from the competition.

There is also a transaction coordinator department on the team whose only focus is to make sure that all the paperwork is correct and in compliance with state and federal laws. They make sure everything is filled out and ready to go for our buyers or sellers clients.

Finally, our post-closing team works after closing to thank our clients. We sponsor a child at the Los Angeles Children's Hospital for every client we work for, using a portion of the fees from the sale. In addition, our post-closing team sends out "thank you" cards to each client.

The best part of the team approach is that it achieves real results in sales for the business. Working alone, I was a typical agent and could sell one or two homes a month. A team allows for more capacity to get things done. Last year, we sold one hundred and seventy homes. This year, we are on target to sell nearly five hundred. Working as a team has allowed us to achieve more than any one of us ever could on our own.

DELIVERING "WOW" THROUGH SERVICE

At our core, we want to deliver a "WOW" through our customer service. It's not enough to simply facilitate a transaction, or make a sale. We want the client to walk away from the transaction really thinking, "Wow!" and feeling taken care of. We want to exceed their expectations of a real estate agent.

One way that we go above and beyond is by having a satisfaction guarantee for our clients. If they buy a house from us and find that they aren't happy in the first two years, we will either buy it back, or sell it for free. That's how important it is that our clients feel that we are doing the right thing for them. I will help you get into a house that you are happy in, even if it means working for free. That relationship lasts beyond the sale.

Those long lasting relationships are key. Every Tuesday, we host a roundtable discussion here that is open to past and present clients. We gather in the office and talk about everything from deals, to recent business updates, to the economy. It allows for people to feel like they are keeping up with the real estate market and the world, and they get some insight into how our company is doing. Building those connections is part of delivering that "wow" factor.

It's also important to understand our internal customers – the agents and team members that work with me. We do things for them too, like having a fully-stocked kitchen. Ice cream is always available here. It seems small, but it has a huge impact in making our team feel cared for. That builds trust and confidence. It's easy to forget the internal customers, but really, they are just as important.

EMBRACE AND DRIVE CHANGE

Real estate is dynamic, and it can be a challenge to keep up with all the changes. Regulations, laws, and best practices are always shifting. Looking at what we can control, we've decided it's imperative to always be ahead of technology. We budget nearly $20,000 a month in ensuring our technology works, and works to set us apart.

We use technology to provide e-signature and document services so that our clients don't need to be tied to their home to work on their deal. Uploading business documents to the customer portal allows for them to be accessed on the go, and this takes another challenge out of the transaction for our clients.

Every step of the process is logged online, so clients can check on the status of their sale at any point. Making sure that we can provide that service and staying on top of technology allows us to reach our clients in a more meaningful way. Driving change keeps us ahead of the competition.

DON'T FORGET THE FUN

It's not enough to be effective to build relationship. Adding fun to the mix keeps it fresh and makes what you offer more valuable to the client. Our team has client appreciation days twice a year. Every six months, the clients are invited to come out to the office. There are musicians, and a huge barbeque. The atmosphere is really relaxed, and we get to connect with clients in a way that is laid back and more personal.

That idea extends to the team itself. Every month we have an internal team event. Sometimes it involves going out and seeing a show together. One time, the team went to the shooting range for the afternoon. It's nice to step outside of the office and build the relationships we have, because those fuel our ability to work together.

New ideas come out when we're relaxed and not focused on work. The team took a trip to Las Vegas, and ended up bringing back ideas that would work in our own space. Growth and learning come in a variety of experiences, and fun propels that.

PURSUE GROWTH AND LEARNING

In order for the team to be the best it can be, we need to be constantly learning. It can be really easy to become stagnant in the day-to-day of operating a business, but that is only going to erode your results and your dynamic. There are few things as important to me as training and staying sharp.

Our office works on training exercises for an hour every morning. It is the foundation of our day and gets everyone thinking about new things. We cover so many things: negotiations, contracts, assistant training, customer service, and sales. It keeps the team well rounded, and helps us stay on top of what might be changing - regulations on contracts, for instance.

There have been agents in the past who have been uncomfortable with the amount of training I have in the office. They have chosen to leave. If someone isn't willing to constantly be working to improve, they wouldn't fit well on the team.

HONEST COMMUNICATION MAKES THE DIFFERENCE

Sometimes doing the right thing isn't the same as doing the thing that is most profitable. There are times when we find out something about a house during the inspection process or sale, and we have to step in and tell our client what is going on. It may mean losing the sale, but it's important to us that our clients are in a home that is functional, and that the deal is good. If a house is going to require thirty thousand dollars in repairs because it is falling apart, we tell our client.

It may mean that we lose that sale, but the value of the impact is immeasurable. Those clients end up sharing with their friends and family how we were honest and stopped them from getting stuck in a bad situation. It builds trust and confidence, and it brings those clients back, as well as new ones.

Internally, that same idea of honest communication extends to how we talk to each other in the office. The team meets together every morning, so any time there is an issue amongst us, we tackle it there. There isn't an environment or a culture of gossip or talking about each other. The only kind of communication we want about the team is positive communication. We can share each other's accomplishments – not shortcomings.

PASSION AND DETERMINATION

The way to ensure that the team is working their hardest for the clients is to make sure our team is full of people who are passionate about what we do. It can be easy to be swayed into real estate by the money – especially when the company is successful, like ours. It's not enough to simply work in real estate to make a profit. It's a highly competitive industry, and in order to keep up, you need to be there for your client. The people on the team need to be so in love with making connections and selling homes that they would do it even if the money wasn't there.

I am so passionate about having a team that shares that vision that I give new selling agents a chance to leave before training is over. After four weeks of training, I pull them aside and offer them five hundred dollars to quit. If they don't want to come aboard, the money will be easy to take. Over the years, no one has taken that offer.

It makes the hiring process longer, and more involved, but it means that the people that come aboard usually stay aboard, and we get better for it. Potential agents meet with myself, and then with the senior agents. We go to dinner and get to know them in an atmosphere that is outside of the office, really early on. If there is a problem, it can be pinpointed in that interaction and the process stops before it gets too involved. The result is that we have a carefully built team of really amazing individuals that bring something to the table.

BE HUMBLE

Humility is what keeps us moving forward in a positive, genuine way. It's unappealing to the clients if we walk around being flashy and cocky about our position in the market. We need to be honest, approachable people who are focused on developing relationships and helping people through the most important transaction of their life.

With the range of business we do, our agents make an excellent salary. Some of the senior agents do really well for themselves. Walking into the office on an afternoon, and you would never be able to tell the agents apart. We function like a family, and a team, and not a sales-driven competitive office.

The reward in our work is in our clients' appreciation of what we do for them. Having more positive reviews on Zillow means more for the business, and the team, than the paycheck that comes at the end of the deal. That's why the focus has been on passion, honesty, and value.

THINKING DIFFERENTLY AND SEEING RESULTS

I could have muddled along as a solo agent, and many people do. However, building a team allowed for growth and change in ways that I could never have imagined. The best part of that is what it allows me to offer the clients that come to us to help sell their home.

The team concept works like a well-oiled machine, and everyone is an expert in their part of the operation. It takes the weight off our agents that interface every day with our clients, and allows them to really dig deep and connect. They get to guide the client through every step of the process, providing support and resources, without feeling hassled or hurried. That approach to personalized service sets the company apart, and creates business down the line.

It seems too simple to be true, but putting the client first and providing value to them way after the contract is signed is the key to a healthy business. It goes beyond the results on paper, or in the office. The real result is in the number of people who come back to us because they know that what we offer is simple, but paralleled by none.

About Rudy

Rudy L. Kusuma is a home owner, investor, best-selling author, business coach, entrepreneur, and top-producing real estate agent. He is the Founder and CEO of RE/MAX TITANIUM and the Managing Director of TEAM NUVISION, #1 Real Estate Sales Team in San Gabriel Valley. He has been recognized as one of the Top 100 team leaders in RE/MAX Worldwide (out of 100,000 real estate agents).

Rudy and his team have sold over $500 Million in transactions. He has been awarded multiple top producers awards, including The Five Star Real Estate Professional Award as published in the *Los Angeles* Magazine, and named as one of America's Best Real Estate Agents as published in *The Wall Street Journal.*

As a philanthropist, Rudy is on a mission to raise $100,000 for the Children's Hospital in downtown Los Angeles. For every house that his team sells, Rudy and his team are donating a portion of their income to the Children's Hospital. Not only home sellers benefit from his team award winning service, but they donate a substantial portion of their income on every home sale to help the local children in the community.

Rudy has advised and counseled home buyers, sellers, and real estate investors from every walk of life. CEO's, executives, and business owners hire his team because their businesses are "Teams", so they understand and appreciate Rudy's Team Home Selling System. Sales Professionals and Marketing-Oriented Entrepreneurs hire Rudy's team because they quickly recognize the superiority of Rudy's sophisticated System for selling homes as quickly as possible, for top dollars. Doctors, Hospital Administrators, and Nurses hire Rudy's team because, like the executives, they are thoroughly familiar with the benefits of a Team Approach. Exceptionally Busy Couples hire Rudy's team because his home selling system features methods of marketing and selling homes that minimizes their involvement and inconvenience.

Rudy provides numerous public resources regarding how to buy and sell real estate in today's real estate market. In addition, as a Certified Distressed Property Expert, Rudy contributes weekly articles on foreclosure prevention options available to homeowners. His expert advice have been published by community newspapers, including: *Indonesia Media, Mid Valley News, Temple City Life, Temple City Tribune, Arcadia Weekly, Monrovia Weekly, El Monte Examiner, San Gabriel Sun, Duarte Dispatch, Rosemead Reader, Azusa Beacon,* and *Around Alhambra Newspapers.*

Rudy L. Kusuma is the author of *The Ultimate NO HOLDS BARRED Guide to Selling & Buying a Home in the San Gabriel Valley*, and the co-author of the book that will change the landscape of real estate industry, *Death of the Traditional Real Estate Salesperson: Rise of The Super-Profitable Real Estate Sales Team.*

Rudy L. Kusuma lives in Temple City with his wife and two sons. He can be reached online at: www.TeamNuVision.net or by telephone at 626-789-0159.

CHAPTER 43

ROCKSTAR: LIVING WITHOUT LIMITATIONS OR RESTRICTIONS TO ONE'S OBSESSIONS
GENESIS: NEW BEGINNINGS

BY DR. RALPH LeBLANC

It has been said that you will become what you think about most; for me, in 1985, I was either going to become a Rockstar or a seventeen-year-old girl. I had no idea which of these choices was the driving force in my life, but if by nature we are moved by pleasure and pain then both of these desires moved me. One thing was clear, becoming a seventeen-year-old girl was the most unlikely choice.

The night was hot and humid, the beach breeze was perfect, and the Gulf air produced a light salty flavor on my lips. The excitement that surrounded me was absolutely intoxicating, or it could've just been the few adult beverages I indulged in that day. Whatever was happening, I definitely knew inside my soul that something was going to be different, so different that it would change my life forever.

The excitement that I felt was building higher and higher. I could actually feel the energy and waves of people all around me as everyone prepared for the night. As I looked around, I witnessed some of the most beautiful girls I had ever seen in my life at that point. The big hair, their beautiful eyes and smiling faces beamed with life. This may not have been heaven, but I knew it wasn't too far away. The sheer emotion of it all was nothing like I had ever felt before in my life. I found myself taking in deep breaths just so I could process all that was happening to me. It was almost too much for a young man to handle.

It was August 9, 1985, my first rock concert. On the marquee that night was Ratt and Bon Jovi, the location was Biloxi, Mississippi. The anticipation for this night had been building for several weeks. This being my first rock concert, I really didn't know what to expect. I just knew that I was in for a life-changing experience.

It was time and Bon Jovi took the stage. The lights came on and the band began to play; the crowd was going wild, girls were screaming, guys were screaming and the music was absolutely incredible. I was mesmerized by the amount of energy that was flowing through the arena. What was more incredible was the amount of attention that these Rock Gods were receiving from everyone in attendance. Bon Jovi ended their sets, and next to play was the headline band Ratt. As they played the arena erupted even louder than before, and I definitely felt something magical happening. This amazing experience had me feeling so much emotion, so much energy, and so much excitement. I knew in that moment I wanted to be a Rockstar.

The energy of that concert carried me into the next week. I was bitten. All I could think about was becoming a Rockstar and living a Rockstar Life. How would I grab the attention of a crowd and move them on a level that was to the heart and soul of what life can and would be. As several weeks went by, I realized that it wasn't the "Rockstar Life" I wanted, after all, I couldn't carry a tune in a bucket, it was that electric unstoppable power that I felt during that concert. It was that emotional soul moving energy that I wanted to feel in my life every single day. So I set out on a journey to find out what I could do to feel like a Rockstar every day of my life.

I would be given every opportunity to test this; some of those opportunities would be easy; some would quite frankly be very hard and downright scary. Whether it was with my high school friends and being that confident, the soldier in the United States Army that motivated and convince friends to push a little harder, or as Doctor of Chiropractic, coaching people to reconnect with the healing power within them. I was given opportunities to find these Rockstar Moments, the kind of Rockstar Moments that can change lives, communities and the entire world.

For the past 18 years, I have had the pleasure and the opportunity to speak both nationally and internationally, and I have witnessed firsthand people just like you and me making decisions to live their Rockstar Life. I am reminded daily how amazing it is to see the life transformation that happens in a two- or three- day program and even in a town where I live and work. The great news is geography has nothing to do with it, and where you live in the world doesn't matter anymore. The Rockstar Life you deserve and desire is right at your fingertips. The beliefs, the ideas, and the decisions that you make today will create your future happiness, health, and success.

While working with a coaching client that hired me to help her achieve her Rockstar Life, I shared with her four easy steps that changed her life forever. She is a self-proclaimed, "I am a real deal bottom line girl..." However, her true reality was that the life she lived was broken; she lived her life as if she were walking down a long, dimly-lit hallway with many doors. With her roadmap in hand, she lived this dimly-lit reality, the roadmap consisted of biblical principles and teachings that she had learned through the years—teachings and standards that she studied for herself and some of which were ingrained into her by others. These were the beliefs and realities that she clung to every day of her life. The effect was a life filled with depression, chronic neck pain, chronic back pain, and the consistent need to be validated by others. She also dealt with daily disappointment because she felt as though she could never meet the standards that she set for herself.

The first thing we need to find out was exactly what did she want to accomplish? What Rockstar Life did she want to live? Was she capable of this kind of transformation? Was she physically and mentally capable of handling this transformation? The one certainty I knew is that if I can get her to feel more hopeful about her future, and have her recognize that she creates her own reality, then her transformation was possible.

She found out quickly that she was going to have to take massive and immediate action, so that she could embrace and recognize the power that she has in order to re-create her true happiness, health, and success. Time was of the essence because, after all, she had a race to run... a triathlon.

When working with clients, it is never a question of difficulty, it is a process. The proper framework can help clients achieve a higher level of understanding. A higher level of understanding about how life truly works and how they can have maximum influence over the result they create in their health, their relationships, and their successes.

Tony Robbins says, "Long ago I realized that success leaves clues, and the people who produce outstanding results do specific things to create those results."

So when it comes to your health, your relationships or your successes, you can live a Rockstar Life and have complete balance. That is provided you are willing to look for the clues and you are willing to follow the steps. I want to give you the easy four-step process to create Rockstar success in your life. When you do this easy four-step process with consistency, passion and purpose, you can co-create predictable outcomes in every area of your life. Why do you want to follow these easy four-steps for success in your life? First, it's a proven method. It's not Theory. Second, it's proven to help people transform their lives all over the world. Third, you are absolutely worth the time, effort, and resources it takes, so you can transform your health, your relationships, and your success. Remember what others have achieved you can achieve. Your success is just a decision away.

STEP NUMBER ONE

Define your Rockstar Life. Napoleon Hill said, "There is one quality which one must possess to win, and that is definiteness of purpose, the knowledge of what he wants, and a burning desire to possess it." This very powerful statement sets up the basic foundation of how your entire life will unfold right before your eyes.

It is pretty simple. Do you know who you are? Do you know what you want? Do you have a white hot burning desire to achieve it? These are just a few questions that you can utilize to identify and define your dream life, your Rockstar Life. Remember whatever your dream is, big or small. . . *You Can Achieve It!*

STEP NUMBER TWO

Evaluate your beliefs. This is probably the most controversial step in the process. The reason is because the ego does not ever want to be challenged. After all, we have been having these beliefs all our life. Surely they must all be correct. Truth is, that's farther from the truth than you can imagine. Understand that these beliefs, some of which are inherited and others we learned in the first six years of our life, set the stage for every decision we make as adults. So you can now see why it may be a little difficult to let go of your beliefs.

The problem with these beliefs is that at one time they were true and correct, they actually served us in a way that protected us from harm and allowed us to evaluate our emotions. Now, as adults we learned that some of the beliefs we learned as children no longer serve us as adults. This creates incongruences in our life, and ultimately leads to failed health, failed relationships, and failed financial situations.

The easiest way to evaluate these beliefs is to first identify the belief. Then ask yourself, "Knowing what I know now as an adult with more life experience than I had when I was a child, does this belief still serve me in a way that it produces happiness, health, and success in my life?" If the belief can pass this litmus test then hold onto it. However, if it fails to pass the test you must release it, because the very belief that once served you and protected you is now creating disturbances and chaos in your life.

STEP NUMBER THREE

Forgiveness: this is the point where all healing in our body and in the world can begin. Forgiveness has been defined as a decision to let go of resentments and thoughts of revenge. It is the act of untying yourself from the thoughts and feelings that bind you to an offense committed against you. Forgiveness can reduce the power these feelings otherwise have over you, so that you can live a freer and happier life. It has even been known to lead to feelings of understanding empathy and compassion for the one that hurt you.

Jesus said before going to the cross, "Forgive them father for they know not what they do." Then upon his resurrection, it was the first thing he spoke to the disciples, "For those of you who have forsaken me, I forgive."

So forgiveness is a very powerful tool, at its very core forgiveness is giving up the opportunity to ever get even. Here I have outlined the five steps of forgiveness:

1. Forgive yourself
2. Forgive the other person
3. Give that person permission to forgive you
4. Learn the lesson of that situation
5. Release it and wish it well

Understand that forgiveness is less about others and more about you. Forgiveness does not deny the others responsibility for the injury or the wrong. It does not condone bad behavior, minimize or justify the wrong, or excuse the act. Lastly, forgiveness is not an agreement that means you choose to reconcile or remain in a destructive relationship or environment. Forgiveness releases all that binds you allowing for complete freedom of life.

STEP NUMBER FOUR

Recognize the value that vision boards and affirmations can have in your life. Research in brain plasticity has shown on a PET scan that every thought you think alters brain activity. Thoughts can change the activity of your brain and your body, your energy, and can even increase or decrease effect on immune function. We know that the brain creates neurological pathways through pictures and feelings, so now we can imprint ideas and images of success into our consciousness. So what you think and or imagine can change your brain activity and allow for true co-creation in your life. Research has shown that whether the activity is an actual or a virtual experience it shows the same brain activity on a PET scan.

So it is highly recommended that you create a vision board with pictures that excite you and inspire you. Make sure the images you use activate an emotional response when you look at them, this will fire neurons that will transmit and create exactly what you desire to see happen in your life.

When stating affirmations, you want to state them from a position of power. The most ideal position of power is a standing position feet shoulder-width apart and hands wide open. Make the declarative statement, your affirmation, with clarity and authority. This will create an ideal response and get your creative mind working to achieve happiness, health, and success.

There you have it: the easy Four-Step Pattern for Success. This is just a tip of the iceberg as to how deep these concepts can be discussed. I want to encourage you to deploy and implement this easy four-step process into your life, and by taking action you will experience massive transformation in your life and you will live your Rockstar Life.

Oh yeah, the client I mentioned earlier competed in four triathlons in three years. Her fourth race was a National Championship race that she qualified in – for her age group. Prior to this, she had never competed in competitive sports. She and her husband were also able to afford the dream vacation to Europe they thought would never happen. She now looks at the hallway and doors that she has broken through as the stepping-stones to reach greater heights in her life, and she is truly experiencing her Rockstar Life.

I am thankful and grateful for the opportunity to share this message with you; this message will continue to allow me to empower health, wealth, and vitality worldwide. Now, go out, take Inspired Action and Live your Rockstar Life Today!

About Dr. Ralph

Dr. Ralph J. LeBlanc – Practicing the principles he teaches, Dr. Ralph has truly mastered "Being the BEST me ever…Living Life like a ROCKSTAR!"

He combines his inner passion with outward purpose to motivate both individuals and crowds to the maximum! Dr. Ralph is CEO and founder of The Center of Wellness, LLC, a State of the Art Wellness Center, in beautiful Branson, Missouri. He has been in private practice for 18 years. Dr. Ralph is one of four Master Instructors for an Internationally-recognized seminar Company in North America, and one of the fastest growing personal and professional development companies teaching health and wellness techniques for well over 40 years.

An international speaker, Master Instructor, trainer, author, researcher and Doctor of Chiropractic, Dr. Ralph is the founder and developer of Rockstar Genesis, a 3-day immersion program that helps participants define and identify their Rockstar Life. He also assists in worldwide wellness training/treatment programs including the BEST Life Intensive Tour, the ever-popular Health Weekend for Wellness and the rapidly expanding Trainings for health practitioners. Dr. Ralph has also been frequently seen on The Jim Bakker Show, where he shares his knowledge and expertise with the world.

Dr. Ralph LeBlanc's programs reflect his personality of passion for the very best of everything he does! "Exciting," "motivating" and "eye-opening" are typical descriptions of his health, wellness, and lifestyle trainings. Literally keeping participants on the edge of their seats, Dr. Ralph truly takes a humorous, no-nonsense approach to training by incorporating accelerated learning technologies to ensure participants learn at optimum, retain at maximum, and apply immediately the knowledge to ensure peak performance for the rest of their lives! Participants see the changes immediately and the results are lasting!

Dr. Ralph has quietly been considered to be one of the most exciting speakers on the subject of health, wellness, and personal development both nationally and internationally. He has worked closely and shared the stage with some of the top authors and speakers in the world including: Pastor Jim and Lori Bakker, Dr. M.T. Morter, Jr., Dr. Ted Morter, Dr. Tom Morter, Dr Bob Hoffman, Dr. Gorden Pederson, Dr. Don Verhulst, International best-selling author and Master Persuader Dave Lakani, and many more!

Dr. Ralph has helped thousands of clients from around the world. He continues to dedicate himself to Changing Lives Around the World, through teaching the Principals of Health, Wellness, and Lifestyle Development to all that want to learn.

Dr. Ralph LeBlanc can be reached at:

417-336-4848

www.drralphleblanc.com

drralphhelpdesk@drralphleblanc.com

info@drralphleblanc.com

CHAPTER 44

FIVE TIPS TO BIG SUCCESS WITH YOUR FIRST SMALL BUSINESS

BY BRIAN & REGINA McCONNELL

Have you ever looked out the window of your workplace and wondered what all of those people outside were doing. How was it that you were stuck inside working and they were running around out there? Didn't they have a job? Didn't they work for a living? How could there be so many of them zooming to and fro every single day? They have freedom! (Or at least they appear to.) Most aspiring entrepreneurs long for that same freedom. We certainly did.

Some people are just not cut out for Corporate America. They can have tremendous success, be on an upwardly-mobile track, win multiple awards, enjoy great company perks, and yet still be unsatisfied. At some point they realize that they are being paid less than they are worth. They salivate for autonomy, personal responsibility, and freedom - Financial Freedom, Personal Freedom, and Creative Freedom!

The only way to accomplish these goals is to strike out on your own, create your own company, and leave the "Safety and Security" of a corporate job behind! But, be prepared, because what comes next is a whirlwind of learning experiences, stumbling blocks, sleepless nights, and some creative financial manipulation to stay afloat. Consider the experiences a "rite of passage" that every true entrepreneur must go through.

Of course every would-be entrepreneur is familiar with the often-cited statistic that 90% of new businesses fail in the first five years. Our goal is to give you five tips you can use to ensure that your first business is successful quickly and does not become part of that 90% statistic. Examine these five tips against the business you would like to start and then venture into the world of entrepreneurial endeavors with confidence!

TIP #1 – PICK A MATURE MARKETPLACE

Do you have a brilliant idea? One the world has never seen before? If you could only make a prototype, and show the world this new invention, would everyone want to buy one? If so, please STOP! That is not likely a good business to throw your life savings into. There are so many books out there encouraging you to follow your dreams and pursue your passion that you can easily become overly confident and underestimate the amount of work needed to create a marketplace for a new product.

We don't want to diminish your grandiose dreams of building the next great widget, we just don't want you to start there. Yes, a few products will revolutionize life as we know it. A few inventors from our era will become part of history. . . but most never will. Therefore, begin your first venture in a tried-and-true marketplace. Allow yourself to make the inevitable rookie mistakes in a field where acquiring new customers is easy. Learn from those mistakes, then move on to more exciting endeavors.

For any start-up, the most critical factor for determining success is "cash-flow." Many first-time entrepreneurs put their life savings at risk to fund R&D and advertising of a product that the world may simply not be asking for. They are content to watch the cash flow out on the hope that one day, someone will recognize their greatness and sales will skyrocket! Unfortunately, it is rarely that easy, and many financial lives have been needlessly ruined.

Fortunately, there are billions of dollars to be made in existing marketplaces. Marketplaces where, instead of you having to find customers, millions of consumers are looking to make a purchase from you! We love service businesses such as landscaping, plumbing, insurance, construction trades, or bookkeeping because the barriers to entry are low. You do not have to invest your start-up funds into R&D, inventory, real estate, or major equipment. Yet, there are billions of dollars flowing through these markets so you can begin generating cash flow almost immediately.

Our first entrepreneurial venture was a pest control company. We were both highly educated professionals, looking for a side business when our personal pest guy told us he was selling his business. While neither of us had any desire to work outside in the hot Las Vegas sun all summer, we did buy the company. We have yet to spray a bug, instead we found the perfect partner to run the operational aspects of the business. That company was part of our portfolio for over seven years and more than tripled in size during our ownership. The cash flowed consistently at about a 40% margin before we sold the business in 2012. The lesson here is to be passionate about the cash flow – not the business.

We always offer this story to new entrepreneurs . . . Two friends are walking through the woods. All of a sudden a bear appears on the trail in front of them and growls ferociously! One friend sits down, takes off his hiking boots, and slips on his tennis shoes. The other friend panics and says "What are you doing? You can't outrun that bear!" The first friend calmly replies, "I don't have to outrun that bear. I just have to outrun you."

If you are entering the world of entrepreneurship for the first time, do not try to invent your own marketplace. First, jump into a healthy marketplace with lots of competition, and be just a little bit better than they are! Believe me, most business owners get lazy quickly. If you compete in a healthy market, and employ the other four tips of this chapter, you are going to have a very successful first venture. From there you will have a solid foundation on which to build future success!

TIP #2 – BUILD SYSTEMS

Systems are the difference between building a business, and building yourself into another job. McDonald's doesn't have a great hamburger, but they have an amazing system to deliver that mediocre hamburger. You have to approach your business that way. In the beginning you may wear different hats, but you need to know (and define) each of those hats. One day, you will pass the hats on to employees who will work the same systems, in the same way you did.

For example, when we purchased the bug business, we focused on building the systems which would make the business run smoothly and consistently. Our role of working *ON* the business was separate from our partner's role of working *IN* the business. We took time at the beginning of the venture to define the roles and responsibilities of every position needed for the business to perform profitably. Had we been passionate about the bug business, we would have likely jumped right into doing everything ourselves and not taken the time to prepare a scalable business model. Instead we were passionate about the cash flow the bug business provided for us.

The most important system, and the hardest to get right is that of your brand. Most people think of their brand as the logo they bought on Fiverr, but it really encompasses everything that your customers experience when dealing with your company. Create a brilliant logo to draw people into your business, but then take as much time to design the system that controls their experience once they step inside. Be intentional about how you greet them, what materials you educate them with, and then make sure that a client who enjoyed their first experience with you can expect to receive the same experience when they visit the next time. Differentiate yourself from the dozens of other players in your market and give your customers a reason to tell their friends about you. If you create a powerful system to deliver your brand experience, you will quickly stand out in your marketplace. Your market share and cash flow will quickly grow.

Beyond your brand you need systems for taking in money, for paying bills, for inventory control, for depositing money into the bank. Take the time to define a system for every activity that must be performed in your business. You may feel like you don't have time to do that, but believe me, you don't have time not to!

TIP # 3 – KNOW YOUR NUMBERS!

Ok, this one gets almost every business owner I know, except accountants. Numbers are boring! Nobody except Scrooge McDuck wants to sit around and look at the numbers. As long as there are checks in the checkbook, everything is fine – right?

There are three financial statements that you must keep current and review often. Thankfully, we live in the digital world and we no longer have to keep these records by hand. QuickBooks software is your friend in the digital age, but buying it is not enough. Take a class on how to use it effectively and then keep all of your financial records there. Don't forget to schedule regular backups. (It is software after all). Once your data is entered into QuickBooks, the following statements will be just a click away. USE THEM!

1. Profit & Loss Statement – Your P&L is your first line of defense to catch anomalies in your daily business situation. All of the income you receive is listed on the top. All of the expenses you pay are below that. On the bottom line is a number; positive is good, negative is bad. This is where the term "Bottom Line" comes from and represents a company's "Net Income". Depending upon the volume of transactions in your business, you should update and review your P&L anywhere from daily to monthly. For example, in the pest control company, we collected hundreds of checks over the month. We found that accumulating checks through the week, and processing them inside QuickBooks every Friday was sufficient. You have to decide, but it is critical to view your P&L reports a minimum of once each month. Compare them to each other so you can see trends developing from month to month and so you can investigate any unusual anomalies.

2. Balance Sheet – The balance sheet shows you the overall health of your business. The balance sheet works on a simple formula:

$$Assets = Liabilities + Owners\ Equity$$

Do you see why it is called the balance sheet? Because all of your assets have to be in equal balance to your liabilities plus your equity in the business. There is a ton of detail we could go into here, but for the purposes of this chapter, just understand that for most small businesses, you want to gradually increase your equity by generating more assets (usually cash) and reducing your liabilities (debt). Review your balance sheet at least quarterly and before you make any long-term financing arrangements.

3. Statement of Cash Flows – The statement of cash flows is a way to see, as radio host Paul Harvey used to say, "The rest of the story!" Cash flow is to your business what blood flow is to your body. (Without it, you won't survive!) There are three types of cash flow: (a) Operational cash flow refers to the cash generated from

the operation (this comes from your P&L Statement above), (b) Investment cash flow refers to cash you make through the buying and selling of assets, and (c) Financing cash flow identifies the cash you spend to pay debt or loan payments you may have. Every owner should review and understand their statement of cash flows at least quarterly and before any significant financing or investing activities occur.

The good news is that if you take a little bit of time each week to update your QuickBooks information, all three of these statements can be automatically calculated and available to you in seconds. The key is not to get lazy and let a backlog of transactions build up. Watch for trends in your numbers and make adjustments as required.

TIP #4 – LEGALLY PAY LESS TAXES

This may be the most important reason for owning your business. Your largest expense each year will undoubtedly be the taxes you pay, but as a business owner you can lower your tax burden legally.

As an employee, you are used to having taxes taken from your check before it is deposited into your bank account. Then, you buy things with whatever amount is left over. However, with a business, you gain the ability to purchase the things your business needs *before* paying taxes. You only pay tax on the amount of profit you have at the end of the year.

Here is a simple example to show you the difference in paying taxes before or after expenses:

If an Employee makes $100 and pays 30% in taxes, she has $70 left to spend. Let's assume she buys $50 worth of goods. She then has $20 left over to put into her bank account.

If a Business makes $100 then buys $50 worth of goods, it has $50 of taxable income. $50 less 30% in taxes = $35 left over for the bank account.

Most people think of the U.S. Tax Code as a scary document, but there are only a few pages that increase your tax burden. They basically state that everything is taxable unless another page says it isn't. There are thousands of pages full of ways to help you pay less tax every year. That is good news! You can fund retirement accounts, write off expenses, and legally pay thousands of dollars less in taxes each year when you own a business. You just need to find a professional accountant who works with small businesses to develop a plan that will work for you.

TIP #5 – HAVE A CASH FLOW PLAN

Think of your business as an asset that generates cash flow. Most owners will put the cash into their checking account and spend it as if it were their paycheck. Our approach, however, is to create a plan for our cash flow. Here is a formula which we use:

1. Every individual should have six months' worth of living expenses stashed away in a "rainy day" fund. Your small business is no different and, in our opinion, you should have the same six months of cash reserves on hand at all times.

2. As stated in Tip #4 above, utilize professional tax strategies to put money away for your retirement years in a tax-advantaged fashion.

3. Take the remaining excess cash flow and invest in additional assets. Once you have your first business running smoothly, take the excess cash flow and build another business. That will provide you with two assets generating excess cash flow. Continue buying additional assets – which will generate additional cash flow.

4. Utilize excess cash flow from your businesses to invest in real estate. Real estate has different tax advantages than your business does. Treat real estate as a way to generate long-term, low-effort cash flow for your future.

We sincerely hope that this chapter has been helpful to you. We know it can be scary to leave your job and pursue freedom! We have tried to deliver the five things we wish someone would have told us before we started that first business. Now, use this new information to break free of the corporate machine and find the freedom you have always dreamed of!

Best of luck to you and your endeavors!

Brian & Regina McConnell

About Brian

Brian McConnell loves small business! He loves the challenge of taking an idea and seeing it generate revenue. He loves creating systems which help that business run on autopilot. Moreover he loves the freedom that comes from owning his own fleet of companies.

Brian graduated from Indiana University in 1996 and went on to earn his MBA from the top ranked Kelley School of Business in 2001. He joined Harris Corporation as a Sales Manager in 1999 and spent 9 years in Corporate America. During that time he was a three-time recipient of the President's Award for "Significantly Exceeding" sales expectations and won multiple other sales awards.

During his corporate career, Brian realized that he was built for more than just driving sales. He found it more personally rewarding to focus on the strategic and financial planning aspects of running companies and creating long term value from their assets. In 2008 he dedicated all of his time to entrepreneurial endeavors and has founded or acquired eleven companies. Those organizations focus on diverse industries including intellectual property licensing, commercial and residential real estate, human dynamics consulting, B2B software, and consumer services.

Financial literacy is key to the approach Brian takes with his companies. He has acquired multiple organizations by finding value in them that their original owners either didn't see or couldn't attain. For example, in 2008 he and his wife Regina purchased a law firm called "Family Law Centers". They immediately split the company in half, creating both an intellectual property company to license the "Family Law Centers" brand to other law firms, and a local law firm, which became the first licensee. Even though they later sold that local law firm (at a 440% ROI), the licensing company continues to pay them royalties every month.

Brian has always loved music. He is an active member of "Central Live" which is the worship band at Central Christian Church, a Las Vegas Mega Church. Their worship set rivals world-class entertainment options such as *Cirque du Soleil*. He regularly tours with the group and is credited on two of their albums. One of which, *Love Can,* hit the top of the Christian charts in 2014.

His greatest passions are his wife Regina and their three kids. Like most families with young kids, Mickey Mouse rules their vacation time together so they enjoy Disney Cruises, Animal Kingdom, and Disneyland. They also love to jump into a motorhome and head to the mountains for a weekend of hiking, skiing, or fishing adventures.

You may connect with Brian at:
www.BrianMcConnell.com
www.linkedin.com/in/mcconnellbrian

About Regina

Regina McConnell, Esq. was born and raised in Muncie, Indiana. She obtained a Bachelor of Science in Business Administration from Indiana University, with a major in Management and a Minor in Economics. She then obtained her Juris Doctor from the Indiana University School of Law – Indianapolis.

Her legal experience began at CMG Worldwide, the premiere Intellectual Property Marketing Firm representing celebrity individuals such as Marilyn Monroe and James Dean. She is a published member of the Indiana & International Comparative Law Review. Regina is admitted to practice law in the States of Nevada and Indiana as well as the United States District Court of Nevada. She has had two cases in front of the Nevada Supreme Court, one of which resulted in a published opinion in favor or her client and another which resulted in an Order of Affirmance, again in favor of her client. Her professional activities have included membership in Phi Delta Phi, the American Bar Association, Defense Research Institute, the Clark County Bar Association, the Nevada American Inns of Court, and the Southern Nevada Association of Women Attorneys.

Regina is passionate about making a difference in the lives of kids. Her current volunteer efforts include the Children's Attorney Project (a program of the Legal Aid Center of Southern Nevada) where she provides legal representation to abused and neglected children so they can have a voice in the court process. She is also actively involved in her church volunteering as a leader for the Fuse Junior High student ministry. Additionally, she has served with the Teen Court Pre-Trial Diversion Program (a Reach for Youth initiative) and the Protective Order Pro Bono Project, wherein she helped victims of domestic violence obtain necessary legal protection.

She enjoys speaking and is a frequent author and speaker at legal seminars educating other attorneys. Her seminars include: Skip Tracing in Nevada, Insurance Coverage Trends, Collection Law from Start to Finish, and Handling the Auto Injury Claim.

Regina has won many awards and accolades for her commitment to excellence and ethics. Her most prestigious award was being named an AV Preeminent Attorney by Martindale-Hubbell. This distinction is obtained by less than 5% of attorneys nationwide and it achieved by having a minimum of 20 other Attorneys and Judges anonymously grade your professional and ethical performance. Other awards Regina has received include Avvo Superb Rated Attorney; Desert Companion Top Nevada Lawyers, 2014; Vegas Inc's Top Nevada Lawyers, 2013; and she has been listed for several years in the Directory of Distinguished Attorneys.

In addition to her law career, Regina has owned several other businesses ranging from real estate to a pest control company. She owns an intellectual property firm which helps other attorneys put the power of a national brand behind their local law practice.

Regina and her husband, Brian have been married for twelve years and have three children together. She loves spending time with her family and being involved in their school and extra-curricular activities.

Connect with Regina at:

www.ReginaMcConnell.com

www.linkedin.com/in/reginamcconnell

CHAPTER 45

THREE KEY INGREDIENTS FOR BUSINESS SUCCESS

BY ANTOINE SIMMONS

It seemed my whole life had been building up to this point; and I did not even know it. By the year 2000, I had been working for Intel Corporation for over 7 years, was married for 6 years, had two children and one on the way. I enjoyed the success of Intel with a good salary, stock options, and great benefits. I worked in the HR Department of the mergers and acquisition group. While working for Intel, I began investing in real estate. I purchased fixer-upper homes and duplexes and remodeled them on the weekends. During this time, it was very stressful to balance my career at Intel with my side business.

Investing in real estate was a family business. My dad was a high school math teacher and real estate investor. My five brothers and I grew up working alongside our father building and remodeling apartments and homes. I remember telling my father many times how I couldn't wait to grow up and make my own money; and not break my back remodeling real estate.

In my mind, I believed I had struck a good balance, working for Intel during the day and building my nest egg in real estate on the weekends. However, in February 2000, signs of cracks started to show in many of the dot.com companies that were built with little to no foundation. I soon realized that the writing was on the wall and my future was now in jeopardy.

My wife and I decided to getaway to the beach to clear our minds and talk about the future. During this trip, I did what I always did and drove around the town, looking for distressed properties for sale. I found this old house with a *For Sale By Owner* sign staked in the front yard. I called the number on the sign and struck up a good conversation with the owner and soon found out that he also owned the motel across the street. When I hung up, I knew that all my life experiences, from childhood with my father to managing projects for Intel, had prepared me for this moment. We took a leap of faith and within four months sold all of our properties, cashed in our stock, bought the old house along with the Blue Gull Inn and moved to Cannon Beach, Oregon.

"A bend in the road is not the end of the road...
Unless you fail to make the turn."

~ Helen Keller

We have been very fortunate. Through a lot of hard work, our business has grown over the years; and we now own and operate four Inns located in the north Oregon coastal towns of Cannon Beach and Seaside. During the early stages of starting a business, I made many costly errors and felt like a hamster running on the wheel, not going anywhere. I only started to get good traction when I asked myself and others the right questions:

- What is my expertise?
- What do I specialize in?
- How do I plan and follow up?
- What do I want my company to be known for?
- What type of people do I need to surround myself with?
- How am I helping others?

We all desire to have control in our lives and be able to find the balance between family, work and fun. I want to be honest here; there is no magic recipe to create this balance that we all seek for in life. There have been many books written on this subject, but the reality of what makes someone happy is different for each of us. In the search for my own personal recipe to find balance, I have discovered ingredients and truths that are universal. All of us will have different measurements of these ingredients, based on the different phases of our life, so the recipe may change, but what goes into it includes the following:

KEY INGREDIENT #1: DISCIPLINE

We must find our focus. It is my belief that we are in a constant battle between the natural-man and the inner-man. The key for the successful entrepreneur is to control the natural instincts and learn to chart a course from within. The foundational ingredient to the work/life balance is to be disciplined on how you approach each part of your life. When we hear the word discipline, at least in my mind, we have a tendency to revert back to our childhood. When I broke rules at home and at school, I was disciplined. In my child-mind there were all these rules given by parents and teachers that took away my freedom. If I broke these rules, then my personal freedom was normally taken away, being sent to my room or in detention. We need to reprogram our natural-man view of the word discipline – the natural-man hates discipline. The inner-man learns to embrace discipline and finds that once applied at the smallest level, it provides freedom.

"True freedom is impossible without a mind made free by discipline."

~ Mortimer J. Adler

Making the engine run without you takes discipline.

Have you found yourself stuck in the middle of a good business that if you took a day off from or wanted to take a vacation, it would literally close? This is a problem for many small business owners who wear all the hats from marketing, sales, production, ordering, accounts payable, accounts receivables and running the front office. I understand from personal experience how in the beginning of starting a business, it's important for the business owner to work in all areas within the business in order to better understand it. But the question is: *how long should it be this way?*

How to get yourself out of the middle:
   1. Define your business:
      One of the vital transition steps from a start-up business into a self-running business is documenting what works. I know the saying; I have said it myself – "No one can do it or cares about my business as much as I do." Well that is true; so write it down. Develop specific procedures for how to manage every aspect of your business. Create phone scripts on how people should handle each problem the way you would. The procedures should

be a reflection of how you want to manage your business. This step takes a lot of time and discipline, but once completed, it will be a base from which to train, teach, and reflect. The procedures manual is a living document and needs to be frequently reviewed and refined. The review process should be added to your monthly planning session.

2. Assembling the right team:

We are fast to hire and slow to fire. Finding and hiring the right employee is difficult and expensive. Sometimes when the season is upon us, we rush to have bodies in place, but find out too late that the person hired cannot be counted on or has been dishonest about the skills they possess. My best advice is to create clear expectations from the beginning with success milestones that must be reached within a certain amount of time. This takes discipline to follow-up on each milestone and requires honest assessment of how your employee is progressing based on the expectations. It is critical to be specific with your employees about what they are doing well and what needs to be improved. You should reset expectations and the timeline after each meeting. I have found that a calendar for each employee that alerts you and your employee of upcoming follow-up meetings is the best way to manage the process. I believe the key outcomes of following a process to help each employee succeed does two things: (i) it shows the employee that you care about them and the business, and (ii) it documents the progress and provides the evidence to remove those who are not meeting the expectations. The goal should always be to create a team that is empowered to make decisions on their own. As an entrepreneur, you need to create the engine that is self-running and your job is to stand back and fine tune. True business success is to get out of the middle and instead, stand on the sideline to cheer and encourage.

3. Training:

Always sharpen your saw. Another key to independence is scheduling monthly training with each department to review changes, discuss what's coming up, complete a specific training and then leave time for questions. Keep it simple and be prepared. To do this, I have taken a section out of the operating procedures and created some questions and scenarios based on them. Having a simple agenda that is clear and precise is essential as is employee development. Invest in your employees and it will pay you back. Research classes taught at the local Jr. College, like managing QuickBooks, accounting and business management, etc. I have found that providing educational opportunities for your employees builds loyalty and shows the entire team that you care about them. After taking classes, some of my staff have moved on to better jobs at other companies. I have always supported and encourage each employee to develop skills that are marketable to better provide for themselves and their families. When you read this you might say, "Well, that was a waste of money." – but I have found that when people know you really care about them, the solid team members stay, continue to grow, and take ownership of the business. Who are they taking ownership from? You.

4. Make a Plan and follow it.

It takes discipline to follow a plan. Create a schedule that you religiously follow. Start with setting your annual goals, then monthly, followed by weekly, and finally daily ones. The only way to take control of your life and business is to set a plan and do your best to follow it. There will be many times that the best plans get scrapped and you need to focus on something unexpected. But then you need to regroup, pull your daily plan and review, regain your footing and continue forward.

"If you fail to plan, you are planning to fail!"

~ Benjamin Franklin

We all desire to find that balance in life; and we have a lot of external factors that work against us daily. As an entrepreneur we need to tune in, away from all the static around us, and focus on our inward voice. We need to stick to one thing and become the expert and authority on the subject. The desire to be the best will get you to the starting line; and daily discipline will carry you through the finish line.

"Your ability to discipline yourself to set clear goals, and then to work toward them every day, will do more to guarantee your success than any other single factor."

~ Brian Tracy

KEY INGREDIENT #2: MENTORSHIP

If you employ the concept of mentorship early when you start your business, it will increase your speed to success by tenfold. All of us have heard the statement, "Let's not reinvent the wheel." Business is a war. There are many business armies out there striving to kill any and all competition with the intention of being the only one left standing. We need to research, find the map and get directions from Generals who have experience successfully navigating through the minefields of business. It has been reported that 80% of all business fail within the first 18 months. Why do so many businesses fail right out of the starting gate? It's because they don't ask for help from the right people.

I would recommend that before anyone starts a business, they first spend the required time doing the research, find the people who have been successful within their field and interview them. The secret is people love to talk about themselves. Dale Carnegie's book How to Win Friends and Influence People is an annual read for me. I would recommend this book to all those who want to start a business. Learning how to influence others and subtlety obtain the information you need is an important skill in creating successful relationships.

Mentorship not only comes from direct relationships, but is also derived from reading good books. Be on the constant search for books that provide an inside look at successful business models. Large corporations hire and pull the brightest business minds into their board of directors. As a small business, you should also have the same goal, creating your board of directors with people that you trust and who will be honest. Successfully building a group of mentors will not only provide safe navigation, but will create a network of resources and more opportunities to strengthen your business. The key takeaway from mentorship is to always seek out those who will inspire you. This ingredient will keep you fresh and focus on what your priorities should be.

"If you light a lamp for someone, it will also brighten your own path."

~ Buddhist Proverb

KEY INGREDIENT #3: SERVICE

Many of you might not find this as an important ingredient in your recipe of finding a work/life balance, but for me, service has been an essential influence on how I look at the man in the mirror. By serving others without expecting in return, you move away from the natural man and find your strength from within. On many occasions in my life, I have found myself struggling with an important decision. After I discuss the decision with my mentors, if I still don't have a clear answer, I turn to serving others for inspiration. I am not going to sit here and preach to you – all I can tell you is what this action has done for me. The feeling of peace that I receive from helping others has always opened my mind and allowed me to find answers. The key take-away from this ingredient is to find ways to set aside the troubles of our minds and replace them with activities that will humble and inspire. I turn to this ingredient often; it keeps me grounded, simplifies life and increases my focus.

"The best antidote I know for worry is work. The best cure for weariness is the challenge of helping someone who is even more tired. One of the great ironies of life is this: He or she who serves almost always benefits more than he or she who is served."

~ Gordon B. Hinckley

As an entrepreneur, we strive to see our dreams become reality. We experience profound gratification by taking an idea from its infancy and, through great care and nourishment, watching it grow. We can hold its hand as it takes its first step and be there when it graduates into something meaningful in the world. True success is achieved when the idea can stand on its own as an independent gift to the world.

About Antoine

Antoine Simmons has been an entrepreneur from childhood when he started his first business of selling fresh vegetables and fruits door-to-door out of his family's garden. Over the years, he has started eight different businesses ranging from a clothing line, financial services, translation services, coffee stores, property management to software developer and hotel operator. Antoine has developed many businesses from the ground up and has found what separates failure from success in business is discipline.

Antoine is a graduate of George Fox University. He is the CEO of Haystack Lodgings, a property management company that owns and operates four boutique Inns located in the Oregon coastal towns of Cannon Beach and Seaside. His story was recently featured on "Builtoregon.com", a website that promotes and shares stories of successful entrepreneurs in Oregon. He has taught and shared his keys to success with entrepreneurs across the country through a webinar series put on by "Builtoregon. com." Antoine and his wife have been recognized and awarded the "Volunteer of the Year" for their community service from the city of Cannon Beach.

Antoine is becoming one of the leading experts on online hotel marketing. Antoine also built a patent-pending marketing software and strategy for the hotel industry to drive direct sales. Antoine's philosophy is to develop incredible value for your customers that they will seek you out.

You can connect with Antoine at:

asimmons@haystacklodgings.com

www.facebook.com/haystackas

CHAPTER 46

THE ICARE DREAM TO SUCCEED METHOD™ — HOW TO LIVE YOUR DREAM LIFE!

BY BECKY CAGEN

"Dream Big, it doesn't cost more!"

Congratulations Mr. President and Mrs. Obama. We are so honored to meet you! Thank you for choosing our band to perform at your Inaugural Ball! ~ Becky Cagen, backstage with President & Mrs. Obama at their Inaugural Ball, Washington D.C. 2009

Seriously? Could this really happen?

Well, it really did, and how it happened is the basis of my latest big dream: helping you live your dream life.

After the inauguration, I realized that the specific steps I took which led to my band performing at the Inaugural Ball were all part of a process I had developed. This process is what I affectionately call: The ICARE DREAM TO SUCCEED Method™:

- Intuition
- Create
- Action
- Release
- Enjoy

Let's start with your dream. "Dream Big, it doesn't cost more!"

Sounds so simple, right? If you are taking the time to dream in the first place, why not dream big? Perhaps it feels ridiculous and sometimes even scary to imagine yourself living your biggest dreams. Once judgment and fear are on board, you soon find that you are not dreaming at all, yet alone dreaming big.

However, when I toss judgment and fear aside, and allow myself to dream big, my dream becomes my guiding light, leading me to my greatest accomplishments.

But "dreaming big" is not enough – it is just the start. Making your dream a reality requires more. It requires a process. Every time I use the ICARE DREAM TO SUCCEED Method™, I live beyond my wildest dreams, and you can too!

I = INTUITION

Trust your intuition.

It is your knowing, your gut feeling. It is that little voice inside your head, which is always guiding you and keeping you safe. Trust what you hear and feel. Your intuition is correct 100% of the time, because it is the universe inspiring you.

My dance band, "The Don Cagen Orchestra" has been performing for parties and events around the country for over 30 years. In January 2008, my husband Don suggested I become involved in political fundraising as a way to make connections that might lead to our band playing at the next inauguration. When he said that to me, something clicked and I just KNEW we were going to perform at the Inaugural Ball. I felt it in my gut and the little voice inside my head was cheering, "Yes, you will be there!"

I trusted my intuition and told Don that his idea sounded like too much work. I have a better way to get us the gig: "Let's manifest it instead!"

C = CREATE

Create a vision of living your dream, which will in turn, manifest it to happen!

Close your eyes, and incorporate all your senses in order to visualize you living your dream. See where you are and what you are wearing. Listen and hear the sounds around you. Take a deep breath and imagine how wonderful everything tastes and smells. Touch your arm and pinch yourself, so you know it's real. Lastly, allow yourself to feel the joy and happiness you created.

Now open your eyes, and create things in your environment to remind your brain what you visualized and what it needs to achieve. This works because the brain does not differentiate between visualizing something and actually doing it.

Here are some examples:

- Hang photos of what you want in places where you will see them everyday.
- Listen to music, watch a TV show or movie that will remind you of what you will be hearing.
- Choose what you will be wearing when you achieve your dream and hang it in the front of your closet.
- Write your dream on paper and tape it to your mirror. Post it on your computer screen and to your social media networks.

In order to create my vision of our band performing at the Inaugural Ball in Washington D.C, I entered the date January 20, 2009 in our bookings database, printed out the signed contract along with a driving map from Chicago to D.C. and hung them both in my office.

Since I'm a superfan of the TV show *The West Wing*, I had DVD's of the show playing in every DVD player in our home and office. During the next 11 months, every time I turned on the TV, *The West Wing* was playing.

Lastly, every morning I visualized singing for the president and how wonderful that made me feel.

Create whatever will remind you of living your dream and makes you smile. Do this everyday. Creating and visualizing will manifest your dream into a reality.

A = ACTION

Take the action steps necessary to achieve your dream.

When you take action, you are focusing your energy towards your desired goal. Where you focus your energy will position you to receive what you want to achieve.

A good plan today, is better than the perfect plan tomorrow. This is one of my favorite quotes because it reminds me to Take Action Now!

Some of your actions may not turn out the way you dreamed, but rather lead you down a better path. Success is never a straight line. One of the many things Jack Canfield taught me is, "When someone says NO, you say NEXT!" Take action! Re-design your website, send e-blasts, post on social media, email, call, and set-up appointments with the people who can help you achieve your goals.

Right before the election, I told a friend that I knew we were going to perform at the Inaugural Ball. She said, "Trust your intuition, but make sure at every juncture, you take the necessary action steps." I immediately called Don and relayed her advice. He said we would need to renew our musicians' union membership to even be considered to perform for The President. When we hung up at 4:45 pm, he called the musicians' union which closed at 5:00 pm. Turns out the deadline to renew was the next morning at 9:00 am. If either of us had waited to act, my dream would have evaporated – ACTING NOW set the stage for the rest of our action steps.

At that time, we only had a one page website. We hired a web design firm to finish our website by Election Day.

Every day after the election, we made calls to people in Washington D.C. who we thought could lead us to The Inaugural Committee, the people in charge of planning the Balls. We also contacted some of our past clients, political and influential families who were involved in the campaign. Not one of these calls materialized into the introductions we needed. We changed our course, and finally connected with an Inaugural Committee member, who said she would keep our name on file. Although it didn't sound very promising, I bought Don a new tuxedo – white tie and tails – so he would have a special tuxedo for the Ball.

Christmas Eve we received a call from the Inaugural Committee requesting our DVD. Since most of our band's bookings are by word-of-mouth, we didn't have a DVD. We spent the next few days making a DVD from video clips of our past performances and quickly sent it off to Washington. They said they would get back to us shortly.

Taking action steps, altering and repeating them as needed, is required if you want to live your dream.

R = RELEASE

The only way to get what you want is to release on it!

Now that you have trusted your intuition, created your vision and taken the action steps, you need to release them and let go of the outcome.

How do you release and let it go? Besides, why would you want to? You have worked so hard trying to get what you want!

When you find yourself wanting something, it implies that you are lacking something and that you are not enough just as you are. However, the fact is, in this moment, you are already whole, complete and perfect, just as you are. The more you feel complete and content, the more you will attract what you want.

It's January 10th, 2009, twelve days have passed and still no word from the Inaugural Committee. I am in the shower, (where I do my deepest thinking) and I am feeling completely frustrated and at a loss. I trusted my intuition, created my vision and took the action steps necessary to achieve my dream. The inauguration is ten days away, so why isn't this happening?

All of a sudden, I hear Lester Levenson's voice in my head. Lester was the developer of a releasing process that I studied called The Sedona Method®. Lester said "the way to get what you want, is to release on it."

Using The Sedona Method® I asked myself a series of questions in order to release on the outcome of performing at the Inaugural Ball. These questions made me realize the reasons I wanted this dream were about my need for security and others' approval. I realized that I don't need any of these things in order to be who I already am. I am enough, just as I am. After releasing, I was able to take a deep breath for the first time in weeks. I felt complete, content and free.

As I get out of the shower, the phone is ringing. The caller ID says "Presidential Inaugural Committee!" "We are good to go!"

In order to live your dream, you must detach from the outcome of your dream. When you CARE and love yourself unconditionally, you realize that you are already enough.

E = ENJOY

Enjoy the Ride of living your dream!

Once you are in alignment, things will start to occur at record speed. Everything around you will fall into place effortlessly. Your dream will be surpassed in ways you can't even imagine. Enjoy the ride!

After receiving the call "We are good to go," the next ten days were a magic carpet ride! Here are some of the highlights:

1) There were ten Official Inaugural Balls. My band was chosen to perform at the most important one, "The President's Home States Ball."

2) When the AP (Associated Press) release announced the entertainment for Official Inaugural Balls, my band was on the list along with Stevie Wonder, Beyoncé, James Taylor, and twenty other superstars. This AP release went worldwide! When we googled "The Don Cagen Orchestra" a box popped up "Topics related to The Don Cagen Orchestra" and listed these superstars as related to us! Our band was on these superstars' websites!

3) In the days leading up to The Inauguration, we performed live on

CBS, NBC, WGN, and Fox News.

4) We were interviewed on national radio and featured in newspaper articles including *USA Today, New York Times, Washington Post, Toronto Star, Chicago Tribune* and *Chicago Sun-Times*.

5) Dress designers sent me gowns. Being politically correct, I chose a purple gown (blending the red & the blue) by Ines di Santo and Cartier lent me jewelry to match.

6) The night of the Inauguration, CNN had our name on their news ticker for over 30 minutes.

7) We were asked to perform patriotic songs just before the President arrived to dance at the Ball. As I was on stage singing "God Bless America" my eyes were welling up with tears, I felt such an overwhelming sense of patriotism.

8) Meeting President and Mrs. Obama backstage was the greatest thrill of all!

We were so honored and grateful to be chosen to perform at this historic event. Through it all I felt I was in complete alignment, exactly where I was meant to be. I felt no doubt or fear anywhere, but instead, I felt faith and love everywhere. Most stunning was the love and joy we felt from family, friends, clients and acquaintances. The emails and cards we received made us realize that we were spreading happiness and excitement during a time of uncertainty in the world. I realized that this is what life is supposed to feel like. What a different world it would be if everyone lived their dream life!

What is your dream life? Whether you dream of working out, losing weight, being in healthier relationships, being a better sibling or parent, being a better caregiver or buying your dream house – The ICARE DREAM TO SUCCEED Method™ can help you live your dream life, the life you are meant to live.

The applications are endless. I used the ICARE DREAM TO SUCCEED Method™ when caring for my beloved Australian Labradoodle, Ella. It enabled her to live a normal, happy life, far exceeding her doctors' predictions!

The ICARE DREAM TO SUCCEED Method™ continues to allow me to achieve my business goals. Recently, I produced a show with my band and four-time Tony Award nominee, Gregg Edelman. Its success has led to designing a national tour.

Your dream can manifest into your magic carpet ride, because when you are in alignment, there are truly no limits to where your dreams can take you.

ICARE to live my dream life.

ICARE that you live your dream life.

ICARE, that's my dream. What's yours?

About Becky

Becky Cagen is an "idea person." When Becky has an idea, she is like a happy dog with a bone! She will not give up on her idea until it comes to fruition. Becky's tenacity, combined with her caring and compassionate personality make her latest idea, The ICARE DREAM TO SUCCEED Method™, a natural progression in her quest to help others live their dream life.

Working with people is Becky's specialty. As a life coach and motivational speaker, her intuitive nature allows her to see beyond the surface and delve deeper into the issues. Becky's creativity and positive energy are contagious and seem to propel others to do their best work. She knows how to inspire people to get the job done. Becky doesn't understand the word "no". She is a very fast thinker and problem solver and knows there is always another solution. Becky believes in others' abilities often times more than they believe in themselves. These skills combined with her quick wit, enthusiasm, and encouragement enable people to overcome their fears and produce beyond what they thought was possible.

As President of Cagen Music LLC, a nationally-renowned special event music production company, Becky has been helping people live their dreams for over 30 years. Career highlights include singing at President Obama's 2009 Inaugural Ball in Washington DC, sharing the stage with international superstars. She has produced and performed at over 6000 corporate shows, weddings and charity galas. These events have provided her the opportunity to make other peoples' dreams a reality. "I love every aspect of my job," Becky says, "whether it's singing, songwriting and performing, or planning, producing and bandleading. But most of all, I love the relationships I have formed with my clients and feel honored to share in the most important days of their lives."

"The Don Cagen Orchestra" co-led by Becky and her husband and business partner, Don, have performed on WGN, CBS2 Chicago, NBC5 Chicago, Fox Chicago, Fox National, CNN and MSNBC. Becky was cast as a singer in the film "Opportunity Knocks" with comedian Dana Carvey. Becky and the band have been featured in *USA Today, New York Times, Washington Post, The Chicago Tribune, Chicago Sun-Times, Variety, Pioneer Press* and *North Shore Magazine.*

You can connect with Becky at:
becky@beckycagen.com
becky@cagenmusic.com
www.beckycagen.com
www.cagenmusic.com

Photo by JenniferMordini.com

CHAPTER 47

RESTORING YOUR HEALTH AND BALANCE... NATURALLY

BY DR. MARC S. CUTLER, D.O.M. (NM), L.Ac. (NC), DIPL.Ac.

When I was 7, I was diagnosed with asthmatic bronchitis. My struggle to breathe would scare the heck out of my parents who would, with great urgency, escort me into the bathroom and turn on the shower. The steam would calm my breathing back to a regular pattern. At that time, I also started to get allergy shots for horsehair, dust, pollen, dogs and cats. After our first assessment, the doctor, presented to me the hugest syringe that I had ever seen (turned out it was for horses). As soon as I saw it, I ran for the door of the Dr's office and headed down the hallway of this New York 10-story building and pressed the elevator to escape. At that point, my dad scooped me up and brought me back to the office so I could get my shots. I'm sure I cried all the way down the hall and past the patients in the waiting room to the shot room.

I used to think about this at night, "How can I possibly be allergic to something on this planet? Didn't we evolve with plants and animals and dust." It just seemed absurd – even to a seven-year-old it didn't make sense.

So, after my first appointment, my Grandparents transformed my room from one of carpeting and horse hair mattresses and down pillows to one of linoleum, cotton mattresses, foam pillows and a very expensive air cleaner. No dust or pollen could ever escape this machine, let alone get into my body. I bet they wished I could have strapped that 50-pound air cleaner to my back as I went through life!

I continued to receive these allergy shots until I was about 12 years old, at which time my immune system was supposed to mature and my body would no longer be allergic to many things any more. However, the allergist wanted to start me on a new round of testing, looking for a new list of allergens. The interesting thing though was that I knew intuitively I was no longer allergic to the things I was getting shots for. In fact, I don't think I was really ever allergic to begin with. And now, as a Doctor of Oriental Medicine and a Functional Medicine specialist, I believe that my allergies stemmed from a weak adrenal system – due to stressors in my life making me unable to handle the stressors of common allergens like dust and pollen and cat dander.

The first experiences I had with the healing community was, in fact, when I was sick. Funny as that seems, we often experience things via the opposite flow: when we are healthy, we are going along well . . . then boom! . . . something upsets the natural balance of things, and we have a "problem to solve."

I got interested in Integrative Medicine when I was 27 and was diagnosed with Type 2 Diabetes. I worked with a traditional American doctor and was put on medication for about a month. It was too strong for my body and made me hypoglycemic. It was at this point that I really started to investigate other methods to balance my blood sugar. After a few months of investigating and really finding my calling, I applied for and was accepted into Acupuncture College in beautiful Santa Fe, New Mexico. This turned out to be one of my best decisions in my life.

While in school, I came to find out that I would be the two hundredth generation acupuncture doctor, a tradition I was proud to part of. In the olden days of China, people in the Orient did not have a choice of going to an allopathic doctor (one who prescribes drugs) or a doctor of Oriental medicine (one who assists you in staying healthy). While training, we studied how powerful modern "Allopathic" medicine is in its treatment of acute problems. It is awesome in emergency medicine such as when one needs stitches, has a ruptured spleen from a car accident or an infection that came on suddenly.

It is also quite amazing in how it uses technology to assist in diagnosing a great many aliments. MRI's and CAT Scans give us a picture of what is deep within us that only a generation ago was not possible. These tools are powerful and quite remarkably useful.

About 14 years ago, my father woke up one day with a leg that was not working; it was partially paralyzed, and a few days later, the other one was as well. My immediate diagnosis was that he had a neurological problem, maybe even MS.

We got my dad to the emergency room where they did a nerve conduction test. He was advised that his femoral nerve was not functioning well and that could be the reason that he couldn't move his "left leg". When he questioned his physician as to how they intended to fix it, the MD replied, "Fix it? We can't fix it." What is usually done, is to manage it. That's right, manage it - whether it is pain, or inflammation, or high blood pressure or psychiatric problems, or high blood sugar or . . . there aren't cures for these things – at least not chemically. Medications are not designed to cure you – they simply can't. They are not created for cure. They are designed to suppress the symptoms so that you are simply not aware that the symptoms are there.

Have you ever run out of a particular medicine that suppresses the symptoms of your illness? An example is blood pressure pills. Take them for a few months and it appears that your blood pressure is normal. But if you run out, you would see a spike in your blood pressure pretty quickly. This has happened to thousands of my patients over the years. An interesting case study was a 58-year-old man who was taking drugs for: high blood pressure, diabetes, and thyroid problems. He had been taking these meds for 10 years at 10 pills per day for seven days a week. So when we did the math this came to 33,000 pills!

When I asked him if he had ever run out of his meds, without hesitating he said "yes."

During a storm, he ran out of his diabetes pills and his HBP medicine within two days he started noticing his blood sugar and blood pressure were rising to very dangerous levels. To the patient, this was a surprise; however, when I asked him about how it was possible after taking 33,000 pills he was still sick he retorted, that as long as he took his pills, he felt fine! but I said, 33,000 pills? And once the medication is stopped, the illness comes back? He leaned back in his chair in my conference room and said, "How about that! 33,000 pills and I am not fixed – what a scam." I agreed – what a scam!

So, allopathic medicine is great at diagnosis but not good at treating disease.

What I am proposing are ways to not have to search for cures. And the best way to do this is not to get sick at all. I know this may sound a bit different or even a bit absurd, but it is the simplest way to keep out of the medical model where, when you do in fact get sick, the only real answer is to take drugs (chemicals) to get you well.

Have you ever seen the commercials on TV telling us that we are sick and to ask our doctor for a "purple pill"? I believe that these messages suggested to us that it is normal to be sick, and being healthy is more of the exception. So the key here is to begin to understand that we really don't have to be sick. It is not an inevitable state that we have to be in.

The idea behind this is not far fetched, but take a moment or two to realize that depending on medications to regain your health is not really possible. I do want to say to the people reading this book or those listening to me on CD or MP3 that I don't want you to stop taking your medications, at least not right now.

But I do want you to consider a different way to stay well.

Being in a healthful state takes focus, interest, personal responsibility and also the willingness to make the conditions in your life better. Today there are medications on the market that help stop coughing, diarrhea, sneezing, and inflammation, vomiting and even stop emotions (like depression and anxiety).

But the medicines that stop these natural processes also rob the body of the way that it heals. It is very smart of the body to have you vomit and have diarrhea to rid itself of food poisoning. Sneezing is another example of a natural way the body rids itself of small particles that enter your nose. So many modern medicines block the bodily functions that would help to cure us.

I'd like to introduce you to what traditionally has been referred to as the 8 Limbs of Traditional Chinese Medicine. But I refer to them as the 8 secrets of successful living! The eight secrets have been passed down from generation to generation for over 5,000 years. And it seems to me that it may have been easier to follow these secrets for thousands of years up until most recently.

In this chapter I will be writing about three of them. Look for the next five in full detail in my next book.

LET'S TAKE A LOOK AT THESE THREE SECRETS OF HEALTHY LIVING

1. The first of these secrets of healthy living is Diet.

Our culture has changed in the past 100 years in how we eat, where we get our food and how it is prepared. We went from sourcing our food directly from the farm to getting our food mostly from grocery stores.

"Let food be thy medicine and medicine be thy food."

~ Hippocrates

A. Everything in Moderation...

However, did you ever eat too much of one thing?

- The result is that your body gives you a signal, in many cases it is digestive, that you over did it. Gas, bloating, diarrhea, etc.

> Did you know that approximately 60% of the population is overweight in 2015?
>
> - In 1925 it was 13%.

B. Eat foods that are organic.

The argument is often cost, however, we can pay now or pay later for what we put in our bodies. We were not built to process pesticides!

So what changes in diet can you make today to eat in moderation, eliminate pesticides and eat organically?

2. Hey Sleepy Head!

Research points out that about 60-80% of the people in the United States have some form of sleeping disorder, whether it is trouble falling asleep or staying asleep the whole night. Yet we know that the better quality of sleep we have, the better our daytime activities wind up being.

When we sleep, our body detoxifies itself, the cells regenerate and believe it or not, most of our fat is burned during deep sleep and not at the gym the day before. And most importantly, we now know that adequate sleep allows our body to stay healthy!

So how is your sleep? Are you getting 7-8 hours of continuous sleep? If so, awesome, if not, this is a key area that needs to be addressed.

3. Acupuncture!

In my practice I utilize acupuncture as one the tools to guide my patients back to health. Acupuncture, as a part of Oriental Medicine, can remedy physical and emotional ailments, improve state of mind, enhance recuperative power, strengthen the immune system, and also heighten one's capacity for work and creativity.

The medicine itself has a history of over 5,000 years and is one of the oldest continuously utilized medicines in the world. It is the science of stimulating the body's innate ability to heal. By stimulating "neurological nodes" it sends a signal to the nervous system to release endorphins, neurochemicals and hormones, as well as increasing blood flow and oxygen to the cells of the body. Thus the body is able to start the healing process itself.

Acupuncture should not be painful and most of my 116,000 patients rarely, if ever, notice the tiny hair-like filament placed into these acupuncture points. In my practice, we have used close to two million acupuncture filaments without side effects.

> Did you know that we could put 34 acupuncture filaments into a traditional vaccine needle? That's how small they are.

Acupuncture is also one of the very few medicines that address the root cause of an illness versus management of symptoms. The ancient Chinese took the time to study the body and discover why a person had a symptom, and then address the underlying cause.

For example: "If you had a pebble in your shoe, how would you get rid of the problem?" The correct answer is to take the pebble out of the shoe! The pebble is the problem, so get to the root of the problem and stop it. But what we are offered in medical models is a "symptom cover up": instead of removing the pebble, you could take something for pain, maybe you take "Pebble-Ez." "Guaranteed to block the pain for 2 hours, when the pain reoccurs reapply, may be reapplied up to 6 times per day." Or the other option is a "Pebble-Ectomy": where we cut a small hole in your foot where the pebble is hurting so that when you step down on the pebble it goes into your foot and goes deep into the muscle so that you don't feel it on your skin anymore.

But this is how we are told to deal with things in our modern world of medicine and perhaps how we deal with problems in general: numb them out or create a secondary set of problems so that the initial problem is forgotten.

Wouldn't it make sense to try something natural, with a high success rate and few side effects, something that strengthens the body, has been around for 5,000 years with no recalls, class action lawsuits, or side effects?

Our bodies are resilient; they have marched through time. We wouldn't be here if they were too fragile. However, something to consider, we are carbon burning (food sourced), 98.6 degree biological beings that need adequate drinking water. We can't go more than 15,000 feet high without an adequate supply of oxygen and can't go deeper than 200 feet without special diving gear in the ocean. So as tough as we think we are, we have a narrow band of survival that we thrive in.

The three secrets are simple ways to begin to thrive. We have to create health again. – It used to be taken for granted, but now we have to earn it back from nature.

About Dr. Marc

For 25 years Dr. Marc S. Cutler, D.O.M. (NM), L.Ac. (NC), Dipl.Ac., has been helping people across the country reach their health and wellness goals. He is also known as "The Health and Wellness Advisor" who is a best-selling author and health and wellness expert. Marc has worked with many famous actors and musicians from around the country and has appeared on CBS, ABC,NBC and PBS television and radio shows including National Public Radio and People's Pharmacy, to share his knowledge of Holistic Healing, as well as the *Triangle Business Journal, Raleigh News* and *Observer* and other media. In addition, Marc is a sought-after public speaker who enjoys sharing his message of Natural health and healing.

As the Medical Director of Advanced Healthcare Solutions based in Raleigh, North Carolina, Marc has introduced the idea of "wellness care" rather than sickness care to more than 116,000 patients. His patients come from his local community as well as around the world. His philosophy behind wellness care rather than sickness care is that it replaces the old approach of waiting to become ill and then searching for a cure, which is often hard to find. So with simple strategies, preventative measures and personal responsibility, getting sick is a lot more difficult.

Marc attended the prestigious Southwest Acupuncture College, in Santa Fe, New Mexico, where he received his Doctor of Oriental Medicine Degree and where he trained with some of the most experienced doctors of Oriental medicine. Prior to that, Marc received his double Bachelors in Psychology and Sociology and his Masters Degree in Psychotherapy and Social Welfare from Stony Brook University. At the age of 7, Marc was selected to be in highly-accelerated classes in school that put him into College at the age of 16.

As a leader in the acupuncture community, Marc has held the position of President of the North Carolina Acupuncture Association and currently serves as a Board Member to the Acupuncture Licensing Board. Marc also served as a Professor at the Southwest Acupuncture College in Santa Fe, New Mexico, where he taught many classes. In addition, he was a Clinical Instructor at the student clinic where he supervised all three levels of interns.

As an author, Marc's forthcoming book, *Soul Of Success* with co-author Jack Canfield expects to impact healthcare in America. Marc is currently working on his next book project, *Making Your Health Your Hobby*. Marc enjoys spending time with his wife, two sons, and his extended family and loves hiking in the woods to connect with nature.

To learn more about Marc Cutler, "The Health and Wellness Advisor", you can connect with him at:

www.advancedhealthcaresolutions.org

Marc@advancedhealthcaresolutions.org

www.facebook.com/advancedhealthcaresolutions

CHAPTER 48

BUILD A LIFESTYLE BRAND IN SEVEN STEPS

BY BEN DAVIS

I own and franchise **The Gents Place**, a one-of-a-kind, membership-based men's grooming and lifestyle club. Imagine country club meets barbershop! Headquartered in Dallas, Texas, The Gents Place differentiates itself with the conviction that we're not selling haircuts; we're selling something even more valuable to our members' lives. We're selling the feeling that we generate in our clients. To do so, we've trained all of our service professionals in the best life coaching strategies for changing an individual's emotional state to make sure our members have an out-of-this world experience.

I recognized this 'feeling' phenomenon as I was building the business. I had members who fanatically preferred The Gents Place over the numerous competitors; amazing, since the marketplace for men's grooming had become so saturated that I'd often referred to Dallas as the "men's grooming capitol of the world." I noted there wasn't a huge difference on the outside between all of our businesses, so I questioned my members. "Why do you come here versus go there, since we're more expensive?" When they responded with comments like, "I don't know, it just feels better here," I continued with, "Why? Can you be more specific?" I heard a range of generalities: "I guess it's the people. You just hire better people," and "You're accessible; I can reach the owner at any time," and "It just feels right. It just feels like others are trying to do this, but it's not the same as Gents."

When I surveyed satisfied members, the word 'feel' came up over and over again. But, exactly *what* feelings were we giving them? I needed something more precise to continue in the right direction.

With the help of my Executive Team, I determined that we were offering something much more than a haircut… even more than an experience. It was a lifestyle! AND that lifestyle generated feelings in our members that our competition couldn't rival. This concept could apply to virtually any business! How do you know if you're a lifestyle business? After your customers interact with you, they'll inevitably feel better than when they started. A lifestyle business must have a lifestyle brand — it could be a website, dry cleaner, flower shop, coffee shop, or even a Gents Place. The defining question is: Are your customers leaving with better feelings than when they arrived?

We answer that question successfully at our club locations. We have members that visit The Gents Place after traveling all week, who may have problems at home, or whose careers are taking a toll on them. Successful men will walk in with the weight of the world crushing down on them, feeling defeated, unloved, or unimportant, but when they walk out of our establishment, they radiate confidence, empowerment, and positivity… by design!

We operate under the belief system that our emotional state determines the decisions we make, and those decisions determine our destiny. If we can successfully put a member in the right state of mind on each visit, we can help him achieve better outcomes in his life!

I'll share with you the process that evolved from my success with The Gents Place. I've been able to further develop and articulate from my own experience how to help you successfully build a lifestyle brand that makes more money and changes more lives than you've ever dreamed of! Once you do this, you can make price irrelevant and share in the immense profits of the world-class organizations out there crushing their competition. There are seven critical steps.

1. SEE A BIGGER VISION FOR YOUR CLIENTS THAN THEY SEE FOR THEMSELVES

A potential member approaches the salesperson of a health club with a simple weight-loss goal and asks if it's achievable. The salesperson (who looks like he must also be a trainer, because he's in such great shape) returns with an even bigger vision of the health and fitness potential the client can achieve, and then guides the client toward the unique and targeted programs the health club has to offer to help the client achieve that bigger vision. In a subtle way, the salesperson is saying, "You're telling me you want X, but I'm really seeing this 2X, 3X or 4X for you, and we provide a customized program that will make this a reality for you!" The result is that the new client goes away saying, "Wow! I never thought this was possible for me. I can't wait to make this happen!"

In order to build a lifestyle brand, you need to build on something bigger than what you're really selling, and do it on an individual level. Creating a bigger vision for each client will create new goals for them and thus, initiate an inspiring journey to fulfill these needs.

2. ANSWER THE QUESTION, "WHAT BUSINESS ARE YOU *REALLY* IN?"

You need to ask and answer this question at least three times to drill down to the core of what you're actually selling. If I walk up to a hair stylist and ask, "Hey, what business are you in?" she might first respond, "I cut hair." To this, I'd say, "Oh, really? Well, how would you answer the question if you couldn't say that you *just* cut hair?" A typical second answer might be, "Well, I guess I provide haircutting services, manicures, pedicures, and other related services." Then, I would further challenge the stylist by saying, "Okay, what business are you *really* in if you couldn't answer *that* way?" The response might be along the lines of "Well, I suppose I make people happy all day." To which I would point out, "Okay, so is it possible you could really be in the business of making each client's day?" With this realization, the stylist would almost certainly smile and enthusiastically agree.

Here's another example. If I ask this question to a chiropractor—someone passionate about his or her craft—the conversation might go something like this:

What business are you really in?

"I'm a Chiropractor."

If you weren't in *that* business, what business are you really in?

"I provide chiropractic services and products to my clients that make them feel better when they are in pain."

If you weren't in *that* business, what business would you be in?

"I improve the well-being and overall quality of my clients' lives."

Asking the question, "What business are you really in?" should push you to arrive at the FEELING(S) that you're selling. When we talk about building a brand, especially a lifestyle brand, drilling down to what you're actually selling people is essential. Lifestyle brands charge a premium, not for the products they sell, but for the feelings they generate in their clients and the meaningful identities they create as a consequence.

I've developed a conceptual hierarchy to identify what any brand *really* sells if it's doing things right. The basic business sells just a commodity. Companies that take it to the next level sell an experience. The most successful and admired companies in the world ultimately sell a feeling. In my experience, the most progressive business owners understand that the next level up from selling a product is selling an 'experience,' but they stop there.

Typically, companies that aren't the lowest cost provider in their market are programmed to say, "We provide an experience." Then they tell all their staff members, "Go provide an experience!" The problem with that direction is that it's so vague that it amounts to no direction at all. One employee's definition of experience might be to remember the customer's name and where he went on vacation. Another employee's definition of providing an experience might be to remember the customer's name, where he went on vacation, the age and names of his children, what he does for a living, and his biggest business sale since the last time he visited, and then document all the information in a system – so it'll be available for reference the next time he visits, no matter who serves him next. Totally different experiences, right?

With the "We provide an experience" companies, as a customer, you consistently get *inconsistency*. If you want to get your business to the level of a lifestyle brand, you must understand that it's not the *experience* that matters, it's how that experience makes them *feel*. The ultimate goal of your business is to reach this top level of the selling hierarchy.

3. DECIDE AND COMMIT TO THE FEELING(S) YOUR LIFESTYLE BRAND IS GOING TO SELL AND COMMUNICATE THIS TO ALL STAKEHOLDERS

It's worth repeating. Lifestyle brands charge a premium, not for the products they sell, but for the **feelings** they generate. Here are a few examples:

a. Starbucks. Not in the **coffee** business; it's "inspiring and nurturing the human spirit."

b. Ritz Carlton. Not in the **hotel** business; it sells "significance."

c. The Gents Place. Not in the **haircut** business; it sells "confidence."

d. The local flower shop that successfully created a lifestyle brand. Not in the **flower** business; it could be selling "gratitude."

In my business, the primary feeling we generate in our members is confidence. If we can give them this feeling successfully and consistently, they'll make better decisions and have better outcomes in their personal and professional lives. If we can help them live out the best moments of their lives and focus on what they love most about their wives, children, and careers, they just might show up differently at home that evening, possibly hugging their wives for the first time in days or closing the multi-million dollar business deals that they previously thought were impossible! Thus, it's our belief that confident men can and do change their lives for the better and the rest of the world around them!

This is why determining what feeling(s) you're selling is so important. You can change the trajectory of your clients' lives if you consistently hit the mark. Ask yourself and your clients what business you're really in, and identify one to three core feelings that you can consistently generate for your clients. Then, share this with all your internal (employees) and external (vendors, partners, clients) customers so that you've set clear expectations about what defines a successful interaction with your company. Once you do this, you'll be well on your way to revolutionizing your business.

4. PAINT THE PERSONA

Once you know the feeling(s) your new lifestyle brand is selling, combine that with the important demographic criteria used to identify your target market (e.g., location, gender, income) to allow you to *paint a picture of who your BEST clients are*. Here are examples of three personas we target at **The Gents Place**:

a. **The Good Life Guys.** 25 to 55-year-old men that want to experience the best that life has to offer. They might be your Scotch-drinking, golf-playing, cigar-smoking, blackjack-playing friends that are always looking for a good time.

b. **The Alpha Males.** 25 to 55-year-old men that are the leaders in their chosen field. They could range from the CEO of a Fortune 500 company to the Fire Chief to the local City Councilman. No matter what profession, they like to be the Alphas.

c. **Successful Businessmen.** 25 to 55-year-old men that enjoy the game of business, and they play it *really* well. They play to win and know that looking and feeling their best is a competitive advantage.

5. BE THE PERSONA

Immerse yourself in these personas. ***Become*** your BEST client — feel what your clients feel, see what they see, think how they think, and become one with the clients you want to attract to your business. It's imperative! BE your own client! Experience your products or services firsthand! If you don't actually enter into the reality of your best client, you'll never truly understand him or her. Then, you'll struggle with how to tap into providing them with maximum value and optimizing their experiences with you. Whether you're a coffee shop owner, real estate agent, or CPA, you can easily immerse yourself in your ideal client's world and learn how he or she wants to be served!

6. MARKET TO THE PERSONA(S)

Speak to your persona(s) directly in your marketing efforts. Your marketing content should use the same or similar vocabulary that your target personas use in their daily lives. Talk to them the way they talk to you. Meet them where they are so you can take them where you want them to go! People want to do business with someone like them or who they aspire to be, so you might want to use inspirational content to help lead them to a better version of themselves.

The key takeaway is that your brand and marketing content should seamlessly and effortlessly engage your core audience in natural and meaningful conversations. With this approach, you'll quickly build rapport and trust, enabling your customers to achieve an emotional connection with your brand.

7. BUILD THE SERVICE SYSTEMS TO CREATE AND SERVICE INDIVIDUAL IDENTITIES

Great service systems create the illusion of *MAGIC* for your clients. Once you have clients in your presence, your primary focus is to serve them so well they're begging to come back to buy from you. The first step is to use a CRM (Customer Relationship Management) system to create an individual record for each client; aka, an IDENTITY. A client expects that when you have met him only once, you should no longer treat him as if he's a part of a 'persona' group. He has his own identity, and you should customize everything you provide him from that point forward based on who he is, to the most granular level possible.

The second step to building great service systems is to leverage the power of marketing software. If you aren't currently using an automation platform, you're not serving your clients in the most personalized way possible and are losing up to 60 percent of the potential lifetime value of each client. There are many products on the market and a simple Google search for small business marketing software will lead you in the right direction.

Building a lifestyle brand is equal parts art and science. Effectively implementing the principles I've described will lay the foundation for you, your employees, and your clients to feel the unique impact you can make in peoples' lives beyond the product or service you sell.

Follow the seven steps and get on the fast track! Achieve that competitive advantage over your competition, make prices irrelevant in your clients' eyes, and realize the profit margin you deserve from the business that captures your heart and soul!

About Ben

A serial entrepreneur with a portfolio ardently invested in the confidence and refinement of gentlemen everywhere, Ben Davis is the founder of The Gents Place as well as its online subsidiaries, The Gents Blog, and The Gents Store.

Since attending The University of Texas at Austin's Red McCombs School of Business and New York University's Leonard N. Stern School of Business, Ben has earned national recognition in *Forbes, GQ, Men's Health, Esquire, Huffington Post*, and the *Dallas Business Journal's* "40 Under 40 Awards" for his success in turning the oft-ignored niche of men's grooming into an expanding commodity.

The primary vehicle fueling Ben's passion of revolutionizing the men's grooming industry is The Gents Place, a membership-based men's grooming and lifestyle club aptly described as 'country club meets barbershop' — with a speakeasy feel. The club is differentiated from traditional barbershops by providing ancillary benefits such as a complimentary top shelf full bar, shoe shine services, straight razor shaves, cigar smoking patios, proprietary and niche toiletries, and quarterly members-only networking events, among other premium amenities.

Most importantly, The Gents Place provides a feeling of community and camaraderie with like-minded gentlemen that money simply can't buy. As one of its first members poignantly noted, "It's a place where personal relationships are formed and deals are done." Ben is most excited about the value his business adds to his members' personal and professional lives and the empowering feeling it provides that goes well beyond the haircut.

Ben started The Gents Place at the end of 2008 in Frisco, Texas during the Great Recession. Nearly seven years later, The Gents Place has locations in multiple states, and Ben is franchising the concept to meet the needs of the underserved market of discerning gentlemen all across the United States. Ben is actively seeking qualified franchisees that are just as passionate as he is in revolutionizing the men's grooming industry.

What is Ben's guiding doctrine through all his endeavors? A contagious philosophy that **men who look their best do their best** and a steadfast devotion to helping them achieve their goals (with the helpful accompaniment, of course, of straight razors, good company, and complimentary whiskey).

Ben was born in Wichita, Kansas, but as the son of military parents, he moved frequently throughout his childhood. He wasn't born in Texas but got there as fast as he could and currently resides in Dallas with his amazingly supportive wife, Lauren, and three children, Benjamin, Pierce, and Caroline.

You can connect with Ben at:
ben@thegentsplace.com
facebook.com/benjaminldavis

CHAPTER 49

THE EVOLUTION OF THE MODERN MOM-PRENEUR

BY JINJIE RAMOS, J.D.

I felt *alone* when she wasn't there to read me a story and tuck me in at night.

- Especially when I just missed her face and was looking forward to sharing something about my day, like winning the school spelling bee.

I felt *alone* when she wasn't there to wake me up and take me to school.

- Especially when the other kids' moms walked them all the way into the classroom, where they'd show off their desk and their pictures that were proudly displayed on our school walls.

I felt *alone* when I was the only kid at school who didn't have a parent in the audience.

- Especially when I was recognized for a special achievement and no one was in the audience with a proud smile beaming back at me.

And I felt even more *alone* when she was physically present.

- Especially when she dragged me around town showing property to her clients. She was stressed, overworked, and preoccupied the entire time.

A LITTLE GIRL'S VOW

My Mother sacrificed her life working so that I could have a better one, and I have the utmost respect for her for that. I felt conflicted as a child because I thought that in order to build a decent lifestyle, sacrifices HAD to be made, but I nevertheless made a vow to myself as a young girl, that when I had kids I would find a better way – a way where sacrifices didn't have to be made, so that my kids wouldn't feel…alone.

MY MOM WAS THE O.G MOMPRENEUR, EXCEPT…

My Mother was the original MOMpreneur, she was passionate about helping people find their dream home, had a crystal clear goal of giving us a better life, and a dogged determination to succeed. She believed in her dream and her ability to achieve it, never wavering. She never made excuses, and always found a way.

The countless hours spent riding in the back seat while she showed property and sitting quietly during her client appointments were filled with valuable lessons of entrepreneurship that have served me well in my business, but they also taught me how I didn't want to live my life. I didn't want to spend my entire life working, while my kids grew up without me.

LIKE MOTHER, LIKE DAUGHTER

I did what we were all told to do to be "successful" in life. I got good grades in school, got my business degree in college, went on to law school, and even opened my own private practice. So why didn't I *feel* successful? Instead I was heading down the same path as my Mother. I felt pressured and guilt-ridden for not spending enough time with my kids.

MY LITTLE GIRL'S TEARS BROKE ME

There was one particular day that was a turning point for me, when I picked my kids up from the daycare and my youngest daughter looked up at me and tears welled up in her eyes. The reason she was so upset was because I, again, wasn't there for her performance at school like I promised I would be. It was so important to her that she saw my face out in the audience, and I let her down, again. I didn't get out of my meeting in time and I wasn't there for her when she needed me. I knew exactly how she felt, because I had been there so many times as a child.

Not only did I break my promise to my daughter, I broke my promise to myself, that my kids wouldn't grow up feeling the way that I did, and I was crushed. I was tired of working so many hours, tired of feeling like no matter how hard I worked we didn't have enough, and tired of feeling guilty about not spending time with my kids. Just as when I was a child, I instinctively knew there had to be a better way, and I was determined to find it.

GET OFF THE CORPORATE LADDER
AND DO WHAT MATTERS

When I decided to quit law to pursue online entrepreneurship, my Mother was in disbelief. She couldn't understand how I could give up a career in law to pimp products and services online. "But the Internet is for uneducated lazy people with no ambition who are just looking for a get rich quick scheme. You have a business and law degree!" she declared.

But I knew in my soul that I was making the right decision. I knew I could design a business that wouldn't require me to make the same sacrifices that my Mother had made for me. I knew somewhere in the virtual world there was a place for me to monetize on my passion, to feed my soul AND my family.

HIGH SCHOOL DROPOUTS, EX-DRUG ADDICTS
AND EX-CONVICTS...MY PEEPS??

There's a misconception that online businesses are just for high school dropouts, ex-drug addicts, and ex-convicts. It's true, the Internet is the great equalizer of modern times, and you certainly don't need a J.D. or Ph.D. or any special letters after your name to be successful. But that also doesn't mean that if you do have a degree or a corporate background, that you can't take advantage of the inter-webs to monetize on your education and experience. It's time to use your talents to build your own business, instead of building someone else's, so that you can reap the benefits of your expertise and reap the luxury of spending more quality time with your kids.

ENTREPRENEURSHIP DURING
THE DIGITAL GOLD RUSH

It couldn't be a better time in history to be both a mother and an entrepreneur, or as I like to call us, MOMpreneurs. With the power of the Internet we now have the influence and global reach of billion dollar corporations. The world is your market and you're open for business 24 hours a day. You have unique gifts, talents, and experiences to share with the world that others would gladly pay you for, I promise. We just have to figure out what that gift is, how it can be used to help others solve their problems, and how you can package and position yourself above the competition.

ONLINE ENTREPRENEURSHIP, A MODERN
MOMPRENEUR'S MOST POWERFUL TOOL

I value entrepreneurship because it gave me a better life than I would have had if my mother continued to work at the hospital trading hours for dollars.

As a product of being raised by an over-worked Mom, and also once being one myself, I understand firsthand the profound emotional turmoil that both children of working moms as well as working mothers, experience. I truly believe that I was given these experiences to inspire me to find the ultimate solution in online entrepreneurship and to share it with other mothers.

I'm passionate about online entrepreneurship because it's the gift that empowers mothers to not only generate income to support our families, but to do so in a meaningful way that also allows us the freedom to spend quality time with our children.

Leveraging technology and the power of the Internet are the tools that distinguish the O.G. MOMpreneurs from the Modern Day MOMpreneurs. They're what allows us the ultimate freedom to run our businesses when we want and where we want. To generate full-time incomes in part-time hours, around our kids' demanding schedules. This is why I'm so passionate about what I'm going to be sharing with you in this chapter.

Although I teach a multi step-by-step system for starting an online business that you love, around the ones you love, in this chapter I will only be focusing on the most important foundational steps in Phase 1, Designing Your Business From The Inside Out.

FIVE STEPS TO DESIGNING A BUSINESS YOU LOVE FROM THE INSIDE OUT

Step 1: Are you Wiling to Ride or Die for Your Why?

When you are crystal clear on your desired outcome and "why", it won't matter what people have to say about you or your business, nor what obstacles may come your way. You will be a woman with a laser-focused purpose on a very specific mission. Refer to your "why" daily to keep your mind focused on your desired outcome.

Step 2: What are Your Gifts, Passions & Talents?

What lights you up inside? What subject can you talk about for days? What makes you feel happy? The answers to these questions are clues left by your heart, guiding you to your zone of genius. We all have innate gifts in the form of unique perspectives, talents, knowledge and experiences that we were born to share with the world. Follow your bliss, you'll be surprised where it can take you.

Step 3: How Can You Use Your Unique Gifts to Solve a Specific Problem, Serve, and Add Value to the Marketplace?

Oftentimes we take our gifts for granted because they come so easily to us. But guess what, they don't come so easily to others, which makes it a perfect opportunity to create a business around your strengths. Create a business around your strengths and find out who else is offering a similar product or service. When other people are experiencing success selling similar products or services in your chosen area of expertise, then that means that there's a definite market for your idea.

Step 4: Find Out Who Your Perfect Peeps Are

It may be true that everyone needs what you have to offer, but if you speak to everyone, you speak to no one. Think about who will be best served by your product or service? Next think about who you want to work with? Just because someone would be served by your product or service, doesn't mean that they're someone you'll enjoy working with. One of the luxuries of having your own business is that you have the power to choose who you work with.

You also want to think about who you want to repel and be clear on who you absolutely do not want to work with. For example, I choose to work with ambitious, savvy moms who want it all. They are ready to use their talents to build their own businesses. They want the financial freedom to live the luxurious lifestyle of their dreams, to give their children the best life has to offer, and the time freedom to create amazing family memories. They have a desire to make a difference in the world. They have a positive attitude and are willing to put in the work to be successful. I choose NOT to work with anyone looking for a get-rich-quick scheme, people who are lazy, those with a victim mentality, those without a sense of purpose, and those who do not prioritize their families.

Now that you know who you want to attract and repel, create an imaginary perfect customer, I like to call her your "Perfect Peep". You have to know her like she's your best friend since Kindergarten. Think of specific demographics and psychographics like her age, race, income and education level, does she have children? Does she live in the city or country? What are her greatest fears and frustrations? What makes her smile? What does a day in her life look like? What are her pain points and how can you serve as the best person to help her solve them?

Step 5: Why Should Your Perfect Peeps Buy From You?

Since you've done your research on competitors in your marketplace, think about how you can differentiate and position yourself above them. Focus on what makes you unique. Another way to distinguish yourself is to become the "go to" expert in your field. Completely immerse yourself in your area of expertise. Read, listen and learn as much as you can about your chosen specialty. Aim for excellence and to know more about your subject than anyone else in the world. Arm yourself with knowledge that will serve your Perfect Peeps and impeccably solve their problems.

MY LIFE NOW...YOUR LIFE SOON?

I love the freedom of being able to stay at home with my kids and watch them flourish and grow. I love having the financial resources to live a dream lifestyle that fully supports my family, including my mother. I LOVE being in a position to impact so many lives by sharing this gift of online entrepreneurship. And I absolutely LOVE giving children their mothers back, as well as mothers their lives back.

With the power of online entrepreneurship, you don't have to make sacrifices and choose between your work and your family, like my Mother had to do. You can design a meaningful business that creates both lifestyle AND time freedom. Yes, you can have it all. GO HOME AND GO BIGGER! I'll show you how.

About Jinjie

Jinjie Ramos, J.D. is an internationally-recognized speaker and online business expert who helps mothers across the globe design six-figure online businesses they love, around the ones they love.

After feeling unfulfilled in her private law practice, and guilty for not spending enough quality time with her children, Jinjie decided to find a better way. Her quest to achieve both financial and time freedom led her to online entrepreneurship.

Being raised by an over-worked Mom, and also once being one herself, she understands first-hand the profound emotional turmoil that children of working moms, as well as working mother's, experience.

As a mother of five children, this is why she is so passionate about teaching other mothers to leverage the power of the Internet to design a meaningful business around their gifts, knowledge, passion, and experiences that will not only give them lifestyle freedom, but also time freedom to spend with their children.

Jinjie's signature online program, "Millionaire MOMpreneur Master MIND", offers a comprehensive, step-by-step system. This system guides her clients starting with specific techniques to master the mindset for success, and works with them to cultivate the perfect product or service based on their specific strengths, to attract their ideal customers with their personal branding, and finally create the automated infrastructure so they can profit from their passion 24 hours a day, even while they're out creating family memories with their kids at the beach.

It is the only program of its kind that is specifically tailored to the needs of the modern mom who wants it all: Lifestyle freedom to give herself and family the best life has to offer, time freedom to spend creating fond memories with her loved ones, and a meaningful business to make the impact she knows she was destined to make in the world.

Jinjie's mission is to inspire a movement of mothers to use their gifts and talents to build their own dream businesses, rather than using their resources to build someone else's. Her work has illuminated the idea that with the power of the Internet, women no longer have to choose between having a career or spending time with their families. Working moms can have it all. They can "Go Home and Go BIGGER!"

Jinjie has a business degree in Marketing as well as a law degree from Santa Clara University. She is the CEO of Jinjie Ramos International, an online company specializing in teaching online entrepreneurship, marketing and personal branding, She is the creator of the YouTube channel Jinjie TV, and The Millionaire MOMpreneur Master MIND podcast. Jinjie was selected as one of America's Premier Experts and has been seen in magazines like *Huffington Post, Entrepreneur*, and *Forbes*.

To learn more about Jinjie, you can connect with her at:
www.JinjieRamos.com/SoulofSuccess
WEBSITE: www.JinjieRamos.com
FACEBOOK: www.facebook.com/JinjieRamos
INSTAGRAM: www.instagram.com/JinjieRamos
YOUTUBE: www.youtube.com/jinjieramos

CHAPTER 50

LIVE THE LIFE YOU LOVE

BY MICHELLE MOJICA

Most people relate success to money, the kind of car you drive and how big your house is. Truth is only YOU can define your success. At the peak of my 13-year career in the timeshare industry – we owned a 4,500 square foot house; I drove the Escalade truck I've always dreamed of, along with a lucrative six-figure income. I had everything I ever wanted but at the end of the day, I felt empty and unsatisfied. This was an ongoing roller coaster since I was 17 when I started earning an incredible income at such a young age. I loved the challenge and loved to work – the only problem was I didn't know when I needed to stop working and didn't have a meaningful "WHY" for working.

The funny thing about being in the timeshare business was that we sold vacations for a living, we encouraged prospects to invest quality time with your loved ones, and to take vacation every year to relax and unwind. But for us who worked in the industry, there was "never" the perfect time to go on vacation. We were either doing so well that we didn't want to break the momentum, or we weren't hitting our numbers so we couldn't leave.

Success meant high numbers and money. I celebrated my success in those years by buying "stuff" I didn't need. Reaching my financial and material goals came way too easy.

So if money doesn't make us happy then what does? How do we build a life or a business that will not only make us happy but will also fulfill us? Here's what I have learned over the years about working for money and working to be fulfilled.

THIS IS MY SOUL TO SUCCESS.

I. Believe in yourself:

"Don't let the noise of others' opinions drown out your own inner voice."

~ Steve Jobs

When I opened my brokerage May 2012, I received negative comments such as:

- Don't you know the election is coming?
- You need about 60k to start a business.
- Do you know how much work is required to run a brokerage?
- Do you know 85% of small businesses shut down their doors the first five years in business?

I have to admit some of those comments were valid; I opened the brokerage because I was bored and needed a challenge, I had no experience in running a business. I had just graduated from ASU the year prior and completed 5 to 6 classes at a time while still working full-time in real estate. One weekend, I attended a three-day seminar and at the end of the seminar we all had to write down our 30-day goal. While the rest of my group had weight goals, working out goals, etc. - I decided I would open a brokerage in 30 days!

My goal was very specific: I would open a Real Estate brokerage in Scottsdale.

The seminar ended Sunday evening and first thing my husband and I did Monday morning was drive around Scottsdale to look at commercial properties for lease. That day, I had a wide awakening - it was more expensive than I thought. I didn't have 30k-50k to build out a space, I had to step back for a moment and really evaluate. I refused to give up, I believed in myself.

After not having any luck on the commercial properties, I took a look at my contacts. With all of my clients as well as contacts from timeshare, surely one of them would know someone who owned a building or better yet can give me some direction of where to go.

As I made my phone calls, I was humbled by the positive reinforcement I received, I was determined to find an office through my relationships and I did! I was able to find an office suite with a courtyard view with enough room for three people. Best part? - Rent was only $700 monthly, and it provided us with a full-time receptionist and conference room space when we needed it.

Only three weeks later, we were open for business. A few months after that we opened another branch, one of my investors had extra space in Phoenix and he offered to allow us to rent the extra space very inexpensively. Today, we have 3 branches and 29 amazing agents.

When you believe in yourself and your vision, you will attract who you are and others who are aligned with your values, mission and vision. Be clear, be persistent and be confident!

II. Be different:

"It takes nothing to join the crown. It takes everything to stand alone."

~ Hans F. Hansen

Most entrepreneurs believe their business idea is the best and can change the world! How is your business different? How are you adding value to your industry?

Within four months of opening the brokerage, we had eleven agents and grew without any recruiting efforts. This was when I came to realize that we were growing a little too fast. We were becoming like any other brokerage office, I wanted to provide more value – I wanted to be DIFFERENT.

To offer more value I needed to fill a need in the Real Estate community. My first eight years in real estate prior to opening my own office, I had the opportunity to learn from three different brokerages as well as other offices I had the pleasure of doing cross transactions with.

In order to be different, I took the gaps from all three brokerages and decided to closed those gaps and create our own culture. I wanted to help new agents with their start up costs; I wanted to give new agents the confidence of knowing how to professionally serve a client fresh out of Real Estate school; I wanted to create a positive TEAM culture where we can all be servant leaders to each other and our clients – and this is who we are today!

As Realtors, we are all independent contractors, so unless you are part of a team – you are pretty much on your own. It is very common to have your license in one office and not know or meet the other agents in the office. Also, what you learn from real estate school is not enough knowledge to give you the confidence to get out there unless you have the support.

Real Estate coaching services are available but very expensive, as high as $1,400 monthly, so I decided that even though it is very time consuming, I would offer one-on-one agent coaching, as well as team-mastermind meetings twice a week. Today, with having three different offices throughout the valley, I wanted to make sure the agents knew each other, so they knew who to go to should they need assistance in other parts of the valley.

Our mission is to create a culture of givers and servant leaders and these are the agents we are attracting. I truly believe that the only way to live a fulfilled life is through giving and serving others.

Stay true to your vision, stand out, and be different!

III. Be fulfilled:

"Too often in life, something happens and we blame other people for us not being happy or satisfied or fulfilled. So the point is, we all have choices, and we make the choice to accept people or situations or not to accept situations."

~ Tom Brady

Don't aim to be happy, aim to be fulfilled. Why are you in business? Is it to make lots of money so you can buy a bigger house, a more expensive car or take that "bucket list" vacation?

Many times, we depend on money and "things" to make us happy. What I have found is that the things that make us happy can also be temporary. For example, once you reach that goal of buying the "dream" car, you're on a high for a moment then we look for something else to get us excited. From 2004-2008, we purchased a house each year, in 2008 was when it got ridiculous – we moved from our 2,500 square foot one-level home to a 4,500 square foot tri-level home, around the corner on the same street, very unnecessary. It all came too easy and too fast. I found the biggest thrill in buying properties and it made me happy – for that moment – but those things weren't enough to sustain the happiness I longed for. I was working to make money to buy "things," I wasn't working to be part of something bigger, I was unfulfilled.

It came as fast as it went! The market crashed around 2008, all four of our properties were upside down, our investments turned into a huge upside-down liability. We had to file bankruptcy and lost it all. As much as this was one of the toughest time of our lives – this is what made me stronger! This made me NOT be afraid of anything, I survived.

2008 was the time when I decided to dive into real estate full time. It was the best time since everyone else was leaving. After four years of traveling and finishing my Bachelors degree at ASU, I was ready for a new venture. The first two years of opening the brokerage was what I called my "discovery" phase.

The first two years, I battled with what my true purpose was in Real Estate, I battled more with myself and my financial motivation. Since I had been conditioned with 13 years of focusing on money and numbers in the timeshare industry - I battled with focusing on personal production, which is what I have always been great at, or focusing on team production. I have told myself over the years that I am not a good manager and that is still true today. I can't help those who do not want to help themselves. What I did discover about myself was that I am amazing coach. As much as I loved coaching my team one-on-one, I found my personal production suffered. The business was not at the point where it was able to supplement my income, not enough to sustain our lifestyle anyway.

This is when I turned to God's will and trusted that he would take care and keep his promises to take care of my family while I took care of others.

I did suffer temporary defeats, my personal bills weren't paid on time, but most importantly, I found myself to be fulfilled and had peace in my heart. I decided to surrender; I decided to have full faith in God and His plans.

Once I focused on serving my team and trusted God to do the rest, I was rewarded in many other ways. Business and success came naturally!

Most importantly, I not just happy, I am fulfilled and satisfied. What I found out was that when I trusted the money, I was unfulfilled and unsatisfied, and when I trusted God, I am happy and fulfilled.

IV. Do what you love:

"You can fail at what you want don't so you might as well take a chance on doing what you love".

~ Jim Carrey

How can your business provide a lifestyle that you love? How can you integrate that into your business?

My family and I love, LOVE to travel! We have four children and we want to show them different cultures to explore, we want to show them the world. Last year alone, we travelled 15 times, and this year we'll be visiting St. Thomas, New York and six other destinations.

Most people vacation to get away and disconnect, I vacation to enjoy God's creations. If I can work at the beach or take a call on top of the mountain, it's all the better. We also encourage our team to do the same. We offer our travel memberships to our team so they too can reap the benefits.

The Real Estate business has provided us with the means to travel and still be able to stay connected to our clients and agents. I love to travel; my team also loves to travel. Create a business that will allow you to enjoy life and provide an amazing lifestyle for others.

Do what you love, this is The Soul To Success!

About Michelle

Michelle Mojica, was born on a small Visayan Island in Philippines and grew up in a small beach town called San Andres. She is the middle child of four siblings who moved to the US when she was only 12 years old. She gives credit to her fearless parents, Eduardo and Maureen Mortel for leaving a very comfortable island lifestyle in the Philippines to pursue the American Dream! She believes that she is here for a higher purpose and is on a mission to fulfill God's promise to change the spiritual culture of real estate.

Michelle Mojica is the Designated Broker and Owner of Mojica & Associates Real Estate. Mojica & Associates Real Estate opened it's doors May of 2012 in Arizona. Today, they have three branches located in Scottsdale, Phoenix and Goodyear – serving all throughout the valley. She currently serves 31 Real Estate professionals in her brokerage where she continually invests time coaching her agents to be servant leaders in the community.

Previous to owning her own brokerage, Michelle Mojica held a Director of Marketing position with Princeton Resorts Group also located in Arizona, which offers 13 years of proven track record in marketing and sales in the timeshare real estate industry.

In 2011, in pursuit of her dreams of becoming an attorney, Michelle Mojica finally succeeded in finishing her bachelor's degree in Criminology and graduated with highest honors – *Summa Cum Laude* – from Arizona State University. She plans on attending law school in the near future to pursue Real Estate law to provide additional value to her clients and the Real Estate professionals in her brokerage.

Her biggest accomplishments today consist of celebrating her 11th year anniversary with her incredible husband: Juan Mojica, who is also a Branch Manager and a Real Estate professional with Mojica & Associates Real Estate. Her proudest moments are being part of raising four amazing children: Elijah (16), Dachelle (16), Isidro (9) and JJ (7). Her family is her biggest inspiration and they are her motivation to lead as an example to be a giver and a servant leader.

Michelle also loves to give back. In 2014, her team put together 200 boxes for Operation Christmas Child and raised funds for other non-profit organizations. This year, her biggest goal to give back is to build a home and a children's church in the Philippines where she grew up.

Michelle's passion is to travel the world and to teach others the lifestyle of traveling, and how the real estate business can provide the means to live the life that you love, while exploring God's creations throughout the world.

Through her own experiences in success, challenges and lessons, her true heart's desire is to lead others to trust in God – not the money – for true, fulfilling success. She believes that if you follow your own journey and not the journey of others, that you can truly find your purpose and live a fulfilled life.

She believes that the *Soul of Success* can only be found through giving and serving others!

CHAPTER 51

BIZTUITION:
THE AUDACITY TO LEAD
WITH YOUR TRUTH

BY JULIE CHRISTOPHER

Steve broke out in a cold sweat. . . He was under the gun and knew a decision had to be made. . . quickly. He'd been analyzing all the data his team had presented to him. It was SO overwhelming. What if he chose the wrong path and it was a huge mistake that could cause everything to come crashing down?

Have you ever experienced a situation like this in your life? One where you had to make a critical decision, felt overwhelmed by mountains of information, and *didn't feel confident in making the right decision?*

THE INVISIBLE BUSINESS DISEASE

Today, there's an invisible disease paralyzing every entrepreneur and company, and it's spreading fast. This epic disease is called "infobesity"!

With technology evolving at blazing speeds, companies are battling information overload. Innovations like the Internet, apps, sensors, analytics, software, etc., all provide vast amounts of data that help business people to make logic-based decisions.

However, the challenge is NOT having enough information to make intelligent business decisions.

The REAL problem facing today's business leader is having the confidence to make correct decisions quickly, even when those decisions contradict the information itself!

No matter how much data we collect with spreadsheets, statistics, and reports, it's ultimately up to a human being to interpret these findings and make the best decisions possible. In business, the pressure's always on. People's futures are at stake. Mistakes are costly and devastating. Poor leadership and indecision can wipe out companies and startups instantly.

Fortunately, there's a cure!

It's a secret skill, developed by elite leaders, that allows them to conquer infobesity and achieve business victory. Once developed, these leaders radiate an aura of confidence that gives them the audacity to lead with their truth and succeed in business. Would you like to discover and develop this skill, so you can be true to yourself and fulfill your purpose?

BIZTUITION... THE NEW "SECRET" SKILL OF LEADERSHIP AND BUSINESS SUCCESS!

Let me share a true story with you...

There was this little girl born and raised in Southern France. She always felt a little different than other kids, as if she knew in her heart that she was destined for a big and amazing life.

Eventually, she graduated from the French Music Conservatory and followed her dream to become a professional musician in Paris! With no family or support, she quickly discovered the music industry was cold and abusive. In fact, one night, when things couldn't get any worse, she had a huge fight in the streets of Paris with her producer.

If you're intuitive, you knew it... this is my story!

In that moment of chaos, a clear vision hit me like a ton of bricks. My gut instinct told me to move to America. . . immediately. In days, I was on a 4:00 am flight to Los Angeles with my guitar and a mere $50 in my pocket.

When I landed at LAX, I felt reborn, exhilarated, and scared, all at once. To survive and thrive, I knew I could only rely on my inner voice and raw instincts. I strode out of the airport into a strange new world, not knowing where I would be sleeping that night.

OUCH! Can you imagine my shock coming to America, with no friends, no resources, no money, and **no English?** Thank goodness for Baby Food! You can just imagine how often I stumbled and struggled over and over again, **only to discover that the struggle revealed itself to be my gift.**

It was during this difficult journey that I was forced to develop my skill of intuition.

Thank goodness I did! During that decade of hard work and sacrifice, I followed my heart, and I was fortunate to jam with famous recording artists like Willie Nelson, sing at Fess Parker parties, and perform at the Grand Ole Opry!

Today, I'm blessed to be co-authoring a book with legendary best-selling author, Jack Canfield! Jack, thank you! I'm eternally grateful and honored to contribute to this book.

If I hadn't developed my Biztuition, as an entrepreneur, I would not be where I am today. My mission is to empower executives, entrepreneurs, and professionals to enhance and develop their own Biztuition. That's exactly what I do with my clients, teams, and companies, during my consultations and workshops. It's an extraordinary feeling to help people realize their full potential!

WHAT'S BIZTUITION AND WHY SHOULD YOU CARE?

Well, Steve Jobs cares about Biztuition. So does Oprah, Jack Canfield, Daymond John and other ultra-successful people. Keep reading and I'll prove it to you!

Now, if you've already used YOUR powers of intuition, then you've wisely realized that. . . **Biztuition** stands for **Business Intuition**.

According to Wikipedia, Intuition is defined as a gut-feeling based on experience, and *"has been found to be useful for business leaders for making judgement about people, culture and strategy. It also has application in the fields of Management, Finance, and High-Risk situations."*

Simply put, Business Intuition, aka Biztuition, is the application of intuition within the business world!

> *Don't let the noise of others' opinions drown out your own inner voice. And, most importantly, have the courage to follow your heart and intuition. They somehow already know what you truly want to become. Everything else is secondary. Intuition (is) perception via the unconscious.*
>
> ~ Steve Jobs

If Steve Jobs, CEO of the world's first $700 billion company, cares about the power of business intuition, then shouldn't you too?

HERE'S WHY YOU SHOULD CARE. . .

I believe that one's ability to develop and hone their skill of Biztuition is THE single most important characteristic to becoming a great leader and achieving massive success! The answers that we seek are already within us! Unfortunately, many of us experience fluctuations of the mind and residual imprints from our past that get in the way. With Biztuition, you can learn valuable skills to clear your mind, so that you can "seize the moment," lead with your truth, and be better. . . at everything.

Here's what Jack Canfield, bestselling author, says about intuition:

"I meditated about the title of my best-selling book series, *Chicken Soup for the Soul.* And I've always sought "inner advice" for every major decision I've made in my life and my business. You, too, can use your intuition to make more money, make better decisions, solve problems more quickly, unleash your creative genius, discern people's hidden motives, and create winning business plans and strategies." (http://jackcanfield.com/learn-how-to-meditate-and-trust-your-intuition)

WHY IS BIZTUITION CRITICAL TO YOUR SUCCESS?

You need to know in your gut that you're making the right decisions! Our intuition is designed to help us avoid mistakes, make better decisions, and follow our purpose.

Your brain is designed to protect you from danger, not lead you to success. When you develop your intuition, you'll transcend and go to a state of love. Success is love. You can achieve that state of consciousness with proper training and practice!

Unfortunately, most people neglect or discount their natural gift! Sadly, most entrepreneurs and executives neglect this essential skill, which typically results in their failure.

That's why I teach professionals, executives, and entrepreneurs to transcend from fear to love, from the brain to the heart. I can help you to achieve a higher level of consciousness. That is the true dynamic of success.

Ask yourself, "Who's the most beloved entrepreneur of our time?"

Learning to trust your instincts, using your intuitive sense of what's best for you, is paramount for any lasting success. I've trusted the still, small voice of intuition my entire life. And the only time I've made mistakes is when I didn't listen.

~ Oprah Winfrey

Remember, we live in a society that's constantly bombarded with information, change, and new technologies. Successful people must make correct business decisions, with confidence and speed. Biztuition is a powerful skill that everyone should develop.

However, Biztuition isn't just about data and information. Would you like to make better decisions in these business situations?

- Would you like to know if you're developing the right partnerships?
- Want to know if you're hiring the right people?
- When to launch a new product or expand your business?
- What about making better decisions regarding Branding and Marketing your company?

Corporate executives and entrepreneurs make **hundreds** of these decisions daily. When contemplating pivotal decisions, it's crucial to leverage your Biztuiton to make the best decisions possible in all areas of your company.

THE NEW BUSINESS TREND

In today's modern world, business and leadership skills are evolving beyond MBAs and resumes. Successful companies are seeking to improve performance with innovative workshops and new ways to inspire their teams.

Search Inside Yourself.

No, I'm not asking to do that.... yet.

Actually, *Search Inside Yourself* is a Google program created by its 107th employee, Chade-Meng Tan, that uses meditative and relaxation techniques designed to teach people how to manage their emotions, which ideally creates better workers. It's so popular that more than 1,000 Google employees have completed the training!

Infusionsoft is the market leader when it comes to automating the process of marketing and sales for small business owners. My husband recently toured Infusionsoft's headquarters in Chandler, AZ, and during that event, Infusionsoft's full-time dream coach conducted a live exercise with everyone on how to accomplish their dreams.

Have you ever heard of a company that had a full-time dream coach on staff?

These companies are **NOT** isolated instances. Just ask Soren Gordhamer, Founder of Wisdom 2.0. According to his website, "Wisdom 2.0 addresses the great challenge of our age: to not only live connected to one another through technology, but to do so in ways that are beneficial to our own well-being, effective in our work, and useful to the world."

Fresh from a divorce and losing his job in 2009 , Gordhamer reflected on his purpose, withdrew his last $10,000, and started Wisdom 2.0. Today, executives and employees from big companies like Facebook and Twitter are attending. In fact, Pierre Omidyar, the founder and chairman of eBay, shared the stage with the Dalai Lama's English interpreter, Thupten Jinpa, and attributed eBay's success to human goodness and trusting between strangers.

The trend of successful companies empowering their people to express their innate gifts, talents, and spirituality is happening at a rapid pace, with no signs of slowing down.

Biztuition is the convergence of science and spirituality in the business realm. If these successful companies are investing in non-traditional methods to improve business performance, shouldn't you as well?

ISN'T INTUITION SIMPLY LUCK? OR IS IT A SKILL? WHAT DOES SCIENCE SHOW?

Despite the volumes of scientific studies supporting the value of intuition, some people are still skeptical. They believe that only rational-based decisions matter, based on data and logic. They claim intuition is simply random chance, or luck.

In his book, Answers for Aristotle: *How Science and Philosophy Can Lead Us to A More Meaningful Life*, CUNY professor Massimo Pigliucci reports, "Intuition works in an associative manner: it feels effortless, and it's fast. Rational thinking, on the contrary, is analytical, requires effort, and is slow. Why, then, would we ever want to use a system that makes us work hard and doesn't deliver rapid results?"

Ask yourself, *"Would you rather work harder or smarter?"*

Scientists who study the phenomenon say intuition is a very real skill that can be identified in lab experiments and visualized on brain scans.

Joy Hirsch, PhD, director of the fMRI Research Center at Columbia University Medical Center, has demonstrated that our brains react with anxiety to images of faces expressing fear—even when such images are shown so quickly that people have no clue they'd seen them.

"The amygdala, which plays an important role in emotional processing, activates in response to these pictures even when they're displayed for only 33 milliseconds—too fast to register in our conscious awareness," states Hirsch.

DOES YOUR INTUITION WORK?

Have you ever encountered someone at a party and were instantly attracted to them? Did you look for subtle signs that they might like you too? Were you nervous and excited? Of course! Why? We fear rejection and making mistakes!

When we do, we're conditioned to learn from our mistakes in order to survive. We replay them over and over in our mind's "eye", and ask, "What could I have done differently, so I could have made a better decision?"

Here's what legendary branding expert and Shark Tank celebrity Daymond John says about what his "gut" tells him:

"As I recall past mistakes I've made in business and personal relationships, I always ignored my gut feeling that something wasn't right in the beginning. Now, I will walk away no matter how good things may appear if my gut says no. How many of you have learned the same lesson?"

In the business world, we rely on our powers of intuition, past experiences, and non-verbal cues to quickly assess situations and make rapid decisions. Entrepreneurs, executives and professionals encounter these scenarios every. . . single. . . day.

HOW TO START DEVELOPING YOUR BIZTUITION

Here's a very simple 3-step exercise to instantly connect with your higher self. It's a basic exercise to start developing your skill of Biztuition.

1. Place your left hand on your heart, your right on your abdomen, close your eyes, and take deep, cleansing breaths. With your mind's eye, slowly count down from 10 to 1.

2. Ask yourself, "How do I feel?"

   Don't wait for a specific answer, as this isn't relevant now. This is intended for you to evaluate your feelings in the moment and letting go.

3. Then simply ask yourself, "Who am I?"

   As you feel relaxed, guidance and answers will come. Trust in the wisdom that you receive. Continue to focus on your deep, relaxing breaths. Simply listen and be aware.

Many people say this seems too simplistic, but once they try it, many say it's challenging to stay focused, calm and still. However, after practicing a few times, most people feel more focused, peaceful, and energized.

You should apply this process NOW. Did you do it?

If yes, how do YOU feel?

ARE YOU READY TO DISCOVER YOUR TRUTH?

When you meet your true self, it's like falling in love all over again, except that it's with the real YOU! You will merge into your inner-divine self and you will no longer feel separation between you and someone else. We live in a material world, where we forget that everything and everyone comes from the same energy and spirit.

Congratulations! By reading this, you've just started your journey to develop your power of Biztuition!

As we progress into the future, companies and entrepreneurs are going to continue to accumulate vast amounts of data and information. This trend is accelerating quickly and is only getting worse. As 'infobesity' balloons to epic proportions, one little prick is going to pop open a massive 'datalanche.' Only progressive enterprises and leaders who actively develop their powers of Biztuition will thrive.

With companies like Google, Facebook and Infusionsoft already embracing the science and art of higher consciousness to achieve even greater success, shouldn't you be developing your Biztuition too?

YES! But you knew that already, right?

Love, Serve, Celebrate! I wish you great success and abundance!

Namaste!

About Julie

Julie Christopher is an accomplished recording artist, songwriter, Reiki Master, Yoga Therapist, Intuitive Business Coach, Consultant, Author and Speaker. Julie's first career started in Paris, France as a full-time professional recording artist and musician. Julie experienced great success in France, with her music syndicated on various media channels and performing live shows at multiple venues. Despite her success, her intuition guided her to pursue a new life in America.

Julie continued her music career in the United States and published her first US album, titled: Ecstasy. Julie traveled across the country and was able to jam with recording artists like Willie Nelson, sing at Fess Parker's parties and even performed on the Grand Ole Opry stage.

During her journey, Julie was drawn into a new career as a professional yoga therapist, publishing her own yoga training DVD. Many of her clients were entrepreneurs and executives who confided in Julie their challenges and obstacles in business.

With her keen powers of intuition and heightened sense of consciousness, Julie realized that many of her clients complained about being overloaded with information, change, and new technologies. Many of them were seeking a solution to quickly handle these challenges and become better decision-makers and leaders. Julie foresaw that the trends of infobesity and datalanche were only going to worsen in the future, and that entrepreneurs, executives, and professionals desperately needed a way to cope.

As a result, Julie created a proprietary process using a blend of meditation, yoga, and intuition to coach executives, professionals, and teams to develop their own innate skill of Biztuition, become better leaders, attract abundance, and grow their companies.

She's successfully helped entrepreneurs from all walks of life to navigate the challenging pains of growing a business, by helping them make better decisions by leveraging their own powers of Biztuition. As a high-level intuitive, Julie's been interviewed on nationally-syndicated shows like Dr. Drew, Nancy Grace, Legal View with Ashleigh Banfield, and others.

Julie Christopher is available for private consultations, group coaching, workshops, corporate events, corporate trainings, retreats, conferences, and speaking engagements. Her specialty is working with CEOs, executive teams, HR teams, and startups.

Want to be interviewed on Julie's podcast? Julie is always looking to share success stories of leaders who followed their truth and believed in their Biztuition, in spite of risks and contrary opinions. Anyone with a great experience or story to share is invited to be a guest on her podcast.

If you'd like to book Julie for an interview, or inquire about her services, please contact Julie at: www.Biztuition.com

http://www.Facebook.com/Biztuition

http://www.Twitter.com/Biztuition

CHAPTER 52

CREATING MISSION-DRIVEN CHANGE

BY NICK NANTON & JW DICKS

He was tired of being left out in the rain in the middle of the night in San Francisco.

As a young, hotshot hi-tech entrepreneur, he would routinely be up late in a favorite restaurant, spit-balling new start-up ideas with other colleagues who were as ambitious and driven as him. Unfortunately, after those marathon sessions, he would find himself out in the street at 2 or 3 in the morning, unable to get a taxi to take him home.

That was a pain.

Suddenly, on a cold winter's night in Paris, the entrepreneur was doing yet another one of his late night brainstorming sessions, when he complained about the SF cab situation to his friend, another entrepreneur looking for something new to do. The situation sparked a thought for a start-up. A new kind of limo service. Maybe, when they got back to their home city, they could split the costs of a Mercedes, a driver and a space in a parking garage? Each man could access the car and driver when needed. If that worked out, they could expand the concept to other potential customers.

A couple years later, they were ready to bring the idea to life – only as more of a taxi substitute, rather than a limo service. They sent three cars and drivers out to roam the SOHO/Chelsea/Union Square area in NYC. The cars could be summoned through a special smartphone app, which was given to a circle of select people. If everything went smoothly in New York, New York . . . well, as the song says, if they could make it there, they could make it anywhere.

New York proved the idea would work – so they prepared for a proper launch back in San Francisco a few months later. The service was an instant success and they were easily able to get additional financing to expand their new business. That success mushroomed to such an extent that more and more investors were banging on their door, ready to put in as much as it took to get a piece of what was looking like *The Next Big Thing*.

The service continued to lengthen its reach – it expanded back to New York City, and then continued on to Seattle, Chicago, Boston and Washington, D.C. Even overseas to Paris, where the whole idea originated. And everywhere they took the service, it was an immediate hit. It became such a huge operation, that the company had enough clout to negotiate a deal with automakers to make vehicles more affordable for its drivers.

At the moment, Uber, which began life as UberCab, is valued at an estimated $40 billion dollars[1] and has almost completely changed the way people get around in metropolitan areas. In the San Francisco area alone, traditional taxi use has dropped 65%.[2] In New York, the price of a taxi medallion, which gives a driver a license to drive a cab, has dropped by 17%.[3] Other Uber-esque companies like Lyft have begun to sprout all over the world. There is now even a Uber-type company for helicopters called *Blade*.

Uber's company mission completely changed the transportation business model.

Here's a very powerful, liberating and, yes, scary, truth of life in the 21st Century: It's never been easier to change the world.

Think of the words that we all use on a daily basis today that didn't even exist ten or fifteen years ago, words like YouTube, Facebook and

---

1. MacMillan, Douglas. "Uber Snags $41 Billion Valuation," *The Wall Street Journal*, December 5, 2014.

2. Buckley, Sean. "The Uber effect: how San Francisco's cab use dropped 65-percent," Engadget.com, September 17, 2014 http://www.engadget.com/2014/09/17/sf-taxi-decline/

3. Carr, David. "When the Forces of Disruption Hit Home," *The New York Times*, Monday, December 1, 2014.

Twitter. The companies that brought these new words to life were able to quickly penetrate the public's consciousness at record-breaking speed simply because the Internet exists – and they had found a new, fun and useful way to connect with its users.

And ironically, these social media tools, along with many others, now enable a company like Uber to also progress at a supersonic rate. It can happen so alarmingly fast that everyone involved can get a case of operational whiplash. The competition has to scramble to survive the new rules of business (a bad problem to have) – while the company that led the charge has to deal with overwhelming growth in a very short span of time (a *good* problem to have).

In this chapter, we're going to look at one of the ultimate benefits of a specific form of being Mission-Driven – and that's the capacity to create enormous change in the way an entire business sector operates. When a company chooses the right mission and implements it in the right way, it's not only able to create that change – it's also able to leverage it so that it's able to experience incredible success. In other words, change can absolutely be the soul of your success, giving your clients and customers new and exciting services that make their lives easier and even more fun.

So - how does an entrepreneur key into this incredibly powerful, profitable and pro-consumer positioning?

Here's the answer in two words – *Disruptive Innovation.*

UNDERSTANDING DISRUPTIVE INNOVATION

The buzzwords for what we're talking about in this chapter are "disruptive innovation" or "disruptive technology." Both terms were coined by Clayton M. Christensen, a professor at the Harvard Business School who first identified this kind of rapid and radical change in his best-selling 1997 book, *The Innovator's Dilemma*, which received the Global Business Book Award for the best business book of the year.

Christenson, identified by *Forbes* magazine as "one of the most influential business theorists of the last 50 years,"[4] first explained how big established companies could easily be brought down by smaller

---

4. Whelan, David. "Clayton Christensen: The Survivor," Forbes, February 23, 2011.

companies delivering the same service in a cheaper, more affordable and/or more convenient way. Uber, of course, is an excellent example of this process, but it's far from the only one in recent memory.

For example, remember when Encyclopedia Britannica used to sell you a set of encyclopedias for over $1000 – and then you'd be left with a set of giant, unwieldy books that together weighed over 100 pounds? Oh yeah, and then you'd have to wait a year for an updated version, at which point you'd have to spend another $1000 for another set of giant books?

That sounds like ancient history - even though it's only been since 2010 when the company finally gave up the ghost and stopped printing physical copies of their flagship product. And even though they still deliver their encyclopedic information online, Wikipedia.org (despite its occasional accuracy-challenged entries) delivers the exact same service absolutely free. As a matter of fact, Wikipedia is even more comprehensive and covers a wider array of topics – and even though it's a nonprofit, it still jumpstarted the disruptive innovation that brought a fatal blow to Encyclopedia Britannica's 230 year-old business model.

Now, disruptive innovation isn't new to this day and age. Henry Ford certainly disrupted the horse and buggy business when he first offered an affordable Model T in 1905. And Alexander Graham Bell certainly disrupted the Western Union telegraph business when he came up with the telephone (even though Western Union had the opportunity to buy all the telephone patents for $100,000 from Bell).

The difference today? How quickly disruption can occur and how many different industries continue to be vulnerable to it. The Internet, combined with the widespread usage of mobile devices, has enabled instant communication and incredible access to a wide variety of products and services – making it much easier for a new company to not only build a better mousetrap, but also quickly deliver it to your doorstep after you've punched a simple few keys on your smartphone.

Think about this stunning example of disruptive innovation: In 2003, Apple introduced the iPod along with the iTunes store. Both of these developments revolutionized the music industry and created two new

5. Johnson, Mark W., Christensen, Clayton M. and Kagermann, Henning. "Reinventing Your Business Model," *Harvard Business Review*, December, 2008.

giant markets for the company: the iPods and the *songs* to play on the iPods. In a span of only three years, the iPod and iTunes were bringing in $10 billion, which accounted for almost *half* of all of Apple's revenue. In 2003, Apple's market capitalization was roughly $1 billion. By the end of 2007? That figure was over $150 billion.[5]

THE KEYS TO EFFECTIVE DISRUPTION

When your mission is disruption, you should probably think about leaving your MBA at the door, if you have one. That's because, according to Christensen and his colleagues, creating disruptive innovation doesn't begin with traditional business models. No, this kind of company mission actually begins with what they call a Customer Value Proposition (CVP).[6] The CVP is all about analyzing what kind of "job" a customer needs to have done – and how to help that customer get it done in the best way possible. In the words of the Harvard Business Review, "Customer value propositions can be a guiding beacon as well as the cornerstone for superior business performance."[7]

By "job," the authors specifically are talking about how the customer would *prefer* to have a product or service sold or delivered - rather than the old-school traditional way it's always been done in the past. For an example, let's return to encyclopedias. Consumers, in order to get access to an encyclopedia's facts and figures in the past, had to spend a lot of money to get a very cumbersome product that quickly became outdated and obsolete. The "job" they really wanted to have done was to be able to get that same information quickly, affordably, and conveniently – a job Wikipedia accomplished like gangbusters.

The greatest opportunity for creating a powerful CVP comes when the job is important to the customer and the current alternatives to getting it done aren't very good. Another great example: The scenario we presented at the beginning of this chapter, in which a man standing out in the rain late at night in San Francisco can't get a taxi to take him home. Uber was expressly created to get that job done in a much better way – and their solution hit the CVP "sweet spot."

---

6. Johnson, Mark W., Christensen, Clayton M. and Kagermann, Henning

7. Anderson, James C, Narus, James A., and Van Rossum, Wouter, "Customer Value Propositions in Business Markets," *Harvard Business Review*, March 2006 issue

8. Johnson, Mark W., Christensen, Clayton M. and Kagermann, Henning

In the words of Christensen and his associates, *"Opportunities for creating a CVP are at their most potent, we have found, when alternative products and services have not been designed with the real job in mind and you can design an offering that gets that job—and only that job—done perfectly."*[8]

They also identified four obstacles that consumers generally face that a CVP should attempt to overcome:

1. **Unaffordability:** The average consumer doesn't want to (or can't) pay the current price for a certain product or service.

2. **Access:** Customers aren't able to easily obtain the product or service.

3. **Skill:** Customers lack necessary professional training to get a job done, so they must hire someone who does.

4. **Time:** The process of getting a product or service takes up too much of a customer's day.

Now, most CVPs can only address a couple of these barriers. For example, Uber solved the problems of access (the guy can't get a cab) and time (it takes too long for a cab to come if you call). But a product like QuickBooks, the small business software package, solved the problems of skill (small business owners could now do their own books), unaffordability (it cost mom and pop operations too much to hire accountants) and time (QuickBooks makes doing the books a lot more efficient and faster).

Technology enables many companies, particularly online retailers, to overcome all four. They create *affordability,* by allowing customers to crosscheck the prices of a wide range of products. They grant access by offering a wide range of products that you wouldn't find in a traditional brick-and-mortar store. They overcome a lack of *skill* in shopping, by offering recommendations and advice on what to purchase, and, of course, they also save *time* for customers by enabling them to pick products at their leisure when conventional stores might be closed, and get their purchases instantly shipped right to their homes or offices. This is the kind of disruptive innovation that allowed Zappos to dominate in online shoe sales, Warby Parker in online eyewear sales and Bonobos to become the largest clothing brand built on the web.

All of the above cases show that *focus* is an incredibly important element of a CVP. Whatever customer "job" your CVP tackles should be nailed down precisely and perfectly. There's a reason the online retailers we just listed all concentrate on just one particular type of apparel – it's easier to create and market a specific positive experience related to a single product category than it is to try and sell everything at once. Trying to do too many things will dilute your mission in the eyes of your potential clients/customers - and also compromise your ability to perform at a high level. Too often, when you try to do everything at once, you end up excelling at very little.

Now, you might respond to that, "What about Amazon? It sells everything and it's phenomenally successful." Well, we're glad you brought it up (even though we're the ones who actually did it for you) – because Amazon is actually the exception that proves all the rules we just discussed. And that's why we're going to close this chapter by taking a closer look at this incredible Mission-Driven company's disruptive ways.

AMAZON'S AMAZING WEAPONS OF MASS DISRUPTION

When it comes to carrying out disruptive innovative, Amazon brightly illuminates what works through the "Weapons of Mass Disruption" it has employed over the past twenty years. That means regularly changing up its mission – at least its public one – while secretly clinging to its actual one: Flat-out owning the commercial possibilities of cyberspace.

Don't believe that was the initial aim of Jeff Bezos, the founder of Amazon? Well, if you type "Relentless.com" in your web browser, you may change your mind – as the web address will take you directly to Amazon's website. That's because Jeff Bezos, the founder of Amazon, initially considered naming his world-famous Internet business Relentless. Maybe he changed his mind because that name would have given away his ultimate game.

But let's not get ahead of ourselves. Instead, let's start with Bezos' first Weapon of Mass Disruption:

Weapon #1: Focus
Bezos began his professional life on Wall Street, where, in 1990, he became the youngest senior vice president at the investment firm D.E.

Shaw. Four years later, however, he abruptly quit the world of high finance. He had always been fascinated by computers and he noted that usage of the Internet was skyrocketing – in the past year, it had mushroomed by 230,000%.

To him, that meant the timing was excellent to try an online business.

Three years before anyone ever articulated the theory of disruptive innovation, Bezos instinctively knew he needed to have a narrow focus to his fledgling business. That focus became books. Since online shopping was still a very new and untested concept, he knew he had to make sure to offer the right product. Books turned out to be that product. In terms of costs, books were easy to ship and hard to break. There wouldn't be many returns or replacements necessary.

Weapon #2: Customer Value Proposition

As noted above, from a sheer operational standpoint, books were an excellent commodity to focus on for the launch of Amazon.com. They also provided, however, an equally excellent CVP.

In that regard, the main "job" it performed for its customers was providing incredible *access*. A physical bookstore could only stock so many different books – just a tiny fraction of all the books in print around the world. So, frequently, when a customer wandered into a bookstore looking for a specific title, the book would have to be ordered by the bookstore and the customer would have to return in a week or so to pick it up. With an online bookseller, however, *every single book in print* could be ordered online directly from Amazon and delivered right to the customer's home.

That powerful CVP allowed Amazon to become an instant success; the young company was already selling $20,000 worth of books in a week after only two months of being in business - and Bezos' first full year in business generated over half a million dollars in sales.

Weapon #3: A Long-Range Plan

Most consumers back in the early days of Amazon assumed Bezos' goal was simply to become THE online bookseller – which it quickly did. Amazon completely turned the traditional book-selling business model upside down. Over the past two decades, local bookstore after local bookstore has gone out of business, along with such big national book chains such as Borders, B. Dalton and Waldenbooks. Book-lovers have mourned that loss – but, at the same time, they hastened that loss, because they couldn't help but gravitate to the incredible choice of books that Amazon offered.

Owning web-based book sales was an incredible achievement all by itself – and, if the company only thought as far as Zappos, Warby Parker or Bonobos did, Amazon would have reached the end game of its disruptive innovation. But Bezos didn't care all that much about books – and certainly didn't want to be limited to only selling them.

Because being a bookseller was NOT his mission.

During the first year of its operation, Bezos ran an Amazon booth at a publishers' convention in Chicago. Roger Doeren, a bookstore owner from Kansas City, saw a sign at the booth that read, "Earth's Biggest Bookstore." According to a New Yorker article, Doeren wanted to find out more - and the conversation went like this:

Approaching Bezos, he asked, "Where is Earth's biggest bookstore?"

"Cyberspace," Bezos replied.

"We started a Web site last year. Who are your suppliers?"

"Ingram, and Baker & Taylor."

"Ours, too. What's your database?"

" 'Books in Print.' "

"Ours, too. So what makes you Earth's biggest?"

"We have the most affiliate links"—a form of online advertising.

Doeren considered this, then asked, "What's your business model?"

Bezos said that Amazon intended to sell books as a way of gathering data on affluent, educated shoppers. The books would be priced close to cost, in order to increase sales volume. After collecting data on millions of customers, Amazon could figure out how to sell everything else dirt cheap on the Internet.[9]

---

9. Packer, George. "Cheap Words," The New Yorker, February 17, 2014

In other words, Bezos originally had a huge long-term disruptive goal: He wanted to sell everything under the sun and use the massive consumer data it was collecting from its book buyers to do it. And, of course, now Amazon sells everything from lawnmowers to diapers – and U.S. book sales only make up around 7% of its annual revenues. To quote that same New Yorker article, *"…books were Amazon's version of a gateway drug."*[10]

Weapon #4: Continually Building on Your Base

Earlier, we detailed how Apple upended the music business with its iPod and iTunes Store. Bezos couldn't help but take note as well – and wanted to make sure Apple didn't cut into his control of the cyber book market. In 2004, he set up a lab in Silicon Valley to build the first home-grown piece of technology from the company. In 2007, the result was the unveiling of the Amazon Kindle e-reader, which could be used to download and read digital versions of books. It did, in fact, further Amazon's disruptive innovation by making physical copies of books unnecessary. By 2010, Amazon controlled 90% of the new industry it had created, the digital book.

The development of the Kindle also provided Amazon with an entirely new revenue opportunity. Just as the selling of books opened up all areas of ecommerce to Bezos, the Kindle resulted in Amazon being taken seriously as a provider of technology. A few years later, Amazon released the Kindle Fire, a competitor to the Apple iPad. The company now has its own smartphone (which has yet to gain much traction) and is now producing its own content, including original programming and films designed to compete with Netflix offerings.

The right business mission that creates change can be hugely beneficial for both consumers and entrepreneurs. Consumers get what they want more easily and the businesses who make this happen are rewarded with a dominant position in the marketplace – if, like Steve Jobs or Jeff Bezos, they're smart enough to capitalize on that position.

Think about your industry. How can you create disruptive change in your business – in a way that benefits both you and your clients? Finding the answer can definitely become the *Soul of Your Success*!

---

10. Packer

About Nick

A 3-Time Emmy Award Winning Director, Producer and Filmmaker, Nick Nanton, Esq., is known as the Top Agent to Celebrity Experts® around the world for his role in developing and marketing business and professional experts, through personal branding, media, marketing and PR.

Nick serves as the CEO of The Dicks + Nanton Celebrity Branding Agency, an international branding and media agency with more than 2200 clients in 33 countries. Nick has produced large scale events and television shows with the likes of Steve Forbes, Brian Tracy, President George H.W. Bush, Jack Canfield (Creator of the *Chicken Soup for the Soul* Series), Michael E. Gerber, Tom Hopkins and many more.

Nick is recognized as one of the top thought-leaders in the business world, speaking on major stages internationally and having co-authored 36 best-selling books, including *The Wall Street Journal* Best-Seller, *StorySelling*™.

Nick has been seen in *USA Today, The Wall Street Journal, Newsweek, BusinessWeek, Inc. Magazine, The New York Times, Entrepreneur® Magazine, Forbes,* FastCompany. com and has appeared on ABC, NBC, CBS, and FOX television affiliates around the country, as well as E!, CNN, FOX News, CNBC, MSNBC and hosts his own series on the Bio! channel, *Portraits of Success.*

Nick is a member of the Florida Bar, a voting member of The National Academy of Recording Arts & Sciences (Home to The GRAMMYs), a member of The National Academy of Television Arts & Sciences (Home to the EMMYs), The National Academy of Best-Selling Authors, and serves on the Innovation Board of the XPRIZE Foundation, a non-profit organization dedicated to bringing about "radical breakthroughs for the benefit of humanity" through incentivized competition, best known for it's Ansari XPRIZE which incentivized the first private space flight and was the catalyst for Richard Branson's Virgin Galactic. Nick spends his spare time serving as an Elder at Orangewood Church, working with Young Life, Downtown Credo Orlando, Entrepreneurs International and rooting for the Florida Gators with his wife Kristina and their three children, Brock, Bowen and Addison.

Learn more at: www.NickNanton.com and
www.CelebrityBrandingAgency.com

About JW

JW Dicks Esq., is a *Wall Street Journal* Best-Selling Author®, Emmy Award-Winning Producer, publisher, board member, and advisor to organizations such as the XPRIZE, The National Academy of Best-Selling Authors®, and The National Association of Experts, Writers and Speakers®.

JW is the CEO of DNAgency and is a strategic business development consultant to both domestic and international clients. He has been quoted on business and financial topics in national media such as the *USA Today, The Wall Street Journal, Newsweek, Forbes*, CNBC.com, and *Fortune Magazine Small Business.*

Considered a thought leader and curator of information, JW has more than forty-three published business and legal books to his credit and has co-authored with legends like Brian Tracy, Jack Canfield, Tom Hopkins, Dr. Nido Quebin, Dr. Ivan Misner, Dan Kennedy, and Mari Smith. He is the resident branding expert for Fast Company's internationally syndicated blog and is the editor and publisher of the *Celebrity Expert Insider,* a monthly newsletter sent to experts worldwide.

JW is called the "Expert to the Experts" and has appeared on business television shows airing on ABC, NBC, CBS, and FOX affiliates around the country. His co-produced television series, *Profiles of Success,* appears on the Bio Channel - along with other branded films he has produced. JW also co-produces and syndicates a line of franchised business television shows and received an Emmy Award as Executive Producer of the film, *Mi Casa Hogar.*

JW and his wife of forty-two years, Linda, have two daughters, two granddaughters, and two yorkies. He is a sixth generation Floridian and splits his time between his home in Orlando and his beach house on Florida's west coast.

CHAPTER 53

CREATE YOUR OWN HOME COURT ADVANTAGE

BY MICHELLE BACA

Have you heard the term "home court advantage"? It describes the psychological advantage that the home team is said to have over the visiting team as a result of playing in familiar facilities and in the presence of supportive fans. Have you ever experienced it? What if you could create this feeling of being comfortable, confident and "at home," not just in the sports world but in other areas of your life? Imagine the positive results you could produce if you felt fully confident, supported, energized and encouraged.

You can create your own home court advantage by practicing and adopting the five PowerPractices that have enabled me and my clients to develop extremely high levels of confidence, self-esteem and positive results. They are the same strategies that I used when I had to figure out how to mentally prepare for delivering a presentation to hundreds of people for the very first time, and they are the same strategies that you can use to generate the state of mind that will help you produce your best results anytime that you choose.

I was asked to deliver a keynote presentation to an audience of over four hundred people at an annual conference. I immediately said "Yes, of course I can do it!" Then I hung up the phone and wondered what I had gotten myself into.

I had always been shy and extremely introverted growing up. I was a loner. And I was still struggling with feelings of self-consciousness and insecurity. But, my instincts were telling me to go for it despite the nervousness and hesitations. There is a voice inside of me that always seems to raise its hand and volunteer me for things that are outside of my comfort zone before the logical, cautious, reserved voice has a chance to object.

Up until then, I had only spoken in front of about sixty-five people so it was a huge leap in my speaking career. I did my research, organized my content and prepared diligently. Then, I practiced delivering the presentation to two of my mentors, Jennifer and Tamera. When I was finished, Jennifer said, "Great job! You know your material, no doubt about that. But there really is no secret formula that will completely prepare you for what it is going to be like to stand up and speak in front of hundreds of people. I can't give you a magic solution for that. It is something you need to figure out for yourself."

What? You mean there's no secret formula! So, I took a deep breath and spent the next few weeks figuring out how to mentally prepare myself. First, I focused on how I wanted to feel when I was delivering the presentation. I wanted to feel confident, capable, relaxed and completely "in the zone."

As I contemplated what would be helpful, I developed five practices and habits that would help me maintain high levels of confidence and tame my negative thoughts and self-doubts. I knew that worries, concerns and fearful thoughts might creep in and I had to find a way to manage them so that they didn't sabotage my success.

When it was time for me to step up onto the stage, I felt completely at home. It felt like I was playing on my home court. I was calm and comfortable, yet energized and engaged. I was surrounded by positive energy and there were no doubtful or fearful thoughts floating around in my brain. I delivered the presentation that I had been envisioning.

I have continued to use this same system for many events and tasks in my life, ranging from high-profile and high-stakes events to informal phone calls and everyday tasks like writing, facilitating meetings, and conducting sales and client coaching calls. You can use these same steps to create your own "home court advantage" anytime that you want to ensure that you perform at your very best. Here are my five

PowerPractices that will enable you to create the conditions for optimal performance:

1. CONDUCT AN ENVIRONMENTAL SCAN

Environmental familiarity contributes to creating a home court advantage that leads to increased confidence and performance. Many people experience some degree of anxiety or nervousness in unfamiliar surroundings. The first day at a new school, the first day on a new job, and moving to a new city are a few examples where you can see the role of nervousness and unfamiliar surroundings in action. When you are in unfamiliar territory, there are some things that you can do to put your nerves at ease and find a state of calm and focus so that you can produce ideal results and outcomes.

My father in-law taught me to always identify the exit in any room or establishment that I enter. For safety reasons, he encouraged me to do a scan of the room and find my bearings in case I had to make a quick exit for any reason. I still do this. But, I have added an environmental scan as part of my ritual.

When you enter the space, take a few minutes to orient yourself with the details of your surroundings. Notice the color of the walls, any designs on the ceiling. Notice the material of the ground or floor that you are walking on. Greet these items that you are in the presence of. Create an internal dialogue that goes something like this: "I am safe and secure in the space. I feel at ease. I feel welcome. I feel at home here." You can do this in a minute or less. Next time someone says, "make yourself at home" – do exactly that by conducting your environmental scan and feel the difference that it makes in your demeanor and confidence level.

2. GET GROUNDED

Consciously move your awareness to the bottoms of your feet, focus on their connection with the surface that you are standing on. Many meditation and relaxation techniques suggest that you imagine a cord extending from the top of your head, down your spine, into your legs and extending out through your feet and into the ground anchoring you to the earth. This creates feelings of being stable, centered and solid. You can do this anywhere. You can also try imaging that you are a grand, magnificent tree and that your feet are your roots, then imagine that they extend deep into the soil of the earth, connecting you to the ground.

Alternately, you can imagine yourself as a massive iceberg, so incredibly grounded that seventy percent of your mass is below the surface!

3. REPLICATE SUPPORTIVE ENERGY

The enhanced performance that occurs on home courts is largely attributed to the cheers, support and encouragement given by the fans. You can use this to your advantage by memorizing the way that the most supportive people you know make you feel. Here are two ways to keep positive people and their supportive energy top of mind for you:

- Think of someone that makes you feel good about yourself. Close your eyes and take notice of the feelings, thoughts and emotions that are present. Imagine that they are with you, engulfing you in their loving, inspiring energy. Memorize what this feels like. Know that you can carry their energy with you and summon it whenever you like. Tell yourself that you can return to this state of being anytime you choose. Regularly practice closing your eyes, envisioning that person's supportive energy and bringing yourself back to the way that they make you feel even when they are not around.

- Maintain a "Pick-Me-Up File." Anytime I receive a positive acknowledgement via email for example, I save it and place it in a special folder that I call my "Pick-Me-Up File." If someone posts a glowing review on my website or social media sites, I copy and paste it into my file so that I can go back and review them whenever I want. Sometimes I look at it at the start of my workday or when I am feeling a little bit down or just not feeling especially competent and capable. It works. It brings me back to when I first received the note that made me feel so good.

For most of us the problem is that the "victories" that we experience are short-lived. We feel a sense of accomplishment and fulfillment, but then time passes and we tend to forget. We may become prone to letting setbacks, challenges and negative feedback overshadow our positive accomplishments and results. Make it a habit to review and add to your "Pick-Me-Up File" at least once per week.

4. CREATE YOUR OWN PLACEBO EFFECT

The positive voices of your biggest supporters and inspirational sources certainly have a positive effect on you, but what about your internal voices? These play a crucial part as well because even if your supporters are cheering loudly, if the voices in your own head are negative and are speaking even louder, then they will drown out the supportive voices of even your biggest fans. One of the most valuable skills you can develop is the ability to create a positive internal dialogue. When you learn to do this, you can essentially create your own placebo effect.

The placebo effect is a phenomenon experienced by patients in clinical trials who think that they are receiving a fancy new drug when, in fact, they are simply taking a sugar pill. But, what is so cool about this is that between eighteen and eighty percent of patients experience improvements in their physical ailments simply because they think that they are getting better because of the medicine they think they are taking. It becomes a self-fulfilling prophecy and by consciously flooding your mind with positive thoughts you can duplicate this phenomenon and manifest positive results for yourself.

Working with affirmations on a daily basis is the best method that I know of for generating a positive and productive mindset. My ritual includes repeating my affirmations at least once in the morning and once at night before bed. I purchase spiral bound index cards and write one affirmation per card. This allows me to keep them all together and flip through them effectively. It is the best way that I know to bombard my conscious and subconscious mind with beneficial thoughts and images. I say "images" because I frequently incorporate visualization with the repetition of my affirmations. I'll read it once and then close my eyes repeating it again while visualizing myself doing or being what the affirmation describes. One of the benefits of repeating these daily is that I begin to memorize them and then I can say them to myself whenever I want.

It is especially helpful when I catch myself thinking a negative thought and I know I have created an affirmation to counteract it. For example, I may start thinking the thought "Oh no – I am not feeling well again, I hope I don't have a serious illness." Then I'll stop myself, recognize the negative, destructive and paranoid thought-pattern and instead, begin saying, "I am perfectly healthy, whole and complete from the top of my head to the soles of my feet." If I catch myself walking into the conference center getting ready to deliver a keynote presentation and I start thinking, what if they don't like me, what if they don't think I'm smart or knowledgeable enough, I can interrupt that thought-pattern and start thinking, "I am great at what I do, I am a master of my craft and I was born to do this." My whole face changes, my body posture changes, I suddenly start standing taller. My shoulders are back and a confident smile comes across my face. What are some of your recurring, negative or un-empowering thoughts? How would you like to feel instead? Use your answer to craft an affirmation that reinforces your new and empowering thoughts and feelings.

Start your own collection of affirmations and incorporate visualization to magnify their effectiveness.

5. PRESS YOUR "INTERNAL RESET BUTTON"

It is difficult to perform at your very best if you are carrying around negative or nervous energy. If you want to be able to consistently create your own "home court advantage," then you will need a strategy for "resetting" your mental and emotional state. You will need a method for letting go of thoughts and emotions that are un-empowering and for filling yourself up with possibility, positivity and good vibes.

Meditation is the best way that I have found to release excess emotional baggage such as irrational fears, concerns, worries, resentment, regret and anxiety while simultaneously recharging and re-energizing.

When I found my "internal reset button," and learned how to activate it through meditation, everything changed for me. I began practicing meditation after attending Jack Canfield's *Train the Trainer Program* in February 2014. It rocked my world. I remember sitting in the training session after one of our guided meditations and thinking, "Oh no. I think I'm addicted to this meditation thing." I was scared that I was going to become an irresponsible, unproductive meditation junkie – who just wanted to meditate all the time because it made me feel so good. It was like a wonder drug.

Instead, something miraculous happened. I continued to practice guided meditation and incorporated it into my hot yoga practice. And, I discovered that if I meditated consistently, it would actually help me accomplish my responsibilities with more confidence and more ease. I still became addicted, but it made me more productive and gave me the greatest sense of safety, love, confidence, possibility, wisdom, guidance, compassion and power I have ever felt.

If you have never tried meditation before, you can start with guided meditations. Eventually, you will find that you can meditate on your own without guidance, whenever you want or need to.

These five PowerPractices will increase your ability to put yourself into a state of mind where you are calm, confident, powerful and effective. You can use these habits and practices to prepare for job interviews, important client meetings, work presentations, proposal deliveries, court appearances, first dates, and the list goes on. And, remember you don't have to reserve these techniques only for the "major" events in your life. You can use them for everyday tasks and activities like going to the bank or the grocery store and you will find that you carry yourself with more confidence and assurance.

The next time you are presented with the chance to do something that makes you nervous and excited at the same time – say yes! Then, apply these practices and let go, knowing that the Universe has your back!

About Michelle

Michelle Baca helps her clients develop the confidence and mindset they need to succeed. She specializes in the application of positive psychology to increase self-esteem, productivity and success. She helps people overcome mental and emotional blocks, create game-plans to achieve their goals and develop unshakeable confidence.

As a recovering "worry-aholic," Michelle is dedicated to helping others experience less worry, anxiety, stress, frustration, fear and uncertainty and more energy, mental toughness, confidence, assurance and clarity.

Her "Hardwired to Succeed" process is designed to help people transform negative thought-patterns into a more productive mindset. Michelle teaches this transformational process via personal coaching, workshops and keynote presentations. She has also launched an online coaching program by the same name, helping people all over the world drastically increase their abilities to produce positive results. Michelle graduated from Jack Canfield's *Train the Trainer* Program and incorporates Jack's *Success Principles* into her keynote presentations and personal development workshops.

Michelle is also a consultant with Convergence Coaching, LLC, a national leadership and marketing consulting firm dedicated to helping leaders achieve success by helping them develop and implement leadership, succession, marketing, and training and development plans. She specializes in helping small and medium-size firms build their practices and improve their operations. Michelle provides individual and group coaching in the areas of leadership, strategic planning, business development, recruiting strategies, and communications skills.

Michelle has a background in Management Information Systems as a result of choosing MIS strictly for the money-earning potential despite the fact that her heart was not in that line of work, so she knows what it is like to be in an unfulfilling career. But, she also knows what it's like to successfully navigate a major career change. In her trainings and presentations, she shares the strategies and skills she used to overcome her own self-doubts and the negativity of people who thought she was crazy for leaving a high-paying career to start from scratch.

As a professional speaker, Michelle has addressed groups ranging in size from five to five hundred and always brings her energy, enthusiasm, and expertise to her keynotes, breakout sessions, and workshops. Michelle's most frequently requested presentation topics include: *How to Find and Keep Your Mojo at Work, Developing a Positive and Productive Mindset, Managing Conflict, Customer Service Excellence, Navigating*

Change Successfully and *Peak Performance Strategies.*

Michelle is also the co-founder of one of the largest ignition interlock service providers in the country where she supervised the daily operations of its two service centers. She continues to serve as a managing member and to create awareness about the effects of the drunk-driving problem facing our nation.

Connect with Michelle Baca:
www.facebook.com/SpeakerMichelleBaca
www.linkedin.com/in/michellebacaprofile
www.twitter.com/michellebaca
www.michellebacaonline.com
www.hardwiredtosucceed.com

CHAPTER 54

FROM PISSED TO BLISSED BY CATCHING LIMITING BELIEFS

BY SYLVIA CHAN

It was the third time I pressed the snooze button. My body was aching, I felt exhausted and really did not want to leave my comfortable bed. I struggled to get up, almost lost my balance and crawled to the bathroom. When I looked into the mirror with hazy eyes, I was shocked by the person looking back at me. "Who is this miserable looking person?" I thought to myself. What really hit me was the fact that there was no sparkle in the eyes staring back at me. Something stirred in my heart, and I knew I could not continue living like this. I needed to change! I wanted the sparkle of life back into my eyes!

So the soul-searching journey began. I started reading personal development books, joined yoga and meditation groups, attended seminars and lectures, took online courses, received healing sessions, tried various therapies, placed crystals at home and many other methods. During this time, I regained some clarity and learned a lot about myself and how I was reacting to people and incidents around me. One of the concepts that really resonated with me was the Law of Attraction.

I was intrigued by the concept of the Law of Attraction ("LOA"), which states that we attract into our lives whatever we give our attention, energy and focus to, whether positive or negative. We are active creators of our own lives instead of being passive receivers of things that happen to us. For me, this concept is very liberating. I was most frustrated by things that were out of my control, I felt powerless when life was just happening to me. So knowing that I could be the creator of my own life by directing my thoughts to create positive vibes, and deliberately attracting what I desire in life was very appealing and empowering. So I started practicing LOA by creating my dream board, saying affirmations, being aware of the words I use, the thoughts I produce and the conversations I have with people. I was so serious about LOA that I got certified by Michael Losier, a Law of Attraction expert and the author of *Law of Attraction: The Science of Attracting More of What You Want and Less of What You Don't*, so I was really familiar with the ways of making LOA work. Things turned quite well on all aspects of my life for a while, until I hit a stone wall.

My happiness level in my relationships, my career and my finance just hit a glass ceiling. The handsome and caring guy I was dating turned into a self-centered and controlling person who did not pull his weight in the relationship, and I felt like I was taking care of him but he did not reciprocate. The promising projects that I was working on came to a standstill due to management issues. My expenses increased but my income didn't grow. Given that I was so into LOA, it was extra frustrating that I was not getting the results I wanted. Then I realized there was something sabotaging my positive intentions and efforts – my limiting beliefs.

These limiting beliefs are like ninjas hiding in our subconscious mind, they sneak out and set up traps or throw darts at us when we are trying to move forward. It felt like someone or something was pulling my legs while I was trying to move forward. I was working so hard to make things work the way I wanted. I became frustrated and angry at life. These emotions of being frustrated and angry, were clearly negative, and, needless to say, my life was filled with more roadblocks and delays because I was so focused on these frustrations that I was actively sending out negative vibes. It was quite clear that I was emitting negative vibes when my colleagues and friends were avoiding me at all costs. I was pissed off with life!

One day it hit me. I heard myself saying that "I could never trust others to do anything right" and I was feeling resentful for having to always take care of things and other people, and I also felt that "no one will take care of me." I examined where these beliefs came from and they went all the way back to my childhood. As the eldest child in my family and second eldest in my extended family, I was always put in charge of taking care of my younger siblings and cousins. When they misbehaved, I was held "responsible" for their actions.

Clearly, these beliefs had been affecting my work situation. So I made some changes. Instead of having to look out for people's mistakes as "I could never trust others to do anything right," I acknowledged that everyone has their own responsibilities, so it is not my role to be their caretaker. I could inspire, instruct and support people who work with me, but they are not my responsibility. This realization gave me a great sense of relief, I felt the weight on my shoulders lifted and had a renewed respect for my colleagues' abilities, instead of viewing them as my liabilities. Magically, after I had changed my attitude, my colleagues suddenly became more proactive and came up with many good ideas – which helped to push projects forward. I also felt less stressed as I was not always on the lookout for people's mistakes.

Then I realized that the "no-one-will-take-care-of-me" feeling also spilled over to my love life. I could not trust my partner to take care of me as "I could never trust others to do anything right." So I was like an inspector always looking for things that my partner did wrong. On numerous occasions when he was just starting to do something, I took over with the condescending vibes, like he was doing it all wrong. No wonder my ex-boyfriends eventually gave up doing anything for me as I had always made them feel they cannot do anything right. Of course, I continued to be resentful for not being taken care of and these experiences just reinforced my limiting belief. What a vicious cycle! When I recognized these patterns, I suddenly realized how I had been pushing people away by making them feel they couldn't do anything right. Next time when this limiting belief comes up, I will surely catch it and not repeat the same mistake.

After I liberated myself from this feeling of "no-one-will-take-care-of-me", I decided to take care of myself and go for a long overdue holiday in Bali, Indonesia. So I put out an intention for a Bali trip, I didn't know when I could get time off work or get the money to travel. I just trusted the Universe is friendly and let go of the "how" for my trip.

One day, my colleague sent me a message saying that Cathay Pacific was doing a special on flights from Hong Kong to Bali for HK$2,314 (US$300) inclusive of taxes and surcharge. I had just conducted a small LOA workshop and the net income was enough to cover the plane ticket! Since it was on special so they only had tickets for a certain period of time, I got the tickets to travel in the third week of May. The timing was perfect as there had been no business trip planned, my Dale Carnegie trainer certification would be completed and I could catch up with my Malaysian friends in the second week of May. I even got three free nights from Hotels.com and got upgraded to Business Class on my flight! Then my friend reminded me that I had been contributing to an investment fund for quite a few years; I checked and the gain from this investment was more than sufficient for all the expenses for this Bali trip! Honestly, if you asked me how I would have the time and the funding for this Bali trip, I wouldn't have a clue. Therefore, when we trust that this is a friendly Universe, it would deliver what we desire in ways that we could not imagine. As my mentor, Michael Losier, always says, "let the Law of Attraction figure it out!"

We simply need to practice three core strategies to turn our lives around, so that we could change from being frustrated and pissed all the time to having a blissful life.

1. TAKE BACK OUR POWER

We must give up the victim mentality and our tendency to blame others. It is so easy for us to say that things happen to us – misfortunes, disasters, economic crisis, global warming – when we feel like we are the victim of anything external or when we blame others, we give our power away. No one, absolutely no one, could make us do things that we don't want to do. You can argue and say that your upbringing, your job, your family, your obligations, the economy "made" you do certain things. The truth is that we can choose to "react" to things based on our default setting (our core values and beliefs), or we can choose to "respond" with the awareness of our tendencies and choose to respond differently.

Realization is the path to freedom. We can live mindlessly in our day-to-day life, blame others, blame circumstances, even the weather, for all of our misfortunes. We need to come to terms with the fact that things happen and we have the power to choose how we respond to these situations. Having the awareness gives us the power back. We are still free to choose our normal responses. With awareness, at least we can acknowledge that we are choosing the same pattern.

External factors have some influences, however, at the end of the day we can choose our actions and our responses to any circumstances. Nelson Mandela could have chosen to respond violently to the injustice and oppression of the South African government. In fact, given the circumstances it would have been understandable for him to choose violence, but instead he chose peace and compassion. Some of the people who experienced the tragic events of 911 or Hurricane Katrina have totally lost hope and have become depressed, never recovering from their losses. Others have changed their attitudes towards life after experiencing the same event and became more positive, treasuring everyone around them, and have completely revamped their lives.

So we can choose our actions and how we respond, we can't blame any external factors. When we give up being victims and blaming others or situations, we take back our true power.

2. CATCH AND CLEAR OUR LIMITING BELIEFS

As we grew up, we were building beliefs about everything, what's right and what's wrong, our image of ourselves, beliefs about money, relationships, love, our abilities, our worthiness, our environment and our circumstances. This set of beliefs served us in making sense of the world as we grew up. Most of our beliefs were installed by our parents and our caregivers, and from situations we experienced or observed when we were very young.

Relationship Beliefs
If we observed our parents fighting all the time, we might form beliefs that "relationships are hard," "couples always fight," etc. If we observed infidelity in our own family or in our friends' family when we were young, it would be easy for us to assume "all men are cheaters," "men cannot be trusted," "women are gold diggers," and there is no "living happily ever after."

Self-Worth/Confidence Beliefs
If we were told as kids that we were not smart enough, or needed to work harder to get good grades, we might develop a sense of "I am not

good enough." With all their good intentions, some adults might want us to avoid disappointments by discouraging our dreams and telling us to just be satisfied with whatever life hands us.

Money Beliefs

Our parents or caretakers might have told us "money doesn't grow on trees," "people like us are not going to be wealthy," "don't put your hopes up too high, just do your job." If we saw people fighting over money, we might think that "money will make people change for the worse." By observing how the media portray some rich people as being stingy like Li Kashing, or mean and rude like Donald Trump, we assume rich people are bad people and we might secretly make a decision that we do not want to be like them and hence, we develop a resistance for being wealthy.

Based on these limiting beliefs, our subconscious mind so brilliantly creates the type of negative talks that destroy our confidence, allows us to be triggered by what others say or do and react negatively to some people/situations, thereby destroying our chances to maintain good relationships or to become successful.

We have to be aware of our limiting beliefs and how they secretly ruin our lives. If we are not aware, it is easy to find ourselves living within the same old patterns over and over again – because we are just cruising on auto-pilot. The key is not to let these limiting beliefs rule our lives. Having awareness means that we can catch these limiting beliefs before going into auto-pilot mode, then we have an opportunity to question them, actively deciding whether these beliefs are still relevant to the situation now, and clearing them so that we could choose an alternative path. When we process these thoughts consciously, the "blocks" become "doorways" that we can step through and move forward in our lives.

There are some techniques such as hypnotherapy, emotional freedom techniques (EFT) and Psych-K that claim to be able to get rid of these limiting beliefs for good. However, the power is in the awareness of these limiting beliefs in action and to catch them before we react with the old programming. When we can choose how we respond to any situation, we have the freedom to create the life we want.

3. TRUST THAT THIS IS A FRIENDLY UNIVERSE

Henry Ford said "Whether you think you can, or you think you can't – you're right." When we assume things are not going to go our way, or good things would not happen to us, we send the negative vibes out and thereby attract negative results into our lives. When we have positive expectations but we are fixated on how things are going to happen, we project our limitations, which might hinder the creation of our desired outcomes. However, when we trust that this is a friendly Universe and our desires would be delivered to us in ways that we may or may not have anticipated, we can let go of our expectations and be nicely surprised.

If we practice the above three strategies, we will regain our power, become aware of what is pulling us back and allow miracles to happen in our lives.

About Sylvia

Sylvia Chan helps her clients transform their lives from stressful to blissful. Sylvia has more than 20 years of business experience with 10 years of management experience in project management and relationship building with clients and professional team members. When her high-stressed finance jobs challenged her wellbeing and made her question her purpose in life, Sylvia embarked on a soul-searching journey and dived into personal development. Sylvia is inspired to help her clients create positive changes. Her strong business background combined with spiritual awareness enables Sylvia to offer unique perspectives and experiences to assist her clients in solving their everyday challenges. Sylvia has been helping companies and individuals to develop clear visions and effective strategies that can help to achieve success in their business and personal lives.

Coming from a strong business background, Sylvia has wide experience working in manufacturing, legal, communications, data analysis, direct marketing and finance project management. Sylvia is a senior vice president of a business consultancy and has led several multimillion-dollar international investment projects and created highly effective project teams to manage the investment projects in fund raising, M & A and public listing.

With her personal development, Sylvia read numerous books and studied with many teachers. She is a Certified Law of Attraction Facilitator and Certified Psych-K Facilitator. Due to her interest in Traditional Chinese Medicine, she became a Certified Hand Diagnosis Practitioner, Certified Hand Therapist, and Certified Chinese Food Medicine Practitioner. In 2011, she co-founded LOA Centre Hong Kong, a training, consulting and coaching firm, and has been delivering dynamic seminars and high-involvement workshops to increase enterprise performance and to empower personal transformation.

Sylvia is a dynamic speaker, trainer, and presenter. She uses innovation and humor to deliver her messages and engages audiences with her energy and enthusiasm. She is an effective coach who can quickly assess her client's needs and provide tools to resolve difficulties, enhance learning, and improve performance.

Sylvia graduated *summa cum laude* from Boston University with a Bachelor of Arts degree with Distinction in Economics. She obtained a Master's of International

Communication degree from UNITEC Institute of Technology in New Zealand. Sylvia is a Dale Carnegie® Trainer in Hong Kong. She is fluent in English and Chinese (Cantonese and Mandarin), and is experienced in conducting seminars in these languages.

Singing is Sylvia's passion. She is an amateur singer who enjoys performing live. During her soul searching journey, she has learnt the importance of balancing Body, Mind and Soul. She practices meditation, mindfulness in everyday life, yoga and Zumba dance. She believes we can heal our bodies with positivity and happiness, sensible diet, natural remedies and Traditional Chinese Medicine. She is the organizer of the Law of Attraction Meetup Group in Hong Kong. More than anything, Sylvia is most passionate about empowering people to transform, get clear on their goals and desires, and to derive steps that can help them achieve their dreams.

You can connect with Sylvia at:
Sylvia@loa-hk.com
www.loa-hk.com
www.sylvia-chan.net
www.facebook.com/loa.hk

CHAPTER 55

HOW TO ACHIEVE SUCCESS WITHOUT LOSING YOUR SOUL

BY SURIA MOHD

It was a moment of despair. I found myself in one of the darkest hours of my business struggles when I lost almost half a million dollars and was at the brink of bankruptcy. I lost everything – everything from money to family. Even my health was deteriorating, as I developed a sudden skin rash and hives, and, for the first time, a chronic asthma attack – all happening simultaneously.

Truly, my life was collapsing, my body was breaking down and I found myself at the lowest point of my life. I cried my heart out and for the first time connected to the deepest part of my heart and soul.

Fast forward in my life, I rose to the top of my industry, being hailed as the fastest millionaire – breaking the company's 20-year record as the first person to ever generate such a massive amount of income in the shortest period of time.

My Facebook fan page count rose to over a hundred thousand and had a reach of over 20 million on any given week. I got my life back together, started spending time with my teenage kids, got a house I love and all went back into peace again.

Many have written me asking how I climbed back up? What did I do to get back on my feet? How did I get the courage to stand up again after such a massive collapse in my life? Truly, the breakdown in my life was the spark for the major breakthroughs that eventually happened.

As I reflected back I realized, yes, there is a formula to success that has worked for me. I started teaching that to thousands of people at my events, seminars and workshops.

I call them the *Six Secrets to the Soul of Success* and I now share them with you:

1. EXPERIENCE THE EXPERIENCE

When I broke down and cried in deepest sorrow, I finally acknowledged that I needed help and support. I didn't stay in denial nor did I push away the pain. I simply allowed and surrendered myself to experience the pain, the disappointments, the sadness and everything bitter that was going on in my life. Yes, I cried my heart out.

Allowing myself to feel was the biggest breakthrough for me in that moment. By feeling, I was able to stay in the moment and be present with what was going on inside me. I allowed myself to cry but I didn't drown myself in those tears.

I allowed myself to cry and reframe those tears. They were not of weakness nor making me admit to defeat, rather they were the tears of strength that flowed out from my heart, cleansing away the pain and bitterness.

2. JOURNAL AND REFLECTIONS

After all the tears and angst were felt, I started dedicating those emotions and directing them to a space where they can flow besides the tears.

I started pouring out my emotions in writing. I wrote out all my feelings, what was happening in my life, what I was feeling, what were my thoughts, etc. I wrote all this down without censoring anything.

I expressed them in a flow. I started with:

> (1st) What was not working in my life, what I didn't want, what was frustrating me, the scarcity, the fears, the pain, the angst and the worries. Then...

(2nd) What I wanted in my life – painting a scenario of what the ideal life would be for me if I had it all back together. I would answer the questions, "What do I want to feel again?" "Who do I want to be again?" "What are the feelings I want to feel again?"

These moments and feelings were scenes I painted in my imagination, and they were all written out clearly as if they were a part of a movie scene that was really happening!

3. FORGIVENESS

After all the mind work is done, when I released the images of what I didn't want and replaced them with what I wanted in my mind, I realized I needed to go deeper into my heart space to allow these new images and dreams to manifest. I also knew that as long as I did not release the emotional baggage in my heart space, I would not be aligned with my mind space.

So I embarked on this offloading of the rocks in my heart. All the hurt and pain from those who I felt wronged me, and towards whom I harboured bitterness and blame.

I felt the hurt and pain again, and it was hard to let go and forgive those people – almost an impossible task. However, I simply set out the INTENTION to forgive and release them from my heart space of bitterness. I know that as long as the intentions are set, the process of forgiveness has begun.

I knew forgiving was not something I was just doing for them, but was more for myself, so that I could walk out of this unlocked prison once and for all.

Later in life when I could finally fully release and had forgiven all, I realize that no one that came into my life came to hurt or punish me. They simply were characters sent in different names and roles for my own growth. So life happens for me, lovingly, to allow me to grow, expand and evolve, not to punish or hurt me.

That perspective allowed me to see everything that happened and everyone that came into my life as mentors to guide and serve me, to heal many wounded aspects of my soul.

4. ATTITUDE OF GRATITUDE

To anchor all my feelings of hope and faith in such moments of darkness, I dive into whatever good I can find still available to me at that moment. Yes, I may have lost the money and then nearly lost the business, and have even lost my family – yet there was something that I felt at that moment that kept me going. I was still breathing.

It was then I realized that breath itself is a sign that my work on earth is not done yet, and my existence still carried a purpose and mission. So it started with an attitude of gratitude, first for my breath and then for everything that I still have in me.

I say my thanks and send all praise to the Almighty for still keeping me alive. I say thanks for the body organs that are still functioning, for the pair of eyes that can still see, for the fingers that can still type, for the ears that can still listen to all the positive motivational words, for the technology of the Internet that still can allow me a glimmer of hope to move on in this business, for my two beautiful kids who are still growing up in great protection, care and love.

Suddenly, in that moment, I realized that the counting of my blessings has made all this pain seem insignificant and hope came alive. Further into life, I realized that no one can ever hurt a grateful heart.

No matter how much pain and hurt, when I can see that the situation is for the good, I can forgive and then be grateful.

5. INTENTION SETTING VS GOAL SETTING

Now, after everything has been taken away from me, after I have cried my heart out, after writing it all down through journaling and reflections, and having gone through the forgiveness and gratitude exercise, what's next?

If I were to reset the formula for my new success again – how would I do it differently? I know in Step #2 that I have stated my goals of what I want and how my ideal life would be, yet, I know there's something missing in that formula. There must be something more than just setting goals again.

After all, I did set goals previously and I was always good at achieving them. But somehow it didn't last and the pain became really unbearable when all that I had aimed for in my business and achieved was wiped out. It's almost like I was achieving yet not achieving. When I had my business I was happy; when I lost it I completely broke down to my lowest self.

I pursued success like it was something I could only achieve in the future, so my focus was constantly on the future and working towards achieving that success. I forget to 'stop to smell the roses' and be present. So I knew that if I had to restart my life again, it would come from a different space of redefining success.

This is what started the process of me heading down a new path to success, and this time I was going to go for success without losing my soul.

6. REDEFINING SUCCESS : THE JOURNEY TOWARDS SUCCESS FROM THE SOUL

Many teachings of success focus on *goal setting and tools to achieve goals* such as affirmations, visualizations and principles such as the Law of Attraction and many more. These are great tools to support the pursuit of success and they work when you apply them diligently.

I did just that, and yes, I do agree that these tools of success allowed me to achieve the goals I set out to accomplish:

- Business Success in Sales and Profits
- Personal Success - The family and marriage
- Material Gains - The car, house, etc.
- Career Success - The Credentials, the Degree, the status, including promotions at work

However, I realized that when I had it all I was still not full and whole. I was in a mad chase for something in the future – this mirage of happiness from a distance. So, now, instead of setting goals, I start by questioning why I want those goals.

I ask myself again:

- What is Success?
- What is our Ultimate BE-ing?

- What is the Purpose of Existence?
- What is it that you WANT?
- What is it that you want when you want what you want , when you are chasing after your Goal?

I asked, "What is it that I actually want to feel when I want to HAVE or GET the things that I desire or set out as my goals?" And as I probed further, I realized that at the end of the car, house, money, etc. – all I wanted was Peace and Happiness!

Here is a process you can use to get to your core motives:

- What do I want? – A house.
- Why? – So I can have a roof over my head.
- Why? – So I can now have my kids stay with me.
- Why? – So I can now be happy knowing I can spend time with them in my own home.
- Why? – So that I can be happy with them in their company.

What I truly want is HAPPINESS!

I started redefining success as a State of BE-ing instead of a State of Having...

Success now means to me:

♥ Being Peaceful

♥ Knowing my Calling on Earth, my Mission and Living it

♥ Being Happy

♥ Living with Passion

♥ Be Loving, Forgiving and Compassionate

♥ Be Grateful for simple pleasures in life

♥ Always Learning & Growing

♥ A Life of Heart-ful Contributions & Heart-ful Connections

♥ Servitude, Giving & Contributing Value

♥ Making a Difference in Someone's life

♥ Doing Meaningful work

♥ Making Peace with my Past and People who have hurt me

♥ Praying well for those who hate, condemn and think ill of me

♥ Being the Best I can be Now given what I know and have now

♥ Connecting to and with God Deeply ~ Feeling & Appreciating His Love

The essence and soul of success is not the dollars and cents of the business, but rather the sacred spiritual process of staying connected and mindful to the intention, purpose and WHY.

I am successful when I am mindful, pause and reflect daily amidst my busy schedule and check in the heart, to re-connect back to who I really am.

This is the *Soul of Success* path.

About Suria

Choosing the road less travelled, internal reflections and reaching for the stars seem to be recurring themes in this schoolteacher-turned-entrepreneur, Suria Mohd. Though there are many words to describe the mother of two, one image comes to mind that epitomises her life: the phoenix, the mythical bird that rises from the ashes.

Growing up through trials and tribulations, Suria knows the meaning of hardship and pain. She dropped out of school, living her teenage years 'pretty much as a bum,' working odd jobs and wandering aimlessly without any direction in life.

Growing up into womanhood, she got married only to find herself amidst the remnants of a divorce. She has stood on the brink of bankruptcy, gone into bouts of depression, experienced obesity and felt suicidal.

Yet after everything that she went through, she emerged triumphant and is now happily managing her thriving businesses, which focus on nourishing the body as well as the soul.

Suria states:

My goal is to bring ancient and new age healing wisdoms to the forefront of people's daily lives.

As I ventured deeper into the realm of alternative healing, I came to understand that there are other more powerful aspects of healing, which are centred on the mind and the soul, and are impacted by the food we eat.

My "aha!" moment came when I went through the deepest financial crises of my life, where I almost went bankrupt in my business. I developed a sudden rare skin disorder with a strange rash that covered my entire body except for my face. It kept me home for three whole weeks. It was during this period, too, that I had my first and worst asthma attack.

Within the mess, Suria found a message: I *started realising the areas in my life that were not working, were factors that lead me to the state of unease, anxiety and stress. The concept can be summarised as a body in a state of "dis-ease" thus becomes diseased, and that the body can heal itself only if it brings itself back to a state of ease.*

The secret to true health, Suria has discovered, is within oneself. 'A peaceful heart is the basis of a healthy body,' she says, adding a quote from the Quran: *"Surely, in the remembrance of the Divine do hearts find peace."*

It is by spreading this message through her companies and speaking engagements that Suria has finally found her life's purpose. She adds:

My mission is to inspire and empower the soul to connect with its life purpose. I deeply believe that no matter what path anyone walks in life, inspiration and self awareness are needed to fulfill true life purpose and potential.

Life is always full of its ups and downs, but Suria's serenity and happiness seem to be here to stay, for she has found their eternal keys. *I cherish my nothingness, for I am nothing who has been given everything by The Creator.*

She declares: **You cannot hurt a grateful heart**.

Connect with Suria on: www.facebook.com/SuriaFan

CHAPTER 56

FOUR WAYS TO BUILD A COMPLIANT, SUCCESSFUL CREDIT REPAIR BUSINESS OR PROFIT CENTER!

BY JOSHUA CARMONA

THE PROBLEM:

Credit-based businesses sell products or services based on the ability of a consumer to qualify for a loan, on a consumer's credit file, on an associated credit score, and on the income to repay the debt over time. Unfortunately, there is a problem in the way data is being added, managed and reported, which has placed millions of consumers at risk. According to a study performed in June 2004 by the United States Public Interest Research Group (US PIRG), over seventy-nine percent (79%) of credit reports surveyed contained either serious errors or other mistakes of some kind, twenty-five percent (25%) of which could cause a denial of credit. In 2013, the Federal Trade Commission (FTC) released a study that stated that five percent (5%) of consumers had credit report errors that could result in less favorable terms for loans.

According to Stuart Pratt, President and CEO of the Consumer Data Industry Association (CDIA), there are over 200 million consumers with credit reports. Extrapolating the data from the USPIRG and the FTC reports and applying them to the number of credit reports in the credit reporting system, there are between 10 and 50 million credit reports that could contain material errors that could result in either less than favorable terms or flat-out denials of credit issuance. Despite these oversights, the credit reporting system will not change until the legislation around the system — and the policing of it — expand in scope at all levels. By the time the credit reporting system changes to where it is fair, consumers may be past the point of even needing credit. That is why consumers must examine the system currently in place, and leverage the legislation to achieve more efficient results within the constraints of the law.

THE SOLUTION:

In 1970, the Fair Credit Reporting Act (FCRA) established a dispute process for consumers to be able to challenge erroneous information on their credit report, and it also established guidelines that the credit reporting agencies and data furnishers needed to follow when performing the investigation and storing data. The FCRA dispute process was tedious, bureaucratic and time consuming, and soon after, companies started offering credit repair services to consumers who wanted to pay someone else to dispute their erroneous data on their behalf. Unfortunately, as in all new, unregulated industries, some unsavory players started over-promising and under-delivering on their promises, which meant that many consumers lost their hard-earned money hiring unscrupulous credit repair organizations due to deceptive trade practices.

After many complaints, the Credit Repair Organizations Act (CROA) was enacted in 1996, and started laying the foundation and, more importantly, the requirements that credit repair organizations needed to follow in order to participate in the space legally.

Soon after, many states started introducing legislation as well, in some instances to enhance federal consumer protection at the state level. The FTC is responsible for overseeing and enforcing the intent of the FCRA, and in 2006 started investigating, enforcing, and shutting down credit repair organizations that were not following the CROA. Operations such as "Operation Clean Sweep" were carried out in order to rid the industry of these illegally operated credit repair organizations. The presence of 'big' government enforcing its might was a great concern to these organizations across the country, but time would prove that it was a benefit to the industry. It weeded out the bad credit repair organizations and positioned the others to be more compliant. Credit repair organizations started to establish themselves as serious players in the industry by adhering to the law rather than looking for ways to circumvent it. Since then, the credit repair industry has grown into a $6 billion Industry, according to the 2014 IBIS World Credit Repair Industry Report, and the industry is no longer on the FTC's Top-100-industries-to-watch list.

The number of consumers with less than perfect credit correlates to the need to sell additional products and services on credit from the real estate, automotive, insurance, banking, and employment industries — and the result is a $6 billion annual opportunity for business. Further revenue is earned from the other industries combined because of how those industries benefit by improved credit reports and scores.

If you are in one of these industries, and you want to increase your sales opportunities, one thing must be very clear: the credit repair industry is a highly-regulated space, and when you contemplate starting your own credit repair organization or profit center, think of compliance first when establishing your business.

Here is a list of the top four things you can do to build a compliant and successful credit repair business or profit center:

1. Stay Legal, Live Compliance
The best way to build a successful credit repair business or profit center is to understand the compliance requirements. There are many policies that regulate the industry, but if you understand the impact of the following laws you can achieve long-term compliance and success:

    a. Credit Repair Organizations Act (CROA)

    b. Fair Credit Reporting Act (FCRA)

    c. Fair Debt Collection Practices Act (FDCPA)

    d. CAN-SPAM Act of 2003

    e. State level Credit Repair Organizations Act

      - State-Level Licensing / Registration and Bonding Requirements

There are many other laws as well, but the Credit Repair Organizations Act and the Fair Credit Reporting Act frame the who, what, when, where, and how credit repair businesses can sell and supply their services legally.

The Credit Repair Organizations Act (CROA) is the most important law for any credit repair organization to understand. It defines the credit repair organization and what and how certain activities should be performed legally. According to the CROA, all credit repair organizations should adhere to the following guidelines:

1. They should <u>NOT</u> charge for services before they have been completely rendered.

2. There should be a credit repair service agreement/contract between the consumer and the credit repair organization.

   a. The credit repair service agreement/contract must contain:

      i. A clear description of the services to be rendered.

      ii. A *Notice of Cancellation* statement/clause directly above or below the signature.

      iii. Two (2) original copies of the *Notice of Cancellation.*

3. The Consumer should be given the Federal Section 405 Federal Disclosure Statement.

As it relates to credit repair, the Fair Credit Reporting Act defines who is the credit reporting agency, the consumer, and the data furnisher and how they should all interact together, to ensure consumer data quality within the credit reporting agency data repositories. Fundamentally, credit reporting agencies are responsible for maintaining the consumer's data in the system, and if the consumer notices a discrepancy, the consumer has the right to dispute said item. It is important to understand this and use it to define your dispute process. Credit repair organizations should not dispute items on a credit report unless the consumer has:

1. Authorized the item to be disputed.

2. Given you the reason for disputing their knowledge of the process.

The FCRA also defines the dispute process cycle, as well as the efforts the data furnisher and the Credit Reporting Agencies must take, to ensure consumer data accuracy. Once again, this will help the credit repair organization define its dispute process. Remember that credit repair organizations are truly custodians of the quality of data inside their customers' credit reports. Credit repair organizations can never guarantee or forecast when something is going to be deleted, updated or repaired, because they do not perform that action — only the data furnishers and the credit reporting agencies can do this. All successful credit reporting organizations set the correct expectations with their customers by never over-promising results. While out of their control, this is something all CRO's should refrain from doing.

2. Be Focused, Build a Business

One of the most challenging things for any entrepreneur to sustain is focus and avoid a mindset called "shiny object syndrome." Entrepreneurs have an innate ability to see opportunities where others see problems, a trait that probably got them thinking of becoming their own boss and going into business for themselves. Yet the fundamental problem is that most entrepreneurs cannot shut that off. And if they are not careful, they could recklessly add more products, projects, and personnel without a clear plan, which could take up most of their time and consume their money and other resources, and often drive their business to the point of failure.

If you are lost in the desert, how do you move from Point A to Point B? In a desert, there are normally no visible reference points, so you need a plan that takes that problem into consideration, and by executing the plan, you get from Point A to Point B successfully. In other words, the better the plan, the better the execution. It also keeps you from running around in circles, which in this scenario, could be detrimental.

According to Forbes, eight out of ten businesses fail in the first 18 months and the things the failed businesses had in common were as follows:

1. Lack of contact with customers through deep dialogue.

2. No real differentiation in the market, or no unique value proposition.

3. Failure to communicate value propositions in clear, concise and compelling fashion.

4. Leadership breakdown at the top (founder dysfunction).

5. Inability to nail a profitable business model with proven revenue streams.

All of the items mentioned in the Forbes article are fundamental parts of a plan. The bottom line is that you need a plan, but a plan spawns from a goal — and that goal comes from a mission, which is itself based on a company's purpose and core values. In other words, your company can have a plan that always works if the purpose, core values, and mission are all in harmony. This is what stops entrepreneurs from executing opportunities that are out of their vision and what provides focus when presented with a "shiny object syndrome" scenario. When you build a business that has a purpose, core values, and a mission, you can establish strategies to achieve the goals defined in that mission.

3. Have An Automation Mindset

Have you ever heard of the saying: *build it and they will come?* To keep your business competitive in this century you must automate. With the advent of the Internet, and social media platforms like Facebook, Twitter, Instagram, and LinkedIn, consumers socialize in a multitude of different ways. It is important to leverage technology in order to compete at a higher level. Automating the following will help you maximize your sales opportunities:

　　a. Customer Life Cycle Marketing

　　　　i. Attraction

　　　　ii. Sell

　　　　iii. Overwhelm

　　b. Billing and Invoicing Process

　　c. Lead Generation

　　d. Employee Development

　　e. Compliance

　　f. Business Management

It is important for all of these things to be automated with technology, but that can be quite expensive. If you plan correctly, you will be able to prioritize the automation based on your immediate needs.

For example, if you do not have enough sales, then you must focus your resources on tools such as CRM's, Sales Funnel Software or services that can help you automate your sales process first — in order to understand when and where your sales are coming from before you start developing a sales force. If you hire a sales force without getting your life-cycle marketing strategies in place, you might miss out on many sales opportunities.

When you apply this concept to Credit Repair Organizations, they all need to have complete systems that not only manage their dispute process, but also their compliance, billing, sales, and marketing processes as well. Systems are increasingly online nowadays, so be very careful when selecting software that has the right security and business-continuity strategies in place in order to protect your investment.

4. Model Your Product and Market

Have you ever had an idea for a product or service, created it, and started to sell it like hot cakes? This probably happened because there was an immediate and clear need for the product and the benefits outweighed the costs. But it can eventually backfire and sales slow down, at which time it's important to create content around the product or service, and we are asked questions that we have difficulty answering, such as:

- What is the market you're selling to?
- What are the problems the market faces because they do not have the product?
- What problem does the product solve?
- Who are your early adopters?
- What are the unique value propositions?
- What is the cost? . . . and why?
- What is the sales price? . . . and profit margin?

Isn't it better to know all of this before you actually invest in creating or delivering your product to market than to see if there is first a market fit by running some controlled tests or proof of concept? Ash Maury talks about this in his book *Running Lean,* which outlines a systematic methodology for quickly vetting product ideas and raising the odds of success.

Credit RepairOrganizations are normally small businesses that are underfunded and require an enormous amount of focus to determine their unique value proposition (UVP) and what problems their service resolves within their demographic or buyer personas.

Most small businesses fail because they cannot make the cash register ring consistently, which is often because they do not understand their market or their product. They do well selling their services to their existing lists, friends and family. They understand their market and can easily fit the service to it. Yet when their business starts growing outside of their initial customer base, it gets complicated, and the unique value proposition has changed and the revenue associated with it decreases. It is important for Credit Repair Organizations to model their products and services to their demographics and understand exactly the problems and solutions each requires to establish the correct UVP for the right buyer persona.

Resources:

1. Jan 21, 2015 FTC Press Release: (Contains summary info for 2012 FTC Credit Accuracy Study; and 2013 Follow-up study) https://www.ftc.gov/news-events/press-releases/2015/01/ftc-issues-follow-study-credit-report-accuracy

About Joshua

Joshua Carmona has been an unmistakable leader in the credit repair industry for many years. He has combined three decades of technology, automotive executive management, enterprise sales, enterprise customer service, business coaching, and enterprise level credit repair experience; and he has used it to empower hundreds of entrepreneurs, in multiple verticals, by helping them find their path to success.

Joshua has applied his vast process knowledge and experience by creating Scoreinc. com's World Class Dispute Process, based on his "Technical Factual Dispute Methodology." He is the founder and vice president of Scoreinc.com, co-founder of the acclaimed CreditRepairSummit.com, co-creator of ScoreWay Credit Repair University, designer of ScoreCEO and consultant to thousands of credit repair businesses in the United States, Puerto Rico, and Canada. When he was in the credit repair retail space, his business managed over 3,000 clients per month. Joshua has trained hundreds of companies in his "Technical Factual Dispute Methodology."

Joshua is an Infusionsoft Elite Forum Graduate, and has also trained with Joe Verde Group, Disney Institute (World Class Customer Service, Toyota Excellence Program) Graduate, Microsoft Business Consultant, IBM Best Team Engineer, US Army (Infantry Officer), and has achieved his FCRA and CROA certifications. As GM for FG Auto Corp (dba Autoland) in 2004, he was responsible for increasing revenue 300 percent from $25 million to $104 million per year in just two years.

With his specific set of skills and experience building successful businesses — with some entrepreneurial failures — Joshua has come full circle. He truly understands what it takes to create, build, manage, and prosper as an entrepreneur.

Joshua was born and raised in New York and currently resides in Puerto Rico. He is the proud father of a 14-year-old daughter and is happily married to Ariana, his life partner of 13 years.

CHAPTER 57

DO LESS TO DO MORE

BY SUSAN SLY

"At the center of your being you have the answer;
you know who you are and you know what you want."

~ Lao Tzu

I humbled myself and got down on my knees, the cool floor pressing into my bones. *"God,"* I sobbed, *"if you will show me the way, I will do the work."* Exhausted, overwhelmed, feeling shredded to my core, tears streamed down my face. How could it have come to this?

Only a few months earlier, my physician delivered the life-altering news that the fatigue, numbness and headaches that I had been experiencing were, in fact, progressive multiple sclerosis. Shock, despair, anger and disappointment flooded me at once. In that moment, his words fell away. What seemed like an inevitable future in a wheelchair and an early death haunted my reality. I went home to feel sorry for myself; consumed with self-pity.

Three days later, through a series of events, my marriage fell apart. We had chosen to handle the mounting stress in deliberate and self-serving ways; none of them healthy. We decided to separate; however, we continued to cohabitate for the sake of our three-year old daughter, attempting to go on with business as usual.

I travelled to Florida to train and coach triathlon. Hundred-mile bike rides in the scorching sun gave me many hours to ponder my life. I wasn't perfect. Maybe I had done something to deserve all of this. I thought about all of the ways in which I had driven myself to succeed. Perhaps pushing myself to exhaustion day after day, getting five hours of sleep every night and driving myself as a business owner, trainer, exercise instructor, teaching at the local college, doing television and radio appearances, training for triathlon and, of course, being a mom, had been too much.

God has a funny way of thrusting the message home. I didn't listen to my body. I didn't make any changes with my life or my schedule. Thus, I broke out with a bizarre rash, which a physician diagnosed as hives. He injected me with two shots of cortisone. Despite running a fever and the spreading rash, I flew to Alabama to participate in a grueling race – The Powerman – which consisted of a 10k run, 60k bike race and then a 10k run, where I was scheduled to race as a pro.

I surged forward with the lead girls and fifteen minutes into the race my breathing was labored, a grey fog started to appear and I found myself on the ground with the ESPN cameras in front of me. I would later be diagnosed with shingles, and, as if to add insult to injury, I was told that the case had been exacerbated by the cortisone.

Running a fever for weeks with red, itchy spots encompassing every square inch of my body, I wondered how much one person could take. I would soon find out. On Good Friday, I went to the health club I co-owned with my husband. There was a padlock on the door. We had been shut down for failure to pay our taxes; I had buried my head in the sand and chosen not to be overly involved with the finances. I stood there surrounded by my students, embarrassed and humiliated, wondering if this was truly the lowest it could get.

This was the point that brought me to my knees. There was no question of asking to be handed something; I knew deep in my soul that faith without works is dead. Still, a small voice within told me that I was capable of much more; I didn't know how it would happen; however, what I did know was that by supplicating myself to God and allowing the next steps to be revealed, my life would change for the better.

The signs had all been there and my ego-filled mind had decided that pushing through was the best solution. Making a decision to bury my head in the sand when exhaustion, overwhelm, and extreme stress were so prevalent was the worst mistake I could have made. Here at the bottom, feeling that there was nothing left to give, my only choices were to either surrender to circumstance or figure out a way to turn my life around.

My goal for anyone reading this is to know that whatever you are going through, or have experienced, you can transcend. This book is about hope; a hope for a better tomorrow. When asked to participate, my first thought was how can I impart the key strategies I used to go from excruciatingly ill, deeply in debt, a broken marriage and living on my brother-in-law's sofa to running five Boston Marathons, becoming a self-made multi-millionaire, and passionately married to the love of my life? In other words, I believe you can have a rich, beautiful, fulfilling life and these words are intended to help you, in some way, to do just that.

I can pinpoint eight things that I did to turn my life around. There wasn't just one strategy; all of these worked symbiotically to create results:

1. GET EXTREMELY CLEAR ON WHAT YOU WANT IN THE PRIMARY AREAS OF YOUR LIFE

I meet so many people who are out of balance – they have money, but their relationship is horrible or they have created a fantastic career, but they are thirty pounds overweight. The primary areas of our lives are health, relationships, money and contribution. When I hit rock bottom and finally came out of the other end of my pity party, I got clear on what I wanted. I created vivid images of what that looked like in my mind.

I knew that I wanted to be healthy, run marathons again, and be free of MS symptoms. I declared that I would meet and marry the man of my dreams; he would be smart, loving, accepting, committed and we would have incredible passion. I envisioned myself as a millionaire. I saw myself travelling to countries and helping girls who had been trafficked. All of this came true within six years, thanks to clarity of vision.

2. LEARN TO SAY "NO"

If you are asked to do something that does not align with your objectives, say "no." For many people, this is the toughest thing to do. Ask yourself, "Is doing this going to get me closer to, or further away from what I want?" You have the answers within. Trust your gut. Ultimately, our lives are as much a reflection of the things we choose not to do, as those things we make a conscious choice to do.

3. END YOUR DAY BEFORE YOU START YOUR DAY

While he was alive, I had the honor of sharing the stage with the late Jim Rohn. Rohn was a business philosopher who also happened to mentor a young Anthony Robbins. Jim used to say that if you wanted to be successful you should end your day before you start your day. He went on to expand on the concept by explaining that successful people write out their day the night before which allows the subconscious to go to work on how to best achieve those intentions.

This singular idea has made me millions. Six nights out of the week, I write out my day the night before. I am much more productive, focused and on point.

4. SURROUND YOURSELF WITH PEOPLE WHO TELL YOU THAT YOU CAN

There were several doctors who insisted that medication was the best method for treating my illness. My personal belief was that there was a better way. I actively sought out practitioners who aligned with those beliefs; putting together a team of people who told me that the plan for my health was possible.

How often do you heed the words of someone who is not supportive? If you want to become successful, you must actively pursue the advice of those who believe that you can achieve your goals. Flooding your mind with the 'you can do it' philosophy is essential to success. In addition to searching for people who believe in you, make it a habit of listening to audios, reading books and watching videos by people who reinforce this positive message. YouTube has great trainings by people such as Anthony Robbins, Jack Canfield and more. Best of all – it is free!

5. UNDERSTAND YOUR PERSONAL R.O.I.

In the investment world, R.O.I. stands for Return On Investment. Everything in our world has one. For example, if you eat fast food and feel sluggish afterward, it has a negative R.O.I. on your performance. If you feel fabulous on seven hours of sleep, then that has a positive R.O.I. People often ask me how I can be a parent to five children, run several companies, write books, speak and run marathons. The answer is that I am extremely conscious of the things that bring me a positive R.O.I., and I choose to do these things more often.

To navigate my failing health, I made conscious choices. I cleansed my body. I gave up meat. I eschewed gluten and dairy. I committed to daily meditation and prayer. Most importantly, I learned to listen to my body and fuel myself with those things that gave me a positive R.O.I.

6. DO LESS TO DO MORE

In my class, *Organize Your Life*, I teach people that lack of organization is the number one enemy of success. I believe it with my whole heart. I think that everyone has talents and gifts that go wasted because they are disorganized. One of the fundamental reasons we become disorganized is that we are trying to do too many things partially well, as opposed to doing a few things really well.

Whether you are a corporate executive, business owner, an employee or someone who simply just has a curiosity about getting better, I can promise you that if you structure your day where you focus on doing just a few things with panache, you will discover that you will accomplish much more than you realized you were capable of. In other words – what appears to be doing less, is actually doing more.

7. DAILY GRATITUDE

The late Zig Ziglar said, *"Gratitude is the healthiest of all human emotions. The more you express gratitude for what you have, the more likely you will have even more to express gratitude for."*

At first, writing out ten items of gratitude was a challenge; the main reason being that I was still operating out of 'victim mode'. Forcing myself to find appreciation for the simplest of things such as a roof over my head, my daughter's laugh and a clear, sunny day, began to transform my life experience.

In the Bible, it is written, *"to whom much is given, more shall be given."* One interpretation of this is that the person who lives a life of gratitude will be blessed with greater abundance. Commit for 90 days to writing out ten items of gratitude every night and see what happens.

8. CONTRIBUTION

When I got my first job after losing the business, I began to donate time and money. Every book on success that I had read spoke of tithing and contribution. It would have been easy to say, "I will do this when I have more money," however, in my soul it was clear that more money would come when I began to contribute. I donated my time, continuously cleared out my closet, offered up excess and also money.

The more I contributed, with love, the more my income grew. Today my husband and I have funded projects for the homeless, helped girls recover from the trauma of human trafficking, built a school in Africa and much more. One of the things that drives the most successful people on the planet is to make a bigger impact with contribution.

Know that you are capable of achieving great things in your life. I encourage you to embrace these eight strategies and go forward creating the life of your dreams.

Lastly, repeat these words after me, 'I am enough.' You truly are enough. You are capable of transcending the odds and creating the life of your dreams. Go for it!

About Susan

Susan Sly is a Balanced Living Strategist. As a speaker, author and entrepreneur, she has appeared on Lifetime Television, ABC Family, The CBN, been quoted in *Forbes Magazine Online* and more. Susan has appeared in the highly acclaimed movie, *Rise of the Entrepreneur,* alongside Robert Kiyosaki, Jack Canfield, John Assaraf and others.

Susan is a mother of five children and loving wife to her husband Chris. Susan believes we can truly have it all.

Her website is: www.susansly.com